PORTRAIT OF THE ROSE CITY

A HISTORY OF
MADISON
— NEW JERSEY —

by Frank J. Esposito
and the Madison History Committee

CONTENTS

Dear Reader,

Among small towns, Madison is exceptional for having a history of its founding and development written by a professional historian, Dr. Frank J. Esposito. That award-winning history, *The Madison Heritage Trail,* was published in 1985 as part of Madison's celebration of the 1776 Bicentennial.

In 2016, Susan Simon, president of the Madison Historical Society, and Nancy Adamczyk, director of The Free Public Library of the Borough of Madison, proposed that *The Madison Heritage Trail* should be updated. This new work would incorporate new research and extend the narrative into the early decades of the 21st century. Simon and Adamczyk successfully recruited Dr. Esposito to revise and enlarge the original work. Another historian would be hired to produce the new chapters. The costs of publication would be shared equally by the sponsoring organizations.

Each organization had received bequests that could be used to fund the new edition. Income from the gift made to the library by Larry Taber, a lifelong Madison resident and town historian, also funded the digitization of *The Madison Eagle,* an invaluable source for the writing of the new edition. The Madison Historical Society also received a bequest from another longtime resident of Madison, who wished to remain anonymous.

A committee made up of individuals representing the Madison Historical Society (Nancy Adamczyk, Linda Connors, Herman Huber, Susan Simon, and Maria Slabaugh) and the Madison Public Library (Louise Easton, David Luber, and Gary Ruckelshaus) was established to review revisions to the original chapters and the new chapters as they were produced. As we were not successful in recruiting a historian to research and write the new chapters, the committee agreed to take on this task. The Madison History Committee has been a strong and hardworking one, committed to producing a definitive history of Madison. Each of the members brought enthusiasm and commitment to the project and employed their many talents to ensure its completion.

Early on in the process, two short-term members of the committee also made significant contributions to the committee's work. Stuart Shippey produced an invaluable digital copy of *The Madison Heritage Trail,* and Jim Malcolm shared information on the Civil War based on his work editing *The Civil War Journal of Private Heyward Emmell.*

The task of creating the new chapters proved more voluminous than originally envisioned. Outlines were developed, and topics were assigned for research and writing. Most members researched and wrote some portions of the new chapters, as well as some revisions to the existing chapters. Whenever possible, Madisonians who had participated in key events were interviewed, and their recollections were incorporated into the text. Some other Madisonians wrote articles about the history of their respective organizations. Committee members applied their editing skills as the new information threatened to overwhelm the book.

As this process of research, analysis, writing, and review progressed, a theme emerged. Throughout most of its history, Madison has been able to muster the resources to deal with the difficult challenges, to focus on finding solutions, and to do this without tearing the community apart. Madison's exceptional experience may offer a useful model for other communities.

Finally, I would like to express my deep appreciation and gratitude to the members of the Madison History Committee, whose dedication and perseverance have made this book, *Portrait of the Rose City: A History of Madison, New Jersey*, possible.

Linda E. Connors
Chair, Madison History Committee

A Review of the Concept and Literature of American Exceptionalism

This book is written with a unique focus on a community's history. We look at Madison, New Jersey, a borough of over 16,000 residents in the 2020s, through a lens focused on examining the possible local applicability of the concept of American exceptionalism, which itself is usually applied by scholars to the nation as a whole. By using this local historical focus on such a highly successful community, we are able to uncover how traditional American political and cultural values have been the driving force behind the town's reaction to the many challenges it has faced in a long and eventful history.

Our Madison is the story of a once-back-roads community that dates back to the early 18th century, and as such, it has experienced all of the same challenges, tragedies, and successes of the nation as a whole. Its history tells the story of how even a small community can provide proof that the founding principles of the American nation can become a reality if people work together constructively to solve the difficulties they face.

Madison's history is replete with countless examples of community action to solve community problems, ranging from fighting Hessians in the Revolutionary War to dealing with racism and world wars in the 20th century to fighting Covid in the 21st century.

It should be noted by the reader, and it is also stated in the text, that we are not suggesting that Madison is the only American community that can be considered successful because it adheres to the basic principles of American democracy and, in particular, their powerful beliefs.

The scholarly term "American exceptionalism" has been used and developed by most scholars to detail the uniqueness of our American (and British) political beliefs and traditions in a favorable comparison with the failures of many of the rest of the world's nations. (See the attached list of scholarly books, most of which emphasize the benefits of the concept.) In recent years, a small number of historians and political scientists have criticized the idea of exceptionalism. These individuals have alleged there exists a growing division with other nations through the perceived failure of the United States to effectively bring American values to the world. There is also the idea that America has not properly valued most other cultures. We, however, do not believe that either is the case. In fact, American values based on constitutionally established rights and responsibilities encouraged many nations to establish and model democratic values and freedoms for their people.

Our current analysis of the latest research on American exceptionalism has also revealed an increase in widely different views of the concept, including the emergence of a view articulated by Godfrey Hodgson, a Fellow of the Rothermere American Institute, University of Oxford, that "Now the common ideals of what has become known as 'the Free World' were claimed as the private property of Americans" (Godfrey Hodgson quoted in Gilligan, Thomas ed., *American Exceptionalism in a New Era*. Hoover Institution Press, 2017).

Several other recent critics claim that the belief in American exceptionalism is declining and cite the failure of America to deliver on its principles with younger generations that fail to see or be taught that these ideals have consistently been achieved. We believe that communities, such as Madison, are still motivated by the principles that created this nation—and that they still believe in them.

The following writers/books have been at the forefront of the recent discussions regarding American exceptionalism:

Gilligan, Thomas W. Editor, *American Exceptionalism in a New Era*. Hoover Institution Press, Stanford, CA. 2017. This is a collection of many of the best studies and articles about exceptionalism by leading scholars, including Niall Ferguson, a Senior Fellow at the Hoover Institution. He quotes that great observer of America, Tocqueville, as fearing that governments can become all-powerful and create total dependence of individuals on the central government. Ferguson wrote, "I share his belief that, at heart, Americans love their liberty too much to allow the exceptional institutions that safeguarded it so long to be completely undermined." Hopefully, that is the case, but fear is now compounded by the badly divided political climate in which we live. One important answer should be to continue to refine and improve our democratic values and not abandon them. There is no better place to do this than at a local or state level.

Hodgson, Godfrey, *The Myth of American Exceptionalism*. Yale University Press, New Haven, CT. 2009. Hodgson argues that America is "not as exceptional as it would like to think." He cites his belief that it is blind to its own history and has created "a disastrous foreign policy." He feels it has made us blind to our weaknesses and even cites the concept of Manifest Destiny as contributing to this belief.

Lemann, Nicholas. *American Democracy*. Library of America, *W. W. Norton*. New York, NY. 2020. Lemann traces the evolution of our national self-image to the creation of our constitutional and political documents early in our history.

Lipset, Seymour Martin. *American Exceptionalism: A Double-Edged Sword*. New York, NY. 1996. He also cites Tocqueville as the first to write that the United States was indeed *exceptional*. In this book, he provides an impressive argument for the belief that the nation has considered itself exceptional because it [America] "was unified by an allegiance to a common set of ideals, individualism, anti-statism, populism, and egalitarianism."

Sewell, Alan. *The Diary of American Exceptionalism: Pivotal Events in American History 1783-2023*. New Ideas Publishing. New Haven, CT. 2023. A detailed review of key events and ideas that created the concept of "American exceptionalism."

Wilsey, John D. *American Exceptionalism and Civil Religion*. IVP Academic. Downer's Grove, IL. 2015. A thorough review of the history of an idea and its impact on civil religion.

INTRODUCTION

The story of Madison, New Jersey, is a study of how an American community met the many challenges it has faced since it was first settled in the 1700s by Dutch and English settlers from New England and Long Island. It all began after some land purchases from resident Lenape Indians. From there, the early settlers created a tiny community in a beautiful valley partially surrounded by a range of mountains the Indians called Watchung, which meant "on the hill" or "mountain wall." The settlement initially became known by the colorful name of "Bottle Hill," which some have claimed was derived from a hillside tavern that featured a bottle hanging from a pole in front of the establishment. (See discussion on the tavern and possible origins of the name Bottle Hill in Chapter Two.)

Madison would grow steadily from its humble beginnings. A war of revolution with England followed, and the tiny hamlet played a significant part in defense of the strategically important Watchungs. American troops under George Washington set up an encampment in the nearby Loantaka Valley. Military leaders stayed in area homes, and the residents strongly supported the war. After the war, the community continued to grow while facing obstacles that all Americans had to endure: the Civil War, two world wars, and wars in Korea, Vietnam, Iraq, and Afghanistan. The turmoil and racial divisions that tore America apart in the 1960s also significantly impacted Madison, as have the recent and present issues of racial and economic equity.

However, one stark difference emerges; many American towns have historically not persevered as well as Madison through these stresses. Some have been abandoned, while others have had a large number of people living in poverty. As a result, crime and homelessness have surged in many formerly well-functioning communities. Madison, on the other hand, has thrived and grown through most, if not all, of its history.

This is not to suggest that Madison is the only exceptional borough, township, or city in the nation. But we submit that the history of Madison, New Jersey, as told in these pages, proffers an attainable yet distinctive model of how diverse communities may be created, grown, and sustained through civic cooperation, mutual respect, and effective political leadership.

Frank J. Esposito and the Madison History Committee

CHAPTER ONE

From Violence: Serenity

Gently rolling, wooded acres, the essence of suburban planet Earth and the upheavals of the prehistoric era now mask the harshness of a violent land that later became Madison.

Long ago is not so far away in Madison if you know where to look. The same land contours that survived the holocausts of pre-historic times that shaped the landscape are still in place here. Walk south up the Green Avenue hill to the Madison Golf Club, and you are on a promontory overlooking the Great Swamp, a one-time island in a vast lake. Travel east on Kings Road toward Chatham and you are on what much later becomes an Indian trail. Take the rise of Park Avenue in the direction of Fairleigh Dickinson University and Saint Elizabeth University and you're on another island in that prehistoric lake. Travel north along Ridgedale Avenue to Florham Park, and you're also treading where, much later in time, Indians, also known now as Native Americans, once made an important path.(1)

In a couple of hours, you could scout these byways and travel back in time to an uncharted age that has left its dramatic telltale landmarks.

Here's how our landscape got the way it is:

Northern New Jersey as we know it today began taking shape hundreds of millions of years ago. Soon after the hardest rock formations of the northwestern part of the state had cooled from the fires of creation, primordial seas rose to cover them. Ancient fossils of sea life covered even some of the highest reaches of the Kittatinny ridge lines. The seas fell, mountains eroded away, and the Earth's crust tilted and fractured and then settled into place.

Most dramatically, ancient volcanoes located somewhere near what is now the northern part of Morris County began to erupt about 125 million years ago. At least three times, molten lava spewed forth and then cooled into solid hills that long have borne the Indian name Watchung.

The molten lava of the Watchungs hardened into diabase rock, popularly known as trap rock to those who quarry it for use as road-building material. The Watchungs, Mount Kemble, and Long Hill, as well as the Palisades along the Hudson River, all represent visible vestiges of this early volcanic turbulence.

The "Terrible Lizards"

While the volcanoes roared in the Watchungs, the sea invaded as far North as an imaginary line between present-day Trenton and New Brunswick. The presence of marl sand beds in southern New Jersey gives evidence that water once covered that region, for marl, is formed only in great depths of water. One marl pit near Sewell in Gloucester County has yielded fossilized skeletons of prehistoric creatures.

The ancient sea teemed with enormous creatures, sometimes as long as 50 feet. Sharks up to 70 feet long also populated the hazardous waters. Closer to "home" (modern Madison), huge, lumbering dinosaurs roamed the land in search of prey or plant food. There is no question that these vanished giants once plodded across this terrain, although no bones or footprints have yet to be found within the borough.

Tracks, however, of the "terrible lizards" (the meaning of the word dinosaurs) have been found close to Madison. Their footprints appeared in 1965 at Lincoln Park in Morris County during excavations for Interstate Route 80. A year later, Paul Ruggierio discovered dinosaur tracks near River Road in Chatham Township. That dinosaur was identified as a six-foot-long, plant-eating creature called *Anomoepus crassaus.*

Children seem to have an affinity for finding dinosaur tracks. In 1966, two fourteen-year-old boys found impressive footprints in a quarry at Roseland. Then, in 1979, ten-year-old Scott Hallock of Chatham found a huge dinosaur footprint in the Great Swamp, evidence of *Eubrontes,* said to be about 20 feet long, eight or nine feet tall and 2,000 pounds on the hoof

Then ten-year-old Scott Hallock who is shown here with a huge rock containing a footprint of a Jurassic-period dinosaur called *Eubrontes,* which he donated to the Morris Museum. The rock was so large that it had to be removed from its site with a crane.

Terrible lizards were here, sure enough, some 100 million or so years ago. Then they disappeared, although science has never been able to explain exactly why. A plausible theory of cataclysmic disappearance has since emerged. This theory attributes the sudden demise of dinosaurs to a huge flaming asteroid that plunged into the sea near Central America, releasing an explosive force and gasses that ended life for most living things.

For whatever reason, relative peace descended for a time. What is now Madison was basically in place. Somewhere close, perhaps even through Madison-to-be itself, an ancient ancestor of the Passaic River flowed south, then east through a gap in the Short Hills. The gap, still there, is now a passageway for Route 24.

Those forces that control the universe toyed again with the earth, this time placing the Northern Hemisphere in a deep freeze that would last for millions of years. The Ice Age would be nature's last major outrage against our planet Earth. At least three glaciers had advanced into what is now New Jersey. The most recent, therefore, the one to leave the most evidence, was the so-called Wisconsin Glacier, which began inching southward about 100,000 years ago. Some 20,000 years later, plus or minus a few thousand years, the Wisconsin Glacier invaded New Jersey. The ice cap ground implacably across the land, pushing boulders, sand, and gravel as an immense bulldozer might clear a vacant lot.

Imagine an ice block a mile or more deep over much of northern New Jersey. This awesome ice sheet came to rest along the terminal moraine, that place where a glacier dumps all the ground-up debris it has scraped off the surface of the earth. Deep beds of sand, pebbles, and gravel are visible evidence of the moraine. In what is now New Jersey, the glacier terminated on an irregular line from Perth Amboy to Summit, Madison and Morristown, then on toward Phillipsburg and beyond to the west.

Locally, the southernmost extension of the glacier is marked by Terminal Moraine Road. From there, a portion of the moraine can be traced today along Woodland Road to Green

Village Road. From there, it extends through the Drew University campus, a portion of the former Dodge estate, now known as Giralda Farms, on Loantaka Way, then proceeds along Madison Avenue to Morristown. The moraine bequeathed Madison the hill that slopes upward on Samson Avenue, Prospect Street, Maple Avenue, Green Avenue, and Green Village Road.

Madison's glacial drift in the moraine is as much as 100 feet deep. When excavation work was finished for the National Methodist Archives building on the Drew campus in 1982, layers of glacially deposited sand and clay were found 30 feet deep, as far as the excavators went. Other evidence of the terminal moraine are "kettle holes," small depressions in the earth that seem to be bowls. The *Environmental Resources Inventory*, prepared in 2011 by the Madison Environmental Commission, describes kettle holes as being "formed when large chunks of ice broke off from the retreating glacier and were subsequently buried in the outwash sediment. As the ice melted, the sediment collapsed into the empty spaces, leaving the depressions."(2) A fine example can be found in the Drew Forest Preserve on Glenwild Road near Loantaka Way.

A Mighty Lake Appears

The glacial ice cap stagnated along the terminal moraine for at least 200 years, perhaps a thousand years, before it began receding northward a few inches at a time. Old natural waterways had disappeared. Glacial deposits blocked off the gap at Short Hills, leaving the prehistoric Passaic River in search of a new outlet to the sea. That was unimportant at first. The receding glacier melted as it went, dripping cold water into the lowland west of the Watchung Mountains. With the Short Hills Gap closed, a giant lake built up between the Watchungs to the east and high hills toward the west. Geologists call it Lake Passaic.

Lake Passaic stretched from what is now Liberty Corner northward for 30 miles to beyond Boonton. It was 8 to 10 miles wide, with a maximum depth of 240 feet. If Madison had existed then, the entire downtown business district would have been deep beneath the surface. The southwestern area of modern Madison, where land elevations average about 350 feet above sea level, would have been little more than small islands, green and pristine in the prehistoric sun.

Let your imagination recreate Lake Passaic, for there were no known humans to see it, no historian to write of it. Imagine, too, that precise time when the ice melted sufficiently at the northern end of the lake to permit the pent-up water to break through in a mighty roar, emptying the lake as awesomely as if a reservoir dam had broken. A totally relocated Passaic River had, at that moment, found a new outlet to the sea.

How long did it take to drain Lake Passaic—hours, days, centuries? No one knows for sure, but even to this day, remnants of the lake are evident in the marshlands that skirt the Passaic River nearly everywhere along the sinuous stream bed carved as the Passaic made its way toward the powerful falls of Paterson.

Passaic River

Of all the boggy remains, the most enduring and most vital has been the Great Swamp, a vast and brooding presence that has been noted on maps since Revolutionary War days. The Great Swamp is just south of the Shunpike Road boundary that Madison shares with Chatham Township. It stretches from Green Village to Meyersville, with the swampland interspersed with rising hillocks where hardwood forests grow.

Swamplands were a torment in primitive times. Certainly, the Lenape Indians went around the Great Swamp's periphery rather than challenging its soft, wet bottom. Colonists also avoided the swamp, naturally preferring the gentle hills that rose on all sides. During the American Revolution, the swamp provided a measure of protection for Continental troops and perhaps even the Tories of Morris County.

The Mysterious Swamp

Even deep into the 20th century, the Great Swamp was considered a mysterious wilderness where people who liked solitude built their homes. It was a place for blueberry pickers as well as hunters who followed baying hounds across the bogs in quest of foxes and raccoons. Wolves prowled in the night, relentlessly preying on smaller animals or stalking an elk. Few outsiders knew of such beauty as the swamp's flourishing laurel and azalea bushes or that the "swamp" was not a place of danger.

After the ice was gone, nature was at peace. Within the confines of Madison, along with hardwood trees and blueberries, the undercover growth began to build atop the gravelly terminal moraine. Another current memento of the Ice Age was a gentle stream (Spring Garden Brook) that rose in the springs below what is now Ridgedale Avenue. The surge flowed across the valley and merged with the new, glacier-induced northward flow of the Passaic River.

Wildlife moved into the area again, welcoming the warmer weather and lush growth that inevitably would cover the bottom of a vanished lake. The region teemed with still-familiar small mammals, lizards, and birds. Lizards and other amphibians lived in the wetlands. Wolves prowled in the night, relentlessly preying on smaller beasts or stalking a towering elk.

Of all the wildlife, the mastodon loomed the largest. Mastodons might have been here before the glacial onslaught; authorities disagree on that point. However, the huge beasts definitely ambled across this terrain after the ice receded, for in 1865, the remains of a mastodon were unearthed at the Morehouse farm off Parsonage Hill Road near Chatham. Shaggy-haired, with long tusks, mastodons were as large as elephants. Except for their size, they could not have been fearsome, for there is strong evidence that prehistoric Indians were able to slay them with primitive weapons or traps. Many other mastodons simply foundered in swamps and died; these became the skeletons most likely to be found by latter-day paleontologists.

Were mastodons here when the first Indians, now also called Native Americans, arrived?(3) That is not known for sure, although mastodons found elsewhere have been dated in a time frame that would make it possible that Paleo-Indians and mastodons came face to face in what is now New Jersey.

The Lenape

Indians were the first humans to inhabit New Jersey. Their very name, Lenape, most likely meant, among various interpretations, "common people."(4) They were descended from ancestors who long before—thousands of years in all likelihood—had begun migrating eastward from what is now Siberia. They reached the eastern United States about 10,000 years ago.

Inevitably, some of them found what is now called Spring Garden Brook. This was their kind of land: clean, with plentiful water, ample game, and areas of open ground between patches of trees. There is not yet evidence that a permanent Indian village ever existed there. Rather, it was likely a place for comfortable camping on the way to someplace else. The Lenape also hunted a wide range of animals, including elk, deer, and beaver, in these forested areas.

The terminal moraine ridge made a natural route through the wilderness, and the Lenape gradually widened a path presently known as the Minisink Trail. It meandered from the Delaware River to the seashore, near Sandy Hook. In present-day Morris County, the path ran from Dover through Morris Plains to Madison, where it followed present Hanover Avenue, Park Avenue, and Kings Road to Main Street in Chatham. A branch of the trail wound through the Hobart Gap of the Watchung Mountains and southward toward modern Plainfield.

Numbering between 8,000 and 12,000 people in all of New Jersey just prior to the arrival of Europeans, the Lenape lived in small hamlets along the rivers and streams of New Jersey, eastern Pennsylvania and southern New York.(5) Other eastern Indians knew the Lenape as one of the oldest Indian groups.

The Lenape could certainly claim to be among the first tribes in this part of the world. Other Indians frequently called them the "grandfather tribe," probably because of their long history. Although it is not known if recent PaleoIndian sites discovered in New Jersey are linked to the Lenape, the age of the finds dates to more than 10,000 B.C.E. Most scholars now agree that the Lenape lived in New Jersey for at least 6,000 years, even if the Paleo-Indian may not have been a direct ancestor of the modern Lenape.

The Lenape living or camping in this region called the nearby river by some variation of Passaic, such as Pachsajeek or Passaick, or whatever a colonial settler or deed writer thought the Indians said. It is usually translated as "peaceful land" or "peaceful valley," although Charles Philhower of Westfield, a noted educator and Indian researcher, thought it might have meant "black silty earth." Neither exact spellings nor meanings will ever be fully known, for the Lenape had no written language of their own other than pictograph drawings used to tell tribal history.

Since colonists tended to call the Indians by the name of the river nearest them, regional Indian names (including Passaic) were used as both a place name and as a label for the group of Indians found there. After a short time, the Indians themselves began to use these same names when they were dealing with the colonists. Therefore, in much of historical literature, the Lenape of this region are known by the name Passaick or Passaic, although some writings indicate they might have been called "Pomptons." The name "Lowantica" was also applied to the Lenape who dwelled in the Lowantica Valley, or as it's known today as Loantaka. Eventually, the Lenape became known as Delaware after the river of the same name. This name is commonly used today by their descendants.

Lenape Artifacts

The Lenape left material evidence, or artifacts, of their culture in Madison's Memorial Park, where they camped along Spring Garden Brook on a site that later became the farm fields off present Rosedale Avenue. The late Susan Kent Hubbard, a long-time local resident and former archeological student, first discovered evidence of this Indian occupation while searching the plowed fields of a farmer named I.S. Brown. She unearthed spear points, arrowheads, net sinkers, a stone mortar, and other implements. Her most exciting find was a rare Lenape religious amulet.

In 1966, archeologists uncovered a 9,000-year-old Indian campsite in the Great Swamp. Two years later, a 3,000-year-old campsite was also discovered there. Amazingly, in 1969, archeologists unearthed a 4,000-year-old wooden bowl in the Great Swamp. Although wood normally rapidly deteriorates in most soils, the remains of this bowl were found in remarkably good condition.(6)

Disease, especially smallpox, undermined the Lenape population. Indians had no natural immunity to the disease, which was transmitted by contact with colonists. They experienced smallpox epidemics in 1654, 1663, 1679, 1715-1717, and 1731. Malaria also decimated the Lenape as early as 1677. Mary Smith, a settler at Burlington in West Jersey during the 1679 smallpox epidemic, recalled how "God's providence made room for us in a wonderful manner, in taking away the Indians. There came a distemper among them that they could not bury all the dead."(7) Many perished in the 1679 epidemic, while others began to emigrate from New Jersey as early as 1690. Most, but not all, were gone by the mid-point of the 18th century.

Those who would take over the land viewed Indians in widely varying ways. The first explorers found them handsome, friendly, and hospitable. However, after a crew member aboard Henry Hudson's Half Moon was found dead at Sandy Hook with an arrow in his throat, the native Indians immediately became "savages" for those who soon coveted the Indian land.

They also found the natives to be "heathens," or without religion, according to a journal of the voyage by crew member Robert Juet. Some also thought they worshiped the devil. This led to many later atrocities. The worst one in New Netherlands was the massacre in 1643 when Dutch soldiers from New Amsterdam massacred 80 innocent, sleeping Indians at Pavonia (now part of what is Jersey City). Lenape conflict with the Dutch lasted for the next 21 years as constant warfare with the Dutch further drained the shrinking Indian population.

The Lenape were doomed. Settlers and government representatives piously exchanged trinkets, guns, and alcohol for acres of land, completing the transactions with documents that the Indians signed without apparently having the slightest idea what they were selling. Originally, Indians had the traditional notion that no one *owned* the land but merely had temporary rights to use it for hunting. As such, it was permissible to share the land with the European arrivals.

Indians were once a vital part of the area, but their time was gone in the Madison region by 1715. They left the land as it had been—pristine, clean, uncluttered. Their trails opened it to human communications, and a few Indians would remain to show others through. Yet, the Lenape would not be heirs of the land. Instead, the white man would ruthlessly inherit it, as settlers originally from another continent were about to wend their way further westward through the gap at the Short Hills.

CHAPTER TWO

The Mystery of the Beginning

Most of Madison's earliest settlers lie in Hillside Cemetery. Locked forever within their graves are the first years of this community. Unlike the dead in Thornton Wilder's *Our Town,* they will never emerge to tell of those who began a village along Spring Garden Brook.

There they lie, the Carters, Burnets, Bruens, Wards, Hands, Genungs, Millers, and many others. They left few diaries, reminiscences, mill records, not even hand-drawn maps, much less letters that told of either business or love. Except for their headstones and very meager church records, it is almost as if they had never existed.

Even traditions and stories handed down generation by generation were not recorded until 1855, when the Rev. Samuel L. Tuttle, pastor of the Presbyterian Church, pieced together remembrances of old-timers and available records into a handwritten diary. We must be thankful for the Reverend's tireless efforts to preserve Madison's history. (1) By 1855, the past had grown cold. If tradition is to be believed, the first person to set down roots here was Barnabas Carter of Elizabethtown, who, according to the widely accepted story, found his way here in 1715. Thus, Tuttle was struggling against 140 years with little to guide a historian.

Tuttle revealed that his task was further complicated by the loss of all church records from August 1795 "back to the time of its organization—a period of nearly 55 years." Tuttle surmises that these records may have been destroyed by "some evil-disposed"(2) persons whose disciplinary cases were under investigation by the church session (the body of elected elders governing the church) at the time.

The web of events of these early days is further tangled in confusing deeds, careless allocation of land, casual-place names, and quixotic changes in state, county, and governmental bounds.

A broader, if still vague, awareness of Madison's beginnings can also be found in the *History of Chatham, New Jersey,* assembled in the first two decades of the 20th century by wealthy amateur historian Ambrose Ely Vanderpoel.(3) Fortunately, Vanderpoel concerned himself with a far larger area than Chatham. He began with the chaotic situation in England between March and June of 1664.

Reverend Tuttle

A Disputed Beginning

Briefly, when the English decided to take the so-called "New World" from the Dutch, the Swedes and the Indians, King Charles II, during the restoration of the monarchy after the Puritan revolution, acted on March 12, 1664. He cavalierly gave his brother James, the Duke of York and later King James, all the region between the Connecticut and Delaware Rivers. James dispatched Col. Richard Nicolls and Sir Robert Carr with four ships and 450 soldiers to seize the land from the Dutch and Swedes. Nicolls would rule as deputy governor. Then, astonishingly, on June 23, 1664, James gave away the territory between the Delaware and Hudson Rivers to two court favorites, Sir George Carteret and Lord John Berkeley.

Carteret and Berkeley were friends who had remained with the Duke and his brother through their years of exile. James thought the territorial gift would be an adequate reward for their loyalty. Unfortunately, he set in motion a chain of events that lasted for years and resulted in confusion for those colonists who thought Nicolls was in command.

Knowing nothing of James' gift, Nicolls conquered the Dutch and the Swedes in late summer. Nicolls seriously began looking for settlers, and in September 1664, gave a group of "associates" (English colonists from Long Island who had formed an association for the purpose of establishing a settlement beyond the Hudson) the right to deal with the Indians in New Jersey. This led to the so-called Elizabethtown Associates' purchase of a huge tract of land that stretched westward to the Delaware River from Elizabethtown (present Elizabeth), the hamlet they founded, to the present locations of Perth Amboy in the south and Newark in the north. That was important because Madison's first settlers would come from Elizabethtown, and the mystifying tangle of land ownership rights in New Jersey had begun.

The Carteret-Berkeley ownership evolved into two colonies, East New Jersey and West New Jersey, each controlled by separate boards of proprietors. On their own, they began selling or granting land. West New Jersey's land extended diagonally from Cape May far northwestward into the wilderness and included all of what in time would become Hunterdon, Warren, Sussex, and Morris counties. Theoretically, if there had been a Madison in the 1680s, it would have conducted county business in the town of Burlington on the Delaware River. At that time, the eastern edge of West Jersey was the Passaic River.

Strongly influenced by Philadelphia Quakers, the West Jersey Proprietors divided land westward from the Passaic River. Actually, they were declaring land dividends to their partners in good standing who would be, from their viewpoint, equal and impartial in their decisions.

William Penn received in 1715 a large tract that included the southern edge of Madison and ran out into the Great Swamp. In May 1715, John Budd, a wealthy Philadelphia merchant, bought over 15,000 Morris County acres, including 1,250 acres that covered parts of modern Chatham, Florham Park, and Madison.

Origin of "Bottle Hill"

Between Budd and Penn lay a peculiarly shaped piece of property given in 1716 to John Hayward. The 870 acres included nearly all of present-day Chatham and reached westward to what now are Rosedale Avenue and Cross Street in Madison.

Historian Vanderpoel put these transactions on a map and overlaid it with modern streets and the railroad.(4) With Vanderpoel's clear depiction, the Hayward tract takes on a highly significant meaning. It apparently belonged to John Budd, obviously through some kind of chicanery known only to the West Jersey Proprietors. At any rate, Budd called this his "bottle lot" because of its odd, long neck. The land rolled gently over a hill at modern Brooklake Road, on the eastern edge of Madison, and reached its western edge at the slope that begins near Cross Street. A bottle lot, two hills. What could be more natural than to call the area "Bottle Hill," Madison's earliest known name?

This complicates a long-accepted and possibly more appealing story to which the Rev. Tuttle gave credence in his history: "This place was almost universally known by the name of Bottle Hill, a name which it is said to have received from the fact that a bottle was suspended from a signpost designating the first public house ever opened in this place..."(5) This tale, Tuttle said, came from Major Luke Miller, who "stated repeatedly that he had himself seen the above sign."(6) However, in a footnote by Barbara Parker in a 1980 reprint of the Tuttle history, it is disclosed that Luke Miller could never have seen either the tavern or the sign, since "by the time he was born, James Burnet had a house on this spot."(7)

Thus, perhaps deviously, through the maze of real estate deals, faulty memory, and some possible fiction, a place called "Bottle Hill" came into existence. It is likely the first settler was Barnabas Carter of Elizabethtown, noted as such in Tuttle's history and designated as a major landholder on the Vanderpoel map. According to Vanderpoel, Carter's land was immediately north of the "bottle neck" and ran around John Budd's property. Its eastern edge would have been today's Brooklake Road, its western boundary near modern Central Avenue.

Vanderpool Map

However, another mystery emerged: How did Barnabas Carter get this land? Certainly, he was not entitled to one of the 1714 dividends of the West New Jersey Proprietors. Equally, he was not likely to have endeared himself to the East New Jersey Proprietors, who must have seen him as an obstreperous, cantankerous foe.

Carter's roots ran deep in America. His father, Samuel, had moved from Newtown, Long Island, to Elizabethtown in 1686 and was a member of the Elizabethtown Associates. This group comprised the men who had founded Elizabethtown in 1664 as well as others who subsequently were accepted as Associates.

The Associates disliked the proprietary system, correctly believing that it deprived them of the rights given to them by Richard Nicolls, deputy governor of New Jersey and victim of the Duke of York's duplicity in 1664. Nicolls permitted the colonists to negotiate directly with the Lenape Indians for land purchases based on Nicolls' patents. The next governor, Philip Carteret, who arrived in December 1666, required them to secure patents from the government for the land. He forbade direct negotiations with Lenape leaders. Worse, Carteret ordered the colonists to pay quit-rents (a form of land tax) on the properties occupied and previously paid under the Nicolls government. There was much confusion, as well as persistent questions about its legality, as public hostility to these taxes grew. Local residents led a colony-wide revolt against the quit-rents, and Governor Philip Carteret was recalled to England in 1672. For many, the quit-rents went unpaid.

The Cantankerous Carters

Samuel Carter leaped into the controversy. As an associate, he hoped that the English monarchy would recognize the abuses of the proprietary system and bring it to an end. Carter and 64 others signed a petition in 1696 that called for greater protection of the interests of the Associates. One section of the petition asked the English King to "appoint indifferent Judges to administer Justice between your petitioners and the said pretended Proprietors."(8)

The King and Parliament were not impressed. Tension mounted; the proprietary courts heard harsh words of confrontation and vilification. Samuel and Barnabas Carter and other Elizabethtown Associates jammed the March 12, 1700, session of the East Jersey proprietary court, the Essex County Court of Sessions. When the court rendered a decision against the interests of the Associates, Samuel challenged the four judges to step out of the court several times and uttered a few obscenities. (9) He was arrested, but court records do not show how long the older Carter was jailed.

The Associates were not alone. Anti-proprietary feelings also ran high in Piscataway, Middlesex County, where angry colonists nailed shut the doors of the courthouse. In July 1700, several men assaulted John Stewart, a sheriff in Shrewsbury, Monmouth County.

Riot in the Courtroom

A few months later, Samuel Carter was out of jail, but his temper had not moderated. On September 10, 1700, the Carters and several allies unleashed their full ire on the court. Samuel shouted at Court President William Sandford: "By what authority does the court sit?" Sandford replied, "By order of the King." The courtroom erupted in a riot with Barnabas Carter in the center of the attackers, who tore off Sandford's powdered wig and pulled him off his high bench. The court clerk noted the judges were grossly abused, some of their clothes torn off their backs, and many abusive words were shouted. Chaos soon swept through East New Jersey.

Finally, in 1702, Queen Anne sent her cousin Edward Hyde (Lord Cornbury), to be governor of a united East and West Jersey. It was a slight victory for the anti-proprietor movement: The proprietors gave up their right to govern the colony but retained control of the distribution of the land, which is all that they really wanted. Tensions continued to mount throughout the colonial era eventually leading to major land riots by 1747 as well as very prolonged legal battles.

It was time to move westward, for the second and third generations of the Elizabethtown founders were finding the streets crowded and the land scarce. They wanted freedom from family as well as from government, and they looked westward to the hills and to the more alluring wilderness beyond the Watchung Mountains.

Surveyor John Reading mentioned in his 1715 diary the Lenape Indian plantations "back of the Great Swamps" and that on several occasions noted that he used Indian guides as the land was often difficult to explore. Reading usually traveled along Indian trails that were sometimes obscured by dense forests and swamps. He apparently met few settlers in his journeys through the wilderness.(10)

Tuttle's history declared that Barnabas Carter and his son Benjamin were "among the very first settlers in this immediate vicinity, so far as I have been able to ascertain...."(11) He was vague about details beyond that point. Only this is certain: Barnabas Carter did occupy the land in 1715, as proved in the West New Jersey survey of that year.

Tuttle also credited Barnabas Carter with damming the Spring Garden Brook in order to create a pond where the lower part of Hillside Cemetery now stands. He may have used the water to run a gristmill. According to Tuttle, he also built a home nearby, perhaps at the southwest corner of what is now Cross and Main Streets.(12)

That raises more questions. If Carter had a mill, where are the ledgers and records that he must have kept? Why a mill in this location at all, since Chatham, far more important at that time because of its riverbank location, did not get its first gristmill until 1727? West Hanover (Morristown) could not have supplied customers since historian Theodore Thayer wrote that in 1727, "there were reputedly only three families in Morristown."

We may never know the answers to these questions. Yet, there is one agonizing possibility that we could have known had not fate intervened. Edwin Ely, Vanderpoel's uncle, found most of the exquisite detail for his nephew's later history of Chatham in the library and attic of a home occupied by descendants of John Budd. The Budd family had assiduously collected everything it could relating to the area—books, papers, deeds, letters, maps, wills, and items announcing farm sales. Shortly after Vanderpoel combed the collection for Chatham insight, a fire in 1883 destroyed most of the Budd house and nearly all of the accumulated records.(13) Is it possible that the record of Madison's early history blew away in the smoke?

Actually, the only important place of note in this area was Whippanong (Whippany) in Hanover Township. It was vital because iron was discovered near Succasunna in about 1700. Soon, iron ore, on the backs of horses, went eastward to Whippany. There, the ore was smelted in an iron forge. The raw metal was made into bars cut to be carried in bags on horseback.

Hanover's industrial activity made it also a religious center, the most important influence in colonial days. Hanover Township, created in 1720 as the first township in present-day Morris County, included all of modern Morristown (West Hanover), Madison, Chatham, and Chatham Township (the latter three loosely called South Hanover).

Changing Boundaries

The population grew very slowly but enough to create change. Hunterdon County was separated from Burlington in 1713 in a section of land that included all of modern Hunterdon, Warren, Sussex, and Morris counties, with a bit of Mercer. Morris County was created in 1739. Political boundaries were closing in on newly created settlements.

How did all of this activity affect Bottle Hill? Actually, very little good came of it. As the population of the new county grew, authorities sliced it into three townships: Hanover, Morris, and Pequannock. Unfortunately, the boundary between Morris and Hanover cut the small hamlet almost clearly in half. Kings Road, the main street, was the new political line, with the scattering of Bottle Hill homes in the north lying in Hanover and those in the south being in Morris. As Bottle Hill was not a major center of population or commerce at this time, this division made it even more difficult for Bottle Hill to claim a clear identity.

For the time being, though, we can doubt that anyone living in the area cared. While little documentation on the matter survives, there was no formal protest about the boundary by the few residents. Perhaps some did not even realize that the new division line had been drawn. In any case, the government then neither collected property taxes nor provided services to out-lying villages. It would matter later when taxes were indeed levied, courts established, and the militia called up. But in 1739, the division of Bottle Hill seemingly made little difference.

Life in the Wilderness

Aside from the inactivity of government in this period, there were other good reasons for the early settlers to attach little importance to their lack of a unified village: simply getting a living from the land was concern enough. It was not easy in those early years. If Tuttle is correct, we can assume that the Carters and other early families did well enough. By virtue of arriving first, they had the pick of the best land, and by hard work in home and field, life gradually improved.

For most settlers, however, life in the wilderness was a grinding, wearying, lonely struggle to survive. These first settlers cleared the land by girdling trees so that they would wither and let the sun into the garden patch to nourish corn, buckwheat, rye, and barley, as well as beans, squash, pumpkins, and always a few fruit seedlings.

With no roads, they came westward through the Short Hills Gap, herding a few pigs and a cow, possibly with a coop of chickens aboard. A team of oxen would be a luxury. On their backs, they carried basic utensils and tools to build a shelter, clear land and plant a garden.

Their abodes were certainly primitive by today's standards. Some took advantage of the ridge (now Ridgedale Avenue) in the western part of the settlement, digging into the bank and plac-ing their structures in the cut as protection from north winds. These shelters faced south to take full advantage of the sun.

Life centered in one room not more than 20 feet square, possibly with a sleeping loft above. A large brick fireplace dominated the room, vital for heat, cooking and light, for there were sel-dom any windows. Later, homemade candles supplied additional light.

Life literally began in this one room. Here, children were conceived and born. As they grew, the parents' sleeping area might be partitioned with curtains, although the material for fashion-ing such a luxury might be better used in making clothing.

Edgar Land, the founder of Madison's Museum of Early Trades and Crafts, summed up those early survival days in this revealing account:

> During the first generation, some children were teenagers before they saw anyone other than members of their own family. There were no schools; most children grew up with-out learning how to write their own names. With illiteracy so prevalent, paper so scarce and very little worth writing about, New Jersey's earliest families left little written record of their life and work.(15)

Existence was simple, rough, and lusty. Drinking of alcoholic beverages was common, even among women and children—and not always as a preventive medicine. The discipline of the wilderness was severe and harsh. Death was ever near—especially in the pain of childbirth. Still, it also represented a chance to earn one's way with a freedom unknown in a settlement. Others came to share the hard life.

First Families

Madison's early pioneers were from Long Island, Elizabethtown, and Newark. Among the earli-est settlers were David Brant, Josiah Broadwell, Ellis Cook, Jeremiah Genung, John Harris, and Josiah Ward. Other early family names included Lum, Corey, Post, and Hand.

In addition to these families, another early settler who came to Bottle Hill was Aaron Burnet. Aaron, a son of Thomas Burnet of Southampton, Long Island, was believed to be 90 years old at the time of his arrival locally in the years between 1744 and 1748. He died in 1755 at age 100. Aaron Burnet lived along the ridge. His grandson, James, extended the family property to almost 190 acres, from present Condurso Way to Elm Street. According to Barbara Parker, an authority on the history of the Burnets, family holdings included acreage that extended from Park Avenue into Florham Park.

The David and Daniel Burnet house on Rosedale Avenue.

In the 1750s, David Burnet bought property on both sides of Rosedale Avenue. By the 1770s, his son Daniel was living in a home, no longer extant, at 100 Rosedale Avenue, opposite what is now Memorial Park and the Madison Community Pool. It is not known if Daniel Burnet built the home or if he inherited it from his father.

According to local tradition, this Burnet home had a clear spring of water flowing beneath part of the cellar floor. The natural spring, called Kalamazoo by the Indians, likely flowed underground into the Spring Garden Brook. Several years ago, the Borough of Madison sank a well nearby. According to local historian Henry W. Pilch, it was a "duster," or completely dry of water. If the tradition was indeed based on fact, the underground stream has long ceased flowing.

Some of Madison's oldest homes shed light on the early history of the borough. For instance, the Luke Miller house at 105 Ridgedale Avenue may be the oldest home in Madison. Built circa 1730 by Andrew Miller on a portion of a tract of land purchased from David Burnet, Luke Miller was born here in 1759. Nearby at 31 Ridgedale Avenue is the Sayre House, built circa 1745 by Daniel Sayre and considered to have been used as a station on the Underground Railroad.

The Luke Miller house.

Residence of the late Deacon Ephraim Sayre.

Historic Sayre House on Ridgedale Avenue. A beautifully preserved showplace in today's Madison.

A Presbyterian Hamlet

As was the case throughout much of colonial American society, Presbyterianism was dominant—even overwhelming—in the social fabric of life. Bottle Hill was a Presbyterian settlement, and the source of religious comfort or harsh messages was the church in Whippany. By 1718, a Presbyterian Church had been erected near the old Whippany forge. Bottle Hill residents then joined other area pioneers in the arduous weekly trek to services in Whippany.

This arrangement lasted for nearly 30 years until 1747, when the residents of South Hanover, Bottle Hill, and Chatham broke away and formed their own congregation. However, according to Tuttle, that action "appears to have been made in opposition to the judgment and advice of the Presbytery of New York to which the parent society was connected."(16) It took great courage to defy the Presbyterian hierarchy.

The Rev. Jacob Green, who won considerable fame as pastor of the Hanover Presbyterian Church, wrote his personal objections in the Hanover church record: "But some families in the south end of the town and neighboring parts, thinking they should not be suited with the position of the Meeting House in Hanover Neck, went off, contrary to the endeavors of the Presbytery, and erected a new meeting house...."

THE OLD MEETING-HOUSE.

Presbyterian Meeting House.

Building of the new meeting house commenced in 1749 and marked Bottle Hill's first major impact on history. Despite the fact that Chatham (then called Day's Bridge) had slightly more commercial importance, the newly formed congregation chose Bottle Hill as the site for the center of worship.

A leisurely walk within the boundaries will bring to mind again the hopes and endeavors of those whose names to be found on the pages of this book. Aaron Burnet was one of the first to be interred here. His great age (100) was said to be a favorable omen to settlers, indicating health and longevity.

Deed for Original Meeting House Plot.

Having a local church also helped counter the problems associated with the political divisions of the townships and assisted in forging an identity for the Bottle Hill area. In colonial society, the founding of a church was a bold proclamation of identity for an area. The church also served as a social center for the village by drawing people together, and thereby, over a period of time, forming a distinctly local entity.

The meeting house stood on a high hill overlooking present Kings Road. The Carter millpond would have been at the foot of the hill (along what is now Main Street). The aging sandstone headstones in the southwest corner of Hillside Cemetery delineate the original church site; people in those days were buried just outside the church.

Building a Church

Tuttle's history declared: "The work [on the church] advanced, however, but slowly, and at one time on account of the want of means to proceed, it was actually arrested."(17)

Into the slowdown period stepped Luke Carter. According to Tuttle, Carter said that "if the congregation would not complete the work, he would do it himself."(18) That shook up the laggards, the work was resumed, and the church finally finished.

The meeting house was quite imposing for its time as a two-story, wooden house of worship that measured 48 x 50 feet. The shingled building was sturdy and spacious enough to serve for more than 75 years until 1765.

Inside, worshipers sat on rough-cut boards and slabs, with a plain oaken table or desk for a pulpit. It also lacked a steeple or a bell. This simple arrangement was good enough for about 15 years until 1765, when the edifice was regarded as being completed. The meeting house was important, but not vital enough to be rushed to completion.

That said something about the vaunted industriousness of early settlers. It may also have said something about the males in the area. Tuttle, who certainly would not have gone out of his way to be adversely critical, also jarred another tradition when he wrote bluntly: "From all that can be ascertained at this late date [1855], it is believed that but a very small portion of the male members of the congregation were members of the church." According to Tuttle, the slack was made up by some "leading men, who though they made no profession of religion, were commendably active in erecting a house of worship."(19)

The first church elders, according to Tuttle, were Paul Day, Joseph Wood, and John Pierson, who brought about the organization of the church and were active in erecting a house of worship. That they worked on building the church was as much a reflection of developing local pride and identity as of religious devotion. Turtle also listed as other original church members the wives of Day, Wood, and Pierson; Barnabas, Benjamin and Luke Carter, "and their wives," as well as the Burnets, Bonnels, Eastons, Bruens, Genungs, and other Day family members. The Hands, Millers, and families named Harris, Roberts, Burroughs, and Hedges were also very involved. And, said Tuttle, there were "others," a designation not likely to bring cheer for those tracing ancestry.

The meeting house was surrounded by wild cherry, oak, and walnut trees. According to *An Intimate History of the Presbyterian Church of Madison,* NJ, edited by Viola Shaw and Barbara Parker and based on the journal of Samuel L. Tuttle (pastor from 1853 to 1862), horses were hitched to posts placed beneath the trees.(20) Kings Road, then at the same level as the hilltop meeting house, ran close to the front door. Today, Kings Road passes under the railroad at this point on a much lower level than originally.

Ministers of Salvation

In 1750, church members decided to call a regular preacher, and they settled on the Rev. Nehemiah Greenman of Suffolk, L.I. The youthful minister was engaged on a "stated supply" basis.(21) That meant that he would regularly preach sermons but was not installed as pastor. Greenman, who received his license to preach at Yale College in 1748, came to Bottle Hill in April 1750, but he was something of a wandering free spirit and stayed little more than a year. He departed to become a traveling pastor to "poor congregations"(22), leaving the Bottle Hill assembly to rely once more on the services of ministers of other towns.

Late in 1751, after several months of itinerant preachers, the Bottle Hill congregation was fortunate enough to secure another Yale graduate, the Rev. Azariah Horton. Installed as the first regular minister, he found a haven here for nearly 25 years. Horton was in the same class as David Brainerd and Jonathan Dickinson. All were vital links in the Presbyterian Church structure in colonial society. As a group, they shared a great concern for the salvation of the souls of Indians. Horton had served as a missionary to the Shinnecock Indians of Long Island.

Azariah labored among both Indian and white congregations for nearly 10 years before he accepted the invitation to be pastor of the Presbyterian Meeting House at Bottle Hill, South Hanover. According to historian Barbara Parker, Horton was a grandnephew of Aaron Burnet, an early local settler.

Since many records are lost, little is known about the first 10 years of Horton's pastorate. However, Samuel Tuttle wrote in his journal of a meeting of the congregation held on January 11, 1759, to settle a stormy dispute over what version of "Scottish Psalmody"(23) should be used in services. Horton and two colleagues suggested a vote on the issue. Those written by Isaac Watts won out over those of Rouse.

In 1763, the congregation purchased land for a parsonage near the site of the present Presbyterian Church on Green Avenue. The house was an excellent example of "Salt Box" construction. Horton lived in this parsonage until his resignation in October 1776.

Although it is difficult to know with certainty, it appears that the local congregation had some trouble raising his annual salary, "never amounting to more than 70 pounds or $175 per annum."(24) Samuel Tuttle suggested that "... it is more than probable that this had something to do with his leaving." It is also possible that his health was weakening. Horton relocated to Chatham to live with his son, Foster.

Pastor Horton had been here nearly 25 years, shepherding the regional Presbyterian Church through countless difficulties that ranged from indifference to squabbling to meager funding. He was regarded as a "venerable Father" to the church and to the community. Perhaps more than anyone, he gave the village a conscience.

Madison's First Businesswoman

Horton was also blessed with a vigorous, enterprising wife—another asset. Most colonial women were ignorant of business affairs, and many were illiterate, for it was not considered necessary to educate women. One exception was Eunice Foster Horton.

Mrs. Horton opened a tiny store on the parsonage property (presently on the southeast corner of Green Village and Kings Road). She operated the store in a building that was only 15 feet square, offering tobacco, groceries, ribbons, linen, clothing, and buttons. Apparently, she managed so well that the Hortons lived comfortably despite a minister's small salary. After her husband's passing, Horton moved her business to Chatham.

Significantly, Eunice Horton is the first local woman in what was then a male-dominated world to be acknowledged as having a critical impact on the community during the time of the American Revolution. She died in August 1778, one year after her famous husband.

Riddle of Bottle Hill Tavern

Naturally, the village had a tavern, for this institution was nearly as important in colonial life as the meeting house. It could be the seat of local government, the post office, the stopping place for weary travelers.

The original tavern in Bottle Hill is believed to have stood on the south side of what is now

Park Avenue at Ridgedale. A bronze plaque marks the empty spot in James Park. However, no records have yet been found to show when it was built. By 1753, a date established through research by Barbara Parker, the property was owned by James Burnet, who never used the site as a tavern.(25)

Moreover, if David Brant did indeed operate a tavern at the present James Park location, it was likely relocated in 1753 to another site at the easterly corner of what is now Woodland Road and Loantaka Way. The 1779 DeWitt map showed Brant's Tavern at the intersection of these roads.

Just prior to the start of the American Revolution in 1776, Bottle Hill was a rural crossroads cluster of homes along Kings Road and Ridgedale Avenue. Traveling westward toward Bottle Hill from Chatham, a visitor would have encountered only two or three farmhouses along Kings Road. At a bend in the narrow, dirt lane, the Presbyterian Meeting House could be seen on a hillside along the north side of the road. A short distance west of the church, on what is now Green Avenue hill, was the Presbyterian parsonage farmland, with Eunice Horton's little store still farther west by the road leading to Green Village.

Proceeding along Kings Road (now Park Avenue), the colonial traveler encountered a group of homes at the intersection with Ridgedale Avenue. Known as the "road to Whippany and Hanover," present Ridgedale Avenue was an Indian trail that served the colonists well. It had good elevation—located on a small glacial ridge—and it had access to water on both sides. Along this road were built some of the first homes of tiny Bottle Hill.

Kings Road then forked west, up present-day Elm Street and followed a straight path to the Loantaka intersection, where it continued along what is now Madison Avenue in the vicinity of the former Dodge Giralda estate. The north fork at Elm Street proceeded up Park Avenue as it does today.

A 21st-century tourist can travel this same route along the old Kings Road. In place of smooth macadam, visualize a dusty country byway where weary colonial soldiers once marched to help establish a beginning for the easy passage we now enjoy in this part of democratic America.

By the time of the American Revolution, Bottle Hill was a settlement of perhaps only 20 families. However, a village identity was taking form. Kings Road was becoming a main route into the interior. Although it divided Bottle Hill, the road would prove important commercially to the village in later years. Even then, a traveler had to pass through Bottle Hill to journey either east or west.

Three factors—a road, a church, and a tavern—provided the key ingredients in the making of this crossroads village of Bottle Hill. Despite the difficulties encountered by settling in a strange wilderness, Barnabas Carter and other early colonists succeeded in their efforts. A community was created along the ridges and valleys of the Spring Garden.

Future generations would find their choice to be a very wise one.

CHAPTER THREE

Bottle Hill: In the Midst of the Revolution

W ar clouds filled the skies of America in 1776. For the residents of Bottle Hill, events that had seemed distant in 1775—Lexington and Concord, Bunker Hill and the siege of Boston—edged ever closer as time went on.

As early as May 1775, the rebel provincial Congress had ordered existing militia units to prepare for war. Towns and villages without militia organizations were directed to form them immediately. A month earlier, Congress had created a militia system with the requirement that communities raise taxes locally in order to support it. The militia recruited men from the ages of 18 to 50. However, Luke Miller, a youth from Bottle Hill, signed up at age 17. Among the early New Jersey militia leaders appointed by May 1776 were William Alexander (Lord Alexander), William Maxwell, and Elias Dayton. Local militia committees roamed the coun-
tryside in search of military supplies, arms, and equipment; the sight of militiamen drilling in towns and villages quickly became commonplace. At the same time, active recruiting began for New Jersey regiments of the Continental Army—

According to legend, General Anthony Wayne was headquartered at Sayre House.

General Anthony Wayne

Washington's regular troops—and the first companies left the area (then still a colony) for duty in Canada in November. While no redcoats were on her soil then, New Jersey was in the fight.

Morris County quickly became a hotbed of support for independence from England. Pursuant to the First Continental Congress, local patriots also took regional control and formed shadow governments. Referred to as Committees of Inspection (or Safety or Observation), these groups dispensed justice, collected taxes, and monitored the behavior of the local Tories and the British.

Hanover Township established a Civilian Committee of Observation, and the chair was Matthias Burnet, Sr. (1). The committee members' names were often published in the news-
papers, along with the actions the committees took. Matthias was recognized as chair of the Hanover Committee in the *New York Gazette* and *Weekly Mercury* on March 4, 1776 (2), four months before the Declaration of Independence was signed. Because their names were published, these committee members were known patriots, and as such, they were some of the most sought-after targets by the British army.

On July 2, 1776, in the town of Burlington, a committee headed by the Presbyterian Minister

Reverend Jacob Green from Morris County took the lead in drafting a state constitution for New Jersey. That Rev. Green and the others, including William Paterson and Samuel Tucker, did so was a supreme act of courage as the delegates to the Continental Congress in Philadelphia had not yet completed their voting on what became the Declaration of Independence. In fact, the final section of the Burlington document, which created the first New Jersey Constitution, was highly ambivalent regarding independence. The end of the Burlington document states that if the colonies reconciled with England the document was voided.

Other than the disastrous American surrender of Fort Lee, which presaged a very difficult struggle ahead, no major battle had yet taken place in New Jersey. However, the initial battles at White Plains, Brooklyn, Kip's Bay in Manhattan, and Fort Washington were disastrous for the Americans. As Thomas Paine brilliantly described those difficult days in *The Crisis* in the fall of 1776:

> THESE are the times that try men's souls. The summer soldier and the sunshine patriot will, in this crisis, shrink from the service of their country; but he that stands by it now, deserves the love and thanks of man and woman. Tyranny, like hell, is not easily conquered; yet we have this consolation with us, that the harder the conflict, the more glorious the triumph. What we obtain too cheap, we esteem too lightly:—'Tis dearness only that gives everything its value. Heaven knows how to put a proper price upon its goods; and it would be strange indeed, if so celestial an article as FREEDOM should not be highly rated.(3)

Bottle Hill's Rebel Sentiments

As New Jersey girded for battle, localities throughout the province received calls to play their part. Bottle Hill, small as it was, was no exception and, in fact, took a militantly patriotic role from the start. If the local citizens were few (possibly no more than 20 households), they were determined. Their loyalties were typical of much of Morris County, and they stood at first for resistance to the Crown and then, in 1776, for Independence. The zeal of Azariah Horton, Bottle Hill's Presbyterian minister, was apparently indicative of the local mood. He was reportedly so firm in his Whig (at the time, Whig was a popular title for supporters of the American Revolution) convictions that he did not hesitate to use his pulpit to spread the gospel of rebellion. Unfortunately, Horton's sermons have not survived in printed form, and we cannot recapture his exact words. But his sentiments were no mystery and probably were akin to those of his Presbyterian colleague in the Hanover church, the Rev. Jacob Green.

Green, also a fiery Patriot, published some of his thoughts in a pamphlet titled *Observations on the Reconciliation of Great Britain and the Colonies* (Philadelphia, 1776). Writing as "A Friend to American Liberty," Green came out squarely for Independence. There was no future in the Empire, he warned: "If we submit to British government, we shall be continually cramped with Governors, and other officers appointed by The Crown. All those in authority over us will be such as suit the ambitious designs of Great Britain, however contrary to our interest." The local spirit of the revolt was thus very much alive and active.

Words meant little without action. To put force behind their resolves, Morris County men became among the most active in New Jersey in organizing militia units. New Jersey law called for companies to be organized from each township, which came together as county battalions. In addition, the most fit and able to march were sometimes formed into special "minute" companies, prepared to move on short notice (thus the term "minutemen"). Bottle Hill men generally served in the Hanover Township company of the Morris County Battalion.

While militia duty was unpopular in many parts of the colony, particularly as the war dragged on in its later years, Bottle Hill men came forward without apparent hesitation. Among those who served in the militia were John Muchmore, Deacon Ephraim Sayre, Luke Miller, Daniel Burnet, Aaron Carter, and Captain Luke Carter. The research of local historian Barbara S. Parker suggested that Elias Bruen, William Butler, and John Russell also served as minutemen. Local men also elected their own company officers (up to the rank of captain), with field officers for battalion duty (major and above) chosen by the company officers. Generally, only locally prominent men became officers, with the Morris County Militia specifically requesting that their leaders be "men of property, character and at least 21 years" of age.(4)

Bottle Hill was also part of an area-wide warning system. It was used to alert the populace and militia of enemy attacks. Rebel sympathizers in hamlets and villages along Kings Road could quickly signal the approach of any redcoat advance with the use of cannon fire. In the Short Hills at Summit, the patriots manned a famed cannon known as "Old Sow." The gun was an 18-pounder (that is, it fired a ball weighing 18 pounds) mounted atop Hobart Hill, and local forces guarded it day and night.

Also atop this hill was a signal beacon constructed of logs rising in a pyramidal shape. A dry brush was used to facilitate quick ignition, and the beacon would be lit when the enemy approached. The spot in present-day Summit, where the nearest signal beacon was placed, was the highest point in the area. From here, other signal beacons could be seen farther north along the Watchung Mountains. As William P. Tuttle later wrote of the Summit location: "It has been admirably located for both purposes. Indeed, it is the only spot on the whole mountain which would have served." (5)

Major Luke Miller, 1759-1851. His father, Josiah, was a widely respected farmer and blacksmith. Luke continued the blacksmithing. His long and active life brought many benefits to Bottle Hill-Madison. The Miller home on Ridgedale Avenue was the scene of many gatherings of war-weary officers, and Washington was often a guest there.

Whether by bonfire or cannon fire, the uptick in alarm signals in the Watchungs in 1776 was a matter of concern to local residents. By the summer of that critical year, public concern grew considerably as the news reaching Morris County was increasingly grave.

On the Road to War

Forced out of Boston in March of 1776, the British counterattacked in New York in late summer. General William Howe landed his men on Staten Island at the end of August and during September and into October continued to inflict a series of devastating defeats on the Continentals around New York City. Then, in November, while Howe sparred with Washington's main body north of Manhattan, a strong British column under General Charles Cornwallis struck across the Hudson River into New Jersey. This bold move led to the virtual collapse of the patriot military resistance in the central part of New Jersey.

Unable to counter the British, Washington moved his forces through New Jersey, crossing into Pennsylvania in early December 1776. Then he later crossed over back into New Jersey on December 25,1776, in order to attack the British at Trenton. To make matters worse, Washington's second in command, General Charles Lee, was captured away from his command near Basking Ridge while visiting a woman for a possible tryst at the Widow Mary White's Tavern. The Continental Congress, then meeting in Philadelphia, feared a British assault on Philadelphia. They quickly moved their meetings to Baltimore. The patriot military and political situation looked bleak indeed, and most of New Jersey suddenly lay open to British occupation.

Fortunately for local residents, Bottle Hill was out of the direct line of the initial redcoat attacks. But as Cornwallis' men chased Washington across the State, residents of Morris County became understandably edgy. Fears of a major British invasion were quite real, and there were a number of questions in the air. Would the British move to the north? Would General Washington return to New Jersey and engage in battle again? And perhaps more to the point, could the militia forces of Morris County, which had continued to rally to muster points around Morristown, rely on any help from the retreating Continental army units? All records of the period indicate a time of anxious waiting as events developed over November and December of 1776.

Meanwhile, Bottle Hill and the rest of Morris County received firsthand accounts of the fighting from refugee Whigs who fled to the area along Kings Road from overrun towns, including Newark, Perth Amboy, Elizabethtown, and surrounding farmlands. The Bottle Hill-Morristown region, with its highly patriotic citizenry and hilly terrain, seemed to offer the best hope of finding a safe haven for those fleeing the British advance.

Morris County also emerged as a vital strategic center. Aside from its generally Whig populace, the area also had iron mines and forges critical to the war effort. Without the Hibernia Furnace, Washington's army would have had an even more difficult time securing the ammunition it needed to stay in the fight. The region was also protected by rolling terrain well-suited for defense. The marshy land of the Great Swamp to the southwest and the natural barriers of the Watchung Mountains and Passaic River on the east afforded additional shelter. Kings Road also provided quick access to the hills of Morris County.

Bottle Hill represented an important part of this defensive strategy. The village was, in fact, on the main route into the area—the same unimproved passage traveled by fleeing Patriots from Newark and Elizabethtown and, if they had a mind to, by any strike force the British might choose to send. Contemporary maps made this quite clear. The best map was drawn in 1777 by Major Robert Erskine, a geographer for the Continental Army. His map, 75-A, showed the stretch of Kings Road from Morristown through Bottle Hill and Chatham toward Springfield.

Several other colonial pathways had considerable military importance. The grandly misnamed Kings Highway (Kings Road), then only a narrow track, and Park Avenue, a mere trail, provided a direct link between Bottle Hill and Morristown. The stretch of byway now called Madison Avenue also led toward the interior of the county. During the revolution, Ridgedale Avenue was a footpath known simply as the "road to Hanover," and the Erskine map shows the route as the "Road to the Hanover Meeting House." Similarly, Green Village Road was called the "road to New Vernon." That passage then stopped at modern Woodland Road and turned right (west) toward Loantaka. Other colonial dirt tracks were the present Rosedale Avenue and Brooklake Road. Tiny Bottle Hill was part of a communications system rudimentary by 21st-century standards, yet of major importance in its day.

First British Strike

The British could also read maps, and the significance of Morris County was not lost on them. Accordingly, on December 17, 1776, they sent lightning strikes toward Morristown. Many local

Patriots were in a state of panic, but the militia, unlike units elsewhere, remained fairly steady. Indeed, they followed their officers toward the advancing British instead of breaking for safety. For most of that cold winter day, the fighting flared around Springfield as redcoats tried to force their way through Hobart Gap. If they had accomplished that, they would have been free to advance along Kings Road to Chatham and Bottle Hill and into the heart of the rebel country.

This fight was a desperate one, with neither side able to force a decision. Nightfall brought the combat to an end, and the exhausted militiamen slept in their positions. The Americans had given a fine account of themselves, and their stubborn resistance surprised the British. Local citizen-soldiers also had their first taste of the fighting prowess of British regulars. Patriot troops fully expected that the struggle would resume in the morning.

However, the Royal troops had had enough. Not realizing how close to victory they had come, the British commanders decided not to proceed without reinforcements. Extra troops, however, were not available, as General Howe needed them to consolidate his line of occupation across the center of New Jersey. Hobart Gap was as far west in the Watchungs as a major British unit ever penetrated. It was not until June of 1780 that the redcoats would again attempt this at the Battle of Springfield.

The Morris County Militia had held its ground in one of the most critical early skirmishes of the war. The engagement was the first demonstration that the militia could check the enemy and a clear signal that, despite initial redcoat successes, New Jersey was not knocked out of the war. In fact, the New Jersey militia saved the important Morris County region from British control.

The first major battle in New Jersey would come on December 26, 1776, after Washington and his forces crossed the Delaware River. On Christmas night Washington led his troops back across an ice-clogged Delaware River into New Jersey. The great general's surprise attack on the Hessians at Trenton was a decisive victory. He followed with a quick strike on the main British army at Princeton on January 3rd. The tide had turned. He then led his men north, arriving in Morristown on January 6, 1777.

As far as local residents were concerned, the Continentals arrived not a moment too soon. Earlier fighting at Springfield gravely disturbed local citizens as far west as Morristown, and many were planning to evacuate. General William Maxwell, the head of the New Jersey militia, who was simply passing through the area while returning with his New Jersey troops from New York, was prevailed upon by local leaders to take over regional defensive operations. He did so, even commandeering two Massachusetts regiments that were marching by in order to join them with Washington's forces. Maxwell, an effective military leader, maintained his independent command (with Washington's blessing) until the Commander-in-Chief himself arrived with the main army.

The Loantaka Encampment of 1777

The arrival of Washington's men again brought the war directly to Bottle Hill. The General faced serious problems in billeting his command for the winter, as none of the villages around Morristown offered sufficient shelter or supplies to support a large number of soldiers. Instead of trying to concentrate his army, Washington dispersed his units to strategic locations within Bottle Hill and also in modern Chatham Township on land owned by John Easton and Isaac Pierson; others were scattered from the region east of Morristown extending southward to the Middlebrook Encampment near Bound Brook, while other groups were established between Chatham and Springfield. The site plan of the camps, as local historian Barbara Parker has noted, relieved Washington of the burden of having to supply a large central encampment. It also helped deceive the British as there were only about 2,000 men with Washington at this point, but their dispersed positions gave the look of a much larger body.

Parker's *Tours of Historical Madison* (1983) provides the best identification of the Loantaka site. Located in the fields "near the intersection of Woodland Rd. & Treadwell Ave.," the encampment was one of the largest (if not the largest) of all of the Continental positions that winter. Residents at the turn of the 20th century reportedly still found rock piles from the chimneys of the soldiers' huts.(6)

Over the years, more evidence regarding the Loantaka encampment came to light. Bill Styple, formerly a resident of Chatham, in recent years discovered American Revolutionary era artifacts at the historic site. Working at the camp location off Woodland Road in Madison, Bill and his son Brad found over 50 items dating from the Revolutionary period. The items are dated to the time of the encampment, although few are of military origin. However, according to Dr. Richard Veit, archaeologist and professor of history at Monmouth University, that is not unusual on former military sites. (7) That the Loantaka encampment clearly existed is also suggested by references in Revolutionary War pension records for soldiers who served at that location.(8)

Bottle Hill was suddenly faced with finding temporary homes for hundreds of soldiers who, in Samuel Tuttle's words, "were billeted wherever room for them could be found."(9) While most of the troops camped at the Loantaka site, many of their officers stayed in town, quartered in private homes. Few contemporary records have survived to corroborate stories of specific instances, but local legend is rich in at least one particular case. According to Madison lore, General "Mad" Anthony Wayne stayed at the Sayre House on modern Ridgedale Avenue.

Although there is no direct proof of Wayne's temporary residency, there may be something to the story. It is possible, even likely, that he rented land locally to pasture his horse. Certainly, other ranking officers stayed, even if only briefly, in Bottle Hill. There is also confirmed evidence that later in the war, Col. Matthias Ogden, who was a Brevet General and Commander of the First New Jersey Regiment, was also in town. He rented land to pasture his horse next to Luke Miller's house on the road to Hanover, and he may well have used Miller's house as a headquarters. Lt. Colonel Francis Barber, another New Jersey officer and one of the army's most dashing light infantry commanders (he was a favorite of Washington's), also took local accommodations. He and his wife rented the old Presbyterian parsonage on King's Road.

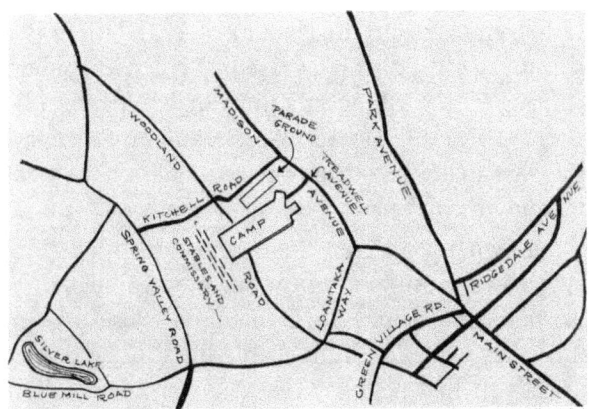

Copy of Loantaka Valley campsite map drawn by William Parkhurst Tuttle from a description by his father, the Rev. Samuel L. Tuttle.

Documented or not, the most important aspect of the Wayne story may have been the fact that the tale was believed by so many people, which was testimony to the pride later Madisonians placed on their town's contributions to the war effort. Tuttle clearly reflected this view in his account of interviews with residents who claimed to remember the Revolutionary years: "There are those," the local historian wrote, "still living among us who remember to have seen officers seated in that sanctuary [the Presbyterian Church] with the families with which they were quartered; and also companies of soldiers entering into that venerable edifice, and taking their places in the southeast gallery."(10) In the strictest sense, this does not replace hard historical evidence, but it says quite a bit about how the town perceived its role in the struggle for nationhood.

If some of the officers lived in town, most of them probably camped with the rank-and-file at Loantaka. The encampment afforded ample water for the men and animals, as well as a good defensive position.(11) According to Tuttle, the entire garrison lived in some "three hundred log cabins, which were built in regular order along a wide central avenue."(12) He based his observations on the testimony of eyewitnesses, including Bottle Hill resident Silas Brookfield. The layout of the camp may have been as described, as it conforms to plans of better documented military positions elsewhere. Yet, 300 huts would have sheltered upwards of 3,000 men, much too high a number since Washington quartered his troops in scattered locations.

Of those who were encamped in the area in early 1777, many were militia. Washington was rebuilding his regular Continental line, and until he had the new regiments in shape, he reported, "I must depend chiefly this winter on the militia, to enable me to act defensively, or even to make a stand."(13) Supplies were also short, and the General was distressed to see numbers of his troops "marching over frost and snow, many without a shoe, stocking, or blanket."(14) The Loantaka encampment was likely not as difficult to endure as the later ordeals at Valley Forge or Jockey Hollow, but that winter was by no means an easy time for the men who lived through it.

The Specter of Smallpox

A lack of supplies and low troop numbers were not the army's only significant problems that winter. In the wars of the 18th century, disease normally killed far more soldiers than combat did, and the war for independence was no exception. One of the most contagious and fatal maladies was smallpox, which had decimated more than a few fighting forces in earlier colonial conflicts. It already had played a large role in defeating the American invasion of Canada in 1775 and early 1776. Washington feared it as much as he feared redcoat bayonets.

What the Commander-in-Chief dreaded became a reality in January of 1777. There is no record of when the first case of smallpox hit the army, but the disease had reached epidemic proportions later in that month. It raged throughout Washington's units in February and, in some areas, lingered until spring. The army faced a genuine medical crisis, and on February 5, Washington reported as much: "The smallpox has made such head in every quarter," he wrote, "that I find it impossible to keep it from spreading thro' the army, in the natural way."(15)

In the hope of stemming the epidemic, the General ordered the inoculation of all troops in Loantaka, Morristown, and Chatham, as well as those joining the service in Philadelphia. The inoculation of an individual was risky and sometimes fatal. Living in close proximity to the army, the civilian population suffered as well, and by the time the disease had run its course, hundreds of soldiers and local residents had perished. In Madison, the old Bottle Hill Presbyterian cemetery offers mute evidence of the impact of the epidemic. According to Parker, of the soldiers and civilian Patriots who are buried there, perhaps as many as 200 were very likely victims of the epidemic of 1777.

These were hard times, but they brought forth local heroes, some not always in uniform.

One such was Bottle Hill's former pastor, Azariah Horton. During Washington's effort to inoculate the army—and civilians willing to risk the procedure—Horton and Presbyterian pastors Timothy Johnes of Morristown and Jacob Green of Hanover came forward to encourage their people to cooperate with the military. Horton had retired in October 1776 after nearly 25 years of service to Bottle Hill, but he saw clearly that the needs of so many afflicted soldiers and civilians could scarcely be met by the practicing ministers. So, at the age of 62, Horton decided that he could not stand by as people were dying. He labored among them selflessly, exposing himself to the disease. He soon contracted smallpox and died on March 27, 1777. He later became a recognized hero of the American Revolution. Remarkably, it was recently discovered that Gary Ruckelshaus, a former mayor of Madison, is directly related to Horton.

In his journal, Samuel L. Tuttle wrote that Horton "doubtless visited many of these poor unfortunate fellows during their dying hours and pointed them to the only true source of consolation; and when they died, he doubtless followed the remains of many of them to the grave."(16) Smallpox very likely killed more Bottle Hill residents than did the war itself.

The Remarkable Connection of Azariah Horton, Bottle Hill's Revolutionary Hero, to Present-Day Madison(17)

What are the chances that a baby born in Troy, NY, who was adopted in 1947 by a couple in Madison, New Jersey, and eventually served as mayor of the town, would learn that one of his ancestors by birth was a founding father of the same town more than 270 years ago when it was known as Bottle Hill? This same ancestor, Rev. Azariah Horton, has become venerated as a heroic figure in the American Revolution.

That is the reason former Madison Mayor Gary Ruckelshaus continues to shake his head in disbelief. For 25 years, Ruckelshaus searched hard to find his birth mother but was stymied by a 1940 New Jersey Law sealing all adoption records. When that law was repealed in 2014, Ruckelshaus was first in line to have his files released on January 1, 2017, the day the law went into effect. This led to the discovery of a half-brother in Seattle, Washington and, two first cousins in California and an unexpected familial connection to Azariah Horton, who had left an indelible mark on the town to which they both devoted years of their time and talents.

The saga began during a casual telephone conversation when Ruckelshaus mentioned to his cousin, Carol Patterson Fisher of San Diego, California, that he was serving on a committee to review *The Madison Heritage Trail*, a history book first published in 1985 and then being updated to include the next fifty years of history. "I mentioned to Carol that Madison was formerly called 'Bottle Hill,'" he said, "and she immediately recalled that in her family ancestry research, she had come across the unusual town name." Literally gasping with anticipation, Carol stated simply to Ruckelshaus' disbelief: "We have a relative from there. The name Horton was prominent in Bottle Hill, New Jersey, in the 1750s."

So gratefully remembered....the grave of Azariah Horton in Hillside Cemetery.

Their spontaneous elation was felt clear across the country. "No one would have ever known anything about the linkage without the knowledge and memory of this incredible woman, my cousin Carol, who lives 3,000 miles away and who was but a stranger to me just three years ago," the former mayor said with great admiration. Carol was equally joyful, saying she felt "the connection with Gary from the minute he got off the plane from New Jersey."

As part of Ruckelshaus' cousin Carol's research, she also discovered the direct link between the Burnet and Horton families. In about 1700, Azariah Horton's Uncle Barnabas married Elizabeth Burnet, daughter of Aaron Burnet Sr, the first Burnet in Bottle Hill. "So, Gary is first cousin, eight times removed to Azariah Horton, and Jim Burnet IV, who currently serves in Madison Borough's government as chief financial officer and assistant administrator, is a grandson seven times removed to Aaron Burnet Sr. I find it extraordinary that two descendants of two of Bottle Hill's most important founders in the 1750s are still active and working for the town. Although I cannot connect a relationship between Gary and Jim now," she said, "I believe that they are distantly related."

There is one final twist to this remarkable story. Matthias Burnet's son, Matthias Burnet, Jr., served in the Revolution in a number of positions, including as First Sergeant of Captain Israil Ward's Company of the Eastern Battalion of the Morris Militia. His son, Matthias Lindsley Burnet, was Madison's first Postmaster. He was also president of the Bottle Hill Temperance Society. Ironically, he cast the deciding vote in 1834 to change the borough's name from Bottle Hill to Madison, thereby extinguishing the Bottle Hill name that led to the discovery of these exceptional circumstances.

A Lull in the Storm

On February 6, 1777, local forces helped repulse yet another enemy attack near Springfield. As an aide to Washington wrote: "The enemy came out yesterday from Amboy, in a manner, so much more formidable than usual that we expected a general attack, but our advance parties gave so warm a reception, that they made a retreat." (18) Inhabitants of Bottle Hill had to live with the constant threat of British attack. Despite this danger, the rest of the winter proved quiet. In April, Washington expressed surprise "that we are still in a calm; how long it will, how long it can remain, is beyond my skill to determine."(19) Washington then ordered the army to move to the Middlebrook encampment site near Bound Brook.

Despite the tribulations of war, the militia frequently provided inspiration to both soldiers and citizens alike. When the British made some threatening moves in June 1777, Joseph Clark wrote of the Morris County militia in his diary: "They turned out, young and old, great and small, rich and poor. Scarcely a man that could carry a musket was left at home."(20)

By the summer of 1777, the residents of Bottle Hill could breathe a sigh of relief. Bottle Hill and Morris County became chiefly a supply area with little fighting, the most serious action being a skirmish a few months earlier, on April 22, 1777, when local militia surprised a British foraging party near Morristown. Two Royal officers and 14 men died, while another 14 were captured. Americans suffered only three wounded. Such news kept Bottle Hill and other residents on the alert, but the war did not come close again for two years until the spring of 1780.

A Brutal Winter

In the winter of 1779-1780, Washington marched a major part of the Continental Army along Kings Road through Bottle Hill to the camp at Jockey Hollow. The ensuing winter there was as difficult to bear for the poorly clothed and meagerly fed troops as had been the previous winter at Valley Forge. Snow buried the landscape as the elements seemed to be working against the Americans.

At the same time, food was intolerably scarce. Once again, as in 1777, residents of Bottle Hill and other nearby settlements provided supplies from meager hoards for use by the military. These local farmers shared with the American forces their limited supplies of wheat, corn, apples, squash, turnips, and other food. Pigs were another vital foodstuff requisitioned by the army. This animal was prepared in a variety of ways with virtually every part used for sustenance. The few chickens raised by local farmers were often taken into the house at night to protect them from predators, but they probably soon disappeared in order to sustain starving soldiers.

Cows, too, often became casualties to the army's needs. With their means of survival dwindling, Bottle Hill farmers were forced to develop great self-reliance to sustain both themselves and the freedom fighters.

As army surgeon James Thatcher wrote in his journal: "It is honorable to the magistrates and people of Jersey, that they have carefully complied with the requisition, and furnished for the present an ample supply, and thus probably saved the army from destruction."(21) Somehow, the assistance from local farmers sustained the army through the winter.

Raising Arms Once Again!

In the early summer of 1780, warning alarms spread through the Bottle Hill area as militia patrols detected enemy activity on Staten Island.

The Hessian General Baron von Knyphausen landed troops on June 6 at Elizabethtown. He set out along Elizabeth Avenue and Kings Road with some 6,000 men. They were headed toward Morristown and quickly threw the region's Whigs into a panic. Patriot minutemen in Elizabethtown attempted to stop them but were unsuccessful. As word spread of this large invasion, it seemed that the worst fears of Bottle Hill residents were coming true—that they were in the path of a major British assault. Sentinels quickly lit the signal beacon on Hobart Hill, and Old Sow boomed its ominous warning as militia rushed to arms.

After determining that the British move was not a ruse to cover some even larger attack, Washington decided to send reinforcements down Kings Road to confront the enemy. The next day, June 7th, local militia and the army stopped the Knyphausen forces at Springfield, but not before his men had sacked and burned much of Connecticut Farms (now the town of Union). The fighting was serious and local resistance was much more challenging than the Hessian commander expected. He ordered his forces to pull back to Elizabethtown and then to Staten Island. The Americans were in no position to counterattack, but patriot towns were safe for the time being. However, Knyphausen was not yet through.

He came back two weeks later, this time with a larger force and with his commanding officer, Sir Henry Clinton. Again, the British thrust was toward Morristown, and on June 23, there was savage fighting at Springfield. Militia units joined Continental regulars in a spirited and gallant defense of the Springfield bridges. Gen. Maxwell, on the scene with the New Jersey Continentals, reported that the contestants traded the fiercest fire he had ever seen.

The British got no further. Deciding that he would gain nothing from a continuation of the battle, Sir Henry ordered a withdrawal to New York. This time, the attackers did not get away so easily. Whig soldiers, including Morris County Militia, harried them all the way back to the water's edge at Elizabeth. Col. Sylvanus Seeley, who saw a good deal of the fighting, recorded in his diary that "this day the enemy came out and burned Springfield and returned about 3 o'clock p.m., pursued by our people. The enemies [sic] loss this day is thought to be considerable."(22)

During the fighting, Parson James Caldwell, whose wife had been killed at Connecticut Farms, provided an American cannon crew with paper wadding by giving them copies of Watts' Hymnal taken from the Springfield Presbyterian Church. As he passed out the hymnals to the cannoneers, he was reported to have shouted, "Give 'em Watts!" According to local tradition, Caldwell, pastor of the First Presbyterian Church of Elizabethtown and a chaplain in the army was a frequent visitor to Bottle Hill and the Sayre House, where he often preached.

The engagement at Springfield was a significant patriot victory. Had the rebels given way, the British would have faced minimal resistance between the Watchungs and Morristown, where the central artillery reserve of the Continental Army lay only lightly guarded. Moreover, Whig towns along Kings Road would have been at the mercy of the redcoats. Given the earlier fate of Connecticut Farms, where at least 30 buildings went up in flames, the fears of Bottle Hill residents were justified. Fortunately for local residents, the Battle of Springfield turned out to be the last major contest in the north. Until recently, many Revolutionary War historians have failed to acknowledge the importance of the Battle of Springfield. The excellent account by Thomas Fleming entitled *Forgotten Victory* has hopefully helped to alter that neglect.(23)

An old landmark, the Wingate house on Woodland Rd. (Now demolished.)

The War's End

After 1780, most of the heavy fighting (and all of any strategic consequence) took place in the southern colonies. Still, Washington kept on the alert for an opportunity to land a blow against the British garrison in New York. That chance never arose, but an even more spectacular opportunity presented itself in the late summer of 1781. Bottle Hill was to witness at least a beginning segment of the most dramatic campaign of the entire Revolution.

Gen. Charles Cornwallis had taken a post on the Yorktown peninsula in Virginia. He intended to stay on the defensive there until the British fleet could bring him badly needed reinforcements from New York. It was at this point that Washington learned of the impending arrival of a French naval task force and formulated a daring plan. If the French fleet could hold the Virginia Capes and stop the Royal Navy from entering Chesapeake Bay, Cornwallis would be forced to fight with only the forces he had on hand. Washington reasoned that, under those circumstances, the British general's position would be hopeless if the Continental Army, with the allied French army under Count Rochambeau, could trap him at Yorktown. With this in view, he set in motion the campaign that would drive the British out of the war.

George Washington by Rembrandt Peale. This portrait presently hangs in the council chamber of the Hartley Dodge Memorial Building. It is among the many treasures given by Geraldine Rockefeller Dodge to be displayed within the walls of the beautiful building.

Washington and Rochambeau mapped a secret and speedy forced march overland to Yorktown, which began in August. Traversing northern New Jersey, the troops took main roads whenever possible in order to maintain their rapid pace. Before leaving Chatham, the rebels built a long series of bake ovens just south of present Route 124 and east of the Passaic River. Although these ovens made bread for the army on the move, their main objective was to make the British believe that the Colonials would be staying put in New Jersey. The ruse even fooled the local residents of Bottle Hill. According to Samuel Tuttle, who evidently interviewed a number of eyewitnesses to the building of the ovens, Azariah Carter remembered "seeing the troops come through this place, and he and Mr. Leonard Bruen, Captain Luke Carter and others have stated to me that it was upon every mind in this region that the whole army was to be permanently quartered on that ground."(24)

The British, fooled badly by Washington's careful deceptions, did not react until it was too late to save Cornwallis. Battered by besieging Americans and French troops, Cornwallis surrendered on October 19, 1781. As the electrifying news spread north, citizens of Bottle Hill and hundreds of other towns and villages rejoiced. The war would not end officially for almost two more years, but Yorktown marked the final major clash between the main armies.

There was a local postscript to the major fighting. Almost a year after Yorktown, Bottle Hill was the scene of a little-known skirmish involving local militiamen and two Loyalist robbers, Caleb Sweezey and John Parr. On September 12, 1782, Capt. Benjamin Carter and a force of 10 militia surprised the two outlaws. They had committed a series of robberies in the Bottle Hill-

Chatham locality, hiding out in the Great Swamp until spotted by an alert militia patrol. Rather than surrender, Sweezey and Parr elected to shoot it out, although the odds were heavily in Carter's favor. The militia under his command wounded and captured Parr and "shot Sweezey dead."(25) That was how the actual shooting phase of the War for Independence ended for the citizens of Bottle Hill.

There was little fanfare when the Revolutionary War officially ended in April 1783. The conflict produced a small crop of veterans eager to return to civilian life. Violence had come close several times, but Bottle Hill had escaped virtually unscathed except for the decimation of livestock and survival food supplies.

Peacetime in Bottle Hill

The end of the war brought with it a more far-reaching event that moved the pioneer community into the mainstream of early American life. Bottle Hill residents probably received their first wheels for transportation!

Until that time, the all-purpose ox served the army in myriad ways, so when the fighting ended, some of the wagons used by the army to transport weapons and supplies were so worn that they were abandoned at Jockey Hollow. Edgar Law Land, founder of the Museum of Early Trades and Crafts, stated that there is evidence that area farmers purchased five of these wagons and that local blacksmiths repaired them. The impact of this must have been very significant in a village of only 20 households that was barely 60 years from the wilderness.

Life was primitive. People were still wearing shoes of the same shape with no left or right. Beeswax was becoming plentiful for candlemaking to supplement light from the fireplace. Sanitation and germs were unknown quantities, which led to high mortality. No records show that the out-back privy had come into general use. According to Edgar Land, human urine was also collected for use in breaking down flax fibers so that they could absorb dye. It may also have been used for tanning leather.

The village economy still depended largely on agriculture, but there were local business ventures. John Dixon operated a dry goods store on Kings Road at the Green Village Road corner, where Eunice Horton earlier maintained a similar business. In the early years of the war, Dixon advertised in the *New York Gazette* and *Weekly Mercury* "an assortment of dry goods (not before exposed to sale) just opening at the house of John Dixon [sic] near Mr. Horton's Meeting House, in Morris County, New Jersey."(26)

Three years later, in February 1779, Dixon was still in business, but he was seeking out the delinquents. His newspaper advertisement struck a firm note: "This is to request all persons indebted to John Dixon of Bottle Hill, Morris County, on book, bond, or note, to come and settle with him by the tenth of February, or depend on being dealt with as the law directs."(27)

Bottle Hill was also mentioned in newspaper advertisements requesting skilled craftsmen and unskilled workers. One such advertisement by Thomas Gordon appeared in the *New Jersey Journal* on December 17, 1780. It promised that "a wheel-wright, who understands making linen and woolen wheels, will meet with good encouragement by applying to the subscriber at Bottle Hill." The advertisement was a sign that the economy was showing activity.

In an advertisement of November 15, 1780, in the same newspaper, John D. Crimsheir stated his willingness to barter slaves. "As farmers are fond of encreasing [sic] their stock, he has a healthy, strong wench and two children, which he will exchange for a wench from eighteen to thirty-five years of age, who understands housework."(28) The advertisement is proof that slavery did exist in Bottle Hill during the Revolutionary War years.

The Museum of Early Trades and Crafts in Madison, which promotes important research on Bottle Hill, issued a series of informative leaflets. In one of these, Bottle Hill colonial merchants are aptly described in this manner:

> If you lived in the Bottle Hill-Chatham area at the time of the Revolution, there were men who would sell you both rock and shore salt; others would butcher your meat. Captain Carter, John Dixon and John Crimsheir provided salt for the families in and around Bottle Hill. Mr. Crimsheir would accept your cash, barter for your wheat, or ask you to cut and cart his firewood in exchange for salt.

In a *New Jersey Journal* advertisement, Crimsheir advertised that he had "two horses to part with, fit for saddle or gears; in payment, for one of which, he will accept of good hay."(29)

A Time for Change

The facts that are known with certainty about those hardy colonists who lived through the Revolutionary War in little Bottle Hill are so scant that the reader must use a creative imagination to fill in the gaps.

To appreciate growing up in such an atmosphere, the reader must close one's eyes, wipe away modern luxuries, and walk a long, dusty road back to a time when there was no such thing as a vacation. Let alone sufficient energy available after the survival chores for recreation. Yet, we can only assume, as they did in the last century, young boys must have fought imaginary wars with whittled rifles and dime store pistols while girls bound up their playful wounds and scolded their rag dolls.

Older folks had their dreams, too, their ambitions, their determination to make things better. The road into the 1800s was becoming wider and less rutted, and it led to somewhere beyond the imagination.

CHAPTER FOUR

From Bottle Hill to Madison

During the half-century following the end of the Revolutionary War, the area known as Bottle Hill struggled to develop an identity all its own. It was not easy. At the war's end, Bottle Hill still remained divided down the middle by Morris and Hanover Townships, with Kings Road as the boundary line. Village unity was nearly impossible when neighbors on either side of the road lived in different townships. Those neighbors were also represented by different local tax collectors.

The state legislature acted in 1798 to create a new political entity called Chatham Township, recognizing that this section of Morris County had little or nothing in common with Hanover. It could not be termed a sweeping change; inexplicably, the legislation was not acted upon for eight years. The creation of Chatham Township had to wait until 1806. The new township included all the areas now known as Madison, Florham Park, Chatham Borough, and the present Chatham Township.

Within the new township, Bottle Hill gradually became dominant. With its Presbyterian Church on the hill above the gradually expanding cemetery, the village developed a stronger identity, but as the 18th century gave way to the 19th, it was on the edge of dramatic change. The forging of a distinct village identity was spurred by several local factors, evolving from common memories of the Revolutionary years and the breaking away from the shared Presbyterian Church Meeting House at Bottle Hill to form a separate congregation in Chatham. The place was changing rapidly from a strictly Presbyterian town into a more diversified community. The arrival of a small group of French emigres from Guadeloupe in 1783 gave the village a more varied character and, in time, led to the formation of a Catholic Church. As early as 1803, a group of Methodists were also meeting in the area. Shortly thereafter, existing roads were improved, a new turnpike passed through the town's center, and within three decades, a railroad arrived. Thus, Bottle Hill, like the state of New Jersey, was looking increasingly to the outside world as it developed within.

Turnpikes Improve Travel

Roads were the important way for Americans to travel as the 19th century dawned. What once had been hard-packed paths and trails slowly evolved into widened, yet still muddy, wagon roads. Even these primitive early roads were always crucial for Bottle Hill, a community of rural farmers with a need to transport their harvests to market. Farmers frequently constructed these early roads through their own lands thereby creating a resultant hodgepodge pattern of transportation.(1)

As commerce developed outward from seaboard towns and cities, the demand for better roads became urgent. Lancaster Turnpike, in Pennsylvania, was completed in 1794 and connected that town with Philadelphia. Citizens of New Jersey clamored for similar construction in their State. New words such as "turnpike" and "shunpike" brought an air of mobility early in the 19th century.

Always susceptible to public pressure, the New Jersey Legislature chartered the Morris Turnpike in March 1801. The first of 51 such highways to be authorized through Bottle Hill, Morristown, Newton, and northward to the upper Delaware River region, "roughly following the old Minisink Trail through the Short Hills Gap."(2) The section between Elizabethtown and Morristown was completed in the fall of 1804, with the route through Madison following the right-of-way of its modern Main Street (Route 124).

The turnpike would prove important to the future development and commerce of Bottle Hill. A straight-line highway, it was an alternative to the narrow winding Kings Road, which had served the settlement as its main artery for almost 100 years. A major purpose behind the construction of Morris Turnpike was to facilitate the creation of commercial outlets for the farms and mines of New Jersey's western interior. Another closely related purpose was to build a road that would unite the upper Delaware Valley with Newark Bay. By doing so, goods could be easily transported to Newark or Elizabethtown and taken by barge or steamboat to New York City.(3)

After the construction of Morris Turnpike, products from farmers of Morris County flowed easily eastward. In the early years of the turnpike, it was not unusual to see covered wagons being used to ship livestock, produce, and other goods. Known as "Sussex wagons," these forerunners of the more famous western-covered wagon used a flax cloth covering over a large wagon carriage.(4) One local resident, writing in 1889, recalled seeing many of them pass through Bottle Hill. A full trip to New York and back took at least two to three days.

In Bottle Hill, the turnpike toll house was located at the northeast corner of present Rosedale and Main Street. The tollgate was similar to many others on the turnpike. Travelers were halted at the house by a long pole-like "pike," or gate, which prevented further movement until raised or turned out of the way (thus the word "turnpike"). Toll gates were usually spaced between 5 and 10 miles apart on the road. There, toll collectors charged fees, which varied according to the number of horses needed to pull the wagon. A fee exemption was given to churchgoers and farmers.

The novelty of the turnpike was to wear thin, however, as toll collectors aroused public ire. Toll dodgers were everywhere, to the frustration of collectors. Some willfully raced past the collectors by going around the tollgate. Others claimed an exemption from the toll because they were on their way to church (it didn't seem to matter what day of the week it was). As one might expect, travelers took other roads to avoid paying tolls. This generally meant using a parallel road in order to avoid the stretch of turnpike where a toll collector waited. The appropriate name of "shunpike" came into being for these roads since they provided a means of avoiding the toll. Madison still has its Shunpike Road, which runs from Green Village to Chatham, essentially in a parallel line with the former toll road, now Main Street.

The busy and more worldly New York was within easy distance by stagecoach to Elizabethtown. By taking a ferry ride the rest of the way, a person could travel to New York, obtain sleeping accommodations, and then return home the next day. This was a dramatic change, welcome in a town that had been largely isolated during its nearly a century of existence.

Bottle Hill got its first regularly scheduled stagecoach stops in 1798 with the creation of a stage line running between Morristown and Paulus Hook (Jersey City). Stops also were made in Chatham and Springfield. Under the ownership and operation of Benjamin Freeman and John Halsey, the line also had a departing-returning routine of Tuesday-Wednesday and Friday-Saturday. The Bottle Hill homes of Benjamin Freeman and Stephen Halsey and the Chatham home of Israel Day were the local stops. For a ride to Elizabethtown Point, riders changed to a second stage at Springfield. Passengers who stayed on the first stage would go to Newark and Paulus Hook. A ferry, in either case, from Elizabethtown or Paulus Hook, would complete the trip to New York. The fare was eight shillings for the trip via Elizabethtown and 10 shillings for the Paulus Hook route, the respective equivalents of $1.00 and $1.25.

John Halsey was still running a stage route in May 1808 to Elizabethtown Point, departing from Morristown at 6 AM on Monday, Wednesday, and Friday, with returns on each succeeding day. Another stagecoach line was created four years later for the same route.

Mail service, so crucial to the flow of ideas and communications in the early republic, became somewhat more regular with better stage transportation. The first Bottle Hill post office was located near the present site of the James building at Main Street and Green Village Road.

With increased traffic on the Morris Turnpike, the year 1819 was a good time for Col. Stephen D. Hunting to open his hotel on the southeast corner of Waverly Place. It was originally known as the Madison House, then later called the Bottle Hill Tavern, and when it finally moved to Main Street, it became known as Widow Brown's Inn. Sadly, it was razed on July 30, 1991, in order to make way for a bank (see Chapter 15). There now is a more recently opened Bottle Hill Tavern at 13 Waverly Place.

Post Office business was conducted at this desk, which is now in the home of James E. Burnet IV. Residents would pick up their mail from numerous cubbyholes.

Matthias Burnet, a wheelwright, built his home in 1812. From 1830 to 1841, the front hall was the Post Office, later the telephone exchange. Later still, it was Alexander Eagles, Sr.'s estate and insurance agency. It is shown here in 1885.

James Burnet III standing by his great-great-grandfather's desk as Postmaster William Lowe used a rubber stamp for the commemorative Bottle Hill-Madison Bicentennial postmark.

A French Touch

French influence took on more importance in the waning years of the 18th century. Local tradition has it that the area in and around Chatham had great appeal for French officers serving with Washington at his Morristown headquarters. Upon returning home, they apparently spoke of Bottle Hill to fellow Frenchmen.

Vincent Boisaubin brought elegance to Bottle Hill. This courtly and gracious gentleman from Guadeloupe built his mansion on land that once was the Loantaka campsite. The estate and 16 acres of the original 113 acres remain.

One of them was Vincent Boisaubin. His reputation was colorful, and his influence upon his adopted community was undeniable. Boisaubin, a loyalist to the French monarchy, left his native country after the French Revolution. He had been an officer in the bodyguard to Louis XVI. Following a brief residency in Guadeloupe, the Frenchman decided to try his luck in America. Hearing about Bottle Hill's already established French community, Boisaubin arrived and prospered. A man of manners and polish, he made many friends, even among non-Catholics. In fact, until St. Vincent's was constructed, he and his family attended the Presbyterian Church. He also had a reputation for understanding others.

Local history tells this anecdote about him: a poverty-stricken farmer with obvious hard luck was particularly upset because his cow, one of his remaining possessions, suddenly died. Coming upon the scene, with sympathetic neighbors surrounding the man, Boisaubin took pity, reached into his pocket, withdrew five dollars and presented it to the man. The incident swelled the French immigrant's reputation at once, earning him a secure niche in local history. Indeed, he was considered a man of such remarkable generosity that when W.W. Munsell & Co. published a New Jersey history in 1882, the dead cow story involving Boisaubin appeared in print. The five dollars, it seems, were well invested.

In the early 19th century, other prominent Frenchmen settled in Bottle Hill. One was Nicholas du Reste Blanchet, a native of Bordeaux, who also came to Bottle Hill from a previous residence in Guadeloupe. The Blanchets had 12 children. Another ar-

Hyacinthe Nicholas du Reste Blanchet, 1771-1848, a French plantation owner from Guadeloupe, purchased the David Howell house in 1812. A Blanchet descendant stated that her grandfather, a boy of nine at the time of Lafayette's visit in 1825, was taken on the hero's knee and taught to tie his cravat like that of the Marquis.

The Howell-Blanchet house, pictured on the south side of Madison Avenue, was moved across the road circa 1900. It now faces Drew University. A hardy survivor of many owners, it continues on with grace.

rival was Edward Thebaud (1798-1883). Thebaud was a wealthy New York businessman who decided to settle here with other French families. He purchased the property of William Sayre on Morris Turnpike in the 1850s, the present site of Madison Junior School. By 1839, according to the Morristown *True Democratic Banner,* Madison had 14 French families. They were a productive and welcomed ethnic group in the growing village, which by this time also had a Swedish family.

Black Residents

Bottle Hill was broadened by other ethnic minorities as well. Local Blacks were small in number but varied in status. Some were free, some indentured servants, and a few were slaves. To a large degree, Bottle Hill's Blacks were as difficult to categorize as those elsewhere in America in the tense years prior to the Civil War. In some cases, servants also learned a particular trade while in servitude.

In one of the first indentures of Blacks in Bottle Hill, in 1819, William Brittin purchased the services of Hannah, a Black child, from Preston Bruen for the sum of five dollars. Two years later, an auction of the services of indentured servants was held in Chatham Township. Hannah Baldwin was indentured for one year to Phebe Allen for $52, and others were auctioned at prices ranging from $20 to $77.

Early Bottle Hill Schools

In the early 19th century, Bottle Hill possessed only one school, which was probably located on College Road (now Park Avenue). As was typically the case during that time, this school was closely tied to the local Presbyterian Church. In January 1803, the Rev. Dr. Matthew L. Perrine, pastor, presided at a meeting of congregants when they decided to help furnish wood for the school. At the same meeting, village leaders were empowered to act as a committee to draw up a constitution for the school of Bottle Hill. There were six such individuals appointed by "a majority of employers present at a general school meeting" in order to work on the constitution. The six-man committee represented some of the most prominent families in the village: Ephraim Sayre, Benjamin Thompson, Luke Miller, Jonathan Bruen, and Samuel Muchmore, in addition to the Rev. Perrine.

The Madison Academy

The constitution developed by the committee consisted of seven articles that set the rules for conducting school business, the number of meetings, voting procedures, powers of the directors and procedures for raising school funds.

On January 31, 1803, the new document won the endorsement of all those at the school meeting. A quorum was lacking, but subsequent approval was secured from the necessary two-thirds majority (18) of the 24 employers. The rules were designed to produce literate, godly students for the sponsoring employer. A public examination of the students was held each quarter. In addition, students were expected to read each day from the Bible, write a composition, and study religion each week.

On February 16, 1809, the employers met to consider the need for a new schoolhouse. After some discussion, a decision was made to investigate the possibility of purchasing property for the school on Columbia Street (Ridgedale Avenue) on the northwest corner near present James Park. The employers named themselves the "Madison Society" at this time and decided that the new building would be constructed of brick rather than wood. On March 4, 1809, a committee chosen to oversee the building of a new schoolhouse, to be called Madison Academy, recommended that a subscription be initiated to secure funds for the proposed building.

The two-story brick academy (with a bell tower added in 1853) was dedicated in 1809. For 70 years, the structure served Madison well by becoming a respected symbol of the town for travelers and writers. It also served as a meeting place for many community gatherings until being vacated in 1879. It was destroyed by fire in December 1886.

School construction lagged after 1809, but it picked up again in the 1830s. By the end of that decade, the village had two well-known boarding schools: a French school for young ladies conducted by Madame Chegaray on what is now St. Elizabeth University property and A. Chanlet's School for Young Men. In addition, there were three other boarding schools and a public school to complement Madison Academy.

War of 1812

The Academy was only three years old when the War of 1812 began. Initially, the war hardly affected the people of Bottle Hill, as it was basically a sea war between American and British ships. The war, however, came a little closer to home in the fall of 1814 when the Third New Jersey Detailed Militia was organized to assist with coastal defenses at Paulus Hook (Jersey City) and Sandy Hook. Capt. Luke Carter commanded the Company of Riflemen from Bottle Hill, while another local leader, Capt. William Brittin, was in charge of the Company of Fusiliers from Chatham. The men saw little action, but they at least participated in this unusual American-British conflict.

The 1825 Visit of Lafayette

The French hero of the American Revolution, the Marquis de Lafayette, Gilbert du Motier, made a triumphant return to the United States in 1824-25 when he began a tour of all 24 states then in existence. His widely heralded tour took him 13 months to travel to countless American towns and cities. While visiting New Jersey, he made a significant and emotional stop in Bottle Hill while traveling on the Morris Turnpike on July 15,1825. He was en route from Morristown to Newark on one segment of his great American tour. The stop in Bottle Hill was at the Madison House, a hotel of Col. Stephen D. Hunting, located on Waverly Place.

When Lafayette stepped down from his horse-drawn coach at the hotel, the Rev. Dr. John G. Bergen, pastor of the Presbyterian Church, then addressed him on behalf of the inhabitants:

> Reverend and honored father; we greet you welcome to our happy land; as a minister of Christ I address you with my parishioners; I have come to yield to you our congratulations as the early friend of our country, the early companion of our beloved Washington, now no more. Honored sir, may sweet felicity attend you during your stay in our happy land—may the protection of heaven bear you safely on the waves of the ocean, to the

bosom of your family, and the blessings of God rest on you forever through Jesus Christ. To this welcome, the Frenchman replied:

Accept, dear sir, my congratulations for yourself, your village and your country, and my thanks for your kind desire for my welfare.

Lafayette was then escorted into the Madison House. Thirteen young girls, dressed in white, were waiting. After being presented to Lafayette by their teacher, Julius T. Derthick, the girls recited a poem that emphasized the close tie between the French hero and his beloved Washington, to whom he was as close as a son:

Recitation of Poem to Lafayette:

All hail to the hero, Columbia's great friend.
Whose fame will resound till creation shall end;
Now welcome, thrice welcome, to our happy clime,
Where virtue is honored in freedom sublime.
You sought us when weak, and you found us when poor,
But now we are strong, and our conflict is o'er;
We tender our homage, extend you our hands,
With gratitude our every bosom expands.
The loss of our Washington still we regret,
But almost behold him in thee, Lafayette,
And could his good spirit now look from the dead,
The heavens would scarcely retain his blest shade.
Now fare you well, father, we see you no more,
The ocean will bear you away from our shore;
May fortune attend you across the broad main,
Until your own daughters embrace you again.

Laura Blanchet, the daughter of Hyacinthe Nicholas du Reste Blanchet, was one of the little girls reciting the poem.

According to a contemporary newspaper account in the Morristown *Palladium of Liberty*: "The eyes of the general appeared to wander over the interesting group. When the name of Washington sounded on his ear, his countenance became grave and his attention appeared fixed, as if holding intercourse with the spirit of his departed chieftain and friend."

Two of the girls then stepped forward to present Lafayette with a copy of the poem. The Frenchman thanked them "especially for their manner of delivering it." Colonel Brittin then showed Lafayette to the sideboard, where he enjoyed some refreshments before saying goodbye and resuming his journey.

According to an anonymous itinerary for the trip now in the Library of the New Jersey Historical Society, Lafayette and his party may have thought they were in Chatham. Or, more likely, they used the name "Chatham" to identify Chatham Township which then included Bottle Hill. The passage reads as follows:

At 7 o'clock July 15—we left Morristown—stopped at Chatham, a few moments and partook of refreshments prepared—the Rev. Mr. Bergen in behalf of the town addressed the general (;) at Springfield the general was saluted by a discharge of canon (sic.) and other demonstrations...

There is a story told about Vincent Boisaubin during the Lafayette visit by William P. Tuttle in his book, *Bottle Hill and Madison*.(6) Although it had little impact on the community at the time, it is worth telling, for it indicates how strongly emotions brought from the Old World could remain in the New. The story concerns Lafayette's 1825 trip celebrated in poetry by 13 glowing schoolgirls and loud cheers from Frenchmen who had been Republicans opposed to The Crown. They had allegiance to Lafayette, who was considered responsible for the capture of Louis XVI during his attempted escape from revolutionary authorities.

Lafayette had known Boisaubin in France. The latter had pretty well established himself by that time in Bottle Hill, being the owner of a beautiful mansion and a member of the "social set." It was, therefore, a natural response for Lafayette, seeing Boisaubin on Madison Avenue, to order his carriage driver to stop. Lafayette stepped down and proceeded toward Boisaubin in a gesture of greeting. Boisaubin, the old French Royalist, is said to have turned his back on the French Republican, letting others see the snub. It put a minor damper on the general's triumphant parade.

The impact does seem to have been slight indeed. Lafayette resumed his tour and many historians have made no mention of the alleged snub. Instead, such positive stories as the marriage of Lafayette's relative, Count Joseph Louis d'Anterroches, to Mary Polly Vanderpoel in the Bottle Hill Presbyterian parsonage have endured.

During Lafayette's 1825 visit, Colonel Brittin was in command of the military escort. After the reception, he set out to escort Lafayette to Springfield. At Short Hills an axle broke, for which the men in the escorting party substituted a rail. The repair was sufficient for them to reach Springfield, where the elegant French leader stepped from the carriage and reportedly promised, "When I return to France, I will tell my countrymen that a Jerseyman rode me on a rail."

A Succession of Churches

As early as 1808, local Presbyterian parishioners discussed the need for a new church. They appointed a committee to make recommendations on the subject, but the issue remained unresolved until 1822. In that year, a majority of the congregation desired a new church building. Construction was delayed by an extended argument about where the church should be located. When the congregants met to decide the issue, those who preferred a site on Main Street won out over those who preferred an alternate site closer to Chatham Village. Forty residents of Chatham Village signed a petition protesting the decision. Led by Silvenus Bonnel, the dissidents complained unhappily for about eight months before organizing their own church in October 1823. Thus began the Presbyterian congregation of Chatham Village.

In 1824, construction began on the Bottle Hill Presbyterian Church. Community involvement in the construction of buildings was frequently called a "frolic," and, according to the Rev. Samuel Tuttle, frolics were held during the construction of the new church. Women of the parish prepared supper at some place near the site in order to feed the men and to do their part in

The new Presbyterian Church of 1825 served for over 100 years. Its bell, forged by Ephraim Force of New York City, rests now on the grounds of the present church on Green Ave.

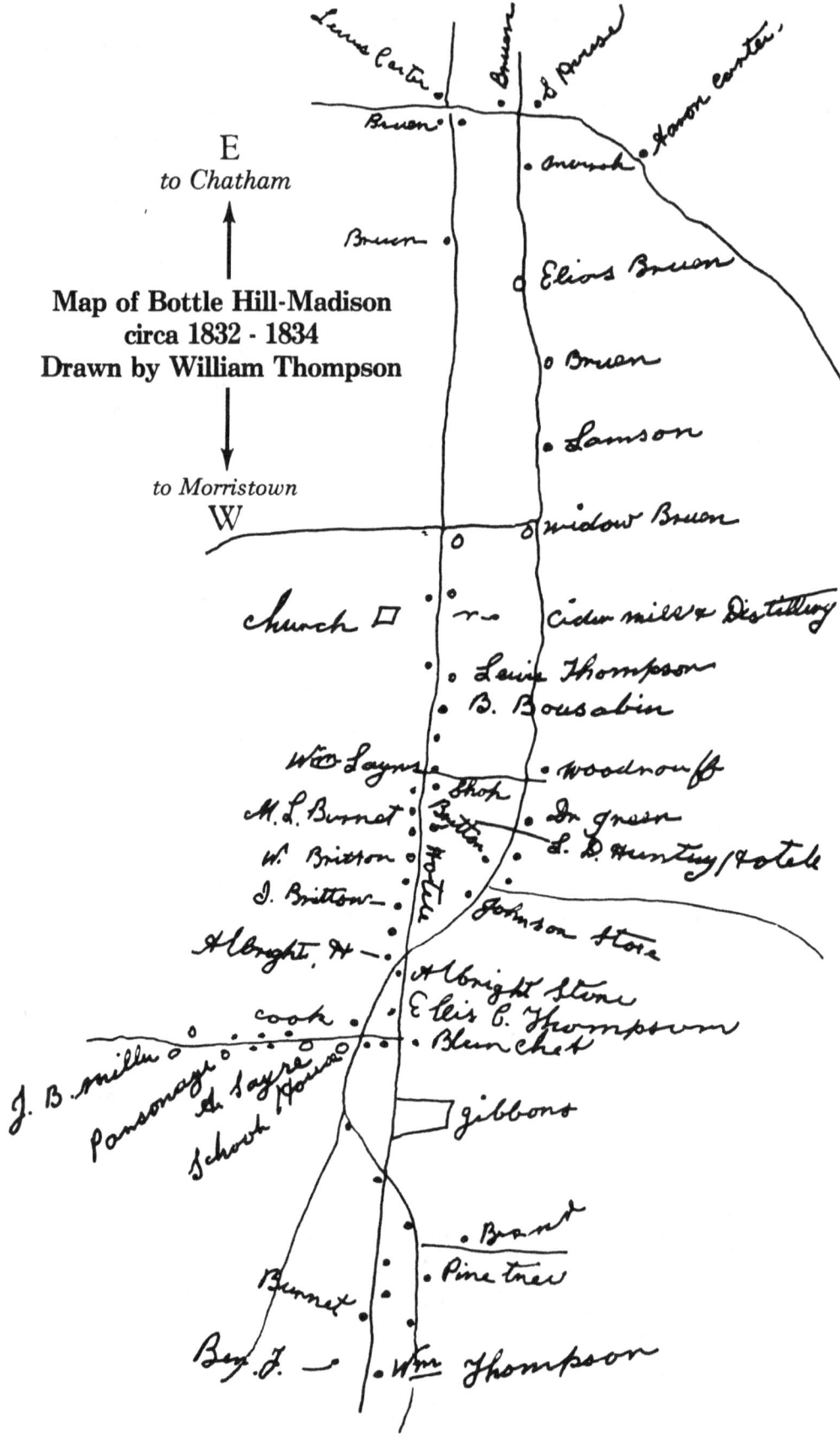

E
to Chatham

**Map of Bottle Hill-Madison
circa 1832 - 1834
Drawn by William Thompson**

to Morristown
W

this remarkable exercise of community spirit. As further testament to the neighborly spirit, the building committee was authorized to take the best timber without cost; according to the Rev. Tuttle, "In order to obtain it, the Committee were authorized to explore the entire wood and timber territory of the whole congregation and wherever they could find what they wanted, to take it."(7)

After the last Sabbath in February 1825, the old church in Hillside Cemetery was taken down by the same workmen who were building the new edifice. Samuel Tuttle, in his Journal, described the dismantling of the old church: "On the day following the workmen engaged on the new church assisted by the members of the congregation met and took down the venerable edifice—stick by stick—and laid its various parts among the tombs of those who originally reared it—a most affecting proof of the mutability of all earthly things." By the spring of 1825 workmen completed the new church on Main Street and placed a bell made by Ephraim Force of New York City in the cupola.

During remodeling 32 years later a memorial board, dated March 8, 1825, and containing the names of those congregants instrumental in building the new church, was discovered beneath the floor of the Main Street sanctuary. The Rev. Dr. John G. Bergen was listed as the pastor, and the congregation leaders named formed a veritable who's who of well-known families, including Muchmore, Carter, Crane, Miller, Brittin, Thompson, Bruen, Roberts, Force, Sayre, Darling, and others.

Dr. Bergen left the pastorate of the Presbyterian Church in August 1828 to move to Springfield, Illinois, then a frontier outpost of log cabins, which would later become known as the hometown of young Abraham Lincoln.

Other Congregations

Madison's Methodists initially met in 1803 in private homes at East Madison, which was also known as "Genung Town." From 1840 to 1843 they met in a room in Henry Keep's Bonnet and Umbrella Factory on the southeast corner of Kings Road and Prospect Street. By 1843 these temporary quarters were abandoned in favor of a newly constructed church on Waverly Place. The building is still standing at 5-7 Waverly Place, although considerably altered and no longer used as a church. In 1870, the Methodists relocated to their present church adjoining Drew University on Madison Avenue.

The present Methodist Church on Madison Ave. was built in 1870. The first church (1844) can be seen today on the west side of Waverly Place. In 1870 it was sold, jacked up, and stores were installed at ground level. The church balcony was floored over, creating a third floor. From 1842, it served as the Masonic Lodge and later as the American Legion Post.

The first Catholic mass in Bottle Hill was celebrated in the Park Avenue home of Lavielle Duberceau in 1809. Father Peter Vianney, an assistant at St. Peter's on Barclay Street in New York City, was the celebrant. The first resident priest in Bottle Hill was Father Pierre Malou, who stayed a few years after 1825. The first St. Vincent's Church, dedicated in 1839, was at present 69 Ridgedale Avenue, now remodeled into a house. Vincent Boisaubin was the most gener-

St. Vincent's Catholic Church, 1839, another landmark of the 1800s. The present church on Green Village Road was constructed by John Corbett.

Grace Episcopal Church was built in 1855. Services were previously held in Col. Hunting's home and in Oriental Hall on Waverly Place.

ous contributor of land and building. The pastor from 1839-1842 was Father Richard Newell.

Early gatherings of Episcopalians began in the home of Col. S.D. Hunting in 1852. Grace Episcopal Church (first called Zion) was founded in 1854 with worship services first being held in Oriental Hall on Waverly Place. The beautiful Gothic Revival structure on Madison Avenue was consecrated in 1857.

Bottle Hill in 1832

William Gibbons, a millionaire who owned businesses and property in New York and New Jersey, as well as several plantations in Georgia, bought land west of Bottle Hill in 1832, known as "The Forest." John Cunningham, in his book *University in the Forest,* relates how the Gibbonses decided to live in Bottle Hill and how their presence changed the area.

While passing through Bottle Hill in June 1832, Cunningham wrote that Mrs. Gibbons "fell in love with the giant oak trees."

> On their return to New York in July, Gibbons stopped in Bottle Hill and asked a local entrepreneur, Abraham Brittin, to assemble as much property as he could in and around 'The Forest.' Brittin first acquired thirty-five acres from Durest Blanchet on July 23, 1832...there the mansion would be built. He assembled 205 acres in The Forest at an average cost of $170 an acre. By 1851, Gibbons owned about 1,000 acres in or near Madison.
>
> Work started on the mansion in 1833. Bricks came from the local area, but the wooden pillars for the front piazza were designed and carved in London and much of the interior trim was imported. A brick stable accommodating 25 horses and numerous carriages, and a brick granary and storehouse were also built on the estate. The family moved in in the Spring of 1836. It has been estimated that Gibbons ultimately spent $300,000 on land, buildings and furnishings for his plantation-style estate.
>
> Residents of rural Madison surely were amazed when they saw the dimensions of this mansion rising amid the oaks. Gibbons' local purchases enriched local merchants and his house and grounds afforded several mechanics and craftsmen a steady income.(8)

The family, including a son and three daughters, enjoyed The Forest together until Mrs. Gibbons died in October 1844. After William Gibbons died of heart failure on December 10, 1852, son Heyward interrupted his attendance at Harvard Law School and returned permanently to Savannah. His spinster sister Caroline continued to live in the mansion, at least part-time, until her death in March 1857. Sarah married Ward McAllister, and her sister Isabell married a Madison neighbor, Frank Lathrop.

"The mansion still stands," Cunningham noted further, "serving as the Drew University administrative center. The stable and granary are in use as university buildings. Drew University and the Gibbons' traditions have merged. As for the Gibbonses, some of them remain in Madison: father, mother, Caroline and Heyward, the Confederate who came back to die in nearby Morristown in 1887. These four lie in Hillside Cemetery under the "most imposing monument on the highest hill, close to the railroad tracks."

A fascinating story concerning William Gibbons was told by Francis Bruen in 1920 when he was 81 years old. According to Bruen, Gibbons was driving his carriage on Morris Turnpike when he passed one of the stagecoaches owned by his own company. As he attempted to pass the stage, the wheels of the vehicles became locked, and both screeched to a halt. The stage driver immediately recognized him, but Gibbons slowly climbed down from the coach and fastened feed bags to his horses. He then climbed back onto the stage and pretended to fall asleep. The driver was resolved to go to New York without backing up an inch, even if the owner of the carriage was his employer. Gibbons then ordered him to move his stagecoach back, but he still refused. Perhaps impressed by the spirit of his employee, Gibbons moved his own carriage backward so that the obstinate driver and his stagecoach passengers could proceed to New York. Gibbons never forgot the incident and talked about it for many years.(9)

Another visitor came to Bottle Hill in the early 1830s to gather information for his pending book on New Jersey. Thomas Gordon, historian and geographer, wrote of the Revolutionary settlement, which then consisted of two main roads, a few houses and little else.(10) Bottle Hill, however, was steadily evolving into a self-contained village. In addition, the population had doubled since the end of the Revolutionary War.

In his now classic *History and Gazetteer of the State of New Jersey*, first published in 1834, Gordon described the newly emerging village as follows:

> On the turnpike road from Elizabethtown to Morristown, 13 miles from the one, and 4 1/2 from the other; 223 N.E. from W.C. (Washington Capital), and 57 from Trenton; contains a tavern, three stores, a Presbyterian Church, an academy, and about 40 dwellings, generally very neat; the surrounding country gently undulating, and well cultivated.

This description of Bottle Hill clearly shows a small community surrounded by farms. In no small measure, the change from a crossroads to a thriving village was spawned by the Morris Turnpike, which facilitated travel and commerce.

Bottle Hill Becomes Madison

The year 1834 was a pivotal one in many other ways. Nationally, it was a year of bitter partisan political fighting on the floor of Congress between the forces of Henry Clay and those of Andrew Jackson, which resulted in the creation of the Whig Party by those opposed to Jackson. Locally, the conflict took on a different focus. Starting about 1830, a temperance movement in the village became increasingly strong and resulted in the formation of a local temperance society. By 1834, local opponents of "demon rum" spoke openly about the intemperate sound of the name Bottle Hill. To some, it undoubtedly conjured a mental image of a village of drunkards.

As a result, a highly spirited public meeting took place at the Madison Academy on August 2, 1834, to debate the issue. Proponents of the name change were led by Matthias L. Burnet, while a significant number dissented. A second meeting was held on August 30, when a vote was finally taken, and those favoring a name change narrowly won out. Burnet served as moderator of the public meeting, with Robert Albright as secretary. The picturesque Bottle Hill name was set aside for a more patriotic and probably more respectable Madison. The namesake was James Madison, the nation's fourth President, who served from 1809-1817. This was yet another sign that the crossroads settlement was emerging as a distinctive American community.

Local Enterprise

Among the best-known Madison residents of the 1830s was the aforementioned Col. Hunting, proprietor of Madison House and host to Lafayette when he made his brief stop in old Bottle Hill. One anecdote about Colonel Hunting was still being told about 100 years after his death. The story concerned the large overcoat worn by the Colonel, which had, over the years, attained an unusual marking. During one night of reveling at the hotel, a tipsy customer accidentally brushed his lighted cigar against the Colonel's back. Since the coat was extremely expensive, Hunting had the circular burn repaired with a patch. The sight of the respectable proprietor with an odd patch on the back of his coat was never forgotten by Bottle Hill residents.

William Brittin was a local justice of the peace through a good part of the early 19th century. He was also highly regarded as a local country lawyer, although he was never admitted to the bar. Typical of the era, William appears to have been self-taught. For several years, he shared his legal practice, as well as his country store, with his brother Abraham. According to the late local history and fire department chronicler Henry Pilch, such non-lawyer judges were called "wooden heads." Brittin had been commissioned as a Colonel during the War of 1812.

Abraham Brittin, who came to Bottle Hill in 1800 from Long Hill, worked as a contractor as well as a self-trained lawyer and storekeeper. In 1804 this many-faceted man built part of the Morris Turnpike from Morristown to Newark. He also worked on the construction of the Morris and Essex branch of the Delaware, Lackawanna and Western Railroad in 1836. He helped build the stone bridge over the Schuylkill River in Philadelphia.

Isaac Brittin served as a mason and later as a contractor. Isaac apparently also had a reputation as a money lender in this age of few banks. When he died in February 1857, his property was inherited by his son, Benjamin Ludlow Brittin, who later sold it to James A. Webb. The Webbs and Brittins also had family ties, as Mrs. Anna Maria Brittin Baker was the mother of Margaretta Baker Webb (Mrs. James A. Webb).

Another figure of note was Caleb C. Burroughs, a talented wood craftsman who opened up shop in 1820 and designed cabinets as well as coffins. Although the furniture business fluctuated, coffin-making was a stable business, and he was Madison's best-known undertaker.

As early as the 1830s, there was one indication of the future development of commerce in Madison. Henry Keep's Bonnet and Umbrella Factory employed approximately 100 women and several men. The first large manufacturing facility in Madison, Keep's produced umbrellas, straw bonnets, and clothing.

The wide range of crafts and trades developing in the area was an indication that the county and Madison were both showing steady growth. Morris County's population grew from 18,500 to 21,500 from 1790 to 1830. Much of this growth was attributable to the development of villages such as Madison and Chatham.

Caleb Carter
Burroughs
1789-1885

The Burroughs' home and business on Main St.,
around the turn of the century.

Coming of the Iron Horse

Striking changes were occurring in the economic life of America as the transition was being made from a stable agricultural-commercial society to modern industrialism. The Industrial Revolution, as it was called, took place in America after the Civil War, but the seeds of that revolution were already taking hold in the years before the war.

The advent of railroads and steamboats greatly sped up the process of industrialization. The arrival of the railroad took on momentous importance to Madison. Statewide, the Camden and Amboy Railroad proved dominant. In 1833, the railroad carried 110,000 passengers and, five years later, 165,800.(11) For Madison, however, the Morris and Essex Railroad became more important. In January 1835, the railroad received a legislative charter, and the idea of a rail line from Morristown to Newark proceeded to become a reality. The charter set maximum rates for passenger and property transportation charges at six cents per mile per ton for commerce and the same rate of six cents per mile per passenger. In March of the next year, the railroad sold shares of stock at sales held in Morristown, Newark, and Elizabeth. William Brittin of Madison was one of the original nine individuals elected to the board of directors.

Seth Boyden, 1788-1870, Newark's celebrated mechanical genius, was asked to design a locomotive for the new Morris & Essex and did so without drawings and at a cost of $6,650.

Railroad construction began almost immediately with work completed by sections. The high reaches of the Watchungs proved difficult for the fledgling railroad. Nevertheless, starting in November 1836, each section was successfully completed. On October 2, 1837, Morris and Essex Railroad service to the community began.

The first trains from Newark to Orange were drawn by horses. These were quickly replaced by the powerful steam locomotives being built by brilliant inventor Seth Boyden of Newark. His first locomotive called the "Orange," was successfully tested on a run from Newark to

A Little Engine that Could...The little "Orange" attained a speed of 60 miles per hour on a trial run and was followed one year later by the "Essex," shown here.

Millville and found ready for the task of pulling cars on the Morris and Essex route. The red-wheeled locomotive was an impressive sight, but few bargained for the ear-shattering noises of the steam engine.

The first railroad depot was an unpretentious structure located near the present Museum of Early Trades and Crafts on Green Village Road. Later, in 1855, the railroad relocated the depot to a site on the northwest corner of present Waverly Place and Kings Road. By that year, at least 50 village residents were commuting to Newark and New York.

Two years after the start of the Newark to Madison railroad route, the *Morristown True Democratic Banner* extolled the skill of engineers as "careful, steady and sober—(cold water men)—and thus far have passed over the road without any serious accidents." If you had to travel by locomotive, the article suggested, it was better to travel with the men who drank only cold water. Alcohol and railroading did not mix safely.

During some early runs of the Morris and Essex Railroad, travelers had rather unfortunate accommodations. Cars were cramped, unheated, and lit by candles. Passengers were also subjected to dangerous accidents, for example, when a man or beast crossed in front of the train, causing it to attempt to stop suddenly. They frequently emerged from train trips covered with coal dust and dirt.

The Morris and Essex Railroad seemed to be cutting a few corners in their installation of equipment along the line. The rails, for instance, were made of wood, not iron, which was deemed too expensive. The top edges of the wooden rails were covered with thin strips of iron nailed to each rail. Excessive use or extraordinary heat would cause the iron strips to curl up-ward, striking through the floor of the car and causing considerable passenger injuries.

During that first arrival of the "harnessed devil," as it was called by at least one citizen, passengers had difficulty holding onto their hats. The brush was so near the track that branches caught many hats of those who peered out of car windows. According to a story told by Charles C. Force many years later, the conductor yelled, "Look out!" as the train neared large areas of brush. One Frenchman apparently took the command literally. He stuck his head out of the window only to lose his hat and scrape his face. The Frenchman then asked, "Why did you not say 'Look in'?"

One story, about the early days of the railroad, perhaps apocryphal, concerned the dangerous habit of racing the locomotive, engaged in by some stagecoach drivers and horse riders. Some of the races centered on a desire of both railroad engineers and stage drivers to deliver mail and goods to a destination before the competitor. In one such race, a locomotive derailed near Morristown, but the engineer would not give up. After freeing himself from his overturned locomotive, he flung the mailbag over his shoulder and "legged it down the railroad track" toward Morristown's post office. According to the story, the long-winded engineer got there first.

Not until 1841 were the dangerous wooden rails replaced by iron rails. In an 1843 advertisement, the railroad boasted that the line "recently re-laid with the heaviest rail, is now in complete running order and offers a commodious and expeditious conveyance to and from New York for passengers or freight." The later invention of air brakes and automatic block signal systems also added to a much-needed improvement of passenger safety.

A Time of Change

The coming of the railroad to Madison also helped establish an important part of the village's emerging identity: it now could be a rural retreat for those who worked elsewhere. The railroad also strengthened the commercial base of the local economy by providing for reliable and quick shipment of products to markets. Rural Madison was now linked with the wider world of commerce. Stagecoach and turnpike traffic were important to the early development of Madison, but the railroad loomed far greater in its potential impact. Progress was firmly tied to a locomotive. All aboard!

CHAPTER FIVE

The Impact of Immigration and the Civil War

By mid-century, Madison was not the only community feeling the impact of the rising Industrial Revolution; the entire nation was quickening its pace as steamships, railroads and big business changed America's social and economic relationships forever. By the close of the 19th century, these powerful changes would make the United States an industrial force with one of the most productive populations in recorded history and a people who shared one of the highest standards of living. As a result, at the start of the next century, Madison would be much stronger as a community.

Change seldom comes easily. Prosperity was not equally shared. There were some jarring and unexpected consequences as the nation had to face up to new conditions brought about by waves of European immigration and the resultant needs to adjust politically and educationally to the new society. The most wrenching adjustment of all was occasioned by the tragedy of the Civil War. While Madison's particular circumstances were local, much of its story is that of the nation in microcosm. As in the 18th century, Madison reflected the challenges and the opportunities facing the entire nation with its unique sense of positive civic engagement.

Irish Immigration

The first half of the 19th century also saw a tidal wave of European immigration surge over American shores. It started in Ireland, where the people fled poverty, political oppression and later, the starvation of the Great Famine. Soon after, Germans joined those flocking to the United States, while to a lesser extent at this time other Europeans began arriving as well. Madison would receive a good share of each group yearning for a new start and the opportunity America and Madison could offer.

Work opportunities brought the first Irish immigrants to Madison. Unlike the French before them, the Irish were poor when they arrived in the land of opportunity. Madison's Irish dug ditches, graded streets, trimmed lawns, and cultivated private gardens. Their homes were on Elm, South, and North Streets, which soon became known as "Dublin." As Mary E. Burnet (a long-time local teacher) wrote years later, "They were hard-working industrious people, hoeing their gardens and taking care of their bits of land as they had done on their own green isle."(1) Despite their initial poverty, some of Madison's Irish, such as the O'Briens and the Corbetts, rose to important stations in local life. In any case, the Irish immigrants found a permanent place in local society, changing it by their very presence and, in return, being changed themselves by the opportunity the village offered.

Jeremy O'Brien, for example, left Ireland in 1852, full of hope for a better life in the New World. After arriving in America, he settled in Madison where his dreams were ultimately fulfilled. Working as a laborer for almost 10 years, the outgoing Irishman finally established his own contracting business. O'Brien was such a success at managing the enterprise that he was soon a prosperous man. He emerged as an active participant in the affairs of St. Vincent's Catholic Church and in partisan politics as a member of the Democratic Party.

Although O'Brien likely was the first local Irishman to start his own contracting concern, he was not to be the most prominent. That distinction went to John V. Corbett, son of immigrant parents, Martin Corbett and Ellen O'Donnell. Corbett was the builder of many Madison landmarks, including the beautiful James Library, now the Museum of Early Trades and Crafts.

Several Germans also arrived in Madison during the antebellum years. Perhaps the best known of these was the Kluxen family. In the old country, the Kluxens had been winemakers for many generations. Setting up shop in 1865 on Fairview Avenue in the rear of a large home, the Kluxens used a rectangular crusher and a presser to crush grapes and a blender to perfect the consistency. Once the grapes were crushed, the juice was put into wooden kegs and barrels for fermentation and then drawn off into the huge casks to age in wine cellars. The Kluxen Winery initially produced sacramental wines, but in the 20th century, the family made other varieties as well, including champagne.

Herman Kluxen, Sr., active citizen. "Governmental watchdog" for the New Jersey licensed-beverage industry.

Wine barrels from the Kluxen winery.

Family patriarch, Francis Kluxen, immigrated to the United States from Germany in the mid-1850s. The Kluxen family property on Fairview Avenue included a home, a three-story winery and barns so the winemaker could watch his or her wine mature under careful supervision.

African Americans Arrive

By the time the Germans and Irish arrived in Madison, there was already an African American, or Black, population. Unlike many other communities, they did not live in any concentrated area in town, and not much is known about their origins. African Americans had been in the area since the Colonial period when some probably were indentured servants or slaves. By the end of the Antebellum period, slavery had been outlawed in New Jersey, and most of the African Americans in town evidently worked as laborers or in other positions on the estates of wealthy residents. The prominent Gibbons family, for instance, had one such employee. Frances Turner, a retired school teacher, recalls that her grandparents also worked on private estates as domestics in the years before the Civil War.

During this pre-Civil War period, the Presbyterian Church provided reading instruction to the largely uneducated African Americans who arrived in town (some of them apparently from the South). While this assistance from the white church was helpful and appreciated, African Americans were desirous of having their own place of worship, which would also serve as a center for their social life. Thus, in 1853, a group of local African American residents founded the Union Church at Cherry Hill (now Fairwoods). The Union Church quickly became the intended focus of much of African American life. It remained a thriving and vital institution as the African American population of Madison grew over the following years. Reorganized in 1885, it became Bethel A.M.E. Church (see Chapter 8).

The Underground Railroad

As the Civil War approached, the Madison and Chatham areas had their share of abolitionist sentiment. Indeed, some local residents took part in the so-called "Underground Railroad," an illegal network of safe hideouts provided to help runaway southern slaves to reach secure havens in the North or in Canada. Legends persist that the "railroad" had a "station" in the Boisaubin mansion on Treadwell Avenue, Chatham Township, and in the Sayre House on Ridgedale Avenue.

The white-columned Boisaubin house originally was the home of Frenchman Vincent Boisaubin. Alfred Treadwell bought the home from the Boisaubin estate in 1853 after the death of Amidee Boisaubin. Treadwell served as state assemblyman for a term beginning in 1865. It is during these years when Treadwell owned the house that the mansion supposedly was used as a stop on the escape route. Still visible today are parts of an emergency "escape" tunnel that ran underground from a nearby barn (razed in 1950) to a hollow portico pillar near the front entrance, through which a fugitive slave could climb by slat ladder into a small attic area. While there is no evidence yet available that any slave ever used this elaborate hideaway, the legend points out the sentiments locally toward the question of slavery that divided the North and South.

Civil War Action

Most of Madison's Civil War soldiers were under 21 years of age, but John E. Brown, who enlisted at age 25, was an exception. While many local young men enlisted, some were drafted. The draft itself was laden with inequity since the wealthy were permitted to hire a substitute "volunteer." For draftees who could not afford the cost of a substitute, military service was required. One important exception occurred in June 1864, when townspeople gathered in Oriental Hall (on the site of present 11-13 Waverly Place) to determine whether the community should raise funds to "procure 30 volunteers for the coming draft." By a vote of 250 to 10, the people decided to hire substitutes for their sons with an inducement of a $500 bonus.

Charles Brant, a Civil War veteran, served under Augustus Blanchet and Gen. George Mindil. He died in 1921 in his home at 85 Main Street.

Madisonians generally supported the Union cause, but they were not always eager to send their sons to the battle-field. Despite parental fears, the boys did volunteer to serve in several state units. Matthias Burnet enlisted with the 27th New Jersey Volunteers in 1862 and became a corporal in October after serving less than a month. Other Madison men served in the 27th and the 14th Regiments of New Jersey Volunteers. Maj. Augustus D. Blanchet of Madison was an officer in the 27th Regiment. As commander of the 27th, Gen. George Mindil commented 35 years after the war: "Madison contributed so many good and loyal soldiers to our regiment." In 1862-1863, Company E of the 27th Regiment numbered 31 Chatham Township men out of a total of 95.(2)

After enlisting on August 20, 1862, John Waters of Madison served as a private in Company C, 14th Regiment of New Jersey Volunteers.(3) He and other members of the unit saw action in such battles as Manassas Gap, Virginia, in July 1863 and Spotsylvania in May of the following year while assigned to the Third and Sixth Corps of the Army of the Potomac. Waters was fortunate enough to come out of the conflict "without a scratch," although he did have some mighty close calls. In 1864, at the battle of Cold Harbor, Virginia, one shot put a hole through his cap near his right ear without touching him. At Spottswood (also in Virginia), Waters' luck again held. A bullet went through his right trouser leg but only grazed his flesh. At the battle of Monocacy in July 1864, Waters had his closest brush with death. According to a *Madison Eagle* interview with Waters, his personal story was a frightening one:

> He was one of a small force engaged in a skirmish kind of fighting, the purpose of which was to hold a large enemy in check until reinforcements might come and help prevent an attack on Washington.
>
> At one point some of the force went ahead and cut holes through an Osage Orange fence for others to dodge back through for safety after firing. Mr. Waters was about to go through one of the openings when a young man named Hedley, from Hedleyville, near Newark, pushed him to one side in order that he might get through first. Then, as the young man was entering the hole he was shot dead.(4)

Local Heroes for a Cause

Isaac Gordon, a Madison African American who was born a slave, became a Northern hero of the Civil War as he unerringly guided Union forces through Virginia. In 1864, Gordon became a hero a second time when he warned the Union Army at Washington, D.C. of an impending attack by Jubal Early's Confederate forces. Early campaigning in the Shenandoah Valley took advantage of Gen. Ulysses S. Grant's preoccupation with Robert E. Lee's Army below Richmond and moved to assault the Federal capital. In part because of Gordon's advance warning, the northern army was prepared and thereby able to reinforce its positions and ward off the Confederates. At the end of the Civil War, Gordon came to Madison with his friend, Union Gen. E.E. Potter. It was Potter who commanded the Union forces that Gordon had aided. Local residents, according to a later newspaper account, felt kindly toward Gordon, who "was not one of the kind to brag about what he had been through. For many years, he was a familiar figure about the borough and was liked and respected by everyone."(5)

Isaac Gordon's Monument.

Another African American, William Henry Kyse, found himself in the center of some of the war's bloodiest battles. Kyse enlisted on July 1, 1861, was wounded in a battle near Atlanta, Georgia, and was wounded again in December 1864 at Murfreesboro, Tennessee. Later, while a prisoner of the Confederates, he was forced to march from Nashville, Tennessee, to Louisville, Kentucky, without shoes. After his release from a Confederate prison, the resilient Kyse served under Union Gen. William Sherman. At one point in the war, he temporarily lost his eyesight but regained it soon enough for him to serve in the battles of Lookout Mountain, Chattanooga, Nashville and Marietta.

Kyse served a total of four long years with the Illinois Infantry before mustering out of service. He left the army with a war record of genuine distinction and, for reasons unknown, chose Madison as his home. He lived in town for 50 years after the war. His son succeeded him, living in Madison also until his death in 1934.

For James D. Kemble of Myrtle Avenue, the Civil War offered an opportunity to travel. Kemble served with a transportation unit that was in every State of the Confederacy during the war, but his greatest feat occurred in Alabama in 1863. There, he and 29 others ferried the bulk of the Union Army across a river in one night's time, even though they were under heavy enemy bombardment.

Merritt Bruen of Madison was a quartermaster with Company K of the 39th New Jersey Volunteers. The 39th was organized in September 1864 in Essex and Morris Counties. Co. K, the only unit composed entirely of Morris County men, was led by Capt. D.S. Allen, while the overall leadership of the 39th New Jersey rested with Lt. Col. James Close. After their initial training, the 39th was sent to Petersburg, Virginia, where they were engaged in several encounters. In the Union attack on Petersburg in April 1865, Company K was out in front as the lead company of the 39th. The successful soldiers planted their flag on the Confederate fort under attack.

By the war's end, 37 Madison men had served in the Union Army, and only one had lost his life. The unfortunate young man was Merritt Bruen. Bruen died at City Point, Virginia, in 1864, during the campaign against the Confederates at Petersburg. Among the veterans of the Civil War were those whose names have long been associated with Madison's history: Muchmore, Horton, Genung, Carter, and Garrison. Sons, grandsons, and great-grandsons of Madison's first families continued to serve their village and their nation as selflessly as their ancestors.

A Critical Congressional Vote

His name was George Helm Yeaman. In his later years he lived in Madison and helped to found the Madison Golf Club in 1896. But 31 years earlier on January 31, 1865, George Yeaman did something that dramatically changed the course of history of the United States. Yeaman was a Kentuckian. Born in Hardin, Kentucky in 1820, he completed his preparatory studies and went on to study law. In 1862, he became a member of the U.S. House of Representatives from Kentucky and held that office until March 4, 1865. In Kentucky, most Unionists were both pro-union and pro-slavery, and they intensely disliked abolitionists and rebel secessionists about equally.(6)

In 1862, Abraham Lincoln issued the Emancipation Proclamation but wanted to expand the proclamation with the 13th Amendment to the Constitution, the amendment that would end slavery. The U.S. Senate

George Helm Yeaman

passed the amendment. The real difficulty came when it went before a terribly divided House of Representatives. Yeaman held a somewhat contradictory position. There is no question that he disliked slavery, but he also feared that abolition would destroy Kentucky's economic and social structure. Lincoln personally lobbied Yeaman at the White House, and when the vote came, Yeaman cast an "aye" vote along with three other Kentucky Unionists—Lucian Anderson of Mayfield, William H. Randall and Green Clay Smith. As a result of his vote, Yeaman's political career was doomed. He became a Republican, stood for reelection in 1865 and lost to a white supremacist Democrat.(7)

George Yeaman served as the United States Minister to Denmark from 1865 to 1870 and then settled in New York City, serving as a Constitutional Law Lecturer at Columbia College. He eventually moved to Madison, and along with other city leaders founded the Madison Golf Club.(See Chapter 9.) George Helm Yeaman died in Jersey City in 1908 and was interred in Madison's Hillside Cemetery.

Lincoln's Secretary

Shortly after his election in 1860, Lincoln appointed William O. Stoddard, later a resident of Madison, to be a secretary on his personal staff. Stoddard was an ardent abolitionist who thought so highly of Lincoln that he earlier wrote an editorial for the *Central Illinois Gazette* of Champaign, Illinois, suggesting that he should be a candidate for president. The Stoddard editorial, reprinted throughout the nation, gave Lincoln's candidacy a major initial push. Lincoln went on to win the presidency, and shortly thereafter, the South seceded from the Union.

William Osborn Stoddard, trusted confidant of President and Mrs. Lincoln; signer of land patents; writer of the first copy of the Emancipation Proclamation taken from Lincoln's personal document.

Arriving in Madison in the mid-1890s, Stoddard lived on Central Avenue. After his service in Washington, Stoddard was appointed by Lincoln as Federal Marshall in Arkansas. Upon his return to Madison, Stoddard spent much of his time writing about his experiences with Lincoln and his well-known book, *Abraham Lincoln: The True Story of a Great Life,* was published.

Stoddard was present at many events in the Lincoln presidency. In March 1908, the *Eagle* printed his retrospective remembrance of the Lincoln inaugural. The former secretary remembered its bustling scene well: the pushing crowds and especially Lincoln's facial expression, which was very solemn, as Chief Justice Roger Taney administered the oath of office. As Stoddard imagined the few years left for the President: "Thenceforward, I saw upon his face the dark shadow that was there at the close of the inauguration."(8)

The Civil War placed a great strain on America and its people. The President and his secretary felt this pressure more than anyone else. Stoddard recalled working late into the night at the White House trying to answer Lincoln's voluminous mail—much of it hateful—when he would see Lincoln pacing about. After the defeat of the Union Army at Chancellorsville, Lincoln "scarcely slept at all," according to his secretary.(9)

A Country Village

When the war finally ended, and Madison's veterans returned home, they encountered a village where Irish and German immigrants were bringing a new cultural dimension. Yet, the community remained a country village where residents knew one another. Madison did not yet have a regular newspaper or a "downtown" cluster of stores. It was not quite ready to be more than a rural center.

While Madison had grown in population, businesses were still typical of a self-contained village. Locally, one could find three blacksmiths, three bricklayers, four carpenters, two wheelwrights, three painters, two drygoods merchants, one ironworker and one tanner.(10) The village also had two physicians in the persons of Dr. Henry P. Green and Dr. George Cole plus one hotel proprietor, Col. Stephen D. Hunting. Boots were hand-manufactured locally by William H. Sayre (in his tannery on the southwest corner of Prospect and Main Streets), while James Keating was a clothing manufacturer. With such a wide range of services, there was little need for the village residents to go elsewhere.

Madison still had a large segment of farmers. As such, they were hardworking people who got up early, worked long days in the fields and then did household chores. Some were craftsmen in the winter, using cold-weather months as a time for working on shoes, carpentry, and similar home crafts. Women tended to the traditional tasks of sewing, cooking, child care, and countless other important household chores. Some children attended Madison Academy, and a few went to private boarding schools, but most completed little schooling. Their skills were learned from working beside their elders, while their social graces were acquired in the intimate village atmosphere of Madison.

Madison in 1868

By 1868, when F.W. Beers, A.D. Ellis, and G.G. Soule published their *Atlas of Morris County, New Jersey*, Madison had grown considerably from its Bottle Hill beginnings.(11) Their map showed many new streets added to the pattern of older roads, all on the south side of Main Street. Hillside Avenue ran from Prospect Street across Green Street (now Green Avenue) to historic Green Village Road. First Street (now Keep) was completed east of Prospect Street. The short stretch of Prospect extending from Kings Road (then called Railroad Avenue) to Main Street was Centre Street.

Interior land on the north side of Main Street was still devoid of public roads between East Madison Road (Rosedale) and Columbia Road (Ridgedale). No Alexander Avenue, Greenwood, or Central! A horseback rider traveling from Chatham to Columbia (Florham Park) could bypass the center of Madison by following East Madison Road. This narrow, muddy lane led in a big arc, crossing what is now Greenwood Avenue, then into present Fairview Avenue and continuing to a dead-end at Columbia Road (Ridgedale). This was the 19th-century bypass around Madison, preceding the controversial 1980s' Route 24 bypass by more than 100 years. (See Chapter 15.)

In the 64 years since the Morris and Essex Turnpike (Main Street) was finished through Madison in 1804, residents built extensively along its "straight as a string" line. A traveler from Chatham on the dusty, rutted road in 1868 would encounter the first cluster of houses in Madison around the Cross Street-East Madison Road (Rosedale) intersection, where a former decommissioned toll house stood on the northeast corner. On its southwest side was the substantial home of Dr. John Albright. Earlier in Madison's history this property was part of the farm of Barnabas Carter, very likely Madison's earliest colonist.

This was a map of the 19th-century Madison area in 1868, from Beers Atlas of Morris Co., (p. 12).

Jonathan B. Bruen house c. 1802, on Morris Turnpike.

Lecture Room; Presbyterian Session House and Sunday School; and Madison Borough Hall (built in 1850). – (Credit: Madison Historical Society)

Several mid-century houses that dotted Main Street in this vicinity centered around the 1825 Presbyterian Church, a landmark on the north side of the highway. (From 1930, this had been converted to Madison Masonic Lodge No.93; it was subsequently purchased by the Borough of Madison in 2023). On a large tract just west of the church, an 1868 traveler could also admire the fine house of New York importer Edward Thebaud, a site later occupied by Madison Junior School at 160 Main Street.

In this post-bellum time, the cemetery across the street did not yet extend to Main Street, and its entrance was off Kings Road. Adjoining the cemetery to the west, the spacious estate of V.S.K. Beaupland made a good impression on our traveler.

The next intersection west on Main Street would be Centre Street (now Prospect), but that byway did not extend across Main into what has become Greenwood Avenue. Instead, the north side beyond the intersection was notable for the cabinet shop of Caleb C. Burroughs, whose business extended to making caskets and undertakings.

At the Waverly Place intersection with Main Street, our traveler would arrive in the heart of this spreading community with the Madison House hostelry, a prominent landmark on the southeast corner. Across Main Street, where Central Avenue would later be opened, a traveler would find Henry Bardon's harness shop and, not too far west of that, the telegraph office.

The next intersection to the west was the venerable Green Village Road crossing. On the site of what is now the impressive brick James building was the Kelley general store. In 1868, the railroad tracks then at ground level crossed the highway just beyond the Green Village Road intersection. On a triangle of land between the railroad and the right fork in the road (now Park Avenue, then known as College Road) was the Presbyterian Session House, used for a variety of community functions. Built in 1851 and also known as the Lecture Room, all mid-week prayer meetings and lectures were held here until the Webb Memorial Chapel was built. After 1888, it was used for town offices until James Park was created on the site.

If a traveler were headed for Morristown, one would proceed on Main Street across the tracks into present-day Madison Avenue, then pass Grace Episcopal Church, and shortly after, the splendid Gibbons mansion would come into view, nestled in its forest. The mansion had just become Drew Theological Seminary headquarters.

If, instead of following this route, our traveler headed along College Road (Park Avenue) toward Columbia (Florham Park), the first intersection at the top of a slight rise would be Columbia Street (now Ridgedale). Proudly occupying the northwest corner was the well-known Madison Academy. The stretch of homes on the ridge toward Columbia was a stronghold of old Madison families. Our traveler might well be impressed with the durability of this nearly 150-year-old community.

Parochial Beginnings

The Civil War era was a time when two of Madison's first institutions for higher education were founded. Just prior to the Civil War, in 1856, the Catholic Church purchased a finishing school for women operated by Madame Chegaray on College Road (now Park Avenue in Convent). This was the beginning of Seton Hall in Madison. The school opened with five students on September 1, 1856.

A major figure in this purchase was the Rev. Bernard J. McQuaid, acknowledged by most scholars as the founder of Seton Hall University. The school itself was named in honor of Elizabeth Seton, founder of the Sisters of Charity in America and aunt of the Most Rev. James Roosevelt Bayley, first Bishop of Newark. McQuaid studied for the priesthood at St. Joseph's College in Chambly, Canada. Ordained on January 16, 1848, he began his work at St. Vincent's in Madison five days later, when he became an assistant pastor to Father Dominic Senez. Within two months, McQuaid became a pastor when Father Senez left to visit his native France.

Father McQuaid's zeal knew no bounds. Builder of churches and parochial schools, he built and rebuilt Seton Hall College, introduced the Sisters of Charity and was foremost in promoting diocesan works; he was named Bishop of Rochester in 1868.

Seton Hall College shown in 1856, is presently the site of St. Elizabeth's University.

Under McQuaid's leadership, the parish expanded quickly. At the time, the parish included Morristown, Dover, Boonton, Mendham, and Springfield. He directed plans for the first Catholic churches to be built in Morristown and Springfield, and in Madison itself, he established the first parochial school in New Jersey. The energetic pastor started classes in the basement of the old St. Vincent's Church building on present Ridgedale Avenue in 1848. Catholic youngsters learned there until 1866, when the church constructed a new school on College Road (on the present Park Avenue site of the former Knights of Columbus building). McQuaid was a renowned speaker and frequently visited other parishes (he even made a trip to the Vatican). Church leaders regarded him as the foremost pulpit orator among the Catholic clergy of the country.

McQuaid provided the Seton Hall venture with strong leadership in its critical early years, but he felt, along with other college officials, that the Madison location of the campus was too far out in the country. The bulk of the New Jersey Catholic population was in the urban areas opposite New York City and Philadelphia, and the pastor feared that Madison was inaccessible to many potential Catholic students. Thus, after a stay of four years in Madison, Seton Hall was moved to its present site in South Orange. The Sisters of Charity subsequently purchased the one building that had housed the school and, in 1860, turned it into the Academy of St. Elizabeth. The Sisters, too, left after several years and moved their institution to its present site at Convent Station. There, it eventually flourished as the Academy and Saint Elizabeth University.

Education in the Forest

In the years just after the Civil War another educational institution was born in Madison. In 1867 Drew Theological Seminary was founded and soon became an integral part of religion and culture in Madison for more than the next 150 years. Unlike Seton Hall, the founders of this school preferred the rural setting available in the wooded area known as "The Forest." For a purchase price of $140,000, Drew found a home on the estate that was previously owned by William Gibbons.

The heart of the new campus was the beautiful Gibbons mansion, which the Gibbons family had enjoyed for only a generation. William Gibbons died in 1852, and his unmarried daughter, the last Gibbons to live in the Madison house, followed him to the grave in 1857. At this point, Heyward Gibbons, son of William, came north briefly from his home in Georgia and closed the family mansion.

With the outbreak of the Civil War, the Confederate government requested that Heyward put the slaves from his rice plantations to work on fortifications for the City of Savannah. Not sympathetic to the Southern cause, he refused. He was consequently arrested; his property was sequestered by the government, and he was forced to fight for the Confederacy in order to save the property. With the end of the war in 1865, Heyward Gibbons' Georgia fortune vanished with the Confederate cause.(12) Trying to recoup a bit of his former wealth, he put The Forest up for sale in 1867 and was happy with the $140,000 it brought.

The man who paid the money was Daniel Drew, an entrepreneur in the mold of the Wall Street barons of the 19th century. Born in 1797 in Carmel, New York, Drew made his fortune through the sale of cattle to the New York City market. Through rather devious methods, he rapidly moved from poverty to riches, placing his investments in steamboat transportation and the stock market. Perhaps his conscience or the influence of several Methodist preachers he befriended motivated him to acts of philanthropy. Whatever his reasons, by the mid-19th century, Drew became known as an important benefactor in the local community.

Daniel Drew

He was also a major benefactor of the Methodist Episcopal Church. By 1866, he was deeply involved in an effort to establish a seminary for the denomination, and it was understood that he was ready to donate a great deal of money for its support if a proper site could be found. After considering a number of locations in New York and elsewhere in New Jersey, The Forest was the final choice.

Mead Hall. A persistent tradition holds that the mansion was patterned after the White House; however, it is more representative of a typical antebellum mansion. Renamed Mead Hall by financier Daniel Drew, the mansion became the main Seminary building that housed a society room, missionary museum, chapel, and lecture rooms.

In recognition of his generosity, the new seminary carried Drew's name, and the Gibbons mansion was renamed Mead Hall after Roxanna Mead Drew, Daniel's wife. The shrewd businessman left his mark on affairs in other ways as well. He was president of the Seminary's trustees and used his influence to secure the services of the Rev. Dr. John McClintock as the first president of the institution. Drew also presented the school with an endowment of $250,000, which the trustees empowered him to invest. It was a promising start to a grand venture.

Later, Drew's initial endowment was lost when the stocks failed. His choice for the seminary's president proved wiser, for John McClintock never failed. He served until his death in 1870, firmly and graciously guiding the school through its critical early years. His successors built on his strong tradition of service and faith. By the late 1870s, Drew Theological Seminary was already developing a national reputation for excellence.(13)

Pursuing Culture

An intellectual widening of the local viewpoint began to be apparent in this maturing community. The Masonic Order founded a local lodge here in 1869. It provided members with informative meetings and ceremonies based on principles of fidelity, charity, and justice, qualities essential to an emerging civic awareness.

Despite the unsettled cultural climate before and after the Civil War, the Madison area seemed to be developing into a center for educational pursuits, with the Madison Academy very well established, Seton Hall giving way to the Academy of St. Elizabeth, and Drew Theological Seminary operating effectively. Certainly, Madison was accruing a new measure of cultural prestige from their impact.

The influx of new ethnic groups was also likely to give the community a broader outlook on diversity, even if it did provoke "growing pains." Such awareness provided an ever-expanding awareness of cultural and religious diversity and prepared the community for the decades ahead.

CHAPTER SIX

Emergence of Small-Town Madison

L ife in Madison in the years after the Civil War reflected a continuing wave of economic growth and development that turned the nation into an industrial giant. In 1865, Madison was still a rural village, but it was a village in an area increasingly influenced by the wider affairs of the state and the nation. Trains now crossed the state from Hoboken to Phillipsburg on the Morris and Essex line. Manufacturing centers arose within short miles of the once relatively remote farming community. Madison residents, for example, could routinely buy coal hauled directly from the Pennsylvania mines and finished goods of all kinds from factories in eastern New Jersey and New York. America was changing and expanding in these decades, perhaps faster and more profoundly than ever before, and Madison was to reflect and react to the process.

Townspeople moved toward the 20th century in a good-natured but steady fashion. Change did not come in a rush, and thus, Madison society never experienced the turmoil of America's larger towns and cities of the era. There was economic development and civic growth, all of which compelled residents to take account of the new age in which they lived. The postwar decades brought improved communications in the guises of the telephone and a village newspaper. A series of natural events, including fire and flood, demonstrated the importance of improved municipal services in the growing region. A maturing sense of local identity, building upon shared prosperity and traditions, finally prompted the creation of Madison as an independent municipality. These steps came, as we will see, in evolutionary ways, rational but necessary responses to a time of transition.

Once a bucket brigade, firemen of 1881 drew no wages, paid dues of three dollars a year and were fined each time they missed an alarm.

Commerce, Fire and Prosperity

Pride in Madison grew steadily after the Civil War. Local residents clearly thought of their town as the equal of any in the state, with its businesses, cultural pursuits, and homes;

Green Avenue School, built in 1879, with an addition in 1897, remained in use until 1950; now the site of a parking lot and Presbyterian Church.

a community sense of exceptionalism was clearly developing. The brick school building on Green Avenue near Kings Road, for example, was a source of particular pride. It was soon known as one of the finest in the region and employed three teachers at the time. Besides this, a newspaper article confirmed, "...we have one or two private institutions of learning."(1) Stores and businesses were also growing, giving Madison the image of a bustling center of commerce amid the more idyllic farming countryside. In fact, the development of a downtown district was one of the clearest signs of both Madison's postwar prosperity and its emerging identity as a special place.

The development of Madison's downtown was given a severe setback, however, on October 21, 1877, when a major fire broke out in the commercial area. "Oriental Hall (owned by David Sayre of N.Y.) was destroyed by a disastrous fire...which was the most appalling conflagration that Madison has ever known."(2) Starting at 9:00 p.m. in the I.J. Ayres Grocery Store on the first floor (presently 11-13 Waverly Place, west side), the fire grew in intensity, consuming the entire building, including the upper two floors which housed the YMCA. Among the other buildings burned were Mrs. Dunn's home, the adjoining house owned by George P. Cook and occupied by George W. Squire as a dwelling and confectionery store and a three-story building owned by J.N. Allen, in which much of the stock of clothes of the Allen & Crane business was saved. Solomon Sam's Cigar Store, however, was soon engulfed in flames. Drew students helped carry cigars out of the building to a spot where they would presumably be safe. However, in "a short time," the *Madison Journal* reported, "boys as well as men availed themselves of the darkness to supply their individual wants in that line of goods."(3)

Others also helped themselves to burned goods from the destroyed stores, so much so that the *Madison Journal* editor vowed to take severe action if such looting ever took place again: "In case of another fire, we will...publish their names, showing no partiality whatsoever."(4)

When the fire was over, a good part of Madison's downtown section lay in ashes. Even the Delaware, Lackawanna, and Western Railroad depot, on the northwest corner of Kings Road, was burned to the ground. Several buildings were saved, although they suffered great damage.

The fire of October 1877 was not easily forgotten by Madison residents. The newly created fire company picked up some new volunteers and solicited public donations for the operation of the firehouse. The town's single horse-drawn fire wagon was unable to handle a fire of this magnitude. A *Madison Journal* writer disagreed and could see "no reason why it should not prove as efficient in case of a fire in our village as a larger one."(5) Luckily, they never had to find out, for a blaze as devastating as the one in 1877 never struck Madison again. The tragedy, however, was a vivid demonstration of the necessity of adequate fire protection in a town with a growing commercial sector.

Recovery from the fire began as soon as the ashes cooled, although it was some time before life returned to normal. By the spring of 1881, Madison's downtown had fully recovered from the fire. Stores were opening along Main Street in locations where few businesses existed a decade earlier, and the town's economy was more diverse than ever. The community had two bakeries, that of F. Neis and one owned by the Linaberry family. Traditional crafts still existed side by side with the newer businesses. E.R. Starr and Michael Mulcahy were blacksmiths, while L.B. Mulford ran a harness shop. Other popular stores were Muchmore Brothers Grocers and E.L. Cook's Dry Goods store. George C. Smithe operated the Gent's Furnishing Store, while Martin Senger was a barber.

Merchants on the Rise

Recovery from the 1877 fire continued unabated as the November 11, 1882 edition of the *Madison Eagle* continued to run advertisements for local businesses. David J. Duncan, one of three pharmacists, advertised the sale of "pure drugs and chemicals" in his Main Street shop. There were a number of grocers, but among the most popular was George E. Bardon, whose store (at 54-58 Main Street, north side) was "opposite the post office" (then at No. 57 on the south side) near Central Avenue. Bardon advertised the sale of tea, coffee, flour, and molasses. George was the son of Henry Bardon, a harnessmaker, and father of Fred B. Bardon, the first editor and publisher of the *Madison Eagle*.

The fact that George Bardon ran a successful grocery store is known because of the survival of his business ledger. The book, now in the Madison Public Library, offers a view of the volume of his business, the nature of goods sold, and the names of his customers. Bardon entered the names of those customers who owed him money and the items bought. He then placed a check mark by the entry when the debt was paid. It was customary in that age to buy groceries on credit. Among the many well-known local names in the ledger are those of Francis Lathrop, a wealthy town benefactor, and William Brittin, a civic leader. Others who patronized the Bardon grocery store included Frederick A. Seaman, Alfred M. Treadwell, and Edward Thebaud. There is also an entry for the Sisters of St. Elizabeth, who paid in cash. All of this was important, of course, to the Bardon family, but in a larger sense it was also a reflection of the continued economic growth of Madison generally.

The Bardon store was, in fact, typical of others in the village. By 1882, Madison had some 2,000 residents. This small community formed the basis for a thriving and diverse commercial sector that led Madison away from its days as a farming town. The more discerning members of the community saw fully what was going on. An editorial in the November 11, 1882 edition of the *Eagle* pointed to precisely this kind of business development, noting that Madison had six grocery stores, two dry-goods outlets, three pharmacies, two butcher shops, and three livery stables that "always seem full of business."(6) The town also had a lumber yard, a saw and grist mill, a cement and plaster store, and two bakeries. Not surprisingly, the beginnings of the local rose industry caused the establishment of 10 florist shops as local flower outlets. In all, the article concluded, there were 83 business houses in town which was remarkable given the small population.

In May 1883, W. Andrew Boyd published his *Morris County Directory for 1883-84*, in which he devoted 25 pages to a listing of the names, addresses, and occupations of Madison's people. (7) The occupations listed run a full range of those needed in a small town. There were carpenters, farmers, laborers, salesmen, storekeepers, shoemakers, and blacksmiths. In comparison with the occupations listed for Bottle Hill village in the 1830s, several new ones emerged. For instance, gardeners for the large estates were now listed. Other jobs previously unlisted were those necessary for small-town America: watchmakers, men's furnishings, druggists, physicians, printers, and even a junk dealer. Clearly, Madison was becoming a town of increasing economic and social complexity.

There were still throwbacks to the village days with an abundance of tradesmen who cared for horses, carriages, and the like. J.T. Hanlon advertised himself in the summer of 1888 as a "practical horseshoer" with "Horses shod on the latest and most approved principles."(8) His age-old business was located on Central Avenue near the First National Bank (present N.E. corner of Main and Central). The Boyd directory also revealed a new part of the growing population of Madison—college professors. One such listing was for "Rev. Dr. Samuel Foster Upham, professor, Drew Theological Seminary," while a similar entry was for "Rev. John Miley." Thus, the Madison outlook was moving toward changing demographics, as were many small towns in America.

Firefighters to the Rescue

As the community prospered, however, it could not forget the disastrous fire of 1877.(9) Madison moved to assure a public service vital to a growing business and residential community: the town strengthened its fire department.

On May 12, 1881, as the *Morris County Chronicle* reported the story, a meeting was convened in order to consider the purchase of a hook and ladder wagon. B. Warren Burnet was chosen as the fund-raising chairman. Two weeks later, Marcus B. Crane, Samuel Brant, Henry R. Burnet, Henry W. Harman, and a few others joined together to produce and sign articles of incorporation for the Madison Hook and Ladder Company No. 1. Madison's fire-fighting service was, for the first time, a legal entity.

Anderson B. Gee (10) remembered well the horse-drawn hook and ladder days in Madison. In the 1880s, Michael Frenz was the road overseer, and Edward F. Frenz ran the family business of sprinkling the streets. When the fire wagons were needed, firemen borrowed the horses used by Mr. Frenz to water the roads. This sometimes created comical situations. As Gee put it: "When the alarm was sounded, we would all gather on Waverly Place and watch for the sprinkling cart. It was usually seen coming down Green Avenue, horses on a gallop and water shooting like Niagara Falls in order to

Prompted by the 1877 fire and lack of fire equipment, William J. Brittin donated a lot at present Elmer Street and Central Avenue (SE corner), where the truck garage was built in 1882. A truck with equipment had to include buckets since the town had no water hydrants.

lighten the load." The drivers were able to unhitch the sprinkler wagon and hitch the fire wagon in as little time as 57 seconds, an amazing feat, causing a "roar to go up among the multitude of onlookers."

With tongue-in-cheek, Gee recalled that the title "hook and ladder" baffled him until he saw the firemen in action at a Green Avenue fire. Then, he said, he knew that the ladder was used by the firemen "to climb to the top of the building before falling off." He remained puzzled regarding the use of the hooks until the fire started to dry out; then, the firemen pulled down "a nearby shed to keep her going."

It was becoming increasingly evident that the village of Bottle Hill had ceased to exist. Main Street businesses were now being established in brick and frame buildings so typical of the emergence of small towns in America. A flourishing school was also proudly in evidence, reflecting an awareness of local educational needs and reflective of the community's continued growth.

An Emerging Local Press

One of the most significant developments of the post-Civil War period was the rise of the local press. There was a need for it in Madison; much was happening in the town, and people needed a means of keeping up with events, with commerce and with the outside world.

One of the earliest papers was the *Madison Eye Opener*, born in April 1877. Largely the result of the creative ability of Fred B. Bardon, *The Eye Opener* got off to a fine start by finding 29 advertisers for the first issue. It ran as a monthly for three issues until Bardon took a partner and changed the newspaper's title to the *Madison Journal*. The *Journal* was then published weekly instead of monthly, and in March 1879, Lorenzo H. Abbey bought the paper.

The *Journal* was a lively effort and did much to bring the outside world into town. The issues of its initial year, for example, noted the death of abolitionist William Lloyd Garrison at age 73 in New York City as well as the opening, in Utica, N.Y., of Frank W. Woolworth's first "five cent" store. Locally, the *Journal* reported the exploits of H.R. Burnet's one-legged chicken to an amused readership.

Three years later, the irrepressible Bardon repurchased the newspaper and took John W. Clift as a partner. The publication was again renamed, and the *Madison Weekly Eagle* was born. Fred B. Bardon was a man of diverse talents. He was editor of the *Eagle*, postmaster, Grace Church organist, member of the Board of Education, bank cashier and vice president of the Building and Loan Association. With the acquisition of the *Eagle*, the *Newark Daily Journal* reported in October 1887 that Bardon was "looking for something else to occupy his spare moments."(11)

The Gee building, which is located on the NE corner of Central Ave and Main St., housed the First National Bank and the offices of the Madison Eagle newspaper. Bardon and Clift are pictured standing in the doorway of the paper's office.

*Eagle r*eaders not only received editorial opinions, news stories, and folksy tidbits in the popular "Eagle Feathers" column, but they also occasionally were treated to medical advice. On January 27, 1883, the column offered this cure for earache: "Take a pinch of black pepper, put it on a piece of cotton batting dipped in sweet oil, and place it in the ear, tie a bandage around the head, and it will give almost instant relief." A short time later, the *Eagle* warned its readers that excessive use of quinine to counter malaria could lead to an addiction as bad as that possible with opium.

The editors sometimes underestimated their own influence. When six years later, the *Eagle* ran an article titled "Mad Dog Beware," many people took note of the warning that mad dogs (12) were roaming through town. The newspaper even advised that "at the slightest signs of queerness it is justifiable to kill them." Unfortunately, at least one young man took their advice and shot an innocent animal several weeks later. Even more seriously, the youth narrowly missed hitting some children who were playing nearby.

The Bardon-Clift partnership flourished for more than 10 years until Bardon became a full cashier at First National Bank and sold his interest in the paper to "a local group of wealthy gentlemen," which included James A. Webb, Edward P. Holden, former Mayor William F. Redmond, former Assembly Speaker Nathaniel Niles, and James H. McGraw, New York publisher.

This syndicate made the *Eagle* a Republican organ and one in opposition to the *Madison*

*Democra*t. The *Madison Democra*t was started on August 8, 1896, by Charles B. Gee and operated by Frank Waters, later a Democratic councilman. During its 13-month existence, the *Madison Democra*t was sold twice to out-of-town operators and eventually was purchased by the *Eagle* syndicate in September 1897 and then eliminated.

Role of the Railroad

The advent of coal hauling along the Morris and Essex route from Phillipsburg to Hoboken brought with it several benefits. The old wood-burning locomotives could not haul heavy cargoes of coal through the Watchungs, thus requiring the upgrading of train routes and the development of coal-burning engines. By 1866, the first coal-burning locomotive made its appearance in Madison.

In the years immediately following the Civil War, Chatham became a major freight area for the railroad.(13) Madison remained an important freight stop on the line and later achieved greater railroad prominence for its growing number of commuters. At the same time, the railroad provided an important economic stimulus for Madison by permitting local businesses—especially the rose industry—to ship products to markets in New Jersey, New York, and beyond.

Such progress, however, did entail a certain amount of risk. Passenger trains could sometimes be hazardous in the early days of commuting. The trains were noisy and dirty. Plus, they were involved in spectacular crashes. One such collision occurred in 1859 on the Morris and Essex Railroad route when a passenger train leaving Newark was delayed by tardy commuters. In Millburn, a westbound freight waited for an hour on a siding for a regularly scheduled passenger train to pass. When the passenger train did not arrive, the freight train started its trip. Meanwhile, the passenger train left Newark and quickly attained top speed as the engineer attempted to get back on schedule. The two trains collided just east of Summit. Miraculously, no one was killed or seriously injured. The good-hearted engineer who waited for his passengers was not seriously hurt, but he was incredibly embarrassed.

Wooing Commuters

Despite these hazards, the number of commuters from Madison to Newark and New York City increased between 1860 and 1880. Between 1880 and 1905, ridership increased further as a wood-burning steam locomotive called the Madison pulled cars along the railroad route to New York. The second Madison locomotive to be called by that name was a coal-burning steam locomotive. Also known as Engine No. 24, it was built in 1880 at Kingsland, NJ, by the Delaware, Lackawanna, and Western Railroad. It weighed 85,000 pounds. A scale model of Engine No. 24 has long been on display in the Madison Public Library.

As new locomotives replaced the older, slower ones, better commuting times became possible. In January 1883, the *Eagle* reported that "a train will be put on the road between Morristown and New York in spring which will make the distance each way one hour."(14) Better train timing naturally resulted in a greater willingness of people to move into Morris County where commuting would be convenient. Thus, even as their town got bigger, the world was getting smaller for Madisonians, who were now only a brief span of time from one of the busiest urban centers in the world.(15)

The railroads were generally quite interested in keeping up their new image as well-maintained lines for the transportation of the commuter. On October 26, 1888, the *Madison Eagle* even mentioned the new "Prince Albert style" uniforms to be worn by the D. L. & W. conductors.

Despite their concern for appearance, railroad operators sometimes proved themselves inflexible in meeting the problems of commuters who lost their tickets. One such case involved Henry C. Ohlen of Madison, who was not permitted to board for the return trip to Madison. Shortly later, the conductor relented by letting Ohlen ride as far as Summit. There, Ohlen was ejected and threatened with arrest if he persisted in boarding the train. It is not known how Ohlen traveled from Summit to Madison, but it was not by train. When the *Madison Eagle* heard of the incident, the newspaper excoriated the railroad for "not giving him a ticket since he was a regular commuter—his name on the books as a 'purchaser of a commutation ticket.'"(16)

Ohlen's troubles, however, did not deter other commuters. By the late 1880s, Madison's place as a bedroom community and as a small suburb for commuters to the larger cities seemed assured. Not long out of its village era, much of Madison's suburban character for the coming century was set by the close of the 19th century. By 1897, an *Eagle* editorial declared that "we really are a suburban town with unrivaled attractiveness and with a city of more than 3,000 inhabitants and increasing rapidly."(17)

That population increase was undoubtedly spurred by the relocation of urban families to the new suburban town of Madison. Still later, in 1903, a similar editorial attempted to get at the reasons for this population shift: "A spirit of discontent for city life, shown through modern literature—the unrest of the man to get back to nature—nearer the green fields and closer to the soil that gives him strength, attracts him to the suburban home."(18) It was not at all a bad analysis of Madison's changing circumstances.

Social Vignettes from the 19th Century

Amid the economic changes of the age, fires, advances in transportation and other local activities, life went on. In fact, as Madison became more diverse, so did the stories of its people. Some of the best of these illustrate the social setting of the growing town as it moved toward the turn of the century.

Because of a higher elevation than that of the area east of the Watchung Mountains, Madison became a popular retreat known for its clean air. This lure brought visitors seeking improved health and a restful vacation. Fred B. Bardon, writing in 1889 as "Incog." in the *Madison Eagle,* described the influx: "Our village seems to be the desired location for invalids, as well as for those who are desirous of improving their somewhat impaired health." Those who came to Madison in search of better health naturally helped those local businesses and boarding homes that catered to them. As Bardon put it: "...the boarding houses are reaping a harvest, as well as our root beer and ice cream caterers, the former of which dispenses a great deal of it, as our physicians prescribe it for persons possessing poor health."

For the infirm, Madison, by 1883, offered the services of five physicians: doctors named Anderson, DeHart, Reed, Van Wagner and Wood, the most prominent of whom was Dr. Calvin Anderson. Dr. Anderson posted unusual hours in his Main Street office, 8 to 9 a.m., 1 to 2 p.m. and 7 to 8 p.m. He accommodated those who worked during the day as well as those who wanted an early morning appointment. Of course, in those days, doctors willingly made house calls as well.

A girl who spoke only German was found nearly comatose near Hillside Cemetery, having almost succumbed to the winter weather of 1883. She was given refuge in the home of Mrs. Robert Jackson, who subsequently found employment for her. Minnie Chirgwin, another woman, was found murdered in Morris County. James Treglown, a 24-year-old Englishman, was accused of the murder in a sensational trial and found guilty. Madison residents were in the crowd when Treglown was hanged outside the county courthouse. Horse thieves seemed to abound, according to newspaper warnings. A horse was stolen on Orchard Street and later found in Parsippany. Police were able to make an arrest.

The winter of 1883 was indeed a difficult one for Madison, with many area deaths due to illness. In February, 21 deaths were recorded and attributed to pneumonia, apoplexy and other causes. Some believed that the brutal weather may have been the cause of it all. The *Eagle* reported that "we cannot perceive the cause, unless it is owing to the inclement weather which we have endured for some time past."(19)

The winter of 1883 was noteworthy in other ways as well. The New Jersey Telephone Company announced that Madison residents would soon have telephone communication with Morristown, Dover, Newton, Paterson, Jersey City, Newark, and New York. The monthly charge was $4.16 for telephone communication with Morristown and Dover, while $5.00 was the charge for New York and Newark. The telephone switchboard and office was located in Henry W. Harman's Drug Store at 16 Waverly Place. Among those telephone numbers first assigned was one for Dr. Calvin Anderson, who received the number Madison 8; B.L. Brown had Madison 3, while Madison 2 went to G.M. Lanning of Afton. The phone directory failed to list a Madison 1 number, which must have been held in reserve for someone special.

The *Eagle* attempted to enliven things somewhat during this difficult winter by offering a $25 reward for information leading to the discovery of the "brainless individual" who placed a false notice of marriage for Miss Maggie Waugh in the newspaper *Sentinel* of Philmont, N.Y. (20) The practical joker used the name of the *Eagle* in placing the marriage notice. The *Eagle* published no response from the young lady.

The spring of 1883 was a more exciting time to live in Madison. Telephone lines being installed were about to expand the local world. The *Madison Eagle* pulsed with the excitement of the event. In the "Eagle Feathers" column of April 21, 1883, the writer told of the event with anticipation: "The telephone poles are being placed rapidly, and it will not be long before we will be able to communicate with our neighboring cities and villages."

Despite these modern innovations, runaway horses continued to be a hazard to town residents. When, in June 1883, William P. Burnett's horse was left untied, the town was in for momentary havoc. The horse ran down Main Street "at a rapid rate," pulling a wagon and causing bystanders to scatter. The wagon crashed into the much-venerated, century-old liberty pole near Green Village Road before the forward movement of the horse could be stopped.

Sports played an important part in the recreational pursuits of small-town Americans everywhere. Competitive walking contests were in great vogue. As the *Dover Index* observed in May 1879: "The walking mania has struck Madison with fearful force." The newspaper thought it humorous to see "big and little, white and black, trudge around the track to come in for a share of the gate money."(21) By July, the walking events stirred great interest in Madison.

Most races were held at a track in the lumber yard of Edward Cook on Main Street near Central Avenue. Twelve laps around the track equaled one mile. In a race later that month, Joseph Bundy, "a noted walker," and Thomas "Blink" O'Neal walked for a period of eight hours. Bundy won by covering 38 miles, while O'Neal finished just over 36 miles. The event was met with "great excitement" and with "a great many being drunk, while others were betting and making a great noise." With temperance being as popular as it was in Madison, this revelry was a little bit out of character. The celebrants must have been out-of-towners.

By July 1881, the ongoing rivalry between Madison and Chatham—a competition likely dating back to the early 1800s when both were small villages—began to heat up along with the summer sun. The *Morris County Chronicle* reported that "our boys" became engaged in a fight in which they were "badly worsted." The newspaper then counseled those involved: "Next time, it would be advisable to take more of the crew along, ain't it." (22) It was not known how the fight started. Maybe there had been a baseball game or other contest between the two towns at the time.

The most notable athlete of the 1880s in Madison was a remarkable man, Charles W. Pinkney, a descendant of a local French family, who showed great athletic skill. Pinkney played baseball in addition to being an outstanding track and field contestant. He ran the 220 in 28 2/5 seconds as a member of the Short Hills Athletic Club and was considered to be the best all-around athlete in Madison.

Even small-town heroes have off days. The *Chronicle* on June 24, 1880, recorded such a day for Pinkney: "The Short Hills athletic games were witnessed on Saturday. C.W. Pinkney of this place, was one of the contestants in the running high jump but was defeated by F.A. Farley by one inch."(23) Later the same day Pinkney entered the half-mile race as the favorite, lost some early ground in the race, then made his move on his opponent. Then, "for some unknown cause," Pinkney stopped and withdrew from the race. One can suppose he might have run faster if his opponent had been representing Chatham.

As with small towns everywhere, Memorial Day was celebrated with deep patriotism mixed with family games and frivolity. The holiday served as a unifying occasion for the community, as most turned out for the parade, a day-long picnic, and a concert in the early evening.

Perhaps Richard Lingeman described it best in his book *Small Town America* (New York: G.P. Putnam, 1980) when he wrote: "A small town in white dresses and straw hats and ice-cream suits celebrating its own life amidst memories of their dead on a warm afternoon of spring flowers and grassy tombs."

Madison Field Club. Anderson B. Gee, Captain, RF; Robert Kelly, P; Harry Waters, C; Carl Lanning, 1B; Heyward Burnet, 2B; Fred B.Bardon, Manager, standing; Robert Troxell, CF; Thomas Fagan, LF; Harry Baker, SS; Robert Paulmier, 3B.

The Fourth of July celebration was much in contrast with that of Memorial Day. The patriotism was more pronounced and more loudly proclaimed through rallies, speeches and parades. Both holidays represented important occasions for Madison.

The only outside entertainment to come to Madison in the 1870s and 1880s was known as Chautauqua. Chautauqua received its name from Lake Chautauqua, NY, where, in the 1870s, a summer institute for Sunday School teachers presented secular speakers who tried to provide moral guidance through motivational speeches. Chautauqua speakers traveled a circuit from one town to another speaking in local halls or preferably in outdoor pavilions.

In an era prior to the development of the radio and motion-picture entertainments, the Chautauqua speakers provided their audiences with culture and enlightenment. Lyric Hall, or Association Hall in the YMCA building on Main Street (present 42-44 Main Street, north side), was frequently used for this entertainment, but the town itself lacked a large meeting hall.

Sometimes, the traveling entertainer had to leave town in a hurry. In January 1880, a Professor Maynard gave an exhibition at Association Hall but, according to the *Morristown True Democratic Banner*, "it proved a sham in every respect, especially in the distribution of prizes." The advance bill announced that Maynard would give out a barrel of flour and a ton of coal, but "no such gifts were distributed."(24)

Anticipating the advent of women's emancipation, the *Eagle*, in one late-century column of "Eagle Feathers," suggested that there were "a number of young ladies in town who would make efficient firemen." According to the unknown writer: "They run gracefully and with ease, and have the faculty of covering a great deal of ground without getting out of breath."(25)

However, the women of the late 19th century could do much more. In 1891, a group of enterprising women formed an organization first known as "Fortnightly Jaunts," which later became the "Fortnightly Club." The club was dedicated to providing intellectual stimulation for the many women who had been limited by Victorian cultural barriers to feminine achievement. Although the women had to get their husband's permission to join, their meetings centered around a member's presentation of an informative, thought-provoking topic. Usually, 15 local women were invited to join by unanimous consent of the membership. Today, the organization is called the Fortnightly Club. The group selects a topic for the year, and each member writes a paper on that topic, which is then discussed by the group.

For similar reasons, Madison women founded the Thursday Morning Club in 1896. The organization provided guest lecturers and became involved with civic improvement projects, the most important being the founding of the Settlement (later Community) House. (See Chapter 11.)

The widening of Waverly Place was an important civic effort, combining both private and business resources. A few decades after the introduction of the railroad into Madison, it became apparent that the depot area on Waverly Place at Kings Road was too small for the increased passenger and freight traffic. Funds for the renovation were raised by donations from private citizens and then matched by the Morris and Essex Railroad. The citizens' action group was spearheaded by Judge Francis S. Lathrop and Mr. Alfred M. Treadwell. In order to widen Waverly Place, additional land was purchased by Judge Lathrop so that buildings could be moved back. The dirt street was also resurfaced with stones and gravel, while the old depot was replaced by a new passenger depot and a separate, new freight depot.

Looking north, the eastern end of the new depot and view of Waverly Place, a hub of activity.

Western end of depot; view of what is now the Waverly-Green parking lot.

The local drug store in most small towns was a meeting place where people gathered to gossip, talk politics, and play cards. Madison had three drugstores. Two of them, Gee's and Harman's, were extremely popular "hangouts."

Anderson B. Gee, many years later, reminisced about his experiences in the drug store. (26) He recalled his father's English Setter, Sport, who would happily greet each customer. For 14 years, Sport stationed himself at the doorway of the store. Gee remembered how his father would take the dog to pick up the newspapers in the morning. Sport was trained to carry the bundle back to the drugstore. The popular pet would also carry packages or letters from Gee's Maple Avenue home but refused to take them from the store to the home. The family never knew why but suspected that candy in the store was the reason.

When Sport died, the *Eagle* reported that "while he was only a dog, he had a larger circle of friends than any person in Madison." Sport also had a better obituary than many humans.

The winter of 1887-1888 was a strange one for Madison. First, local residents were stunned to read of an unusual crime in November 1887: theft of the contents of the cornerstone of Webb Memorial Chapel on Green Avenue. Although the cornerstone contained only a few coins, newspapers, photographs, and toys, the thief opened it, took some of its contents and scattered other items at the site. Although small in financial value, these offerings were given in memory of the late beloved James A. Webb, Jr., who died in early manhood. The chapel was presented to the Presbyterian Church by James and Margaretta Webb as a memorial to their son. The pilfered cornerstone stirred a sense of outrage in the community, where residents had developed a strong awareness of civic values and the nobler qualities of life in the suburbs.

As the *Madison Eagle* stated: "We believe we speak the sentiments of our people when we say, no punishment is too great for the scoundrels who have committed this crime, and we think every man should form himself into a private detective to find out the culprit and secure his conviction."(27) The crime hurt even more because many felt it reflected poorly on the community at a time when Webb, a wealthy fellow citizen, was bestowing a special gift upon Madison. The thief was never found, but he likely had more than a few sleepless nights over this small crime that so stirred the conscience of a community.

The Great Blizzard of 1888 struck Madison with a massive snowfall. The snow continued for several days, according to Anderson Gee, who became "fed up" after three days of shoveling. Of course, the blizzard was not all bad. Snow meant sleigh rides and snowball fights.

During snowy winter nights, the lamplighter on his rounds was a welcome sight. He traveled along some streets west of the railroad station, carefully lighting kerosene lamps that had been placed there by several wealthy citizens. For several years, the lamplighter was paid by Francis Lathrop.

Even stranger things took place with events related to the "Runaway Nuns" hysteria in some communities in the United States. It even led to the infamous "Madison Riot" of April 14, 1870.

The Runaway Nuns and the Madison Riot

The strange case of the 'Runaway Nuns' and the 'Madison Riot' was an early example of the town's growing connection to the outside world. It began when a woman named Edith O'Gorman came to town to speak about her experiences as a Catholic nun who left the convent—to run away—because of the ill-treatment she claimed she received. She wrote a best-selling book, *Convent Life Unveiled* (1871), detailing the depravities of the church and went on a speaking tour. On April 14, 1870, she arrived in Madison to tell her story, and a riot broke out.

The cause of the largely forgotten Madison Riot has its roots in the wider American Anti-

Catholic movement of the nineteenth century. Anti-Catholic sentiment had a long history in America, and the phenomena of Runaway Nuns really came to wide public attention for the first time when, in August of 1834, a crowd of Protestants laid siege to the Catholic Ursuline Convent, Mount Benedict, at Charlestown, Massachusetts. The mob was convinced that American women were being held there against their wills, so they attacked it and burned down the convent and its attending orphanage. It was a national scandal with news agencies from one end of the country to another reporting on the events. It would be the first of several Runaway Nun related incidents.

Runaway Nun Edith O'Gorman.

In her autobiography, *Convent Life Unveiled* (1871), Edith O'Gorman wrote the last and most sober Runaway Nun story.(28) "From infancy," she said, she was "inclined to prayer and piety." She found no pleasure in everyday life, and when she confessed this to her priest, he told her that the only way to save her soul was to join a nunnery. After some balking by her parents (for which the priest called them "agents of the devil") on October 1, 1862, Edith entered Morris Township's St. Elizabeth's convent.

Following the Runaway Nun tradition, it was not long before Edith was troubled by what she claimed went on inside the convent. She talked of "secrecy" and how the Abbess, Sister Mary Joseph, was a nasty tyrant who mistreated the sisters(29) and the orphan children of the school. This mistreatment allegedly included mercilessly whipping a three-year-old and locking another in a closet until she had "gone mad." Edith had a whole list of grievances. In 1864, she was transferred to the new convent in Hudson City (now Bergen Township, New Jersey).

Before long, she reached a low point. Edith hated life at the convent. She hated the other sisters, she hated the priests, and she hated the Church in general. Her problem was that even though she felt this way about the institution of the Catholic Church, she could not leave because not only would they not let her leave, but even if they did, she would suffer damnation. As a result, Edith remained. New developments would bring events to a head.

She had complained to Mother Xavier about the advances of one of the priests, Father Walsh. However, the mother gave her a reply that basically said that the father knew what he was doing, to do what he said, and that Edith could expect no help from her. A short time later, while they were alone together, the priest drugged Edith with the intention of doing her amorous mischief. She awoke at the last second and fled before anything could happen. This was all she could stand. On January 31, 1868, after six years, she slipped out into the cold and ran away, never to return.

On August 29, 1869, she renounced the Catholic Church and became a Protestant. Shortly thereafter, she hit the lecture circuit. Edith O'Gorman's lectures generally centered on the vague 'evil' workings of 'Romanism' and addressed parents about what a bad idea it was to send children to Catholic schools because of the poor quality of instruction and because they would be swayed to 'Popery.'

At her talks, there were always a few irate Catholics in the audience, who often made their presence known with heckles, but she had no fear. That changed, however, at an April 14, 1870, speech at the Methodist church in Madison, New Jersey. Upon her leaving the church, a crowd gathered around her, many of whom were Catholics angered by her speech. According to the Morristown *Jerseyman* (April 23, 1870), threats were made prior to the talk, and a crowd "out of the Irish element" began shouting and throwing stones. As Edith and her escorts were getting into a carriage, someone in the crowd fired a pistol shot at her. Luckily, the shot hit no one, and the group raced away in their carriage with the angry mob in pursuit. Arriving at the home of local Methodists with whom Edith was staying, the crowd pelted the house with rocks. Some supporters, along with students from nearby Drew Seminary, forced the crowd to withdraw, and the incident ended.

The so-called Madison Riot (such as it was) launched the case into a new level of controversy. Lines were more clearly drawn, and more people, especially the press, took interest. The *Jerseyman* backed Edith. They ran an article next to the report of the riot (April 23, 1870), which hammered home the standard complaints about the "showy, theatrical and alluring forms of the Romish church which has a peculiar charm for children," and how "the priests spend a great deal of time in these schools making love to the sisters." The *New York Times* also took Edith's side. A *Times* article (May 22, 1870) gave a quick rundown of the events, describing Catholics as having "Gathered from miles around in a lawless riot" in a "cowardly attempt to shoot her down." The article ended by saying that she had been "providentially saved" and was "resolute" in arousing people to the "danger in their midst."

The Paterson, New Jersey *Daily Guardian* was much less favorable, referring to her as "not an escaped, but an expelled nun" (April 21, 1870.) In the same issue, the paper ran what it purported to be letters from Edith to Mother Xavier begging to be allowed back into the convent because her actions were performed when she was "desperate and crazy."

Not long after the riot and the newspaper reportage, Edith O'Gorman drifted into obscurity, never to be heard from again. Madison residents now realized that the community was not immune to outside influences, however strange or controversial.

Emerging Issues

Sidewalks were a long-time local issue dating from colonial Bottle Hill. When spring arrived after hard winters, the streets and sidewalks often were in disastrous shape. *Madison Eagle* readers were asked to "pick out the loose stones" on the highways so that carriage accidents could be prevented. As the weather warmed, public complaints about streets and sidewalks increased.

In an "Eagle Feathers" column titled "Dust, dust, nothing but dust!"(30) came the frequent lament: "While other towns enjoy the luxury of having the streets sprinkled during this hot weather, we are compelled to take the dust." Two weeks later, the complaint was again repeated. The "sidewalk issue," as it has been called, is a significant one because it symbolizes the problems of transition from a village into a small town. Prior to the emergence of a business district, there was some concern about the condition of the streets and sidewalks, but the feeling intensified considerably after the development of the downtown area. There was little need for sidewalks prior to this development. After its growth, however, they became indispensable as shoppers tried to walk from store to store.

Despite the worsening condition of the sidewalks, people were still coming to Madison in search of good housing. By the summer of 1889, the *Madison Eagle* noted that "the building boom has struck Madison with renewed force."(31) Mention was made by the newspaper of the new proposals for building on Central and Green Avenues. The newspaper reporter was confident that "our mechanics are assured of plenty of work during the summer…"

From Water, Government

The summer of 1889, however, was not one for building or for any other kind of work. Madison residents did not forget that summer for a long time. A pattern of turbulent weather, which had plagued the nation for five years, continued. Scientists blamed the alternate heat waves, drought, winter blizzards, rainstorms, and earthquakes on sunspots. Summer brought with it torrential rains and unusually severe storms. On June 7, the unthinkable happened at Johnstown, Pennsylvania, when a dam several miles above the city gave way, sending a terrible deluge that killed 10,000 people. According to the *Eagle*, Madison residents had "aching hearts" for those suffering in Pennsylvania. This tragedy made them wary of their own Spring Garden Brook, which coursed through the borough, crossing Main Street in two places.

Householders had good cause to worry. In August of that year, another deluge of rain turned the brook into a raging torrent that decimated crops near its banks and caused a railroad wash-out. Statewide, flood damage ran into the millions of dollars. Over the next 80 years, sleepy Spring Garden Brook was destined in 1902 to wash out Hillside Cemetery and in the early 1970s to wreak havoc along eastern Main Street during two "once-in-a-hundred years" rainstorms.

When, in that same year of 1889, a fire swept through Summit, causing considerable damage, the need for adequate water reserves became clear to most citizens. If such reserves had existed in Summit, the fire could have been contained. In his next editorial in the *Eagle*, editor Bardon emphasized the need for an ample water supply for Madison. The issue then was the subject of a town meeting held in Fagan's Hall on Waverly Place, now the site of the former Madison Trust Building.

In a series of potent editorials with headline titles like: "A WARNING," "WATER," and "Water! Water!"(32) during the spring of 1889, Bardon urged residents to create their own water supply. He also sent 300 questionnaires asking for reader opinions on the question. To Bardon, it was clear that a change in government leadership was needed to achieve a proper water system. Since Madison was a legal part of Chatham Township, the expense of a new water supply for one section would have to be shared by the entire municipality, a situation untenable to the Township Committee. The only answer, reasoned Bardon, was for Madison to declare itself a separate entity.

Not everyone agreed. Speaking for a group in opposition to any change, Edgar Beaupland said: "We are not in favor of a borough government or water supply. We have a good well; that is all we need."

The argument for a water system and for a new governmental identity eventually won out after several months of heated debate. On Christmas Eve 1889, the Borough of Madison came into existence by a vote of 308 to 145. With its creation, and the resultant secession from Chatham Township, came a government based on the mayor-council form.

On January 14, 1890, James P. Albright, former New York City lawyer and Morris County legislator, received the highest vote on the so-called Union ticket for election as mayor.(33) Albright attend-

Mayor and Council. Seated: John M. Tunis, Jeremiah Baker, Dr. Stuart H. Reed, Daniel Burns. Standing: Enos Wilder, Mayor James P. Albright, Jacob S. Paulmier.

ed Madison Academy and studied at Princeton and Union College, Schenectady, graduating in 1863. Although he was a Democrat running in a traditionally Republican community, Albright managed to garner bipartisan support for his campaign. At that time the mayor's term was for only one year. The first council consisted of Jeremiah Baker, Enos Wilder, Dr. Stuart H. Reed, Jacob S. Paulmier, Daniel Burns, and John M. Tunis. Council members were elected for staggered terms with Baker and Tunis serving until March 1890. Both Reed and Paulmier won election to two-year terms until 1891, while the terms of Wilder and Burns ran until March 1892. When the staggered terms were completed, the councilmen would then be elected for three-year periods.

Madison Water Department building.

Mayor Albright emerged as an enormously popular and effective mayor. He was reelected each year for 15 consecutive terms, and in 1895, he was elected unanimously with no political opposition. As the *Eagle* reported, the election of Albright was "a deserved compliment and a mark of public confidence."(34) Perhaps as importantly, Madison also had a good water supply in the form of its own water utility plant. Constructed at a cost of $60,000, the brick building housed a Dean water pump capable of pumping one million gallons daily. Within a few years, the community could boast of eight miles of water mains installed and a dedicated water utility. Madison residents also had added reason to be happy with the conduct of their public affairs by a nonpartisan government of their own choosing with the creation of a borough form of government of their own after the secession from Chatham Township.

The creation of an electric system soon followed this significant progress.(35) Based on the principle of municipal ownership, where every resident would pay a pro-rata portion of the cost of lighting public streets, and with the hope that profits from the venture would make it self-sustaining, the new electric utility was funded by the same $115,000 bond issue ($35,000 for electric) that paid for the new water utility. An electric plant consisting of two coal-fired turbines was constructed on John St. and opened on Christmas Day, 1891. Mayor Albright turned the streetlights on, much to the amazement and excitement of Madison residents.

A year later, Madison had 400 streetlights and one residential customer, Councilman S. H. Reed. By 1894, the Webb Memorial Chapel, the Methodist Church, and Drew Theological Seminary had electric lights. Customer growth continued during the next decade, and additional generators and engines had to be installed in 1898 and again in 1905.

The utility rates initially gave commercial customers a considerable price break per electric lamp, but not for residents. Strident complaints about the arrangement were eventually resolved by switching to charges based on kilowatt-hours rather than the number of lamps. Business began to boom, and electric meters were installed in 1911, along with several new dynamos to increase capacity and voltage. The following year, the current was changed to 60-cycle A.C., the current U.S. standard.

Until about the time the U.S. entered World War I, Madison supplied some surrounding towns with electricity. This arrangement came to a halt in 1918 when the state mandated that such transactions would require the utility to be under the authority of the Public Utilities Commission. The fear of losing local control and the view that Madison's aged plant was poorly adapted to the times, the borough council made the decision in 1923 to abandon generation and purchase wholesale power from Jersey Central Power & Light. When this decision was publicly questioned, the council responded: "We have not voted away any revenue, rather we will have increased revenues because we will purchase at a lower rate than we can generate ourselves."(36)

They were right, and the new business model proved to be successful. Four years later, the utility began to provide the borough's general budget with funds from its surplus revenue—as it continues to do today.

The End of an Era

The creation of an independent town government, however, reflected more than a concern over the water problem. That issue was merely the one that brought matters to a head when the broader subject of local growth and development was discussed. The establishment of the Borough of Madison was the result of all the various trends in the town's life.

The evolution of a strong business economy, an active local press, modest but steady population gains, and the need for effective municipal services (as seen in the schools, fire company, electric utility and water system) all worked to bring into bolder relief a local identity. Thus, as the 19th century drew to a close, there was much to be pleased about in Madison. It had evolved from a village in Chatham Township into a town in its own right. Its prospects for the new century looked bright.

Caravan, Waverly Place. As the 19th century closed, fewer caravans, such as Lasley's Traveling Palace, passed through town. An advertisement on the wagon read: "New York 24 July 1902. Look. We have traveled in our only house on wheels 13,712 miles. Please buy one of our books of our travels. Price only 10(cents) and 35(cents). From Seattle, Washington, bound for New York." A painting on the first wagon read: "Climbing Benders Hill in Mo. Remember WE guarantee our books to please you."

CHAPTER SEVEN

The Age of Roses and Great Estates

The process of social change often works in subtle ways. While the Industrial Revolution brought visible results to Madison, with such innovations as steam trains and a growing commercial district, at the same time, there were fewer direct forces in motion.

Economic growth in other regions of the nation created consumer demands of some particular kinds, which reflected the tastes of America's rising middle and upper classes. Two of these blended to form unique aspects of Madison's character—its public image as the "Rose City" and its rise as the home of some of the greatest private estates in the entire country. For those Americans who could afford the best in flowers and real estate, Madison emerged as a special place indeed in the late 19th and early 20th centuries.

Roses Become an Industry

The rose has captured the hearts of millions of people since its blossoming centuries ago as a symbol of love, and for over 100 years, the rose proved significant to Madison. "Fortunately for the world of beauty," recalled Joseph Ruzicka, prominent rose grower, in 1948, "there are few of us who do not respond to the Queen of all flowers, The Rose, whether she blooms along the dusty roadsides or in a garden, or in scientific cultured splendor in our commercial greenhouses...in Madison today, we live in an area that has been, and still is, foremost in the growing and development of roses in the United States."

The rose industry, as it was called in Madison, owed its inception to several factors: the advent of regular, dependable railroad service from Madison to New York and the potential of the local soil and climate for rose production. Still known as the "Rose City," Madison's love affair with roses began in 1856 when Alfred M. Treadwell built several greenhouses on his estate (present site of the Boisaubin mansion and property west of St. Hubert's Giralda off Woodland Road).

Following Treadwell's lead were other estate owners in Madison who began producing roses for the commercial market, having the finances, acreage and gardeners necessary to start growing on a large scale. The subsequent movement of skilled Europeans, especially English gardeners, to the large local estates brought experienced men and proved one of the key elements in the rapid growth of the industry.(1) The future of the rose-growing enterprise was well assured.

A few years after the construction of the Treadwell greenhouses, Judge Francis S. Lathrop built several on his property (later known as Giralda Farms). In 1865, Lathrop hired James M. Littlejohn, considered a pioneer in rose growing, to supervise his greenhouses and to arrange transportation of roses to New York, in what is believed to be the first commercial marketing of Madison roses.

Littlejohn was a native of Strathearn, Scotland, and the first of several European gardeners who became important figures in local rose growing. He opened his own rose-growing range in Chatham in 1872. His son, James Robert Littlejohn, also a rose grower, kept diaries of events (1888-1933) in Chatham which reflect not only community activities, but also the daily chores involved in rose cultivation.(2)

James M. Littlejohn came from Scotland to work on the estate of John Jacob Astor prior to his arrival in Madison, where he worked for Frank S. Lathrop.

"Dellwood," home of E. V. Haughwout and T. J. Slaughter.
Photo source: Madison Historical Society

In 1867, Eder Vreeland Haughwout came to Madison and built his home and estate, "Dellwood," which included several greenhouses that provided local homes with choice flowers. James McCulloch began his floriculture experience here, managing the estate grounds, and was succeeded in 1874 by a young Englishman, John N. May, who became superintendent until 1880, when he moved to Summit and built his own rose range. In 1885, May introduced the beautiful Bride rose, one of the finest tea roses in the market at that time.

John N. May was born in England, the son of a Middlesex gardener. He was first attracted to rose growing at the age of nine when his father brought home the rose, Souvenir de la Malmaison, to show his mother. The *Eagle* of September 21, 1888, told this story: "After listening to their praises of its lovely color and fragrance he resolved to have one of his own..." May then proceeded to emulate his father by attempting some experimental grafts himself, "and strange to relate," he remembered, "one of them grew and blossomed the following summer."

Thomas J. Slaughter, a New York merchant, purchased the Haughwout estate in 1877.(3) He had suffered financial setbacks early in his career but was able to build the successful merchandising firm of Norton and Slaughter of New York. Profits from this business enabled him to raise the capital needed to buy "Dellwood." Although retired, Slaughter quickly developed the estate into a thriving enterprise. He built five greenhouses measuring 200 to 300 feet in length and 15 to 22 feet wide, containing a total of 10,000 plants.

Slaughter spared no expense in this venture. He installed the finest heating and ventilation equipment and was viewed by the community as the consummate businessman. The *Madison Eagle* of August 20, 1886, quoted Mr. Slaughter's business principles: "A judicious employment of capital and a systematic method in business can hardly fail of success."

Slaughter grew thousands of plants at a time with the American Beauty, Catherine Mermet, and La Perle des Jardins among his popular roses selected for cultivation. In 1886, his business practices resulted in the marketing of about 40,000 roses a month during the September 1 to July 1 season. His foreman, James Monahan, a little-known but talented rose specialist, was the most successful of the various foremen employed over the years on the estate. In one season, he exceeded the number of roses grown by any previous foreman.

Half a Million Buds

In March 1888, the *Eagle* reprinted an article from *The American Garden* magazine detailing the rose-growing production of T.J. Slaughter. This "single grower," according to the report, "expects to market this season no less than half a million buds." Slaughter had produced in the preceding two years Niphetos roses which averaged 52 buds per plant. Revenue was figured at $1.78 per plant. The American Beauty rose produced a revenue of $5.09 per plant, with each plant producing an average of slightly over 21 buds. The price of buds differed markedly between the poorer and finer grades.

At this point, the large supply of roses produced by both small and large concerns like that of Slaughter seemed to have no ill effect on prices. Through much of this early rose-growing era, prices continued to climb. By 1889, the *Ridgefield Park Era* called Slaughter "the King of the Madison rose growers, and his roses are famous as far as the growth of the rose is known."(4) Slaughter's success encouraged others. By March 1, 1889, the *Eagle* proudly proclaimed that "Madison is conceded to be the centre and head in the culture of roses." By then, 35 rose-growing businesses were in operation in Madison, with one at Convent Station and four to six in Chatham and Summit. In Chatham, James M. Littlejohn had eight greenhouses in operation. Unlike other rose growers, he sold directly to retail stores rather than to wholesalers.

In October 1888, the *Summit Record* profile of Chatham growers, reprinted in the *Eagle,* extolled the virtues of rose growers. "The rose-growers are a great benefit to any village as they give a good deal of employment and spend thousands of dollars for work and taxes." The editors also could have noted that they brought the "Rose City" significant national fame.

Madison's rose growers created their own organization on September 6, 1894, in order to further their common commercial interests. Known as the Madison Rosegrowers Club, the organization inaugurated a long tradition of Madison rose shows on November 30, 1894. The first flower show was held in Fagan's Hall, bedecked with flowers for the well-attended event. The first prize went to D.E. White and Brothers for their large vase of American Beauty roses.

The *Madison Eagle* reporter who attended the show was

Madison Rosegrowers Club, November 1895. L-R, bottom row: M. Brady, M. Maguire, Wm. Charlton, John Jones, Jas. Jones, J.J. Ryan, P. Cosgrove. Middle row: Ed McGuiness, J.R. Mitchell, D. Shannon, Thos. Conroy, D. McCarthy, G. Fenton, P. Ryan, Thos. Keefe, E. Kerwin. Back row: D. White, Jas. Murphy, Wm. McCormick.

distracted from flowers, as seen in the report filed with his editor for the June 24th edition: "It is a well-known fact that the prettiest roses in the world grow in Madison, but a person attending the flower show would decide, without a doubt, that while Madison roses are beautiful, they take second place to Madison's young ladies."

The rose show was just the capstone on an incredible half-century of progress for Madison's rose growers. By July 1896, the *Eagle* reported that a 7 a.m. train took 80 to 100 boxes of roses to New York each morning. In the same year, there were 45 growers in business in Madison. By comparison, Chatham had only six. Madison's rose growers had a total of 505,740 square feet of greenhouse glass at that time, with Theodore W. Stemrnler (36,000 feet), Harry H. Francis (32,000 feet), and Louis M. Noe (32,000 feet) the leading growers.

Rose Growers' Strong Roots

The early decades of cultivating roses were marked by the accomplishments of several other highly talented individuals who helped the local industry establish strong roots. Names that became synonymous with the industry included John Jones, James Hart, Louis M. Noe, Joseph F. Ruzicka, Charles H. Totty, and the horticulturist Arthur Herrington.

Like so many other growers, John Jones was born in England, where he studied the art of gardening. After arriving in America in the mid-1860s, he went to work on the estate of Governor Jewell of Connecticut before relocating to Flatbush, Long Island, and then the Danforth estate in Madison. Shortly thereafter, Jones accepted an offer by Madison's Judge Lathrop to work on his estate. After Lathrop's death in 1882, Jones continued the rose growing activities of the estate. His greenhouse plant totaled 10,000 square feet of glass. Jones was the first president of the Madison Rosegrowers Club and was active in the Morris County Gardeners' and Florists' Society.

Another local rose grower of the late 19th century was William Bryce. He hired as his foreman James McCulloch, who was considered a successful grower of the Marechal Niel roses for the New York markets. Compared with Slaughter and Jones, McCulloch's rose production was considerably smaller, and his plant consisted of 6,000 or 7,000 feet of greenhouse glass. He also perfected the cultivation of grapes on the Bryce estate.

James Hart may be called one of the pioneer wholesalers of New York City. Born in Ireland, he came to America in 1865, and by 1870, he had established a wholesale florist market in New York. Several years later, he came to Madison and built extensive greenhouses (nine buildings) adapted to rose culture on Ridgedale Avenue.

Young man with bouquet of roses, Amedeo Micone, c. 1900 at Edward Behre greenhouses.

Of French descent, Louis M. Noe established his rose business in 1884 and was the first to develop the hybrid American Beauty rose in Madison. He became the nation's largest producer of that variety within a single decade, and his son, Louis A. Noe, continued the business in the early years of the next century. Indeed, he dealt with an exclusive clientele at times.

In December 1910, his son shipped 100 of the largest of his American Beauty roses to Queen Alexandra of Great Britain, maintaining a tradition that started years earlier when roses were sent to Queen Victoria at Christmas. For many years, Queen Alexandra used Noe roses to decorate the palace dinner table. The *Madison Eagle,* on December 16, 1910, noted that "the present King and Queen will have Madison-grown roses—the very acme of rose-culture perfection—upon their Christmas dinner table." Noe's success with the Queen was part of the thriving rose business. Noe was not alone, for the Rose City continued its leadership role in national rose production.

Two Englishmen, Arthur Herrington and Charles Totty, were attracted to the Twombly estate, "Florham," in the mid-1890s to care for the acres of gardens and shrubs. By 1915, Herrington managed the world-famous International Garden Show in New York and continued in that position for 25 consecutive years.

Herrington arrived in Madison from Sussex, England, in 1896 as superintendent of the Twombly estate. He remained until 1910, when he commenced his own business as a landscape gardener. Arthur often lectured before horticultural societies and was a frequent contributor to gardening publications. He served as the first president of the Morris County Gardeners' and Florists' Society in 1897 and, in 1902, was named president of the National Chrysanthemum Society. In 1947, Herrington received the greatest honor of his career from the Horticultural Society of New York—the George D. Pratt Achievement Medal, one of the highest awards presented to a horticulturist.

Twombly estate greenhouses and potting sheds, located behind the orangery, were dismantled and removed prior to Fairleigh Dickinson University acquiring the estate. Additional greenhouses were closer to Ridgedale Avenue. Credit: S. C. Burden, Fairleigh Dickinson University Archives.

Charles Totty labored to develop new strains of orchids on the Twombly estate. When he later started his own local firm in 1903, known simply as Totty's (Ridgedale-Greenwood Avenues, near Florham Park), he cultivated new strains of chrysanthemums as well as roses and carnations. In 1911, a cultivated sunburst flower was selected rose of the year, and in 1912, a prize-winning carnation, Wodenethe, was exhibited in a London show. By 1925, Totty had developed a national reputation as a skilled rose grower. In the June 1925, issue of *Gardeners Chronicle*, he counseled other rose growers that certain roses, such as the Columbia pink or the Madam Butterfly, were best for garden cultivation. His advice to home rose growers, naturally, was taken quite seriously.

In 1927 Totty built three new greenhouses at his Greenwood Avenue plant at a cost of $250,000. He reported that more than 200,000 orders for his roses had been processed within the year and were shipped all over America and to such nations as Holland, France, England,

and Sweden. By 1930, Totty was producing a million chrysanthemums and half a million roses annually.

Totty's death in 1939 was a great loss to the industry. The control of the business passed to his daughter, Miss Helen Totty, who not only did an outstanding job managing the business but continued to improve on many of his techniques. She was the only woman to operate a range of greenhouses of that size in the country until her retirement in 1962, when she sold the landmark facility.

The Multi-Talented Joseph Ruzicka

Joseph F. Ruzicka, civic leader and rose grower, produced a wide variety of roses for the commercial market. In a speech given in 1948 at a luncheon meeting of the Madison Rotary Club, Ruzicka described the early days when roses were shipped by horse-drawn wagons and later when the railroad added a special express car for roses.(5) Roses were all shipped to New York by Railway Express or a local messenger. Trains which carried the bulk of them left in the early morning hours. It was not unusual to see a sled, an express wagon or even a wheelbarrow used to convey the flowers to the depot. Later, the roses were shipped by refrigerated trucks.

In closing his speech to fellow Rotarians, Ruzicka chided them "not to wait until a funeral to buy flowers" and then told the story of an 80-year-old man who was planning to have his funeral while he was alive so he could enjoy the flowers.

The owner of this humor was yet another immigrant to Madison who fared well in the community. Born in Kutna, Czechoslovakia, Joseph Ruzicka arrived in Madison in 1900 after working briefly on Long Island estates. He became a partner in a rose growing business with Louis A. Noe in 1916 and soon purchased the Brant-Hentz Co. The firm was renamed Noe and Ruzicka, Retail Florists and was active until 1932 when Joseph Ruzicka became sole owner.

Joseph F. Ruzicka, in a 1948 Rotary Club speech in which he described the status of the rose industry: "As the world moves into the cycle of specialization it is only natural that our business should keep pace with the trend. There is little new in the art of Rose Growing—the fundamental principles do not change—but it is man's ability to adjust himself to the changing conditions of the times and environment that counts most today."(6)

"The average grower today is not willing to practice hybridizing, as a man may raise thousands of seedlings only to find them all worthless. There is a feeling of genuine admiration for the pioneers who do much noble work in this direction. It takes several years to test a variety and try it out properly and decide whether it is worth growing and putting it on the market."(7)

Not only a superb rose grower, Ruzicka was also an active citizen. His community activities in the mid-1950s proved extensive and exhausting. At that time, he was the first president of the Madison Rotary Club, a member of the borough council, the Board of Health and the governing board of the YMCA. In addition, he was a trustee of Madison Methodist Church and a director of both the Madison Building

Roses by Ruzicka being delivered for the opening of the United Nations.

and Loan Association and the First National Bank (later First Bank and Trust). Ruzicka was a popular local figure for over half a century, ever since his turn-of-the-century debut in the rose-growing industry.

In announcing Joseph and Emma Culver Ruzicka's 55th wedding anniversary in 1957, the *Eagle* lauded his long service to the community: "There are few people whose productive lives cover such a span of changing times and who still enjoy recalling the days when the classic American Beauty rose with its four-foot stem was one gift supreme to win the heart of many a fair lady."(8)

During the 1930s, the rose industry continued to flourish. One year after the formation of the Noe-Ruzicka partnership, the Duckham-Pierson range was built. William H. Duckham came from England and was first employed as superintendent on the James estate, later the Dodge estate. Lincoln Pierson invented the first practical method of constructing greenhouses of steel and formed the Pierson U-Bar Company. He built the conservatory on the Twombly estate. The Duckham-Pierson greenhouses occupied six acres on the former estate of Dr. Frank Fuller (presently Noe Avenue and Shunpike Road area) and housed 10,000 plants. In 1939, the enterprise was purchased and became the noted Watchung Rose Corporation (to be discussed later).

Coal, Lots of Water, and Fame

These early decades of rose cultivation were marked by continuing improvements in production methods, greater experimentation, and the development of new ideas for securing markets. Growing techniques were rapidly improving and becoming more complicated for growers. Roses were usually grown on benches in five to six inches of soil with a mixture of composted cow manure and surface soil that had been previously exposed to frost action. Bone flour was frequently added to the soil to increase its fertility. The process of maintaining the correct greenhouse temperature year-round was exceedingly expensive and difficult in the heyday of the rose grower.

Water consumption was also quite expensive. In 1886, Fred B. Bardon, editor of the *Eagle,* expressed his estimate for the cost of running the greenhouses at nearly $100,000 in initial expenses and $55,000 in operating costs. In his editorial titled "About Roses," Bardon concluded, "to imagine, as some do, that rose growing is an easy task is a mistake, the utmost care is needed, no precaution towards success can be neglected, the neglect of even a few minutes of heat may ruin the crop, too much moisture may mildew the plants."(9)

The most critical element in rose growing was the control of humidity in the greenhouse. Too much moisture was as deadly for the roses as was too much dryness. Buds could not be permitted to get wet during the night and then have the hot sun shine on them. In regulating humidity and temperature, the watchman played a crucial role in adjusting conditions inside the greenhouse according to the weather changes outside. Yet, most threatening was windy, cold weather with its potential for quickly changing temperatures. For the watchman, a still night with the mercury showing below zero temperature was not as feared as a night when the mercury was from 10 to 20 above with a gale blowing.

If you were lucky, the roses survived these critical conditions until they were ready for cutting. Once fully mature, the roses were cut while in bud so they would not open until reaching the consumer. At the end of the day, according to an *Eagle* editorial of February 1978 by Ruth Churchill, historian and granddaughter of Louis M. Noe, roses were graded by size, counted, and "bundled before being plunged into containers holding water." In the days after the advent of electricity, the roses were hardened off by refrigeration before shipment.

Despite the hazards of growing roses, the business helped to put Madison on the map. As an editorial of the *Eagle* expressed it in 1886: "Rose growing is par excellence the industry of Madison and the proportions it has attained bear witness to its importance."(10) Although they were called amateur florists by themselves and others, Madison's growers were anything but dabblers at perfecting the roses they grew. A product of the highest quality was sent to the marketplace. They were considered nonprofessionals only in that the estate owners did not need to depend on the sale of roses for their income.

By the 1950s, Madison's rose growers were doing very well financially, as the local industry was still a national leader in the sales of commercial roses. The principal local businesses were Rose Farms Corp., built by Henry Hentz, and Watchung Rose Corporation, located on Shunpike Road, Chatham Township and owned and operated by Robert and Wilma Nichols. Watchung Rose Corporation had as many as 100,000 plants, producing three million roses yearly. Even more astounding, especially since most work was done by hand, over 8,000 roses were harvested each day during the heyday of the industry.

In 1939, Robert Nichols, with his wife and Joseph Ruzicka, acquired the range originally built in 1917 by Duckham-Pierson. The Watchung Rose Corporation was founded in an attempt to bring the scientific applications of Nichols' engineering background to rose growing. Wilma Nichols was the daughter of the legendary rose grower Joseph Ruzicka. Nichols did, in fact, start working with his father-in-law when Watchung Rose first started his business. He remembered Ruzicka's amazement at new methods introduced, such as the use of steam sterilization of the soil and chemical fertilizers rather than manure.

Loading new benches with soil in preparation for setting new rose plants.

Robert W. Nichols: his engineering and management experiences became valuable assets in introducing many innovative changes.

Watchung Rose Corp., growing industry at full flower in the 1950s.

Nichols was especially adept at marketing. While most area rose growers shipped only to the New York market, Nichols expanded by shipping to many distant destinations by air cargo. The advent of commercial air flights allowed rosarians to ship across the nation and still deliver fresh flowers to the retail distributor.

Local growers shipped roses by airplane or train after the flowers were packed in 4-foot long, 10-inch high cartons, which had a capacity of 500 roses. Workers carefully packed the roses in layers of ice and wet newspapers. It was with precise skill they were able to make sure that the top layer would be level.

Undoubtedly, Ruzicka also marveled at a tension meter installed in the greenhouses to measure the amount of moisture in the soil. In the past, according to Robert Nichols in a 1948 *Eagle* *in*terview, "...ten men could stick their fingers in the soil and come up with ten different opinions as to the amount of water needed." The flower beds at Watchung were watered automatically by an underground water system, an innovation considered an anathema by some older rose growers. Nichols left little to chance and to traditional methods. The number and quality of his roses showed he was right in his scientific approach. He took the traditional skills developed by Slaughter, Noe and Ruzicka and added a new scientific dimension, which continued to make rose growing a viable industry throughout the 1950s.

Another Madison rosarian, Anthony Sodano, also raised commercial roses for the market. Sodano grew approximately 20,000 rose plants in five greenhouses, which required 60,000 gallons of oil per year to operate at a temperature of 64 degrees Fahrenheit. Sodano learned rose-growing techniques from his father Vincenzo, also called Jimmy, who won many awards in a lifetime spent in the cultivation of the plant. The elder Sodano used his consummate artistry to produce the beautiful rose called Spellbound. This rose, which took him six years to perfect in his Garfield Avenue greenhouses, was of a deep red hue, a velvety texture and had an unusually dark green foliage.

Vincenzo Jimmy Sodano, a horticultural genius, also grew prize-winning gladioli in addition to his patented hybrid roses, Spellbound and Little Princess.

In these years, Madison was the scene of popular rose shows or "Rose Festivals" held at Mead Hall on the campus of Drew University. One such show, held in June 1948, featured "thousands of roses, grown in local greenhouses," by such rose growers as Jimmy Sodano, Joseph Ruzicka, Stanley B. Roberts, Louis Heyl and the Noe Farm Greenhouses.(11) These shows were sponsored by Drew University, the Madison Chamber of Commerce, the Garden Club of Madison, the Madison Rotary Club, and the local commercial rose growers. Among those in the industry, the shows won critical acclaim.

Madison Fire Department and rose-bedecked equipment en route to a parade in Newark, June 1916. Two little boys in the driver's seat: Jim Cavanaugh in his fireman's uniform and Joe Corbett, rear, dressed as Uncle Sam.

In a news release by Roses Incorporated of New York City, local rose growers received praise for the beauty and fragrance of their product. Sodano presented a "breathtaking display of hundreds of roses reflecting the arrangements in two huge floor-to-ceiling mirrors," as well as a gigantic wooden frame filled with long-stemmed roses in the form of a painting.

The seeds of change for the rose industry were already at hand in the 1950s, although few knew it at the time. As people moved into the Madison area in search of suburban housing, land prices increased. With these increases came higher taxes and utility bills. Cathie Coultas recalled that increasing competition from rose growers in warmer climates using air freight for shipping proved to be insurmountable for local growers. Madison growers also began to receive offers for their land, which became increasingly hard to resist. Within the next 20 years, the industry would all but disappear. The sale of the Sodano property in 1984 marked its complete disappearance from Madison.

The Rise of the Great Estates

The success of the Madison rose industry was clearly linked to the establishment of lavish estates in the years after the Civil War. These great tracts required talented gardeners, who were frequently trained in Europe, in order to maintain the extensive grounds. In addition, many estate gardeners knew a great deal about the cultivation of commercial roses. To ply their trades, they needed large growing areas. This need contributed to the rise of great estates in the area.

The late 19th century was a time when "captains of industry," as many of these millionaires were known, held sway over the finances as well as the imagination of Americans. Profiteering from business schemes was rampant. Tax laws were inadequate; this was an age when the rich were not yet castigated in the press as *robber barons*.

While the wealthy accumulated great sums and lived in a flamboyant, extravagant fashion, they were admired by most Americans. Because of this public adulation and opportunities available for the rich to invest in a rapidly growing economy, many Americans have recalled the era as "The Gilded Age."(12)

Madison, as well as the surrounding area, had its share of these "captains of industry." Most prominent of the super-wealthy were Hamilton and Florence Vanderbilt Twombly. In addition to the Twomblys, the region's monied gentry also included Robert F. Ballantine, President of P. Ballantine and Sons Brewery; Marcellus Hartley Dodge, Chairman of Remington Arms Co.; Geraldine Rockefeller Dodge, an heir to the William Rockefeller fortune; Arthur Burdett Frost, one of America's best-known and wealthiest illustrators; Daniel Willis James, an executive of Phelps, Dodge & Co.; James H. McGraw, co-founder of the McGraw-Hill Book Company (now McGraw-Hill Education), and Charles Scribner, President of Charles Scribner and Sons publishing firm. All resided in Madison except Scribner and Frost, who lived in Chatham Township.

While the William Gibbons estate, which became Drew Theological Seminary, was one of the first important large estates to be built in Madison, others followed in the second half of the century. Many of the wealthiest families resided on Madison Avenue in the four-mile area between downtown Madison and Morristown. Alternately known as "Millionaire's Row" or the "Great White Way," the street was a showcase of some of the most opulent homes to be found anywhere.

Millionaires Express

Along with business profits, the railroad made possible the creation of both the great estates and the rose industry. New York businessmen could board a train for the city in the morning and return in the evening with fine regularity. For the well-to-do, the ideal of country-estate living, while still operating a business miles away was now possible.

Called the "Millionaire's Express," a steam locomotive pulled a line of coaches on the route from Morris County to New York. The Delaware, Lackawanna, and Western Railroad began servicing this route in 1883. Soon thereafter, the train depots of Chatham, Madison, and Morristown were crowded in the late afternoon with liveried drivers of the wealthy awaiting the arrival of the express. The train stopped at approximately 4:45 p.m. in Madison and arrived at 5 p.m. in Morristown each weekday. Average-income folk would ride in the forward cars, but the wealthy traveled in the better-furnished club cars at the rear of the line of train cars.

King of the Gilded Age

Hamilton McKeon Twombly was born in 1849, the son of a wealthy Boston shipping merchant. He attended private schools before his graduation from Harvard University, after which he wasted no time in expanding the family fortune through well-timed railroad stock purchases. Wealth frequently attracts wealth, and in 1887, Twombly married Florence Vanderbilt, an heir to the Cornelius Vanderbilt fortune. Twombly began to exert control over the vast Vanderbilt railroad empire as well as other family investments.

Twombly was considered a man of extraordinary wealth even by those who were themselves millionaires. The fortune he built was estimated at between $70 and $80 million at that time. Naturally, he spared no expense in building a country estate in Madison. The estate was called "Florham," a name derived from the combination of the first four letters of Mrs. Twombly's name, Florence, and three letters of his name, Hamilton. The 100-room mansion at "Florham" was a showplace of the era. Designed by the famous architectural firm of McKim, Mead, and White, the mansion was modeled after a wing of Henry VIII's Hampton Court in England. Today, the mansion serves as an administration building on the Florham Campus of Fairleigh

Dickinson University. The estate grounds were designed and landscaped by Frederick Law Olmstead, then America's best-known landscape planner. Olmstead also designed Central Park in New York.

The mansion and grounds were completed in 1896, but the estate was not occupied until a year later. The delay was caused by a long period of mourning for the death from pneumonia of the Twombly's daughter Alice. She succumbed in January 1896 after spending the Christmas holidays in Madison at their first home, "Cecilhurst," located on the same estate grounds as the newer mansion.

Not until May 1899 did the Twomblys recover sufficiently from the tragedy to open

Imposing view of the Twombly Estate from the main entrance.

their new home to the public. At that time, they hosted a well-attended party, which began the springtime round of activities marking the Morristown social season. The season, as writers John Rae, and John Rae, Jr., have noted, "...continued throughout the Spring until July 4—when most of the blue bloods departed for Newport—and then returned in September."(13)

The Twomblys did know how to live. Two years after they moved into the mansion, a $23,000 tunnel under the Delaware, Lackawanna, and Western Railroad tracks on their property was completed at their expense, permitting direct access from the mansion to Madison Avenue. Soon, they also built an indoor riding academy and indoor tennis courts on the estate. They also expanded the cultivated acreage to 750 acres of the "Florham Farms" section of the estate, north of Park Avenue.

To run the estate, the Twomblys employed a superintendent, a butler and a chef. The household staff usually totaled 25 servants at all times when the mansion was occupied by the family. When the Twomblys were in New York City or Newport, a skeleton crew remained to care for the house and grounds. In an age when the average American worker earned less than $500 per year, the Twomblys paid their French chef $25,000 a year.(14)

Mark Twain Visits Chemmiwink

In the early 1880s, Dr. Frank Fuller purchased a beautiful estate called "Chemmiwink," located on a hill on present Noe Avenue near the intersection of Sinclair Terrace.

Fuller was born in Boston in 1827. He later practiced dentistry in New Hampshire where he numbered Robert Lincoln, son of the President, among his patients. Through his subsequent friendship with Abraham Lincoln, he was appointed Governor of Utah. He moved to New York in 1874 and founded a company first known as the Health Food Company, later part of the

Dr. Frank Fuller with his wife, Annie, and son, Louis, on the lawn of his estate Chemmiwink. Chemmiwink is a Lenape Indian word believed to mean "The place of Hospitality," and indeed it was!

The bowling alley was available to guests.

Lavish entertainments and theatrical performances were presented at Holiday Hall, the estate theater resembling a river showboat. Local residents were often the thespians. *The Jilt* is believed to be the last play given in September 1902. Credit: Chemmiwink Album-Madison Historical Society.

Wheatena corporation, followed by several ownership changes and mergers until it is now part of the food giant Conagra.

About six years later, Fuller bought Chemmiwink for use as a summer estate. Best known among the many guests he entertained at Chemmiwink was the writer Mark Twain. Fuller entertained his visitors with horse racing, theatrical performances, boating, bowling and other activities. The theater was housed in a large wooden building called "Holiday Hall." Originally used as a storage barn, the building was renovated by Fuller and a stage with an orchestra pit built for its interior. In 1896, 400 seats were installed, and the theater's ceiling was painted blue with silver stars. The theater also had dressing rooms. With Fuller's death in 1915, however, the grand days of entertainment at "Chemmiwink" became only a glorious memory .

Besides Mark Twain, the great estates attracted other famous people. In May 1889, the *Eagle* reported that Frank R. Stockton was "now occupying 'The Holt,' his newly purchased property on Kitchell Avenue." A popular writer best known for his short story "The Lady or the Tiger," Stockton was related to Richard Stockton, one of New Jersey's signers of the Declaration of Independence. A year after his arrival in the area, Stockton was selected by readers of the journal *The Critic* as one of the top 40 writers of all time. *The Holt* is still standing on Kitchell Road.

Stockton was widely heralded as the originator in his writing of a "new vein of humor." In essence, he was a great storyteller who was able to weave folk tales and history into uniquely entertaining creations. One of his lesser-known works is *Stories of New Jersey,* an excellent recounting of the legends of the State.(15)

An Age Remembered

In the end, the great estates and the Madison rose industry were parts of the same story. Both grew as a result of the interests of the well-to-do who found the area's rolling countryside attractive. (It should be noted that it was not only the rich who enjoyed the romantic lure of the rose.) Often, estate owners provided growing space and even initial capital to launch cultivation efforts. Without either of these vital resources, the commercial rose-growing industry could not have taken hold.

There was another legacy of the estates and the rose industry, however. It was people. Those who came to Madison to grow the roses and to work on the estates added new skills and lifestyles to the Madison scene. They came from America and from abroad, and their settling was evidence that the growth of Madison touched on one of the great social phenomenons of our history—the immigration of millions of Europeans to the United States and from the southern states to the North.

The story of roses and of real estate also reflected the story of the immigrant experience in Madison, which will be a special concern in the next chapter.

"Rosedale Villa," home of Hugo A. Thomsen, presently Elks Club, Main Street and Rosedale Avenue.

Greenhouses

A tour of Madison around the year 1900 would reveal 45 to 50 small ranges of greenhouses growing roses and employing about 200 men. These growers were then in business:

Woodland Road	Dennis McCarthy
	Chas. E. Cook
Gibbons Place	James P. Murphy
Prospect Place	Thomas Kelley
Lathrop Avenue	T. Conroy
Green Village Road	Joseph Querney
	James J. Ryan
	Pat Manning
Loantaka Way	John R. Mitchell
Garfield Avenue	James D. Burnett, later Edward Behre
	Charles A. Work, later Sodano
Prospect Street	Arthur Searing and Thomas Rhedicen
Belmont Avenue	M. Brady
	James Monahan
	Ed McGuiness
Keep Street	Pat Connelly
	Michael B. Maguire
	Thomas H. Keefe
Main Street	Patrick Cosgrove and Son
	Philip F. Ryan
	Geo. W. Bruen
	Kerwin and Bryce
Madison Avenue	Judge Lathrop
	Wm. P. Wight
West Street	Jas. Dougherty
Park Avenue	Pat Donnelly
	Robert B. Holmes
North Street	T. Carr
	Wm. Quinlan
Myrtle Avenue	Eugene Fenton
	William Charlton
	James H. Dunn

Central Avenue	David Shannon
	Theo W. Stammler - Villa Lorraine Rosaries
	(Now Summerhill Park)
Shunpike	Henry Hentz Jr.
Green Avenue	Miss Alice Green
Ridgedale Avenue	James Hart
Fairview Avenue	Warren Barton

To the above list, these names should be added: E.R. Bellman, George Brown, D. Cantwell, H.H. Francis, Alfred S. Force, P. Hickey, M. Tilden, H.A. Thomsen, Mrs. D. McCarthy, Thomas Manion, and Thomas Madigan. During this same period, about 18 new greenhouses came into existence in Chatham, Chatham Township, and Murray Hill.

By 1950, the following rose ranges were in operation in the Madison area (their separate fates are noted in the third column; these ranges produced 25 million blooms annually):

Rose Range	Location	Destiny
Hentz	Shunpike Rd.	Housing
Jos. F. Ruzicka Co.	Shunpike Rd.	Stonehedge Dev.
Jimmy Sodano	Garfield Ave.	Housing
Stanley Roberts	Fairview Ave.	Dismantled
Alphonse Troianello	Burnet Rd.	Dismantled
Charles H. Totty Co.	Ridgedale Ave.	Housing
Abrahamson Co. Inc.	Greenwood Ave.	Housing
Manker Roses	Ridgedale Ave.	Housing
L.A. Noe & Son	Noe Ave.	Housing
Noe Farm Greenhouses	Southern Blvd.	Housing
Noe Estate Greenhouses	Noe Ave.	Housing
Watchung Rose Corp.	Shunpike Rd.	Chatham Twp Athletic Field
Rose Farms Corp.	Southern Blvd.	Apartments
Louis Heyl	Green Village Rd.	Not operating
J.L. Doremus	Spring Valley Rd.	Demolished
L.B. Coddington	Murray Hill	Demolished
Ruzicka	Chatham	Chatham H.S.
DiLauri Bros.	Florham Park	Demolished

Here are some of the roses originating in Madison:

Rose Range	Location
White Shawyer	Totty's
Mrs. F.F. Thompson	Totty's
Vanity Fair	Stanley Roberts - hybridizer;
Copper Lustre	Stanley Roberts - hybridizer;
Totty's Red	Totty's
Matchless	Duckham
Hentz	Nash greenhouses
Spellbound	James Sodano
Little Princess	James Sodano

Data in this supplement are from a history of Madison's rose industry written by Wilma and Robert Nichols of Madison.

Madison Estates

By 1910, wealthy landowners practically took over Madison. A Morris Co. Atlas of that year lists 40 named estates of varying sizes. The chart below lists principal ones together with the housing tracts that later displaced them.

Landowner	Familiar Name	Present Use
William Toothe	Oakwood Farm	Knollwood; E. of Greenwood; inc. Valley Rd., Hamilton St., etc.
H. A. Thomsen	Rosedale Villa	Now Elk's home; Main & Rosedale
Nathaniel Niles	Monatiquot	Niles Ave. area to Delbarton
Paul C. Zuhlke	Fairview	House still stands N.W. corner Edgewood Rd. & Pomeroy. No. 6 Dogwood Dr. was former barn
H.A. Hutchins.	Beechwood	Later Horace Work estate; now Cross Gates between Woodland & Pomeroy
F.A. Seaman	Echo Grove	Beverly Rd Norman Cir, Kensington Rd. area
A.G. Evans	Bellagio	Later Laura Augusta home; now Harwood off Woodland
Mary J. Slaughter	Dellwood	Now Dellwood; off Woodland.
Mary B. Hentz	Melrose	South of Woodland; Broadview & Crestview Aves., Coursen Way
Jennie T. Stemmier	Villa Lorraine	Ridgedale Ave. near Fairview; now Summerhill Park
C.L.G. Harrison	Ess-A-Kay	Corner Ridgedale & Fairview

Adolph de Barrett	Cecilhurst	Danforth & Madison Ave.; site of Bayley Ellard; now "St. Paul Inside the Walls."
Mrs. Henry B. Binsse	Oak Hill	These three estates shared lands between R.R. and Park Ave.; Danforth Rd. to North St.
Lenox S. Rose	Rosewood	
R.B. Holmes	Holmedale	
Mrs. J.M. Young	Ingleside	Cor. Madison Ave. & Morris Pl. extending to Elm St.
H. McK. Twombly	Florham Farms	Fairleigh Dickinson U. off Madison Ave
Mrs. D. Willis James.	Onunda	Later Dodge Estate; now Giralda Farms
Enos Wilder	The Chalet Clingstone	Two mansions in area called "Peach Orchard" behind Drew U.; Woodland, Green Village Rd. to Loantaka
James A. Webb	Wyndhurst	Corner Woodland & Prospect; Now Wyndhurst area, end of Maple Ave.
J.H. McGraw	Edgewood	House remains at No. 82 Prospect St., vicinity of Pomeroy
R.H. Williams	The Oaks	Madison Avenue beyond Bayley-Ellard; now Shadylawn

Other owners include:

John W. Steele	"Kool Kroft"
Frank M. Bruen	"Lawn View"
George K. Hooper	"Pine Knoll"
Anna Y. Condit	"The Knoll"
Emilie F. Condict	"Stone Henge," and "Kewaden"
Mrs. J.J. Humbert	"After Glow"
Annie P. Downs	"Bide A Wee"
Edward A. Isaacs	"Sunset View"

CHAPTER EIGHT

Ethnic Vigor
Diversifies the Community

Immigrants streamed into America in the years following the Civil War. Huddled on the decks of transatlantic ships, these tattered people were fleeing the broken hopes, poverty and persecution of European life at that time. Their faces, as reflected in old photographs, are haunting. Principally from Italy, Ireland, and Eastern Europe, the newcomers followed earlier waves of Europeans in their quest for freedom and economic opportunity. Madison offered both for those who would work for it. And work they did!

When the Scotch-English settlers first laid claim to this region and began to displace the Native Americans, they didn't think of themselves as immigrants. They believed they were "pioneers" with a prior right of ownership through the government they established.

The first real immigrants were refugees from the French Revolution, who received rapid social acceptance because they were wealthy and educated. They also sublimated their Catholicism by attending and supporting the Presbyterian Church.

For succeeding white immigrants—the Irish and the Italians—social acceptance had to be earned over a period of generations because these ethnic settlers lacked financial status. Landless and without property or education, they survived through hard labor and menial jobs. They lived in close-packed sections of the borough as "mainstream" Madison was then largely off-limits.

Yet, the very circumstances that segregated these immigrants were those that made them skillful at surviving in a community that accepted newcomers as soon as they proved their worth to the wider community.

The Irish

Among the best-known early Irish families in Madison were the Corbetts, O'Briens, McCarthys, and O'Donnells. The experience of David and Ellen McCarthy was typical. Grandparents of Helen, Lucille, and Joseph Corbett, they emigrated from Ireland in the late 1800s and arrived at Castle Island, NY, which then served as an immigration processing center. From there, they moved to Binghamton, NY, and shortly thereafter to Madison.

The McCarthys almost immediately became involved in the growing of commercial roses in greenhouses they constructed between Ridgedale and Central Avenues. The Corbett sisters remember the winter mornings when their grandmother, Mrs. David McCarthy, took "boxes of roses by sled to the railroad station."(1)

John Corbett - Irish community leader and builder.

Despite the important involvement of local Irish in the rose industry, their major contribution occurred in the area of construction. The most prominent among Irish builders were Jeremy O'Brien (see Chapter Five) and John V. Corbett. Both later sought and hired Italian immigrants to work on their construction projects.(2)

In an amazing career, Corbett served as the builder of St. Vincent Martyr Church, Central Avenue School, James Library, and the first YMCA. By this second generation, represented by Corbett, the Irish began to be accepted by most of Madison's dominant social class. However, this did not necessarily mean that the Irish were viewed as being on the same social level. Acceptance was facilitated because they shared a common English-speaking background.

John Corbett constructed the beautiful new St. Vincent's Church, rectory, and school to accommodate a growing congregation (1912).

Especially remarkable was the good relationship between the Irish and the Italians in Madison. They worked together and frequently helped one another. Helen Corbett, daughter of John V. Corbett, remembered well her father's fondness for his Italian workers. On many occasions, he lent them money when times were difficult.

Father Rolando and early class on the steps of St. Vincent's School on Park Avenue. The Park Avenue School became Knights of Columbus Hall in 1922.

Surge in Madison's Population

When the development of great estates in the rural countryside surrounding Madison transformed farmland into landscaped grounds and acres of green lawns, farmers who sold their lands often moved into the village. This shift in population, combined with the great influx of immigrants to labor on the estates, caused a surge in growth for the local community. Between 1880 and 1889, Madison's population grew from 1,756 to 3,250, an extraordinary increase.

As the Italians were arriving and some of the oldest families were leaving, a dynamic social situation emerged which had political and religious overtones. Politically, the estate owners gained increasing power because it was widely believed that they could influence the voting patterns of their employees. The new immigrants also created a demand for Catholicism, which must have provided some tension between the "old" and "new" ethnic groups in Madison.

Sons of Italy

Just as the Irish had before them, Italian immigrants moved into the North Street section of Madison in the late 1890s in search of jobs and a better life. Most were able to achieve both of these. With its great estates, its rose industry, and its numerous large homes with lawns in need of care, Madison was a great attraction. Local jobs offered steady pay, and because so many of the new arrivals came from agricultural regions of the old country, they often had skills valuable to Madison employers. Certainly these skills enabled many Italians to win a degree of acceptance in American society.

It was felt that the key to the American dream could be found through hard labor. As railroad laborers, the Italians excavated railroad beds and constructed sidings. Italians also be-

came the barbers and shoemakers of that period. Yet it was in the construction industry that the Italians, as had the Irish before them, made great strides by toiling doggedly in all kinds of weather on bridge, road, and canal projects.

Individual stories of successful Italians were numerous.(3) Samuel Maione, for instance, came to Madison in 1897 at age 13 and quickly found work in the large peach orchard that covered much of the acreage from Lathrop Avenue to Shunpike Road. Maione worked and saved his money before returning to Italy to bring his family to America.

Samuel Maione in his store on Park Avenue, 1926.

Making New Citizens

In 1903, Maione opened a restaurant in a building on Kings Road at the corner of Green Avenue. Later, he founded a grocery store at 13 Park Avenue, which his son Ralph continued

after World War II and then developed into the Bottle Pantry by the 1970s. Ralph Maione was elected to the Madison Borough Council in 1972 and ultimately served three terms on the council. Among others, Samuel Maione, in his day, purchased carloads of grapes, which he sold to local people to make homemade wine. Like others of his countrymen, he assisted many in finding jobs in the new land of opportunity, and he helped them apply for citizenship.

Maione was not alone. Naples-born James Sodano came to America at age 17 and worked in Madison's rose-growing industry for Louis Noe. He was later employed by Lincoln Pierson, but few suspected the significant contributions he would eventually make to the art of developing new strains of roses. (See Chapter Seven.)

Samuel Maione, second from left, and his father, Joseph, on the far right.

Frank Valgenti, Sr., father of local lawyer Frank Valgenti, Jr., arrived in America in 1880 as an orphan from Avellino, Italy.

Frank Valgenti, Sr.

He first lived in Brooklyn before moving to Madison in 1888. By the time of Valgenti's arrival here, there were already over 300 Italians living in the town. Valgenti proved to be a leader of ability for the Italian populace. First, he purchased a shoe-repair business from Amos Rathbun (site of present James Building) and later operated a grocery store.

Just before the turn of the century, he built a three-story building at 14 Central Avenue, where in 1900, he opened a private banking business, believed to be the only private charter ever granted by the State. The building at the corner of Cook Avenue still stands today. He also established a steamship agency here, from which he would arrange passage for people in Italy who wished to come to America. Valgenti also transported carloads of grapes from New York vineyards. He remained in these businesses until his retirement in 1930.

Earning Their Way

One of the most prolific family names in this community is Esposito. One of these family lines was begun by Joseph Esposito, who came to this community around 1891 at age 19. He went to work for D. Willis James, who then was master of what became the Dodge estate. Joseph married a daughter of Antonio and Angelina Allocco. Antonio was a foreman at the D. Willis James estate, and Angelina ran a boarding house at 11 Lathrop Avenue.

Another of Joseph's jobs was as a railroad gateman at the Green Avenue Crossing. He also helped dig the hole for the foundation of Burnet's Hardware store and received one dollar a day for his labor. He and his wife raised four boys and three girls, and like his countrymen, he helped many families to come to America. Among his children was Patrick Esposito.

Eventually, Patrick opened a grocery store at 15 Lathrop Avenue and a storage barn next door, from which he supplied grain, hay, and feed to estates in the region. He recalls that he would deliver as many as 3,000 bags a week. Patrick also claimed that the A & P grocery chain bought bulk sugar from him. He picked up his supplies at the old freight station, off Kings Road, that later served as a part of the YMCA complex. Patrick also later recounted that he had then acquired an early liquor license in Madison, enabling him to carry package goods in his store.

Joseph Esposito   Patrick Esposito in his store on Lathrop Avenue.

When Patrick Esposito built his home on Alma Avenue, the site was surrounded by the old Webb estate. With the help of his boys, he sawed timbers and constructed the house himself. He had learned many trades, such as plumbing, carpentry, and masonry because he had to "do many things" to support such a large family. Among the children were Joseph L. (Brownie) and

Michael P., who owned and operated the Esposito Brothers store at 82 Main Street for more than a decade.

Americanizing the Newcomers

Some Madison residents expressed their concern over the difficulties experienced by some Italians in making the adjustment to the new country. Citizens, led by Curtis Ezra Whittlesey and Charles Fremont Sitterly, rented a room for instruction in English for the new immigrants. In 1903, the library committee of the Madison Public Library offered immigrant children a class in basket weaving and other manual training. Miss Minnie Davis from Newark provided the instruction. The *Eagle* reported this goal in a news story at that time: "The object is to teach the children how to use their hands in delicate work and to rouse their ambition to better themselves when they grow older." Of course, many Italian immigrants were already bringing manual abilities with them to America.(4) Apparently, this came to pass as the future showed that Madison's Italians became even more highly skilled in building and craftsmanship. Another obvious motivation behind the effort was the desire of some teachers to have the Italians learn English in order to facilitate their assimilation.

Ethnic groups that have already been accepted frequently have little patience with those that have not. An *Eagle* editorial in 1903 lamented that the Italians were not trying hard enough to be Americans: "Too many persist in remaining Italian in heart and soul, in habits and sympathies and ways of living, and refuse to cast their lot in this hemisphere to the end of their days and become thoroughly American."(5)

Yet, there were other views that indicated that Italians were succeeding in American society. A youthful Red Cross worker from Italy visited Madison's Italians in May 1921 to study their status in local society. At the end of her brief visit, she reported to the local Red Cross chapter that Madison's Italians seemed well acclimated and able to interact with non-Italians. She expressed pleasure, in an *Eagle* article, that local Italians were given "every opportunity to assimilate the thought, customs and life of the community."(6)

Preserving a Culture

Meanwhile, the strong sense of pride in their nationality led Italians to organize local clubs. Sons of Italy was a local chapter of a fraternal organization for Italian American immigrants. It offered medical and death benefits for its members as well as culture and sociability. The group sponsored plays in Italian, with performers coming from New York City to act in James Hall. On Columbus Day there was a celebration in Madison with a big parade and spectacular fireworks. Pushcart peddlers came out from the city to sell Italian delicacies.

Another organization with a common ethnic interest, dedicated to

Alex Micone, Madison's long-time friend and businessman, is shown greeting a customer in front of his barbershop built in 1911. He arrived in Madison as a youngster of 10, where he worked long hours as a waterboy on construction jobs until his first job in a barbershop at age 13, earning 50 cents a week.

promoting civic activity, was the Forum Club, organized in 1928 with a charter drawn up by Frank J. Valgenti, Jr. Its first president was Pat Franco, a well-known tailor of Waverly Place. The group met in makeshift quarters for a time until they constructed a building on Walnut Street in 1941 and later added a large hall and gymnasium (currently the home of the Madison Civic Center and other offices but slated for demolition in 2023). This clubhouse served as a social center with but one requirement for all Italians: American citizenship. The organization has been recognized locally through programs such as sponsorship of a Little League baseball team, prizes for the annual summer program at Dodge Field and prizes for outstanding football players at Madison High School.

After reciting the organization's history at the 1955 dedication ceremonies, Frank J. Valgenti, Jr., praised its nonpolitical purpose: "It could have degenerated into the usual type of diluted Americanism that has characterized too many hyphenated organizations. However, we have never been a political pressure group. I believe it is for this reason that we have prospered."(7) Other Forum Club leaders responsible for the success of the organization included Ernest Mazzarisi, Dominick Mottola, Joseph Natale, John Cena, and Torey J. Sabatini.

The North Star Athletic Club evolved from a sports group of baseball and basketball players. They built their own sturdy brick clubhouse at 95 North Street with a hall and meeting rooms and became an organized club chartered by the State of New Jersey.

Thus, the first Italians in Madison were able to maintain major elements of their Italian culture: religion, strong family ties, and traditional ethnic ways. However, their initial experiences in the first half of the 20th century forced them to overcome significant ethnic prejudice. For them, the promise of America seemed to be only slowly taking hold.

A Racial Barrier

For Madison's African Americans, the promise of America took longer to be fulfilled, and social acceptance became harder to achieve. This group not only had to contend with the color barrier but also with an ingrained tradition of being classed as "slaves" and unskilled menials. However, many of Madison's African Americans—even before the Civil War—were "free."

This group of people never were immigrants in the true sense. Theirs was a transplanted culture in an inhospitable land. Because of such mighty handicaps, Blacks in Madison always had to try harder while suffering more from the bigotry that penetrated into the fiber of a white-dominated community. This required tenacity and stronger resolution in dealing with prejudice.

Frances Sheppard Turner of Floyd Street, a Black school teacher who taught in the Newark Public School system for 20 years, was born here in 1904. Her maternal grandparents, Dennis and Mary A. Hoggans, came to Madison in the years following the Civil War in order to work as domestic housekeepers for Madison's wealthy inhabitants. The late Emmett A. Turner, Frances' husband, moved to Madison with his parents before his 10th birthday. His father, a painting contractor lured here by the prospect of steady work, was born in Virginia, while his mother was originally from North Carolina. Emmett followed in his father's footsteps as a local painter. (From a private interview on June 29, 1982.)

African Americans had founded the Union Church at Cherry Hill, now Fairwoods, in 1853. This building was moved to a new site on the south side of Kings Road at Cross Street in 1864 when Judge Francis Lathrop made a gift of the property to the congregation.

In the 1870s, this organization came under the supervision of the African Methodist Episcopal Church, and in 1885, the present Bethel A.M.E. Church was constructed at the northeast cor-

Bethel A.M.E. Church

First Baptist Church

ner of Central Avenue and Chapel Street on land donated by Mr. and Mrs. William Jackson Brittin. To build this church, several Black families, including Dennis and Mary Hoggans and William Henry Williams, used their homes as collateral for a church loan. Prior to this time, the religious needs of local African Americans were met by an itinerant circuit preacher. Others who were instrumental in the church's founding were William Mills, Cornelius Molborn, John Keets, and Joseph Johnson.

The organization of another African American church began in 1895 when a group of dedicated people started a Baptist Mission on Central Avenue with the Rev. R.D. Cheek, Baptist state organizer. Pioneers in this mission were George Burroughs, Trim Felton, John Milton, Richmond Barrow, Jacob Boone, Isaac Garrish and others.

William Burroughs, cousin of Abel, father of Bizzell, and grandfather of Harriet Battle, Shelton and George Burroughs, long-time Community House director.

This group was required to attend an organized Baptist Church for one year before founding their own, so a company of 12 joined Calvary Baptist in Morristown. Meanwhile, the Mission ladies in Madison formed a women's sewing circle with Mrs. Emma Burroughs as president.

In 1896, Mission members organized the First Baptist Church in Madison. By 1900, the church began by purchasing a lot on Cook Avenue from B. Warren Burnet, and in June 1901, work began on the present sanctuary on that lot. The first service was held there in 1902. This church and the Bethel Church became active centers for local Black culture.

The Amazing Rebecca Lassiter(8)

Madison produced an African American woman with remarkable leadership qualities. Her name was Rebecca Lassiter. She was born Rebecca Prout on a small farm in Vineland, Cumberland County, on August 31, 1884. Her mother died while she was still a child, and she lived with a foster family. Still, Rebecca felt she had a happy childhood. She first came to Madison in 1920 to conduct an evangelistic service. During this visit, a 13-year-old boy was quite impressed by her. One of his questions to her was startling: "Why don't you come to my house and be my mother?"(9) As fate would have it, Rebecca did subsequently marry the boy's father, James Lassiter, Sr., a widower.

Once settled in Madison, Mrs. Lassiter made her presence felt by teaching music to young children at the Settlement House (now the Madison Community House; see Chapter 11). In the early 1950s, Mrs. Lassiter was ordained as the first female minister of the African Methodist Episcopal Church and, in 1953, became acting pastor of Bethel A.M.E. Church. Four years later, she was ordained deacon of the church. Mrs. Lassiter was a member of the local Ministerial Association, United Church Women, the Fair Housing Committee, Senior Citizens, and League of Women Voters and served as chaplain of the Madison Business and Professional Women. Somehow, Rebecca Lassiter also found time to raise four children. In 1959, she was honored by the Madison Rotary Club as a recipient of their Annual Citizen Award, being only the second woman to be so acknowledged. (Mrs. Dodge received this award in 1953.)

Mrs. Lassiter at her 89th birthday party in 1973.

Madison and *The Negro Motorists Green Book*

In the plot of *Green Book,* a 2019 Academy-Award-winning film, the protagonist, a Black performer traveling through the American South in 1962, is shown using a booklet that listed places where he could stop. In the mid-20th century, automobile ownership and usage boomed, including among people of color. But for African American motorists, driving to a new place meant understanding where they could find the amenities travelers rely on. Many service stations, motels, hotels, and restaurants were strictly segregated in the early and mid-20th century. Knowing where to find businesses friendly to the Black traveler meant the difference between a smooth trip and one potentially filled with social awkwardness, insults, or even violence. Although the movie shows the guide being used in the Jim Crow South, it was clearly needed across the country. *The Negro Motorists Green Book* was published annually from 1936 through 1967, with sites listed in just about every state. In the 30 years of publication, New Jersey had some 581 individual businesses listed in 31 different towns.

The largest concentrations of listed establishments in New Jersey were in Atlantic City, Asbury Park, and Newark. Newark's listings offered a wide range of services, as befit the state's largest city. These included service stations, hotels, barbershops, taverns, restaurants, and nightclubs. In other cities and towns, in addition to the expected service stations and restaurants or taverns, there were often beauty parlors, tailors, and barbershops, reflecting the deep-seated prejudice encountered by African Americans at many personal service businesses.

The two Madison businesses listed in the *Green Book* were both taxi services, and both were located at 14 -18 Lincoln Place, across the street from the train station. Their offices were within the recently demolished Madison Theater. Indeed, a historic photo of the theater shows taxis out front, ready to take passengers from the train to nearby homes and businesses.

Between 1939 and 1953, the *Green Book* listed the Yellow Taxi Service at 14 Lincoln Place. One company, the Yellow Taxi Cab Company, was founded around 1920 by Frank Watson. In 1943, Richard White, Jr. of Madison, announced in an ad in the *Madison Eagle* that he had purchased the Yellow Taxi Cab Company and would continue operations at an office at the theater building.(10) Richard S. White Jr. already owned and operated White Brothers, a taxicab company that first had offices on Main Street from at least 1927.(11) Still, he had adopted the name "Yellow Taxi Service" for the consolidated business after 1943.

Who were the White Brothers? They were members of an African American family with deep connections to Madison and a strong love of automobiles. The parents, Richard White, Sr. and his wife Lavinia (or Luevinia), moved to Madison from New York City in 1900 with their infant son, Richard White, Jr. Ultimately, there would be four White brothers and one sister, Madeline, who never married and spent her working life as a bookkeeper for the family taxi business. In later years, their father, Richard White, Sr., also joined the enterprise and advertised in the *Green Book*. He used his home address of 196 Main Street as the business address. Today's Wells Fargo Bank at 200 Main Street is on the site of the White family home.

Richard White, Jr. died in 1948, and the business continued for a few more years under the leadership of Richard White, Sr. When he retired sometime in 1953, the company stopped listing in the *Green Book*, effectively closing the business his family had built over the previous 30 years.

Stoddard Defends African Americans

William O. Stoddard, Sr. was a very popular man in Madison during the last 30 years of his life. As a former personal secretary to the martyred Abraham Lincoln, Stoddard was highly respected. In an open letter to "colored voters of New Jersey," printed in the September 2, 1910 issue of the *Madison Eagle* under the title: "A Plea from Lincoln's Friend to the Colored Voters of Madison," the former presidential secretary

William Osborn Stoddard, Sr. He is shown here in his later years. He was greatly influenced by his grandfather, John Osborn, a member of the Legislature, sportsman, religious man, and Abolitionist. During his teen years, Stoddard attended N.Y. state party conventions (Whig, Democratic, Abolition, Women's Rights) and listened to great men such as Daniel Webster. He was an organizer of the Union League of America, secured the nomination of Andrew Johnson for VP at the 1864 Baltimore Republican National Convention, and in 1867, obtained passage of an act authorizing the laying of a second Atlantic telegraph cable. During the late 1870s came the greatest change in his way of life: the compulsory devotion to literature. Between then and 1908, he wrote over 70 books, mostly juvenile stories and historical works. Stoddard was known to nine presidents.

urged Blacks to exercise their right to vote.(12)

Stoddard made reference to those who told him that "the colored man is unfit for such a responsibility, that he will never act independently, but will always obey such orders or instructions as he may receive from some other man." To Stoddard, such thinking was nonsense. He urged Black voters to "Know whom you vote for, know why you vote for him, and prove to the people of New Jersey that you cannot be bought for a price, but are men indeed."

By 1910, several family names were beginning to be recognized as active in African American cultural affairs in Madison. Among these were Ader, Borland, Camp, Clark, Copeland, Demby, Davis, Wilson, West, Watkins, Whitehurst, and Willingham.(13)

These families assisted in bringing the doctrine of self-help and civil rights to African Americans in the early years of the 20th century. Frequently, Madison Blacks heard from distinguished lecturers on these topics.

One such speaker came to Bethel A.M.E. Church on October 25, 1910, to speak on "How to Get Up in the World." He was Bishop Wesley J. Gaines, founder of both Payne Institute of Selma, Al., and Morris Brown College of Atlanta, Ga. His coming was a clear sign of the desire of the Black community to advance its interest and to overcome racial barriers in the quest to live as equal citizens in Madison.

Despite the difficulties that the Irish, Italians, and African Americans encountered, they were all here to stay. Their children and grandchildren would continue to build on the foundation they constructed. Madison was enriched by the ethnic diversity these groups provided and strengthened by their contributions to local life.

CHAPTER NINE

Benefactors Create
a Modern Madison

Madison's evolution from a small town to a suburban community was greatly aided by the vision of several wealthy benefactors. The contributions of these key figures to Madison's development are seen not only in terms of dollars, though vast fortunes from inheritance and business acumen were put to work, but in terms of foresight: a realization that the need existed for a church facility, a better police department or modernized civic buildings. Fortunately, the Madison hills attracted not only a prosperous citizenry but activists who were willing to share their good fortune with the blue-collar working community. They were a diverse group of estate owners whose interests and good works ranged widely over many decades.

Among the most prominent were Judge Francis Stebbins Lathrop, whose foresight gave Madison a central focus; James Augustus Webb, business and banking entrepreneur, whose influence made possible a golf course as well as a water utility; Daniel Willis James, who with his wife Ellen Stebbins used their fortune to glorify Madison; and Geraldine Rockefeller Dodge, a canny heiress who with her husband Marcellus Hartley Dodge gave Madison its most memorable civic landmarks. These doers had in common a high regard for the town in which they lived and a desire to take a direct hand in its progress.(1)

Judge Francis Lathrop is recognized as the first of the community's memorable benefactors. A lay member of the Court of Errors and Appeals, Lathrop saw the need for open space around which to build a business center. He purchased properties on the west side of Waverly Place with the idea of widening this thoroughfare.

When the great fire of 1877 destroyed most of the buildings on that side of the block, he and other far-thinking citizens seized the opportunity to make way for the broad central plaza we know today as the heart of the community. He built a hotel on the site but died in 1882 after its completion. It was then sold as a part of his final estate. Judge Lathrop

Judge Francis
Stebbins Lathrop

was also a prime mover in other civic causes. For instance, he donated substantially toward the construction of Grace Episcopal Church and, along with George T. Cobb, purchased 24 acres of land in Evergreen Cemetery in Morristown for the members, clergy, and vestrymen of Madison's Grace Episcopal Church. He played an important role in helping his community evolve from a village to a town.

An influential peer of Lathrop's was James Augustus Webb, who came to Madison in 1862. Webb was born in Norwich, New York, on February 3, 1830, and became, in his lifetime of 80 years, one of Madison's greatest benefactors. Webb was the son of New York merchant Augustus Van Horn Webb and his wife, Phoebe Baker Webb. At the age of 23, James established his own business as a manufacturer of industrial alcohol in New York. He developed this

K. Conklin. Architect; J. Corbett. Builder

This YMCA, dedicated in April 1908, served a growing town until the 1960s. (At right, front row: E.D. Conklin, J.A. Webb, Gov. Fort, Dr. Buttz. Middle row: J.E. Hedges, E.P. Holden, J.H. McGraw, Col. A. Colgate. Back row: D.S. Voorhees, W.M. Kingsley, W.H. Seward.

business into an array of commercial and banking enterprises and moved from New York to Madison. By 1873, his interest in local activities became apparent. That year, he helped organize the Madison YMCA and served as its second president. He was also instrumental in the 1904-1910 fund-raising effort to build the YMCA facility on Main Street (now an office building across from the Museum of Early Trades and Crafts). Webb gave the largest single donation of $15,586 toward the total cost of $75,228. He also served as a Presbyterian Church trustee and was its treasurer for 40 years. As a memorial to his son, James A. Webb, Jr., who died on April 6, 1887, Webb and his wife Margaretta built the Gothic Webb Memorial Chapel and gave it to the church. In July 1903, Webb provided land and donated a new clubhouse for the Madison Golf Club. In what was publicized in The *Madison Eagle* on July 10,1903 as "one of the most *a*ttractive social events of the season," the club "formally opened" amid the usual gala of a Fourth of July celebration. Webb was also influential in the struggle to bring Madison its own waterworks and electric light plant. He helped establish a telephone exchange by guaranteeing the company 20 subscribers.

Local social connections were frequently neatly interwoven by marriage. In 1852, Webb mar-

Margaretta Baker Webb   James Augustus Webb

Webb Memorial Chapel

ried Margaretta Baker, the daughter of Jacob and Anna Maria Brittin Baker, thus uniting two of Madison's best-known families. Of James Webb, it was said: "With [him] business has never been a trade but rather a profession, in which the test was not time service, but a hearty and wholesome loyalty to entrusted interests which served to develop all that was best for the individual."(2)

The Founding of the Madison Golf Club(3)

"There is some talk of forming a small golf club in Madison. The use of a field on Green Village Road has been secured, and the grounds will be put in shape as soon as the snow clears." This brief mention of a "rumor," published in the *Madison Eagle* of March 20, 1896, turned out to be true, and it heralded an important event for the thousands of golfers who, for well over a century, have enjoyed the pleasure of playing the challenging private Madison Golf Club course.

Seven days after the piece of gossip was published, on March 27, 1896, a meeting was held at the 60 Green Avenue home of former US Congressman Judge George H. Yeaman to organize the private Madison Golf Club. With the actions of 11 prominent Madison citizens, New Jersey's sixth golf club was born. The club officially opened with its first tournament on July 4, 1896 and that tournament remains today as one of the most popular events of the Madison Golf Club season. The original course measured 1,200 yards for six golf holes.

It was all made possible through the generosity and encouragement of another Madison resident, industrialist and philanthropist, Mr. James A. Webb. Not only did Mr. Webb offer the free use of his land, but he also encouraged the formation of the Club; he later paid for the construction of a clubhouse pictured below, which he proudly presented to the Club in 1903. Webb continued the free use of his land until his death in 1910. In keeping with his wishes, his estate continued this generosity until 1939, when the estate sold the 26 acres to the Club at a most agreeable price of $15,000. Mr. Webb's original

Madison Golf Club. Then and Now, "Madison is one of the first golf clubs in the United States—a private family-type club for the enjoyment of the game of golf and for association with other members and their families. This has remained. It was then a credit to the town of Madison; it is now and will be for many years to come." 2020 Photo Credit: Herman Huber

1903 clubhouse was expanded several times and used until 2011 when it was replaced by the present-day clubhouse.

The most significant renovation was undertaken in 2002 when professional golf architect Robert McNeil was engaged to bring the course and its conditioning up to current standards. The course was reopened for play in June 2003 to the delight and perhaps some consternation of the membership.

As the iconic Eisenhower loblolly pine tree at Augusta National stood for decades on its 17th fairway, a magnificent specimen silver maple tree stood for years in the middle of Madison's ninth fairway, about 50 yards from the putting surface. A challenge to golfers of every skill level, generations of golfers hit shots over, under and around the club's landmark until it was blown down by heavy winter winds in 2015.

With its demanding narrow fairways, exacting small greens and mildly rugged terrain, in September 2020, Madison Golf Club was named number 25 of the top 50 stand-alone 9-hole golf courses in the world by *Golf.com Magazine*. Despite such worldwide notoriety, its distinct familial atmosphere continues to proudly reflect Madison's small-town charm and character. Although not a golfer himself, Mr. Webb believed in 1896 that a golf course in his adopted hometown would be a treasured asset. As a testament to his inspiring generosity and sharp foresight, the Madison Golf Club now provides its members challenging yet pleasurable recreation. Madison residents enjoy a scenic, green, park-like setting and a well-valued and loved resource that most towns across the country would envy but few can claim.

The Daniel Willis James Legacy

Just as Lathrop and Webb created a positive role model for Madison's wealthy to emulate, Daniel Willis James expanded that role model through his personal charisma. Shortly after Judge Lathrop's death, James bought his property off Loantaka Way and ultimately became a major figure in community affairs.

James Park, completed. A plaque honoring Mr. and Mrs. James is beside the overpass at the intersection of Kings Road and Madison Avenue.

The James Building is located at the corner of Green Village Road and Main Street.

James Library, now home to Madison's Museum of Early Trades and Crafts.

Born in Liverpool, England, in 1832, he was the son of a merchant who emigrated to America with his family. In an age of frequent unbridled greed and excess, James was a notably honest businessman. He earned his fortune through shrewd management and wise investments as a senior member of Phelps, Dodge & Co., as president of Golden Hill Corp., an investment firm, and as a director in several other companies.

While interested in supporting charities and colleges through his generous donations, James preferred to remain anonymous. He was especially fond of his contributions to the Children's Aid Society of New York. From 1897 to 1901, James served as president of that agency. When speaking of the society's work, James frequently referred to a letter he received from a former New York City waif who had been picked off the streets. The waif, Andrew H. Burke, later became governor of North Carolina. The letter which James treasured read in part: "There has never been a day that my heart has not nurtured a grateful remembrance of the fostering care extended to me and noble incentives imparted at the threshold of my life by the Children's Aid Society."(4) Unlike some "captains of industry" of that age, James measured his success in human terms.

The Interior of James Library shows a vaulted ceiling and ornamental ironwork on the balcony.

On July 4, 1898, this benefactor made his first great contribution to the people of Madison: James Park was formally opened to the public as a gift to the community. Its location bordered on three sides of the railroad tracks between Madison Avenue, Park Avenue, and Ridgedale Avenue. The site had been a swampy eyesore for many years. James had the park designed flawlessly with an arched footbridge over the tracks and carefully chosen plantings of shrubs and trees. Grassy slopes replaced swamp land. Madison was assured of a beautiful park near the center of town.

This was only the beginning for philanthropist D. Willis James. In 1899, he made his most remarkable gift to the community when he built and donated to Madison a handsome library now used by the Museum of Early Trades and Crafts. The Richardsonian Romanesque, Gothic building served Madison as a library for 70 years until 1969.

At the same time, James built the large, cream brick business structure across Green Village Road from the library. Called the James Building, it originally housed various businesses as well as the official borough offices. The second floor was designed as a roomy Assembly Hall with a balcony, which served as a community meeting center and fashionable gathering place. (5) Rather ingeniously, James planned that the rental revenue generated by this commercial enterprise be utilized for the upkeep of the library. This was an imaginative plan for the age, and it represented another reason why the wealthy were generally held in such high regard locally.

Ellen Stebbins James   Daniel Willis James

James not only gave publicly to the community but also exhibited privately some of the best traits of Madison's privileged class. Although his gifts to the community are well known, his private acts of humanity are not. On several occasions, he assisted Russian Jewish immigrants who had fled penniless to America.(6) In addition, his Newark-based firm of James, Allman and Company outfitted some of the recent immigrants as tinware peddlers. One such peddler, who later became a successful metal manufacturer, described James as "the only godly man I ever knew. He was the first man in America who held out a friendly hand."(7)

Madisonians appreciated this kind of altruistic man. On July 8, 1898, the day that James Park was dedicated and given to the town, more than 1,000 townspeople, marching to band music, paraded to their patron's home and escorted him to the ceremony. On that occasion, Mayor James Albright said of this popular townsman: "His object is humanitarian; his work is philanthropic; his modesty and generosity unparalleled."(8)

What was most amazing about James was the degree of popularity he received in such a short time in the community. When he died in September 1907, he had lived in Madison for less than 15 years, yet his influence was profound and lasting. On Wednesday, October 2, 1907, his fellow townspeople crowded into the Assembly Hall in the James Building on Green Village Road to pay tribute. As the Rev. William Russell Bennett of Morristown (formerly of Madison) said of James: "He has so identified himself with this locality that we have seen here striking evidence of those elements of his personality and purpose that meant so much and accomplished so much in the larger world."(9)

In his will, James left $1,195,000 to charity. This was given primarily to colleges, including Union Theological Seminary, Columbia University, and Yale University. At his death, his total assets (in a legal appraisal of April 3, 1908) were valued at $26 million.

After the death of her husband, Ellen Stebbins James continued to carry the torch of pride in Madison, indicating that she had always shared in the planning that made this a special community. At the time of the elevation of the railroad tracks in 1914 and 1915, Mrs. James was prominent among those who turned chaos into beauty by making possible a great curving boulevard out of Kings Road in front of the railroad station.

From her mansion off Loantaka Way, later inhabited by Geraldine and Marcellus Hartley Dodge, the widow of D. Willis James financed the rearrangement of the west end of town. It was she who paid for the work involved in changing the course of Madison Avenue, the widening of Park Avenue, the purchase and removal of three properties on Ridgedale Avenue to allow this street to end at Park Avenue instead of crossing the railroad, and for the complete realignment of James Park.

Mrs. James and other Madison stalwarts were steadfast in their efforts to urge the D.L.&W. Railroad management to build a new station that would reflect the elegant status of the area's fashionable millionaires.

Aura of the Rich

Madison had ample reason to be grateful to benefactors such as Lathrop, Webb, and James, but not all of the wealthy chose to share their largess with the town on such a munificent scale. Yet the townspeople seemed pleased to rub elbows with rich Madisonians, even if they contributed little to the welfare beyond their taxes. They helped maintain a bountiful aura.

Opinion in favor of the wealthy was so marked that some out-of-town observers found it hard to swallow. A 1903 editorial in the *Millburn Review* took the *Eagle* to task for its favorable coverage of Madison's upper crust. The *Review* described the *Eagle* as "cautious, dignified, and able, yet it condescends to truckle to the wealthy." This cutting remark generated heat between the newspapers.

The best way to describe the position of the *Eagle* on the growing number of wealthy citizens moving to Madison is found in several editorials that center on the issue of "good works" done by the wealthy. The rich, according to this theory, had an obligation to benefit other people as well as themselves.

The *Eagle* frequently took the position that the affluent who merely amassed millions without social purpose were "not successful." In a 1903 editorial titled "The True Measure of Success," the writer stated that men could make opportunities for themselves: "There is not a millionaire in Madison who was ever given any greater chance to be really successful than the poorest and humblest man in town...men do not have chances thrust upon them—they make chances for themselves."(10) The newspaper described Madison as "blessed in the character of the men and women who occupy the fine residences and own the fine propertys [sic] that make it so beautiful as a community."(11)

This strong sentiment did not prevent the newspaper from taking local capitalists to task when excesses were observed. In this regard, the park-like estate of the late Dr. Leslie D. Ward (present site of Braidburn Country Club in Florham Park) figured in a brief controversy in December 1910 when the *New York World* accused George Gould and a party of friends with the slaughter of more than 1,700 wild ducks within a three-week period on the estate. The *Eagle* refuted the claim of the *World* regarding the number killed with the assertion that "several hundred" in that time period seemed more likely. Nevertheless, the *Eagle* indignantly characterized the "slaughter" as "disgraceful enough." Strong words against the alleged excesses of the wealthy!(12)

Even when considering such episodes with displeasure, Madisonians were to have greater cause than ever to be thankful for the presence of the public-spirited well-to-do. There soon came a grand successor to the departed Daniel Willis James.

"In Love with Madison"

In 1916, Geraldine Rockefeller Dodge and her husband Marcellus purchased the former James mansion off Loantaka Way. Geraldine was the daughter of William Rockefeller, leader of the Standard Oil Company and brother to John D. Rockefeller. Born into fabulous wealth,

Geraldine Rockefeller, at the time of her marriage to Marcellus Hartley Dodge.

Geraldine Rockefeller grew up in New York State and, early in life, revealed her extraordinary interest in animals. On the Rockefeller estate at Scarborough-on-the-Hudson, she raised thoroughbred horses. Her marriage on April 18, 1907, to Marcellus Hartley Dodge united two large fortunes. Earlier, Mr. Dodge had inherited a large fortune in stocks from his maternal grandfather, Marcellus Hartley. His paternal grandfather, William E. Dodge, Sr., was linked to the Phelps-Dodge industrial empire. By age 21, he was the sole heir to the vast Dodge fortune and a year later, he assumed the presidency of the family-owned Remington Arms Company. In many ways, he exceeded the success achieved by his grandfather. This was a major accomplishment for someone so young. Mrs. Dodge's father died in 1922, leaving her a $15 million trust fund. In those sad events, the two large inheritances were merged.

Mr. and Mrs. Dodge on the morning of a dog show.

Marcellus and Geraldine Dodge chose Madison as a place of residence after renting a summer "cottage" in the hills nearby and commuting to New York. Later, Mrs. Dodge revealed that she "fell in love" with Madison the first time she saw it. After a succession of land acquisitions, two separate estates evolved in the expansive Dodge complex: now to be called "Giralda Farms" and "Hartley Farms." The latter became Mr. Dodge's residence. Although separated by a distance of nearly two miles, each mansion could be seen from the other because the couple had an 80-foot wide tree-lined corridor cleared between the two residences.

Living in the 35-room Giralda, Mrs. Dodge began to cultivate extensively her two main hobbies: the collection of art, and the breeding of pedigreed dogs. Her interest in dogs led from breeding fine canine specimens to the competition of dog shows. By 1927, she organized the

Crowds awaiting the opening of the annual Morris and Essex Kennel Club dog show at the Hartley Farms polo field in Harding Township, at that time the largest one-day outdoor dog show in the country.

Mrs. Dodge with Fire Chief Samuel A. Gruver in front of the new Ahrens-Fox Model P-4 fire engine that she donated to the town.

first of the famous dog shows of the Morris and Essex Kennel Club. Nearly 600 dogs were entered, and the winning owners received large cash prizes and silver trophies engraved with the name of the winner and that of her son, Marcellus Hartley Dodge, Jr.(13)

In the 1950s, this show became the outstanding summer event hereabouts with crowds of dog fanciers arriving from all over the world. Considered the largest one-day event in the world, the show was held for 30 years, except for a halt during the 1941-1945 war period.

Mrs. Dodge's concern for her adopted community manifested itself openly in May 1921, when Madison firemen saved her complex from possible destruction when a barn on the estate caught fire. She was then inspired to donate $18,000 for a fire engine. The trusty and popular fire engine was later sold by the borough, only to be repurchased in 2013. (See Chapter Sixteen for the story of the repurchase.) Now named "Geraldine," it was ceremoniously returned to the community where it remains today as a popular attraction for schoolchildren and in community parades. Mrs. Dodge also hired the first motorcycle policeman in the town's history and paid his salary for one year. In addition, she purchased a motorcycle for him to ride! Because of these spontaneous acts, Madison's citizens soon became well aware of this great benefactor in their midst.

A celebration on May 14, 1921, in connection with the presentation to Madison of a fire engine by Mrs. Dodge, drew many fire chiefs and officials to town. The fete included a parade, dinner, and block dance. Said to be the first of its kind, the six-cylinder fire engine carried 122 feet of hose, a 20-foot extension ladder, and a 12-foot roof ladder.

The Lady of Giralda was such an exponent of clean water that she would empty her outdoor swimming pool and refill it if anyone entered the water before her. With a keen eye for recycling, she used the excess water to refresh her gardens. As a woman of strong habits, she was used to having her own way. To some, she seemed idiosyncratic, but her consistent interest in mothering the community outweighed her domineering characteristics.

Perhaps a sidelight on Mrs. Dodge's philosophy of reciprocity in local philanthropy was observed in 1922 when she requested and received a lower tax assessment on her property. In the case before the Morris County Board of Taxation, the Madison Borough Council did not contest the lower assessment figure on the ground that a legal case might prove too costly.(14) Whatever the motive of the council, it was clear that town leaders, as well as area newspapers, held Mrs. Dodge in considerable awe.

A "Million-Dollar" Memorial

Such favored local treatment, perhaps, moved Mrs. Dodge to impressive acts of generosity. In the tradition of Lathrop, Webb, and James, Mrs. Dodge, represented by Carroll B. Merritt, acquired two parcels of land on Kings Road opposite the Lackawanna Railroad station and gave the deeds to the borough council in September 1927. The property later became the site of Madison's so-called "million-dollar" borough hall.

Eight years later, at the dedication of the Hartley Dodge Memorial building in May 1935, the borough presented the philanthropic lady with a resolution thanking her sincerely for her generosity. The resolution characterized her as "a farseeing, loyal, generous friend, and citizen of Madison, donor of lands and money for playing fields [Dodge Field] and parks, seeking nothing for self, while giving richly to ensure enduring beauty to our community and advantages to our people."

The municipal building was a lavish memorial from Mr. and Mrs. Dodge for an only son killed in a tragic automobile accident in August 1930. While traveling in Europe in his

Hartley Dodge Memorial Building dedication on Memorial Day 1935, on the site given to Madison by Mrs. Dodge and Mrs. Webb.

Hartley and his mother.

Princeton Polo Team.

expensive sports car, young Hartley, only 21 years old, died instantly. A friend, Ralph Applegate, survived the crash, and Mrs. Dodge took him into her home for recuperation. With the death of their cherished son, who, from all accounts of those who knew him, was a very personable and talented young man, the Dodges retreated into the seclusion of their estates.

In November 1931, Mrs. Dodge became involved in a local controversy involving the contest for mayor. Just prior to the election, Raymond L. Patterson, Mrs. Dodge's secretary, issued a statement that implied that Mrs. Dodge would give the town a new municipal building if Frank A. Cook, the Democratic candidate, was elected. It should be noted that Mrs. Dodge never personally commented on this alleged promise, but voters took it seriously. In an overwhelmingly Republican town, Democrat Cook won handily. His opponent, James A. Smith, complained: "What a price the people of Madison are asked to pay for a municipal building. In order to secure this benefit, they must sacrifice their right to a free choice."

For the public, the price seemed small since both men had administrative talent. The town could not lose no matter who received the office. Some citizens, however, resented the alleged interference of Mrs. Dodge.

As promised, Mrs. Dodge's contractors broke ground in September 1932 at the peak of the Great Depression. Labor for the project was plentiful with so many individuals unemployed.

Impoverished men came from all over the nation seeking employment. There was always a line at the high fence on Kings Road, which enclosed the construction site.

The cost of building the Hartley Dodge Memorial was estimated in excess of $800,000, with granite shipped from Deer Island, Maine, and marble imported from quarries here and abroad. Owing to an obsession with perfection and delays in the arrival of materials, construction dragged on for nearly three years.

Mrs. Dodge speaking at the dedication ceremony.

On Memorial Day, 1935, the building was dedicated before a crowd of 2,000 people. County Judge Arthur Holland presided at the ceremonies, but the main speaker was Senator W. Warren Barbour, who said, "The building is American throughout and symbolic of the best tradition." Mrs. Dodge said little at the dedication, but she later pledged a $300,000 trust fund to provide income to maintain the memorial. She also installed furnishings and, in the elegant council chamber, placed a stunning collection of art treasures, almost all of which were willed to the Hartley Dodge Memorial Foundation.

The collection includes three Lincoln pieces: a bronze bust of Lincoln by famed American sculptor Max Bachman (1905); a full-length oil portrait of Lincoln (now on loan to the National Portrait Gallery in Washington, D.C.); and a tapestry-covered chair made from timbers of the house Lincoln helped his father build. A fourth item, originally thought to be Lincoln's desk during his time in Congress from 1847-1849, was actually built later and was of the Renaissance Revival style used by members of Congress during Lincoln's presidency.(15) There were also two ceiling-to-floor length exquisite Gobelin 17th-century tapestries that were later sold by the Dodge Foundation. Highly significant was a marble bust of Napoleon by Auguste Rodin, first identified as such in the 1985 publication of *The Madison Heritage Trail*. The sculpture was, in recent years, confirmed to be the work of Rodin. After being on display at the Philadelphia Art Museum, it was sold to a private collector.

The Madison council chamber collection also included a bronze bust of Benjamin Franklin by French sculptor Jean Antoine Houdon (1778), portraits of George and Martha Washington by American painter Rembrandt Peale, and an oil portrait of John Quincy Adams by George Peter Alexander. A portrait of (Ethel) Geraldine Rockefeller at the age of 23 was painted in 1905 by German artist Friedrich August Von Kaulbach. The future Lady of Giralda is seated against a seascape that stretches to the horizon. It is an especially lovely memory to keep of this great philanthropist who left a lasting legacy to this community. Those who attend council meetings may view these museum pieces as a fringe benefit.

During the age of great benefactors, Madison's population was small yet growing steadily. With only 1,756 residents in 1880, the population rose to 3,756 by 1900, then nearly doubled by 1930, when it reached 7,473. Despite such a large increase, Madison was still a small town. However, the legacies of these generous benefactors gave the community a unique patina that was hard to match even in cities of much greater population.

Interior view of the council chamber showing many of the art treasures displayed throughout the building. Note: Doors leading to the mayor's office.

CHAPTER TEN

Memories of "The Old Boys"

They were known as the "Old Boys of Bottle Hill" and still are, though long since gone. Born in the early 1800s, they became childhood pals in the village, running in the fields and fishing in the ponds. By the late 1800s, they had their own careers—machinist, blacksmith, wheelwright, physician, and the like—but they never lost touch with each other and over the years, they could seldom resist the urge to gather for a bit of reminiscing. They emerged as an informal social club devoted to the preservation of local lore, and at its peak, the group numbered 18 men.(1)

Their history started not long after George Washington died in 1799. They recalled, for example, the visit of Lafayette in 1825 as well as the community's discarding of the name "Bottle Hill" in 1834. They were still holding their meetings in 1909, and by the time the last of the Old Boys passed on, the group had witnessed the transformation of Madison from a rural outpost to a thriving town of over 4,700 residents. The Old Boys were an important part of Madison's collective memory, and their stories offer some of the most fascinating insights on life in Madison during the 19th and early 20th centuries.

Origins of the Old Boys

The Old Boys of Bottle Hill represented some of the oldest and proudest family names in the history of Madison; most were residents from before the Civil War and some had their roots in the colonial period. They included Charles C. Force, Pierson A. Freeman, Benjamin Warren Burnet, William Jackson Brittin, Louis Beaupland, Dr. Lewis Sayre, William H. Sayre, and "Uncle" Nelson Samson. Their nominal leader was Force, who was born in East Madison in 1818. At age 16, he was apprenticed to John B. Miller, who taught him the skills of a blacksmith. For nearly 50 years, Force served the village as a blacksmith and machinist. His shop was on College Road, now Park Avenue, just west of present Ridgedale Avenue on the south side. This was the origin of the Madison Iron Works. Before failing eyesight and eventual blindness compelled his retirement, Force had also done good work as a school trustee and a township committee member.

Madison Iron Works prior to destruction by fire in January 1908; rebuilt with brick in August 1908. Eleanor Roosevelt visited the foundry during World War II.

Together, the Old Boys represented the village's past, and the townspeople knew it even before the turn of the century.

As early as 1895, Madisonians were looking fondly at the efforts of the Old Boys to keep the memories of the town's early days alive. On October 31st of that year, former resident Thomas B. Carter paid them a glowing tribute in a letter published in the *Eagle*. Recalling the stories of the Old Boys, he grew sentimental over the town. "Oh beautiful, beautiful Madison," Carter wrote, "how much thou hast changed for the better...." (2) He was right; the town had changed, and the Old Boys remembered the changes.

Two old veterans of the Grand Army of the Republic.

One story Carter recalled from the group was a "great holiday for us youngsters" (Carter was only a boy at the time)—the day on which the first Presbyterian Church in Hillside Cemetery was demolished. He wrote that pieces of the old church ended up as part of Col. William Brittin's barn, while other sections went into the construction of the second church on Main Street.

There were other stories as well. Charles Force liked to tell about the first stagecoach trips through the village and how excited he was to see the arrival of the first locomotive in Madison. (3) At an Old Boys' gathering in May of 1898, "Uncle" Nelson Samson related his astonishment when Force played a recording of John Philip Sousa and the Marine Band on a Gramophone; he "could not conceive how it was possible." Details like these, handed down by the Old Boys, kept the past alive for Madisonians and gave local history a human dimension.

Dr. Lewis Sayre

In addition to telling stories, most of the Old Boys also added significant chapters to the history of the town as they built their careers. Of all the group's members, none was more successful and respected than Dr. Lewis Sayre. Born in Bottle Hill in 1820, he was the grandson of Ephraim Sayre, local Revolutionary War quartermaster and son of Archibald Sayre, a wealthy Morris County farmer. Only five years old at the time of Lafayette's visit in 1825, young Sayre was among the children who greeted the Frenchman. He attended Madison Academy and Wantage Seminary in Deckertown, New Jersey. After two years at the Seminary, Sayre lived with his Uncle David in Lexington, Kentucky, and attended Transylvania College. Sayre graduated in 1839 and moved to New York to study medicine with Dr. David Greer. In 1842, he earned a degree of Doctor of Medicine from the College of Physicians and Surgeons in New York. He was appointed assistant to the professor of surgery at the College of Physicians and Surgeons until 1853, when he was appointed surgeon at Bellevue Hospital. In 1859, he was named surgeon at the Charity Hospital at Blackwell's Island and was made its consulting surgeon in 1873. In October 1861, he became one of the founders of Bellevue Hospital Medical College and was a member of the first faculty as a professor of orthopedic surgery until 1898, when the college united with NYU.(4)

Lewis A. Sayre m.d.

Signature of Dr. Lewis A. Sayre.

This Old Boy was quite at home at the group's

nostalgic sessions, casual to say the least, but he had already made his mark in the medical profession through the books he wrote and the operations he performed using newly developed techniques. He was one of the first surgeons to successfully remove bones from diseased hips, discovered cholera was a contagious disease, pioneered the use of steam inhalation for combating croup and perfected the use of the plaster of Paris jacket for the treatment of spinal diseases.

Sayre visited England in 1877 and received the greatest acclaim ever showered on an American doctor of the age. At Guy's Medical College, Sayre treated a 12-year-old girl who suffered from spinal disease. When the girl was able to walk after a half-hour treatment, those present were astonished at the skill of the American doctor.

Sayre, like the other Old Boys *of Bottle Hill*, remembered nostalgically his boyhood days in the quiet village where life was pleasant and uncomplicated. Even after the accolades of Europe, the great American surgeon would frequently return to visit his childhood haunts and attend reunions with other Old Boys.

Brittin and Burnet

One of the best-known family names in Morris County annals is the name of Brittin. Most bearing that name could trace their lineage back to William Brittin, Sr., an 18th-century immigrant to America from Sutton in Ashfield-Notts, England. His grandsons, William, Abraham, and Isaac, came to Bottle Hill in the year 1800 and built a country store located at what is now James Park. William Brittin lived at this location, while Abraham lived across the street. William Brittin's son William Jackson, one of the "Old Boys of Bottle Hill," was born in this house on April 9, 1816, and in September 1897, he died there. In an era of increasing mobility, it was

Some of the Old Boys—Charles C. Force, Nelson Samson, and Benjamin Warren Burnet frequently gathered in Force's home. Burnet also served as the first president of the Madison Fire Department.

unusual that the younger Brittin spent his entire life as a Main Street resident.(5)

B. Warren Burnet, born in Bottle Hill in 1824, was the son of Matthias Lindsley Burnet, a local wheelwright (who lived at the present 60-64 Main Street, north side). Benjamin Warren Burnet was a member of the local council for six years and a prominent member of the Democratic Party. He served as secretary of the Old Boys for many years and worked on a history of Madison which was never completed. Burnet liked to recall the days when his father, who was the second postmaster of Bottle Hill in 1830 and the first after the name change to Madison, kept the incoming mail in his desk. The post office was then in his house, which stood near the middle of what is now Central Avenue on the north side of Main Street. Townspeople, when calling for their mail, would open his desk, sort through the material, and take what belonged to them. (6)

Joanna B. Tuttle

If the Old Boys ever would have decided to invite a woman into their club, she would have been someone like Joanna Bruen Tuttle. Born at Union Hill in 1823, she married Charles M. Nicholas in 1844. After being widowed, she became Mrs. Edward Augustus Tuttle on December 25, 1855, and began compiling her memoirs.(7) Mrs. Tuttle grew up in the village of Bottle Hill and attended the local school. Committed to church work, she had aspirations of becoming a church missionary but never did. Instead, she married twice, once to a contractor, then to a Sunday school superintendent. Both husbands preceded her in death, and Mrs. Tuttle lived until age 88, passing away in 1911. During her entire life she never drank any beverage other than water. Along with her kindred spirits, the Old Boys, Mrs. Tuttle remembered the coming of the railroad and the building of the Presbyterian Church. This straight-laced, religious woman was typical of many of her era. While she may not have become a missionary, she lived a full life for a woman in 19th-century America.

A Graveyard Destroyed

The Old Boys were not fully prepared for the events of the summer of 1902. Spring Garden Brook asserted its power over the community after a severe rainstorm caused the brook to run over its banks in a wild torrent. Rapid, heavy rainfall cascaded from the hills, forcing the narrow waterway to carry more water than it could handle. At Greenwood Avenue and Main Street, the brook flooded streets to a depth of two feet.

"With a roar that could be heard half a mile," according to the *Madison Eagle*, "it took its course down this tiny brook, along the back of Mayor Albright's, across the road, and into the Beaupland property it dashed with mad fury,"(8) until it met the culverts at Hillside Cemetery.

There, the water rushed through the cemetery, causing washouts of many graves. Bodies were found along the course of Spring Garden Brook, but all were recovered and again placed in coffins. It was impossible for authorities to identify 28 of the dead.

Hillside Cemetery remnant of a furious brook! Residents would periodically be reminded of its potential and power.

The *Madison Eagle* cited Edward H. DeHart for his quick action that night in notifying authorities of the waterborne calamity. DeHart waded through the dangerous waters at the scene of horror to find help. Because of his efforts, workers were able to locate most of the cadavers prior to daybreak, thus saving others from the "awful scene that would have been presented in the morning."(9)

The flood yielded a lively story that became standard lore at Old Boys' meetings during the next few years. It concerned Dugald MacDougall, who was present that night in the cemetery helping to locate the disinterred bodies. He and another worker heard an "awful hair-raising noise." "What the deuce is that?" he cried. He wasn't fully prepared for what he saw. Propped against a bush was a decomposed corpse, which made a noise in its throat as the wind blew through it. "I never heard a sound like it before or since," said MacDougall.(10) Madison Historical Society member Jim Malcolm has suggested that this incident may be connected to the human jawbone found in the brook following the flood. It is now in the possession of the Madison Historical Society.

Close to home, at Seaman's Crossing (on the large Seaman estate near the Chatham boundary), another tragedy was narrowly averted. There, the rain had washed out the sand beneath a 20-foot stretch of railroad track. The rails were thereby "suspended in the air over this chasm for the entire distance."(11). Unaware of the washout, the engineer of a westbound train proceeded at high speed toward the crossing. Unable to stop, the locomotive and cars passed over the washout, with all but the last car making it across. The last car flew off the tracks, causing a derailment, but no one was injured in the accident. For the next two days, while the roadbed was repaired, trains could come only as far west as the eastern boundary of Madison.

Talk of Politics

During the fall of 1902, the events of the rainy summer were forgotten as local conversations centered on politics. On February 13, 1903, the *Madison Eagle* reported that James P. Albright (the town's first mayor, in office since 1889) seemed not to be campaigning for reelection but let it be known that he would "not refuse" the nomination if asked to take it. If he did run, it was obvious that the popular mayor would again present himself as an objective, nonpartisan leader with solid managerial skills.

Albright did run as the Citizens' Party candidate for mayor that year against civic leader Alvah L. Reynolds, the choice of the Republican Party. In the election, Albright defeated Reynolds by 437 to 360 votes. As the *Eagle* later described the outcome: "The result was a surprise to both parties—the Republicans because they did not win and the Citizens because they won by so large a majority."(12) The margin of 77 votes was greater than expected by the Citizens' Party.

A Model Borough

During the election, Madison was given the appellation of "Model Borough" in a speech by Albright. The phrase stuck for many years. To Albright, Madison was "not alone a model" because "of efficiency and progress, but because it has kept free from political wrangles."(13) Albright did not mind it a bit that voters seemed to give him credit for this. They welcomed Albright's call for continued progress.

There were some good-natured barbs among the Old Boys about ongoing problems and their repercussions on public officials. By April 17, 1903, slightly over one month after his election, Mayor Albright was criticized by *Eagle* editor Edgar C. Markham in an editorial regarding the condition of sidewalks. The sidewalk issue first surfaced in Madison when colonial horseback riders and stagecoach drivers complained about the condition of local roads, and it continued to plague every elected official. Markham wrote that, while he did not wish to criticize the mayor and council, "we are very anxious that the sidewalk problem in Madison be solved."(14) It proved far easier to install electric lights, a trolley system and a railroad line than to give Madison the sidewalks it wanted.

New Firehouse

Other improvements were on the way for Madison. On June 19, 1903, the Madison Fire Department announced that a new firehouse would be built at the northwest corner of Cook and Central Avenues.(15) The building (no longer standing) was once the Health Department and is now the location of the Barbara Valk Firehouse Apartments. The first floor would have two large bay doors which opened to allow the movement of fire equipment, while the second floor was to be used for meetings and living rooms for firemen. Construction bids were opened with the result that local builder John V. Corbett was given the contract.

The estimated cost of the building was $9,000, which was raised by a building committee of the Madison Hook and Ladder Company. On August 13, the cornerstone was laid with Mayor Albright presiding at the ceremony. On the occasion, Fred B. Bardon, a man active in every facet of Madison's life at that time, introduced the guest speaker, John J. Gibson, and placed in the cornerstone old copies of the *Madison Eye Opener,* the *Madison Journal* and old photographs of Madison. Today, these contents are in the Madison Historical Society collection.

Madison's first hook and ladder, with its matched dappled grays, in front of the new firehouse. The tower in the background is the bell tower.

In 1903, the school budget continued to grow, yet another price of the "progress" of Madison. Along with James McGraw, Fred B. Bardon helped provide leadership for the school board. McGraw, the founder of the New York publishing house of McGraw-Hill, believed the high school section in the school was "unsurpassed in the country."(16) The school budget of $13,062, of which $9,750 was used for teachers' salaries, received little opposition that year.

In 1905, just over 15 years since the founding of the borough government (December 1889),

Madison elected its second mayor, Dr. Calvin Anderson. As the *Madison Eagle* counseled voters: "It was also evident that the Albright administration had fallen from the good graces of the newspaper and of the people." Albright and the council failed to resolve several important issues involving the introduction of natural gas service to the community (which it tabled), the need for a better means of sewage disposal and, of course, the sidewalk issue. An *Eagle* editorial just before Anderson's victory gave voters this reminder: "The history of the sidewalk improvement is too recent to be forgotten by any of our citizens. It is not necessary for us to point out that it took more than one year…[for our leaders to] complete six crosswalks."(17)

Knowing what kinds of things disturbed townspeople the most, the Old Boys realized the great challenge faced by Mayor Anderson, who immediately set about dealing with the sidewalk issue. He moved to install sidewalks in those areas where voters had petitioned. A correspondent who took the name "Public Spirited Citizen" expressed his hope in a March 1906 letter to the *Eagle*: "Mayor Anderson is determined that the sidewalk problem in Madison shall no longer be so great a hindrance to Madison's growth."(18) While he continued to make steady improvements in the repair of sidewalks the issue never completely went away in the dawning 20th Century.

Madison continued to grow despite its sidewalk issues. In figures released that year (1905), the borough's population of 4,115 people included 317 Irish, 558 Italian and 351 Blacks. The Green Avenue School (the site of the present Presbyterian Church) became so crowded that an annex was needed for the next four years.

Mayor Anderson was succeeded in November 1907 by William F. Redmond, who served only one term as mayor. He, too, failed to resolve the sidewalk issue. After his term, Redmond spent a great deal of time breeding thoroughbred horses at his estate in Madison (on the southwest corner of Woodland Road and Loantaka Way) and in Orange, New York. Redmond's horses competed successfully on the racetrack circuit.

Attention was diverted from the sidewalk issue in 1907 when Civil War veteran William Henry Byram received the book, *Pollack's Course of Time,* which he had lost on the Monocacy Junction battlefield in Virginia on July 9, 1864. The book was returned to him by a lady who found it on the field the day after the conflict. It took her 43 years to find the man who inscribed his name in the volume.

Temperance and Local Option

Almost since the early days of Bottle Hill, local residents believed in temperance. They didn't always practice it, but with the beginning of the 20th century, the temperance movement was extremely powerful in Madison. Led by the Rev. Dr. Robert Aikman, pastor of the Presbyterian Church, the cause was also boosted locally by the presence of a national temperance leader in the Rev. Dr. Ezra Squier Tipple, the scholar with an ironic name.

Dr. Tipple, the colorful president of Drew Theological Seminary, played an important role in the temperance movement. He also was a prominent theologian who authored several books, including the widely heralded *Life Of Francis Asbury* (1916), and who served as a trustee of the Board of Education of the Methodist Church of Madison.

On September 18, 1908, the *Eagle* decried the proliferation of li-

Dr. Ezra Squier Tipple, the dynamic president of Drew Theological Seminary; a builder of resources and goodwill for the institution. Photo credit: Drew University Archives.

quor stores in New Jersey, citing a figure of one liquor dealer for every 195 people. This statistic was labeled the "worst of any state east of the Mississippi River." At that time, the concept of "local option" was popular: a local community had the right to decide whether or not licenses should be granted. Political candidates were divided rather evenly on the question. Opposing forces heatedly argued its merits. By the following July, Madison's local optionists ran their own candidate for State Assembly, George Jenkins of Dover.

The most influential local leader among the supporters was Harold S. Buttenheim, to whom the "local option" concept meant allowing the people to decide whether or not saloons would be permitted. Madison vacillated on this issue over the years, first permitting and then outlawing the sale of liquor until a final decision to go dry was made in 1919.(19)

Despite the battles over questions like the local option, a public sense of "progress" was widespread. There was confidence that the town would continue to grow and prosper. Town publicists seized every opportunity to bring the name of Madison to those who might be interested. In 1909, the newly published *Industrial Directory of New Jersey* devoted almost a full page to a description of Madison, which they called "a fine residential town, possessing all the characteristics usually associated with a select community of homes." The directory correctly identified Madison's most active industry as the cultivation of roses, in which approximately 250 people were employed. According to the directory, nowhere else in the State was the cultivation of roses "conducted on so large a scale." Other local industries and the number of people employed included C.C. Force and Son, iron founders, 16 employees; Charles H. Keys, box manufacturer, 40 employees; J.M. Smith Company, mill and lumber yard, 15 employees.

In 1909, the population of Madison was 4,500, and the value of local property was assessed at $3,300,000. The directory boasted that the town offered "paved streets and macadamized roads," a claim which might have been disputed by some local residents.

In November 1910, Fred B. Bardon published his 64-page pamphlet entitled *The Public Schools of Madison, N.J.* Bardon, who was still school board president at the time, drew upon the Old Boys in securing information for the history. In the preface of the pamphlet, Bardon referred to Matthias L. Burnet, Col. William Brittin, Charles C. Force, Dr. Lewis Sayre, William J. Brittin and several other prominent citizens. In addition, Bardon mentioned that "at a number of receptions held by the 'Old Boys Club of Bottle Hill' there was the usual exchange of

A hub of activity: J.E. Burnet's Hardware Store, 1905. Halsey Doty, W.E. Philhower, James E. Burnet, Sr., Jerry Clark, Fred McPeek, on the wagon, and Harry the Horse.

'schoolboy experiences' which made valuable history and all this I carefully treasured for use on such an occasion as the dedication of this handsome new school." Bardon expressed well the gratitude he felt to the Old Boys at the ground-breaking of the Central Avenue School on October 8, 1909. The community was lucky to have even a few of the Old Boys still around in 1909 to retell the old stories of life in Bottle Hill.

The Trolley Arrives

By 1912, most of the Old Boys were gone, but former Mayor James P. Albright still remembered the days when he "plodded barefooted" as a boy through Waverly Place before it was widened. He also remembered the Old Boys, and perhaps he reflected on how much they would have enjoyed the arrival of the first trolley in their hometown. To men raised on horseback, who had lived through many advancements, this new form of transportation would perhaps have seemed like a boon to the average citizen.

The trolley—the "poor man's automobile"—came to Madison in February 1912, after the borough council granted a franchise to the Morris County Traction Company at its last regular session for December 1910. After slightly more than one year's time, the trolley tracks were laid along Main Street from Summit to Madison. Under the charter agreement, the Morris County Traction Company operated the line and was responsible for keeping the condition of the roadway in good order for a distance of 18 inches on the outside of each rail.

The coming of the trolley on that cold day in February was a momentous occasion for Madison residents. The *Madison Eagle* reported the anticipated arrival of the trolley "over the ice-covered rails" with great expectation.(20) It was soon hoped that "a regular schedule would be adopted" after the ice melted and that the line would, in the near future, be completed to Morristown. The first trolley car finally got through on that cold night of February 9. It worked its way past Greenwood Avenue, braving snow and ice, and received a rousing cheer from a crowd of bowlers coming from the Waverly Alleys as it reached the center of town at exactly 11:14 p.m.(21) Initially, at least, the rider could take the trolley from Elizabeth to Madison for a 15-cent fare.

For several weeks the *Madison Eagle* had printed complaints that Madison was "years behind" other regions because of the lack of a trolley line. Yet the newspaper expressed the fear that: "We do not remember a community that has not had trouble with trolley companies, trouble that could all have been obviated by a little foresight."(22) These fears had some foundation in fact, as there were problems in Madison as well. Not until 1914 was service established the full length of the line to Morristown. That western extension from Madison had been held

The trolley in Madison. Catherine Kelly Kiernan appears in the sixth window from the front of the car. Van de Water's home is on the extreme right.

up for over two years due to legal action brought by Mrs. Florence Twombly, whose estate was being used for part of the right-of-way. Similar legal action was pressed by the Sisters of Charity at the Academy of St. Elizabeth at Convent Station. A decision of the Court of Errors and Appeals in the spring of 1914 cleared the way for the completion of the route. The extension to Morristown covered a distance of 2.6 miles at a total cost of $175,000. In October 1914, brand-new steel trolleys were added to the line. The future of the trolley and the community suddenly looked brighter.

However, a year later, when the trolley owners failed to maintain their legal obligation to keep the center of Main Street paved, local citizens became enraged. Officers of the Morris County Traction Company seemed surprised by the public anger. Apparently, they didn't know that Madison residents and Bottle Hill citizens before them were always very concerned about their sidewalks and streets. If they had still been around to hold their meetings, the Old Boys of Bottle Hill could have told them that. Nevertheless, the trolleys were scrapped by 1927 and quickly replaced by buses.(23) By 1933, the remaining rails were paved over, thereby ending the relatively brief era of trolleys in Madison.(24)

Bottle Hill Changed to Madison

The name of Madison was not adopted by the village until 1834, when a public meeting was called with a result as is shown by the following notice cut from an old newspaper:

"Agreeable to public notice, a meeting of the inhabitants of the village of Bottle Hill convened at the Madison Academy in said place on the 2nd of August 1834, to take into consideration a change of name for said place, and after an interchange of sentiment, it was resolved to adjourn for 4 weeks, to give further time for deliberation and in pursuance of such, the inhabitants again convened at said Madison Academy on the 30th of August, 1834, when Matthias L. Burnet was chosen as moderator and Robert Albright, secretary, and after an interchange of sentiment, a motion was made, seconded and past that the name of said village be changed.

"A motion was made, seconded and passed that the name of said place be called 'Madison.'

"Adjourned.

"M. L. BURNET, Moderator.

"ROBERT ALBRIGHT, Secretary.

"Madison, August 30, 1834."

Bottle Hill to Madison... A Bold Step Into the Future! An important chapter in local history ended with the passing of the last of the Old Boys, who had been so apprehensive of the changes they witnessed and yet left us their fascinating recollections of so many local events.

BOTTLE HILL CHANGED TO MADISON

The name of Madison was not adopted by the village until 1834, when a public meeting was called with a result as is shown by the following notice cut from an old newspaper:

"Agreeable to public notice, a meeting of the inhabitants of the village of Bottle Hill convened at the Madison Academy in said place on the 2nd of August, 1834, to take into consideration a change of name for said place, and after an interchange of sentiment it was resolved to adjourn for 4 weeks, to give further time for deliberation, and in pursuance of such, the inhabitants again convened at said Madison Academy on the 30th of August, 1834, when Matthias L. Burnet was chosen moderator and Robert Albright, secretary, and after an interchange of sentiment, a motion was made, seconded and past that the name of said village be changed.

"A motion was made, seconded and passed that the name of said place be called 'Madison.'

"Adjourned.

"M. L. BURNET, Moderator.

"ROBERT ALBRIGHT, Secretary.

"Madison, August 30, 1834."

This verse, printed in the *Madison Eagle* on December 17, 1897, represented the growing spirit and pride of townspeople regarding Madison. An unknown female poet, who called herself only "X.Y.Z.," captured something of the sentimental feeling felt toward the town at the turn of the century:

Madison, formerly Old Bottle Hill
(The name, don't you know, did fit it quite ill),
Has grown to be a most charming place,
Where many a girl has a sweet, pretty face;
The citizens, too, all are enterprising,
And spend little time in criticizing
Their neighbors actions, good or bad;
And say few words that make one sad.
"Progress and Poverty" go here hand in hand
Headed, of course, by the Citizen's Band.
The town is governed by a council so wise
That they seldom need much of the mayor's advice.
The taxes are low and the place is so healthy
That the doctors, God bless 'em, will ne'er grow wealthy.
The citizens own their water and light,
(The former is pure and the latter quite bright)
And the roads have all lately been fixed,
And the streets are all named for those who get mixed.
Three robust police, strong, stalwart brave men,
In buttons of brass, have naught to do-'hem! .
For the people here are all law-abiding
And rarely is needed stern Justice's chiding.
At the foot of the hill two schoolhouses stand—
They're simple in style, but the work done is grand.
The three R's are taught, with the trimmings along,
Such as French, Greek and Latin drawing and song,
The scenery is pleasant and, in spots really grand;
For nature has blessed us with bounteous hand.
A writing of Madison would fill up many tomes;
It's not a city of houses, but a city of homes
Hurrah! for this town, yell out with a will!
Sing praises forever of old Bottle Hill.
X.Y.Z.

CHAPTER ELEVEN

Prosperity, Prohibition, and the World at War

The coming of the 20th century meant, in many respects, an end to small-town Madison. It was not that the town had grown to enormous size, but rather that national and international affairs imposed themselves upon the community. Daily concerns for Madisonians would never again be mostly local. Rather, they would involve the business, turmoil, and bustle of the age, the coming of World War I, Prohibition, the "Roaring Twenties," the Great Depression, and the tremendous effort to defeat the Axis in World War II.

All of this would bring well-known national leaders into town; new ideas and organizations would take root; local sons and daughters would be sent far from home to serve their nation and sometimes die for it. The years of the first half of the century were at once transforming, crucial, tragic and prosperous. They would directly set the stage for the Madison of today.

Prosperity and Productivity

President Woodrow Wilson appeared to have Madison's confidence. In 1910, while a candidate for governor of New Jersey, an *Eagle* headline at the time described him as a "plain man of the people."

Most of New Jersey's voters also shared this opinion of the Princetonian, and Wilson, indeed, became governor. The following year, still fighting his battle for political reform, he once more came to the attention of Madison's voters, but this time in person. In October 1911, while campaigning for the election of a Democratic legislature, Governor Wilson gave a heated speech in Madison that sounds eerily like recent national political struggles between the major parties.

"The main fight in this and future campaigns," Wilson claimed, "will be between a Republican Party which has rejected progressive measures, and the Democratic power [Party] dominated by its progressive element—call them radicals, if you will."(1) Not all Madisonians agreed, but the governor was well received. It was only a year later that Wilson was a strong candidate for the Democratic nomination for president. These were heady days for New Jersey, with Wilson's rising star putting the state in the national limelight.

If there was increased confidence in the state, Madison fully reflected the mood. Its citizens were involved in a growing number of cultural pursuits that complemented the town's vigorous commerce and politics. They were looking forward to the future, and they had exciting plans for their town. A listing of "Things to be Accomplished" in an October 1909 *Madison Eagle* column reflected the hopes for a better Madison:

> Extension of Sidewalk Improvement; Construction of Sewage System; Attractive Stand Pipe; Larger Appropriations for Borough Forestry; Inauguration of Band Concerts During Summer Months; Encouragement of Playground Movement; Oil Properly

Applied to All Borough Streets; Publication of Tax Assessments; Continuation of Mosquito Spraying During the Season of 1910.(2)

The air of boosterism was evident as well in a brochure titled "Madison, The Rose City," which advertised the many virtues of the borough in the early 1900s. Madison was touted for its healthy air, attractive surroundings, and cultured people. The highest praise was reserved for Madison's location on the Morris and Essex Division of the Lackawanna Railroad, which made access to New York easy with 50 trains a day. Express trains reached Hoboken in less than an hour, and commutation tickets to the metropolis cost only $7.05 per month for a daily round trip. Quite wisely, the unknown author of this brochure believed the future growth of a quiet small town of 3,754 (in 1900) would be tied to the commuter.

A few years later, a similar local pride was displayed in a more reflective *Eagle* column:

The glory of Madison is, partly, in its pathway aisles formed by trees, varied in form and color, that separate the meditating mind of the summer stroller from the rush and rashness of the bordering highways; partly in the refinement of the hills, molded by a Master hand, in forms that win approval by their inviting slopes, what here and there are rounded shoulders imparting strength to the beholder who reads the lines with a mind receptive; complete when the azure haze of the mellow shadowless, winter days softens the outlines of the distant northern hills and soothes, and satisfies the mind until if what the vision grasps were all the world contentment would reign supreme.(3)

William Jennings Bryan

William Jennings Bryan, the "Great Commoner" of the Democratic Party, made two visits to Madison during these years. In the fall of 1896, Bryan stopped at the local railroad station while en route by train from Pittsburgh through Dover to New York. The train pulled into the old station at 3:24 p.m. with Charles Gee, followed by Bryan, stepping off the train. When the crowd saw Bryan, "a great cheer went up." The next day, Anderson B. Gee teased his father about the ovation. He said: "You and Bryan got quite an ovation yesterday." The elder Gee "never batted an eye" but said "most of it was for Bryan."

Bryan, according to Anderson Gee, was not that successful in his brief speech to the crowd, and the cheer had not been for him but for a local boy. Just as the great orator started his speech, Ralph Eagles, a local youth, climbed a telephone pole and yelled, "Hurrah for McKinley!" Bryan tried to laugh it off with the remark, "I'm glad you can't vote," but the damage was done. As Gee later recalled, "Ralph had got in his deadly work. Bryan sputtered, stammered and coughed, he was all done for."(4) The politician quickly got back on the train and headed toward New York.

Years later, Bryan addressed a more enthusiastic audience in James Hall in November 1921. He spoke of the increased possibilities for world peace through disarmament. In a speech that lasted two and one-half hours, the great orator also spoke on many other topics, including Prohibition, business reforms, and the teaching of evolution. Regarding the Darwinian theory of evolution, he urged those assembled to refuse the teaching that man has the "blood of the brute in him rather than the breath of God."(5)

Only four years later, Bryan would become a central figure in the famous 1928 Scopes Trial as the pro-creationist lawyer who debated famed lawyer Clarence Darrow, who, in turn, was supporting Darwin's theory of evolution. The two famed lawyers tried to settle the debate over human evolution in the trial held in Dayton, Tennessee, which ended with a guilty verdict and a $100 fine for teacher John T. Scopes. Scopes became the focal point of the trial for his teaching of Darwin's theory of evolution in his classroom. More importantly, the trial brought this issue into the minds of many Americans. However, the verdict itself remained standing in Tennessee until 1967. The trial remains an important event in American cultural history.

One need not have shared Bryan's ideas to agree that his second appearance in Madison was of importance. Bryan was one of the premier orators of his generation, and by the 1920s, he seldom spoke in backwater towns. When he lectured in Madison, he tacitly added further recognition to the town's growing sophistication and maturity.

In such an atmosphere of increased recognition, even minor local setbacks could be taken in stride. In 1918, for instance, there was a disastrous fire at the Green and Pierson Lumber yards east of Prospect Street and Kings Road. No human lives were lost, but three horses perished. Damage was estimated at $60,000, a hefty amount of money for those days. Only the bravery of the Madison Fire Department stopped the blaze from spreading to the nearby downtown area.

Even a minor crime could have its lighter side, as the proven in the "case of the thirsty dog." The unusual incident occurred in the summer of 1910 when residents of Green Village Road and Loantaka Way complained that someone was opening the milk bottles placed at their door in the early morning hours and spilling the contents over the ground. In order to catch the culprit, Police Chief Johnson spent several evenings "...cautiously crawling through the weeds, near where the thefts occurred."(6)

After he saw no humans at that hour, it finally dawned on him that animals might be doing this mischief. The chief then suggested that a "certain dog from a Madison Avenue home be confined during the early morning hours." Remarkably, the mystery was solved. No further depredations took place. The milk was safe through the rest of the summer of 1910.

Education and the Arts

During the early part of the century, residents established a tradition of local involvement in order to ensure quality in education that continues to this day. Townspeople felt more secure sending their children to schools, both public and private if they had a voice in the operations. For more than 100 years, the Madison Academy had been opening its doors as a private preparatory school for boys and girls. Its advertised purpose was to offer "thorough preparation for the best colleges and scientific schools."(7)

Madison Academy, on Green Village Road.

When the academy opened its 1910 session in September, it had a new look that consisted of significant interior renovations of the main building.

At the same time, the public Central Avenue School was nearing completion, and school authorities were immersed in the details of making final improvements. The Board of Education was also considering bids for sidewalk construction, the installation of electric call buttons for classrooms, and new security arrangements for important documents, including deeds. In fact, 1910 was a time when news of the schools, both public and private, was a constant matter of popular concern.

School leadership was a matter of particular interest. Amos F. Stauffer was the supervising principal for public schools until 1904. Succeeding him was Marcellus Oakey, whose subse-

Groundbreaking for Central Avenue School, 1909 From left, first row: Jerry Clark (with flower), Joseph Corbett, Milton McGargle Police Chief Edward Cooney, Fred Bardon (man with flag not known), King Conklin (dark suit with flower), Floyd Van Etten, builder John V. Corbett (with hat), Steven McCune, Carroll B. Merritt; little girl, Helen Corbett.(Author's notes: Helen Corbett was interviewed in the early 1980s by Dr. Esposito; local architect King Conklin died during the 1918 Influenza epidemic.

Central Ave School

quent leadership helped to upgrade the high school curriculum. When Oakey died after eight years as principal, the town felt his loss. The Madison school system had enjoyed an increasingly enviable reputation through the state during his tenure, and according to a tribute in the *Eagle*, "Mr. Oakey is given largely the credit for this honor."(8)

The Board of Education named Dr. William T. Whitney of Ridgewood as Oakey's successor. Salary was set at a whopping $2,000 per year for the graduate of Teachers College, Columbia University. Whitney recommended some changes in the assignment of teachers as he assured the community that "It is my purpose to place the schools of Madison on the highest plane possible...as great things can be accomplished with teachers who are not mere workers but are willing to give possibly more than they receive."(9) Despite his noble objectives, Whitney resigned from his post in April 1913, after less than a year in the position, to assume a similar job elsewhere.

The following month, the Board of Education appointed Jesse T. Godfrey as superintendent of schools. Within a year, Godfrey hired a teacher for the town's learning-disabled students, a very progressive action for 1913. During the next four years, the school population increased to the point where split sessions were scheduled for the high school. In December 1919, Godfrey resigned as superintendent due to ill health and was replaced by Richard E. Clement of Elizabeth. Godfrey had left the Madison schools in a position to face the future with confidence.

A Writer's Haven

It was also during these years that a local Madisonian gained considerable note as an author of children's books. William O. Stoddard, Jr., the son of Abraham Lincoln's secretary, published his first book, *The Captain of Catspaw*, in the summer of 1914. Following this success, Stoddard wrote several others, including *The Farm that Jack Built* and *Making Good in the Village*.(10) Stoddard's characters were healthy, all-American boys who were ready to meet any challenge. More than any other quality, this talented author was able to tell a good tale while never failing to use an incident from his childhood to enhance the story.

Another popular story writer who called Madison home was Horace Holden, who based his stories upon experiences in New York City and in the woods of Canada. Holden operated a boarding school in Weymouth, Nova Scotia, for several years prior to coming to Madison, and he drew upon this private-school experience in writing his teenage stories. They featured the Westminster School in Simsbury, Conn., and told of situations students faced in their maturing years. Holden's best-known title was *Young Boys and the Boarding School*, which helped bring him a wide literary reputation.

There was also a nationally known artist residing in Madison during these years: Arthur Burdett Frost, better known as A.B. Frost. In 1893, the *Eagle* described a glass model house, which was used as his studio, on his property on Treadwell Avenue. With surrounding glass walls, the artist posed his models in realistic settings. For instance, if snow had recently fallen, Frost would use the snow-covered landscape as a backdrop. This marvelous building was built on a metal frame and, as the *Eagle* described it, "tight as a drum and nicely warmed."

Arthur B. Frost: Madison's nationally famous artist.

Frost prospered as an artist during his years in Madison with much of his work appearing in *Scribner's* magazine, as well as other popular periodicals and books. His Uncle Remus illustrations for the stories by Joel Chandler Harris were prime examples of Frost's incredible talent for painting folksy, yet realistic and natural portraits.

Frost lived at the 22 Crescent Road home of his son John, who was nicknamed Jack. Jack Frost was also an artist who painted naturalistic scenes, frequently of Western subjects. For a short time, elder Frost had an office studio on the top floor of the First National Bank. When an *Eagle* reporter visited Frost in 1917, the studio was marked only by a small business card tacked to the door. According to the unnamed reporter: "Nothing else indicated the workshop of the man who was intimate with Joel Chandler Harris and has met and known most of the celebrities who stand for things in America."(11)

Frost loved the country air of Madison. He enjoyed walking in the woods in all seasons, thereby capturing mental scenes for his illustrations. Whatever the reasons for his stay locally, Madison residents were proud to have such a prominent artist in their midst.

Oak Seats, Marble, and Railroads

Major changes took place in the center of town as growth necessitated new transportation arrangements. On September 21, 1914, the borough council authorized the elevation of the tracks of the Delaware, Lackawanna and Western Railroad. This enormous project involved rerouting streets, moving houses and building a new railroad station.(12) While the work took over two years to complete, trains were routed along temporary tracks laid on Kings Road.

This work was long overdue. Existing rail routes had proven to be unsafe as the downtown became busier over the years. Several serious accidents between horse-drawn carriages and locomotives caused local leaders to urge railroad officials to elevate the tracks through Madison and eliminate grade crossings. In a terrible accident in 1902, a man and his son were killed at a crossing near Chatham when they tried to cross before a speeding train.

Seamon Mansion

The Seamon Mansion, once considered a showplace, would now face demolition. The railroad ran in a wide sweeping curve around steep Union Hill from Samson Avenue, where the curve extended halfway to Main Street to Union Avenue at the Madison-Chatham border. On top of the hill stood the imposing Victorian mansion of F.A. Seaman. To eliminate the roundabout curve in the tracks, it was decided to dig straight through Union Hill. This also entailed the considerable expense of acquiring the land for $255,000.

Work began on "the big cut" in December 1913, requiring a two-mile-long excavation, 75 feet deep in spots. Hiring mostly immigrant labor, the Lackawanna Railroad Co. used hand shovels and steam shovels to clear the right-of-way. Vast amounts of soil were removed in special side-dump cars operating on temporary tracks. The fill was hauled to sections of the line through Madison, where the elevation of the railroad required embankments at Prospect Street, Green Avenue, and Green Village Road. Over 600,000 yards of dirt were removed from Union Hill.

Upheaval in the vicinity of the railroad was horrendous. Temporary tracks all along the route had to be laid parallel to the main line. This meant Kings Road, between Samson Avenue and Green Village Road, became a right-of-way for trains. Much confusion ensued. Merchants were so hampered in conducting business that there were frequent angry confrontations between them and would-be shoppers.

American House. Moved, now apartments with businesses on the first floor, facing Lincoln Place.

As part of the reconstruction, Prospect Street was widened from a lane to a full street width. In order to create a new street connecting Prospect Street with Waverly Place, to be called Lincoln Place, the American House hotel was moved to a site on the new street, where it now serves as an apartment house with storefronts. At the Prospect end of the new street, three businesses selling feed, grain, and lumber had to be vacated. Ridgedale Avenue, which previously extended across the tracks (as Bridge Street), then ended at Park Avenue.

The disruption associated with this major community face-lifting was political as well as physical. Tempers flared as people clashed over the handling of the project. Kenneth Haynes described it in the series "Madison Heritage Tales" written in 1979 for the *Madison Eagle*: "In truth, it did create a local war, as dissidents, uncertain legislators and disgruntled businessmen railed at one another in heated meetings and weekly fiery letters to editor Fred B. Bardon, who through it all remained a calming influence, imparting common sense and a progressive attitude."

The Big Cut

In this 1913 view of the railroad's "big cut" between Samson Avenue and Chatham, artist R. Harmer Smith imagined some of the multitude of workers who accomplished the job and the cars that moved tons of dirt for embankments to elevate the tracks throughout Madison.

As was frequently the case throughout the town's history, a benefactor assisted in the project. Mrs. D. Willis James financed much of the expense of road grading caused by the track elevation. Led by Mrs. James, many local residents insisted that the railroad management build a new station worthy of the prosperous community. The local government passed an ordinance authorizing issuance of $159,000 in railroad improvement bonds, and the present station became a reality. When completed in 1916, the sturdy stone structure was an impressive landmark. Despite the expense, it was a station that still makes townspeople proud.

Designed by architect F.J. Nies in Collegiate Gothic style, the station boasted oak seats, brick walls and marble chip floors.(13) The D.L. & W.R.R. cooperated generously in landscaping and planning for the handsome depot. The new facility and improvements associated with "the big cut" and the elevation of the tracks all served to further encourage the growth of Madison's commuter population. Relatively recently, in the 1980's the station fell into some disrepair. Later in the 1990s, local citizen pressure led to successful efforts to restore the

The Big Cut

In this 1913 view of the railroad's BIG CUT between Samson Avenue and Chatham, artist R. Harmer Smith imagined some of the multitude of workers who accomplished the job and the cars that moved tons of dirt for embankments to elevate the tracks throughout Madison.

Pictorial montage by R. Harmer Smith from Madison Heritage Tales, Madison Eagle

Big Cut by R. Harmer Smith, from Madison Heritage Tales, Madison Eagle

Disruption Brings Safety and Positive Change

Construction of the tracks at Madison Avenue

Temporary station, corner of Green Avenue.

Madison Railroad Station, immediately following completion.

Just prior to the demolition of the old station. Chauffeurs had already replaced footmen for the wealthy commuters.

station. (See Chapter 15.)

Railroads were not the only transportation concern, for shortly after the turn of the century, the automobile appeared on local streets. At first, it seemed an oddity. Gawkers frequently stood along the sidewalks to catch a glimpse of the strange vehicles. To onlookers, it appeared to be a horseless buggy with rubber tires, a noisy engine and a black metal body. The initial cars in Madison inspired some fear among townspeople, who thought that automobiles would scare local animals, ruin the roads, and raise the noise levels. Events proved these fears to be well founded, but the automobile was here to stay.

They were here to stay. Early autos and expanded horizons! Enroute to 1910 Princeton-Yale game were, L-R, Curtis McGraw, Andy Gee, Ted Humbert, James McGraw, Jack Humbert, and Fred Douglas

The Madison Alerts and the *Eagle*

By November 1912, the Alert Social Club was already eight years old. Originally a Democratic club, it was founded by 20 young men led by Fred W. Bardon, son of Fred B. Bardon. The younger Bardon died at age 22 of natural causes, four years after the founding of the Alerts. As a promising athlete, Bardon was typical of the young men who joined the club. Originally meeting in the Dunning Building, now No. 5 Waverly Place, by 1906, the Alerts had moved to the second floor of Waverly Bowling Alleys at 41 Kings Road, which for many years was the home of the *Madison Eagle*.

The Alert baseball team of 1912 was an especially strong one which finished with a record of 18 wins and only 5 losses. The team featured Walter Devitalis, a 16-year-old pitcher, and first baseman "Moe" McCracken, a .309 hitter, both considered to be among the best athletes in the state. Alerts' manager Edward J. Daniher also served as a pinch hitter. Strong-armed Jimmie Bradley was a popular catcher, while Claudio Devitalis led the team in hitting with a .362 batting average.

For small-town Madison, the Alerts provided an exciting diversion. The excitement always mounted in games against arch-rival Chatham. In the 1912 season, the Alerts beat Chatham Athletic Club by a score of 4 to 1. That alone made their season a success. The Alerts helped bring the national pastime, baseball, to a high level of popularity in Madison. Other opposing teams included the Caldwell Field Club, the Gorham "Colored Giants," and the Roseville Athletic Association. Everywhere, citizens were viewing their local teams with pride.

The 1912 Alerts. Front row: Jimmie Bradley, Claudio Devitalis, Stelce, George, and Mgr. Edward Daniher. Back row, "Colonel" Waters, Allen, Cavanagh, W. Devitalis, Kays, and McCracken.

In October 1910, the 34-year-old *Madison Eagle* changed hands as Edgar Markham sold the newspaper to John E. Clarey, Sr. Clarey's ideal for a good local newspaper was quite simple: it should be "intensely local and intensely loyal." To this professional newspaperman from the Midwest, the *Eagle* would concentrate on the local scene and leave national events to other newspapers. To Clarey, the local newspaper should also always be looking out for the community's welfare, that being the quality of loyalty to which he referred.

One of the most lively local controversies surfaced in the *Madison Eagle* in 1910, centered on a request from Public Service Gas Company to lay mains in town. Mayor George Downs questioned the reasons for the request. Despite a muddled response from the company, one thing was quite evident: Madison was viewed as an important potential market.

Some local residents were also skeptical. Harold S. Buttenheim wrote a letter dated February 27, 1911, to the editor sounding "a note or two of warning." Using the successful local operation of the water and electric plant as a basis for his argument, Buttenheim expressed the thoughts of many when he said: "No small percentage of our citizens would favor a municipal gas plant, even though we had to wait a few years for it." The issue was debated throughout the spring and summer when it finally came to a head. A public referendum decided things: by a vote of 391 to 207, the community chose to award a gas-line franchise to Public Service Gas Company, and the borough council quickly made the arrangements. The appeal to the Italian population was written in Italian in the *Eagle* so that all could understand.

If most of the local news was of a positive nature, there were also some dark spots. Following a normally joyous Christmas season, Madison residents were shocked in early January 1911 to learn of the discovery of a horribly mutilated murder victim in a wooded area known as "Burnet's Woods" just off North Street. The body of an unknown man who had been hacked to death with a hatchet was found in a ditch. Within 10 days, police discovered the identity of the murdered man. He was Mazzeo Giuseppe, a construction worker employed by a local contractor. Although several leads were developed, the murder was never solved.

Madison and World War I

Three years later, however, another murder—in which the killer was captured—had much more profound international repercussions. This killing took place not in Madison but in the city of Sarajevo in the Austro-Hungarian Empire. When a Serbian nationalist assassinated the heir to the Austrian throne and his wife, Europe began its plunge into the conflagration of World War.

Despite proclamations of neutrality, America increasingly drifted toward war. The sinking of the British liner Lusitania off Ireland on May 7, 1915, resulted in the loss of over 100 Americans among the 1198 drowned. With that event, American anger toward German submarine warfare increased to a higher and more dangerous level. By December, President Wilson addressed Congress regarding the necessity of preparedness for the expanding European war.

Douglas Simon, Ph.D. Drew University professor emeritus, scholar, and trustee of The Madison Historical Society, described the onset of mounting conflict:(14)

> Like most of the country, during the first two years of the war, 1914-1915, citizens of Madison did not appear to have any great interest in America getting militarily involved in the conflict. Within the borough, the most important *national* issues seemed to focus on women's suffrage.
>
> There *was* significant support for the Wilson's Peace Proclamation of Thanksgiving of 1914 that among other things called on Americans to help relieve the suffering of those at war in Europe. Indeed, the citizens of the borough had already begun to mobilize a relief effort. In early October 1914, plans got underway in a service at the James Assembly Hall... Mayor Benyew D. Philhower was to preside over a meeting called in support of Wilson's Peace proclamation.(15) Toward the end of October, Madison's Red Cross chapter held a benefit concert that raised $177.07 to be used to, "alleviate the sufferings of European humanity" as a result of the war.(16) Further in 1914, there were a number of guest speakers in town relaying their experiences traveling in Europe during the first year of the war.(17)

The mounting world tension made Wilson's 1916 election claim that "he kept America out of war" appealing to many citizens. Certainly, it helped the President in his narrow defeat of Republican candidate Charles Evans Hughes in the presidential election of that year. Continued German attacks on American ships, however, followed by disclosure of Germany's plans to support a Mexican military effort against the American Southwest, pushed the United States into war. On April 6, 1917, President Wilson signed a congressional resolution declaring war against Germany.

With hostilities a reality, Madison rallied to the cause. Within five weeks, Madison women, led by Margaret Buttenheim Powell, were granted a charter to establish a chapter of the American National Red Cross. Local women were continuing to play an important civic role in Madison as community organizers.

Madison's War Efforts

According to Dr. Simon:

> War relief activities continued in Madison during 1916, such as the Loantaka Camp Fire Girls gathering clothes for children in Europe orphaned by the war. (18) But it was also the year that the first hints of battle lines on America's policy on the war began to emerge within the borough with proponents of peace through neutrality on one side and the first hints of support for military action under the rubric of 'American preparedness' on the other. In May, a reception was held in the YMCA building in honor of Miss Elizabeth A. Allan, chair of the anti-war New Jersey division of the National Women's Peace Party. (19)

> The following month, at a banquet of the Men's Club of the Presbyterian Church, Commander E. N. Jessup of the U.S. Navy spoke on "Preparedness and Pacifism." He noted how unprepared the U.S. was for possible invasion and our inability to resist an invading army. He also stated, "The pacifist idea is wrong because it is based on giving up instead of holding what the United States has."(20) The year 1916 also saw increasing calls within the borough for patriotism.

> September saw action underway for the Liberty Bond Drive.(21) In early 1917, as America moved closer to war, so too did the Borough of Madison. During the first week in March, plans were put in motion for the creation of the Madison Home Defense League, in order to muster resources, "whether it be in peace or war."(22) In late March, all male citizens of Madison were encouraged to attend a meeting in James Hall for the purpose of organizing a rifle club as part of the plans of Madison's Home Defense League. The meeting called for the formation of a military company, and to start drilling immediately.(23)

> On the 30th of March, [the former secretary for Abraham Lincoln,] William O. Stoddard called on his fellow Madison residents to plant beans and potatoes to help feed the allies. He urged that citizens should grow potatoes and, "help the democracy vanquish tyranny and shame in the form of the most vicious autocracy the world has ever known."(24) That same day, a short editorial appeared in the *Madison Eagle* that openly challenged the work of the Women's Peace Party and other pacifist organizations. "You cannot arbitrate with a mad dog which has you by the tail," the column noted.(25) Three days later, President Woodrow Wilson called on Congress to declare war on Germany.

Through the spring and summer of 1917, volunteers met three times a week at Madison Academy to produce supplies for American troops being sent into combat. Some of those soldiers were from the Rose City. On May 26, Ex-President William Howard Taft visited the Madison home of F. Hallett Lovell and spoke for an hour to 45 prominent local men. He strongly encouraged U.S. involvement in the war. He compared Germany's submarine campaign as "exactly as if she had landed a regiment at Sandy Hook and fired into homes of New Jersey citizens." As a result, a little more than $5,000 was raised that evening for a national YMCA fund that would provide welfare work for U.S. soldiers and sailors who might see service in the war with Germany.(26)

Several Madisonians enlisted in the services, but most were drafted. To be drafted in 1917 was generally considered an honor, so much so that a reception for those drafted was held in August 1917 at the YMCA. The spirited response of the community to the war effort led to a parade in honor of the draftees in September. By month's end, 23 local men left Madison for military training.

News From the Front

Pvt Thomas J. Kelley of Gibbons Place, with the 308th Field Artillery in France, wrote to his mother in September 1918 describing the German enemy: "They're something like a fox; when nobody is around, they come out of their holes, but just as soon as they hear the Yanks yell 'Heaven, Hell or Hoboken by Christmas!' they run for dear life."

Edgar W. Cheever, of 292 Main Street, received a letter in October 1918 from his son Pvt. L.W., with the 54th Artillery in France. Young Cheever extolled the food provided by the American Red Cross:

> I got my dinner in the Red Cross and it only cost me a franc, or 17 and one-half cents for the following:
>
> One cup cocoa — very good
>
> Two Swiss cheese sandwiches — fine
>
> One jam sandwich — nice and sweet
>
> One big doughnut — just like home and also all the chewing gum or smoking tobacco you want — free.

Friends who made it home again! Maurice Patterson, William O'Donnell, and Edward Cosgrove, before leaving for camp, December 10, 1917.

Pvt. H. Parks Greer wrote to a Madison friend from France in September 1918 about an artillery attack on the Germans:

> One morning at 1 o'clock the Sammies started the biggest barrage the Germans ever saw and in thirty hours they killed thousands, captured 15,000 men, 150 square miles and lots of gas and ammunition. So you see what they are doing, and I hope they keep it up so this thing will be over with.

A Nurse's Sacrifice: The First Nurse to Die In WWI

War, however, demanded a high price, and Madison helped to pay the toll of lives lost. Town citizens were saddened to hear of the death from blood poisoning on January 17, 1918, of Army nurse Amabel Scharff Roberts, a local woman attached to the No. 2 Reserve Base Hospital in Etretat, France. She was the first nurse to die in World War I. Amabel's care of the sick had won her the respect of all with whom she worked, especially her service to the military and to the citizens of Etretat. At her funeral in France, the sick and wounded marched in a long column in her honor. According to one contemporary account, "After these came all Etretat, women and old men...They were here to pay their tribute, and so they came, some in clumping wooden shoes, some leading little children; the lame, the halt and the blind, the old and the weak; they knew of bitter experience, and they could sympathize."(27)

This plaque was for many years located in the Health Department facility on Walnut Street but is now housed in the Hartley Dodge Memorial.

"A life without sacrifice is utterly valueless," wrote Amabel Scharff Roberts from Etretat two months before her death. She attended the Madison Academy and was an honors graduate from Kent Place School and Vassar. In 1916 she also graduated from the Presbyterian Hospital Nurses' Training School. She went overseas with her hospital unit in May 1917; she was the first American Army Red Cross nurse, as well as the first local citizen to give up her life in World War I. "Taps was blown for the first time in Etretat over an open grave. We had become so used to the Last Post that we had almost forgotten the real beauty of Taps, but now its piercing loveliness struck home with an added force, 'Go to sleep, Go-to-sleep.' It was an end and a beginning."

Amabel Scharff Roberts - A hero nurse of World War One.

She came to final rest in Hillside Cemetery in July 1921. A room was dedicated to her memory at the Columbia-Presbyterian Medical Center, and in May 1918, the Madison Equal Suffrage League presented to the borough an ambulance in her memory to be maintained by Madison for the use of its citizens.

The End of WWI

As young men marched off to war, food became scarce and natural supplies, such as coal, had to be conserved. There were nationwide edicts decreeing wheatless Mondays, meatless Tuesdays, gasless Sundays, and other gestures of patriotism.

In fact, there were some examples of patriotic excesses. Madison news dealer B. Kemelhor stopped delivering German-language newspapers in May 1918, as local feelings mounted against the European war enemy. Kemelhor claimed he only delivered a few, "less than half a dozen in all." News dealers all over the country were doing the same thing. Later in May, an *Eagle* editorial supported the action, saying that the German newspapers were harmful because the average American could not read them; therefore, many harmful things could be printed and be undetected.

In June 1918, the newspaper reported that 14 Madison men who were serving as members of the 308th Artillery had arrived safely in France after completing their training at Camp Dix (now Joint Base Fort Dix, Maguire, and Lakehurst, New Jersey). Other Madison youths who had enlisted in the New Jersey National Guard finished training at Camp McClellan, Alabama, and were scheduled to leave for France soon.

Madisonians who were listed as serving in the 308th Artillery were Cpl. Orrin H. Atchison, Michael Brady, Frederick R. Burnham, Francis J. Cavanaugh, Thomas A. Dunne, Charles Foley, Sgt. Joseph H. Fredericks, Forrest W. Jacobus, Thomas J. Kelley, Louis Larson, Richard V. White, Jr., William E. Suiter, and Olaf C. Swenson.

All eyes were on the battlefront. In the fall of 1918, Pershing's 1st Army attacked through the Argonne Forest. By November 7, the German supply line to the

Erected by the grateful citizens of Madison, this memorial commemorates those who participated in World War I.

front was cut off. The armistice with Germany was signed four days later, as Madison citizens and Americans everywhere took to the streets in joyous celebration. Finally, in June 1919, the Treaty of Versailles was signed in France, officially bringing World War I to an end.

Spanish Influenza

The so-called "Spanish Flu" influenza pandemic of 1918-1919 was one of the deadliest in recorded history, killing an estimated 50 million souls worldwide in a short twelve months.(28) Unlike the 2020 - 2021 COVID-19 contagion, where the most vulnerable patients have been those 65 and older, most of the fatalities from the Spanish Flu were young adults. The pandemic swept across the world in three relatively distinct waves: one in the early summer of 1918, a second one in the October-November timeframe, and a third in the early months of 1919. The second wave was the most lethal in most countries, and it was this wave that had the greatest impact on Madison.

This second wave of the Spanish Flu slammed into Madison like a tsunami just as the Great War was coming to a close. The October 4 issue of the *Madison Eagle* reported that "only a few cases have developed here, and none of the victims has been seriously ill."(29) A week later, the *Eagle* reported that 167 cases had been reported, with seven of those being fatal. On October 7, the Madison Board of Health ordered: "the closing...of all schools, public and private, churches of all denominations, public library, Y.M.C.A., moving picture theater, and all places of amusement, hotel barrooms, liquor saloons, lodges, pool rooms and public meetings of any kind."(30)

Another week later, The *Madison Eagle* reported the number of reported cases in the borough had risen to 300, and whole families were devastated. The baggage master at Madison's Lackawanna station, John Forte, reported to the board of health that seven members of his family were all sick with influenza. Only he and his wife had been spared. Among the seven were Mr. Forte's brother, special police officer Daniel Forte, as well as all of his children.(31) On November 1, the *Madison Eagle* reported that Daniel had died at All Souls' Hospital.

By October 18, [Morristown] Memorial Hospital had announced that it could accept no more new cases. In response to this lack of capacity in Morristown and at Overlook Hospital in Summit, the board of directors of the Madison YMCA turned its, by-then-closed, building on Main Street over to the local chapter of the Red Cross to be used as an emergency hospital for patients of the pandemic. The *Madison Eagle* reported that by Monday, October 22, "Madison has a well-equipped emergency hospital for the adequate treatment of influenza cases." And "seven patients were [immediately] conveyed by the borough ambulance to the new quarters."(32)

The crisis ended almost as quickly as it began, and by November 1, the *Eagle* reported that the borough's emergency bans were lifted as "the epidemic [seemed] to be dying out."(33) But that was certainly small comfort for all the families that had been devastated by the disease. As of November 15, there had been 540 cases of influenza and 60 related cases of pneumonia in Madison—then a town of about 5,500—since the first of October. These resulted in 34 deaths, and 25 Madison children left either fatherless or motherless.(34) In comparison, by May 2023—three years after it began—the total Madison death toll from COVID-19 was 33. This was in a town with a population of about 17,000, or about three times its 1918 population.

Much like the experience the New York metropolitan area had with the COVID-19 pandemic, the medical community had little rest during the peak of the contagion and were not immune to infection. Dr. Aldo Bliss Coultas was reported ill and at home, as was Dr. F. I. Krauss of Chatham during the second week of October. The *Madison Eagle* reported that week that: "Every physician in the county was working day and night, and all of them appear to be pluckily standing a greater strain than should be put upon them."(35) The *Eagle* also reported that Borough Health Inspector S. Fred Burnet was "laid up a couple of days" during the following week.(36)

Dr. Coultas recovered from his infection, but his wife, Ella Pearl Bardon Coultas, did not, and she succumbed to the disease on Sunday, October 20.(37) His daughter, Mary Dorothy Coultas, would also fall victim to the disease.(38)

The pandemic reappeared in Madison in early February. By the 21st of the month, there were approximately 200 new cases of influenza or "grippe," with one fatality reported. Although approximately an eighth of all Madison school students were reported absent due to sickness by mid-February, most reported cases in this third wave were relatively mild.(39) They were nothing like what the town had had to deal with the previous October.

Young Students and Athletes of the Twenties

Madison's Rose City Baseball Team (note the uniforms), late 1920s. Front row: Unknown, Frank Crehan, Eddie Bergmann, Bebbe Lusardi, unknown, Vince Spagnolia, Carlton Apgar, Harold Cutler. Middle row: Al Lusardi, Gil Lusardi, Lawson, Bill Fitzgerald, Joe Valgenti, Chick Pedrick, Frank J. Valgenti, Jr. Top row: Michael Mottola (scorekeeper), Mayor Gibney, Reginald Baker.

Girls' Basketball, 1922-1923 Front row: Mildred Washer, Bess Corbett, Margaret Tuttle, Grace Farmer, Edith Walters. Back row: Miss Aldrich, Viola Egbert, Coach Harry, Dot Waters, Aileen McCabe.

St. Vincent's Boys Band, 1925, under the guidance of Fr. Weitekamp. Cornet: Thomas Moore, James Dunlavy, Wm. O'Brien, Walter Gensch, Jos. Giordano, Robt. Sullivan, Ed. Rider, Sam Piccolo. Clarinet: Francis Ryan, John Dunlavy. Saxophone: Angelo Del Luca, Carmen Guerriero, Thomas. Johnson, Vincent McCoy. Trombone: Peter Bartell, August Bartell, Nicholas Esposito, John McCoy. Baritone: Tangred Esposito, Ed. Daniher. Bass: Jos. Vibbert, Anthony Piccorale, Wm. Mahoney. Bass Drum: John Early. Cymbals: Jos. Piccolo. Drums: Francis Carroll, Francis Ford, Gerald Gero. Drum Major: Ed. Stanton.

The Twenties: Roaring and Otherwise

The return of peace saw a continuation of the varied cultural, political, and commercial activity that had characterized Madison's years before the war. The popular image of the 1920s in America has an air of frivolity about it with flappers, bathtub gin, the *American Mercury Magazine,* and sensational trials (Leopold and Loeb and the Scopes cases). Yet the twenties were also years of important social change and, as Madison served to illustrate, of genuine accomplishments.

Historical Society Created

Pressing civic affairs were a visible part of the local scene. For instance, the Madison Historical Society was created in 1922 as a means of providing public support for an effort to save the historic Madison House from demolition. The action was precipitated when the First National Bank, then located on the northeast corner of Central Avenue, bought the site directly across Main Street occupied by the Madison House. This landmark became a hostelry in 1819 when Col. Stephen Hunting bought the property.

It was here in 1825 that the

Looking west on Main Street. Madison House on the left, before the move.

Madison House en route to the new
site. Many remember the slow progress.

Madison House after the move. From red paint
to gleaming new white.

town's dignitaries gathered to welcome the aging Marquis de Lafayette, a major general in Washington's army, as a national hero for his role in the American Revolution. In response to public agitation in 1922 to save this vintage landmark, the bank management agreed to donate the building to a community group willing to pay for its removal.

Fortunately, a band of Madison citizens—most notably Mrs. Calvin Anderson, Mrs. Anderson Case, Mrs. Fitzhugh C. Speer, Lloyd W. Smith, and Arthur W. Buttenheim— came to the rescue. They spearheaded a successful fundraising effort, which, in turn, led to the founding of the Madison Historical Society. Within a year, membership grew from 23 to 82.

During the winter of 1922-1923, the venerable building was laboriously moved east to the trolley tracks in the middle of Main Street past the Prospect-Greenwood intersection to a location nearly opposite Alexander Avenue. The move disrupted trolley service for several weeks. Passengers were required to dismount, then walk around the building that completely blocked the tracks during its transit, and then board another trolley in order to complete the journey.

Madison Historical Society

Once relocated to its new site, the Historical Society renamed it Bottle Hill Tavern and opened a tearoom to help support its headquarters and museum. The tavern had its grand moments: in 1925, for instance, ceremonies were held there honoring the 100th anniversary of Lafayette's visit. In 1946, the society sold the building to restaurateur Mario Torrani, who, with his wife Mary, revered its historic background and made the restaurant a fashionable gathering place. (See Chapter 15 description of this historic building's ultimate demolition.)

The society, dedicated to preserving Madison's historic legacy, then moved to the James Library until the late 1950s, when the historical collection was dispersed to several sites. Throughout the intervening years, the society has continued to publicize and research local history in an office in the Madison Public Library. In the future the actual historical artifacts collection will be housed in the Hartley Dodge Memorial Building.

Women Take the Lead

In the 1920s, Madison women were responsible for giving community service a preeminence that reached far beyond the confines of the borough. Under the aegis of the Thursday

Morning Club, a women's organization was founded in 1896 with a guiding motto of "I Serve." A group of dauntless ladies, in January 1925, opened a permanently based Settlement House on Cook Avenue to serve "the people of Madison as a whole" regardless of "color, creed, or nationality."(40)

The building, made possible by a bequest in the 1920 will of late member Mrs. Mary Brown Cash, is the same sturdy facility, with several appropriate additions (See Chapter 16), that today serves borough needs as Madison's Community House. In the 1950s, the group was said to be the only women's club in the United States to own and operate a settlement house.

Actually, the Thursday Morning Club women made their start in settlement work in January 1909, when they opened a room on North Street to serve as a recreation and medical center and installed the capable Miss Cora Payn, whom they had hired as a district nurse in 1906. She later became settlement director in 1911, when the club rented the Brittin homestead at 36 Main Street, where 10 rooms and a bath were available. Ultimately, a diet kitchen, dental clinic, and baby keep-well clinic were initiated.

These Madison women early realized that a trained nurse was sorely needed to minister to the poor and needy, especially among those immigrants who flocked to Madison with the growth of the rose industry and during the strenuous work of elevating the railroad tracks and

Seated, L-R, Mrs. Dwight F. Morss, Mrs. Alfred P. Smith, Jr., Mrs. J. Frank Chapman, Mrs. Paul L. Hammann, Mrs. Albert S. Johnston. Standing: L-R, Mrs. Earl J. Reddert, Mrs. E. Haskell Hewson, Mrs. Roswell N. Hait, Mrs. James C. Ashley, Mrs. George A. Fenton, Mrs. Louis L. Pettit, Miss E. Van de Water. The Settlement House name was changed to Community House in January 1957.

Lillian Russell and Judy Zanzucchi.

Green Door Players, founded in 1925, derived their name from the green door of the Settlement House.

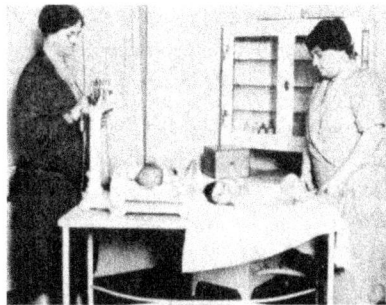

Well-Baby Clinic; Cora Payne, RN (L), assisted with births, deaths and operations, visited the sick and set up the Baby-Keep-Well Clinic at the Settlement House.

in digging "the big cut."

Although the clubwomen had to struggle to secure their own financing, they were always buoyed by a reputation for being able to "accomplish anything they undertake." Such recognition dated back to April 1906, when they organized a town improvement committee at the request of the borough government. In short order, they cleaned up the littered, unkempt sidewalks about town, put the railroad station premises in presentable condition and beautified Waverly Place with flower plantings, as befits the image of "a model borough."

From this perceptive beginning, the various service committees of the Thursday Morning Club have never ceased to function when they were needed most: through two world wars, rationing, killing epidemics, a major financial depression, and the ever-present specter of poverty. At one time during the Great Depression, baths were made available at the Settlement House at five cents apiece, "towel and soap supplied by the bather...."

There were happy times, too, when the clubwomen sponsored indoor and outdoor dancing, supplied instruments and uniforms for the first Madison Bugle and Drum Corps, provided the Green Door Players theater group with their first home, made available a gym for St. Vincent's and Central Avenue Schools, and offered classes in ceramics, woodworking, cooking and sewing. They formed the Committee on Shade Trees, which later became the borough Shade Tree Commission; started the first public playground at Dodge Field; and began the first morning kindergarten, now part of the public school system. This amazing organization also founded the Friends of the Madison Public Library in 1938.

There are many worthy organizations in this borough that have freely answered the call for "public service" over the busy years. Yet, the 126-year-old (in 2022) Thursday Morning Club was the pioneer agency that has, with steadfast aim, continued to make Madison a better place to live.

"Demon Rum" and Prohibition

While Madison emerged from the 19th century with a community identity clearly its own, it nonetheless generally moved with the main social currents of American life. In the early years of the 20th century, the Progressives were pressing for major reforms in American society. Although primarily representative of a movement geared to national issues, the Progressives also had a major impact on local political activity. They supported women's suffrage and Prohibition, two important issues at both the national and local levels.

The Temperance Movement, with its goal of prohibition, was extremely strong in Madison. Local orators, bolstered by the local Methodist Seminary, urged crowds to abstain from alcohol while bemoaning the evils of "demon rum." In January 1920, national prohibition became a reality, although Madison had gone dry six months earlier. On June 30, 1919, revelers in Madison treated themselves to an exuberant final binge. The bars of both the American House and the Madison House, at opposite ends of Waverly Place, were crowded with those in search of that last drink. Throughout the night before Prohibition, customers flocked to these two taverns in a great debauch. Although Madison had been a staunch temperance town for the past 100 years, it seemed as though the teetotalers were out of sight for the night. Only those who enjoyed "booze," as it was called, could be seen—and heard.

Still, later, other leaky cracks in Prohibition appeared. At least one of Madison's rose growers wasn't interested only in horticulture. In November 1932, police raided a greenhouse on upper Greenwood Avenue. They found two stills capable of producing 12,000 to 20,000 gallons of illegal alcohol per week. A janitor at the greenhouse was calmly working the coal-fired boilers within a few feet of the stills when police arrived. Yet, he steadfastly said that his job was only to put coal in the stove. He claimed not to know his employer's name, what was being produced, or even how much he was being paid.

Illicit production of liquor continued in Madison. The *Eagle*, in an editorial titled "The Sale of Beer" on March 24, 1933, claimed that Madison "has more than a dozen speakeasies." The newspaper urged that they be replaced by licensed bars permitted to sell beer with a 3.2% alcohol content, then permitted by legislation signed by President Franklin D. Roosevelt. The year 1933 also marked the formal end of Prohibition; with the passage of the 21st Amendment, Madison's speakeasies vanished.(41)

The Amazing William A. Starrett

William Starrett

With the 1920 presidential election, Warren G. Harding was ushered onto the stage of American history. The "roaring twenties" were not kind to Harding, whose political appointments showed him to be a poor judge of character. The Teapot Dome oil lease and the Veterans Bureau scandals rocked the nation by 1923. Under political pressure and in poor health, Harding died of a heart attack on August 2, 1923. Taciturn Vice President Calvin Coolidge was sworn in as the 30th President of the United States.

Despite the political problems with corruption at the national level, the 1920s were years of real prosperity for millions of Americans. William A. Starrett, Republican mayor of Madison from 1920 to 1922, became one of the town's most successful residents of the decade. Starrett was a man with talents that far transcended his local political office. As a partner in Starrett Brothers and Eken Inc., he supervised the construction of some of the tallest skyscrapers in America.

In the 1920s and 30s, under William A. Starrett's leadership, the Starrett Brothers companies became known for their large-scale construction projects, particularly skyscrapers. The New York Life Insurance Company Building and the McGraw-Hill Building were two notable examples. But the jewel in the crown of Starrett structures was, of course, the Empire State Building. Work on the building began in the early years of the Great Depression. The project employed upward of 3,400 workers on any single day. Many were immigrants from Europe. Of particular note were hundreds of Mohawk Indian ironworkers. The project took twenty months to complete, from the first architectural drawings in September of 1929 to the building's opening on May 1, 1931. The final cost was $40,948,900. Today, that would amount to $691,710,455.(42)

Born in Lawrence, Kansas, in 1877, Starrett was one of seven children of a Presbyterian minister. He studied engineering at the University of Michigan and served as chairman of the construction committee of the War Industries Board during World War I. After the war, he designed earthquake-proof buildings in Tokyo, Japan. Starrett even foresaw the building of 150 to 200-story skyscrapers in the future once people were ready to "live in the clouds." Besides a busy professional career, Starrett found time to write a book appropriately titled *Skyscrapers and the Men Who Build Them*.

William Aiken Starrett Jr. passed away on March 26, 1932, at his home in Madison after suffering a series of apoplectic strokes. To this day, he is remembered in architectural and construction circles as "Father of the Skyscraper."

Madison's next mayor and publisher of the *Madison Eagle,* John E. Clarey, Jr., resigned due to poor health in May 1924, shortly after his release from a hospital where he was treated for pneumonia. In his letter of resignation, Clarey wrote of his "abiding love for this splendid community," which he felt was an "outstanding center of suburban life in New Jersey."

Some Sad Asides of the Twenties

In the fall of 1921, the brutal murder of 11-year-old Janette Lawrence created a sensation in the community. She had been stabbed and killed in the early evening in the Kluxen woods near the corner of Ridgedale and Fairview Avenues. A *Madison Eagle* account was published in 1982.(43)

After lengthy investigations, two suspects, Frances A. Kluxen and Frank Jancarek, were arrested, indicted, and subsequently tried for Janette's murder in separate trials. Neither was found guilty of the crime. An *Eagle* editorial of July 21, 1922, noted that "The patch of woods at the corner of Ridgedale and Fairview Avenues holds its secret of the savage stabbing."(44)

Notable Local Literary Publishers Emerge

The year 1927 was known for its flapper girls, economic prosperity, and automobiles. It was also the year in which Arthur W. Rushmore, design and production executive of Harper & Brothers, and his wife, Edna, of Fairview Avenue, started the famous Golden Hind Press, and the year in which Geraldine Dodge began her annual dog shows.

Edna and Arthur Rushmore at work in their home.
Credit: Delight Lewis for American Artist, May 1941

Golden Hind Press started as a hobby for the Rushmores, but their books quickly became collectors' items because of the intricate and imaginative use of printing typefaces. The Rushmore also used old-style italics and several other unusual types in fashion at the time their work was first published. Within 20 years the Golden Hind Press had printed 180 books covering a wide range of topics, including classics and children's books. (45) Several Golden Hind books were selected for "bookmaking beauty" by the American Institute of Graphic Art.(46)

The Washington Hand Press used by the Rushmores was given to the Madison Library but is now on loan and displayed at the Museum of Early Trades and Crafts (METC). The Rushmore Collection at the Madison Public Library concentrates on the cultural side of the history of printing.

Pathe Photography

On a cool day in March 1927, the great poet Carl Sandburg visited Madison and spoke at the Thursday Morning Club meeting in James Hall. The "Apostle of Americanism," as he was called, read from his poetry, including the famous "Smoke and Steel" and "Accomplished Facts" poems. Sandburg then delighted the audience by singing folk songs of the Mississippi Valley while strumming a mandolin. As part of his lecture, the poet extolled the greatness of Abraham Lincoln as an artist. "That is," he said, "if to possess the grace of human behavior and the poise of soul and mind is an art, then Lincoln was a true artist." His message, that Americans should cultivate their own talents and extol the virtues of their own country, was not lost on Madison's citizens, who looked with anticipation to the future of their community.(47)

Madison has had more than its share of public commentators. Citizens have been unafraid to comment on the past, present, and future conditions in the community. One individual who demonstrated unusual clarity and vision was Carroll Bradford Merritt, an official of Scribner Publications, a former prominent Madison businessman, and an early editor of the *Madison Eagle*. Speaking to a gathering of the Business Men's Association of the YMCA in January 1929, Merritt counseled businessmen to improve the appearance of their downtown section by not forgetting that its main streets are the "show windows of the community."(48) Merritt demonstrated a willingness to forecast the future when he predicted a local population of 20,000. He also felt that the figure would be attained within 10 years. (Madison hasn't quite made it. The Census Bureau states that the borough's population was 16,937 on April 1, 2020.)

Despite this unrealistic timetable, Merritt showed a clear understanding of the factors about to change Madison. Among them were modernization of the railroad and growth of the commuter population. He concluded that "Madison is no longer a country town."

Gypsy King Naylor Harrison.

The Romani (or Roma), those much-misunderstood people popularly known as Gypsies, made Madison the site for an annual camp throughout the years before and after the turn of the century. Led by Gypsy King Naylor Harrison, a large "tribe" regularly descended on Madison in a train of brightly colored wagons. Harrison's wagon was then valued at $2,500, and many in the entourage had servants. Harrison was able to amass this small fortune mainly from horse trading. To some, he was thought to be the wealthiest Gypsy in the world.

King Harrison was a well-built, handsome man who sported a mustache. In a photograph on his tombstone in Hillside Cemetery, he looks like a respectable Wall Street or Main Street businessman. He and some members of his group were active in the local Masonic Lodge. Despite his unusual life as a Gypsy, Harrison was well respected in Madison and Florham Park, where he owned a house and barn that were once part of the property of the former Mauro's Florist and Garden Center near the junction of Greenwood and Ridgedale Avenues.

By the time of his death in 1928 at an encampment in Morristown, Naylor Harrison was a local legend. Some say he died from injuries received when kicked by one of his many horses. His burial in Madison's Hillside Cemetery on July 7 was attended by about 500 mourners. A motorcade of over 100 cars followed his hearse from Morristown. The motorized procession was an ironic twist for this Gypsy leader, who preferred horse-drawn wagons to automobiles.

A University's Influence

In September 1925, Drew Seminary opened for the fall with a record number of students. The *Eagle* urged Madison residents to offer both "rooms and work" to those students in need of them. The newspaper did not want the townspeople to miss an opportunity to help its "most famous institution."(49) The position of the *Eagle* was quite evident: it urged cooperation with the institution. With allusions to Oxford and Cambridge, the editor argued that "There is no university in Summit or Chatham or Morristown, but there is one to rise here in Madison."

This was a reference to the conversion of Drew from theological seminary to university, which was being contemplated at that time.

On February 3, 1929, local and regional newspapers carried notice that a gift of $1.5 million had been given to Drew Theological Seminary by Leonard and Arthur Baldwin to establish a College of Liberal Arts. For the many local admirers of Drew, this was a "time for rejoicing." With this gift and the establishment of a liberal arts college, the institution changed its name to Drew University.(50)

Arthur and Leonard Baldwin, shown at the groundbreaking ceremonies for the Liberal Arts building in 1929 with freshmen of the class of 1932. Photo source: Drew University Archives

During the 1930s, Madisonians were well aware of the mounting problems in Europe. This awareness was cultivated by a talented academic in their midst, Dr. Lynn Harold Hough, a professor at Drew University. A graduate of Drew Seminary, Hough was a speaker with a national reputation who had earlier served as president of Northwestern University. In 1934, he became dean of the Seminary. Although a prolific writer on religious topics, Hough had his greatest local impact through his speeches on national and international affairs.

Speaking before the Men's Forum of the Methodist Church in April 1934, Hough expressed faith in the policies of the New Deal while telling the audience: "Never will we go back to the old life under the former regime." He spoke of his travels around America where, unlike Madison, "Intense ferocities are bottled up, just waiting to explode."(51) As international tensions increased in 1938 and 1939, Hough gave frequent speeches predicting the end of Benito Mussolini's and Adolf Hitler's governments. Hough had little patience with the isolationists. From his point of view, they invited disaster.

Dr. Lynn Harold Hough. Photo source: Drew University Archives

Dean Hough represented the significant impact of Drew University on the townspeople of Madison. The professors at Drew have served as an intellectual stimulus for the community since the creation of the "University in The Forest." They, and frequently their students, were also active in local church affairs. By giving lectures in the community, Drew professors exposed Madison residents to a much wider intellectual horizon than that normally afforded a small town.

The Benefactions of Lenox Rose

Drew University became the recipient of another large bequest in May 1937 when the contents of the Lenox Sheaf Rose will were revealed in the *Madison Eagle*. A Madison resident of 36 years, Rose left the University approximately $500,000 to construct a suitable memorial in accordance with the will of his wife, Nellie K. Rose. The building was to be known as the "Rose Memorial Building." Rose's generosity also extended to other community organizations. To the Madison Fire Department, he left a sum of $1,500, which was to be divided equally among the 97 members. The then 60 employees of the borough also received $1,500, which was to be divided equally. Similar sums were left to employees of the Madison exchange of the New Jersey Bell Telephone Company, the local post office and the Madison Trust Company. Rose also left funds to the YMCA, Thursday Morning Club, police department, public library and each local church.(52)

Rose himself represented a rags-to-riches story. He worked his way up the ranks at Blanchard Brothers and Lane, Newark leather merchants. He apparently saved diligently and valued every dollar he earned. In death, he tried to distribute these savings so that they might do the greatest good for the largest number of people. As the *Eagle* stated in reporting his death: "In his passing, Madison loses a man and gains an ideal."

Lenox Sheaf Rose's bequest to Drew University answered the pressing need for a new library. The Rose Memorial Library was designed to contain 400,000 books, reading rooms and offices. It is one of the finest small university libraries in the nation. Photo source: Drew University Archives

The Great Depression

Business generally prospered in America throughout the 1920s. Locally, merchants thrived, and the Madison population grew from 5,523 in 1920 to 7,481 in 1930. Indeed, the town's growth reflected a regional trend in those boom years. The population of the New York-Newark metropolitan area began to fan out. The farmlands and former estates of Madison, and of Morris County in general, gradually gave way to housing developments. The major improvements in the railroad system tended to make living in these suburbs more appealing for individuals commuting to work in New York City.

However, the economic bubble was about to burst. On the morning of October 24, 1929, prices on the New York Stock Exchange dropped disastrously. The decline led to panic selling, halted only by large banking purchases. Then, on October 28, the bottom fell out, with 8 billion dollars in stock prices lost. Literally thousands of investors were wiped out in the crash.

Alan A. Brown- A Man of Few Words

Yet, as hard as the Depression hit so much of the nation, Madison generally suffered less at first. Indeed, the town kept largely to its steady policies of stimulating local improvements and relative political stability. This was clearly evident in the November 1933 mayoral election, in which Councilman Alan H. Brown succeeded Frank A. Cook. Brown, a Republican, came into office quietly by praising his predecessor and by keeping many of the same individuals appointed by Cook in their administrative positions. During his opening speech, Brown announced there would be no major policy changes.

Perhaps Brown was Madison's version of Calvin Coolidge. The mayor seemed unusually brief with his comments. His inaugural speech and the meeting that followed it only took 26 minutes. Even a *Madison Eagle* writer was moved to comment on the quiet mayor who "conducted his first meeting with such briskness." Brown served the community as mayor during the Depression and possibly thought it best not to make too many promises to the people that might be difficult to keep. Despite the poor national economy, Madison's municipal govern-

Police Department. Just before the big move to Hartley Dodge Memorial in 1935. The three officers in front row: Tony Giordano, Chief Peter Farrell, and Ed Hinch. Back row: Leon Doty, Bill Ryan, Orrin Atchison, Jim Ryan, John Walsh, Bill Kiernan, Marty Jennings. This old building, corner of Central Avenue and Elmer, long faithful to firemen and police, is now attractively remodeled.

ment operated well, he thought, so "it would seem part of sound common sense and political wisdom to continue in our untroubled and quiet way." The mayor felt he was bolstered by the council and the "sage advice" offered by Borough Attorney Henry W. Pilch.

Mayor Brown correctly assessed the positive impact on the local economy of the construction of Hartley Dodge Memorial. In his inaugural address, Brown paid tribute to Mrs. Dodge, who took "every possible opportunity to assist Madison with its problems of unemployment." He praised her "disposition toward civic pride and public benefaction," yet urged all citizens, from wealthy to humble, to be involved in the improvement of the community.(53)

Madison's government was soon thereafter relocated from the James Building on Green Village Road to the new Hartley Dodge Memorial. Dedicated on May 30, 1935, the granite and marble structure was built with bronze doors, a marble staircase, and other lavish embellishments.

Aspects of the Depression finally were felt in Madison, not the least of which were the work projects of the Civilian Conservation Corps (CCC). In the spring of 1935, the CCC initiated a project to clean up the badly clogged Spring Garden Brook from Madison to Florham Park. The project involved regrading and straightening the stream channel in order to prevent overflow from stormwater.

During the cleanup, a positive clue to past use of the waterway was found. About 500 feet south of Oak Street (now Community Place), a network of tile drain pipes was found in a marshy part of the brook, near its source at the foot of the ridge.(54) The discovery clearly indicated the much earlier existence of a drainage system for the marsh at a time of crop cultivation in the area. Nearby, workmen also found over 50 large carp which were living in the swampy water only six inches deep. The Civilian Conservation Corps crew cleared other tributaries of the Passaic and found an 1817 penny, bottles, horseshoes, automobile tires, and rubber balls.

Even in the depths of the Depression, however, Madison continued to look ahead, and there were some signs that the future might indeed be bright. During the 1930s, for example, the Lackawanna Railroad line was electrified. The improvement of commuter service to Hoboken was viewed by the public as a large step toward the completion of a rapid rail connection between Manhattan and Madison. The possible impact of improved rail service on the population was not lost on William Hartwell Ludlow, who, in the May 25, 1934 edition of the *Eagle*, recommended efficient land-use planning before the population increased. Such an outlook was in marked contrast to that in many other American towns, which saw the age only as a time of economic calamity, not of potential progress.

The year 1935 was marked by the retirement from his New York job of William Webb Davis, frequently called "Madison's oldest commuter." Davis commuted on the railroad for 56 years, amassing an incredible three-quarters of a million miles of travel. Among other stories, he enjoyed recounting a tale of the time during the Blizzard of 1888 when he was stranded on the train at South Orange while en route to New York. Snowbound there for 24 hours, Davis and James A. Webb, his uncle, left the train and walked through deep snow to a livery stable, where they hired a sled to take them to Newark. Once in Newark, the pair took a Pennsylvania Railroad train to New York. The trip from Madison to New York took them 36 hours during this famous blizzard.(55)

The Second World War

Throughout the 1930s, local residents watched the events in Europe with interest and fear as German aggression escalated. The European situation intensified in September 1939 when Germany invaded Poland, provoking declarations of war by Britain and France. The winter of 1939-1940 found many Americans continually shocked and dismayed by the events in Europe. Things continued to deteriorate through 1940 and 1941 until, on a day forever etched in the American consciousness, December 7, 1941, the Japanese attacked the U.S. naval base at Pearl Harbor on the Hawaiian Island of Oahu. With anger and shock, the people of Madison, as did Americans everywhere, came to accept the reality of the event: America was at war!

The conflict brought a new routine to the town. There were blackouts and air-raid drills, as well as the rationing of goods for civilians, including such items as gasoline, sugar, and meat. And although dealing with rationing proved to be difficult, nothing could match the horror of war itself as, yet again, Madisonians left their homes to bear arms. Alas, in war, there are casualties. The first local person to lose his or her life was Charles Piccolo, son of Mr. and Mrs. Angelo Piccolo. Others who died in the early years of the war included Sgt. John Geotis and Seaman Alexander Esposito.

These war deaths marked a turning point toward an even greater acceptance of local Italian-Americans by the wider community. Italian-Americans, most of whom were then second-generation Italian families, were fighting on battlefields all around the globe. In attendance at a local ceremony, in March 1943, were 500 parents and relatives of 215 Madison Italian-American

Farewell ceremony honoring those leaving for military service. This early morning scene was often repeated.

servicemen and women. Frank J. Valgenti, Jr., acted as master of ceremonies with a service flag representing those who served in the Armed Forces unfurled at Park Avenue and North Street. The service banner had three gold stars at the top representing the three men who had already died in the war, two of whom were Italian-Americans.(56) That the son of one of Madison's earliest Italian immigrants should preside at this service was a fitting tribute.

Casualty lists mounted as the war continued, and growing confidence in the American war effort was tempered with the knowledge that some local soldiers were never coming home. Among these were four former scouts from Troop 25: John Stoddard, William (Bill) Reddert, Kennedy (Kenny) Blake, and Robert (Bob) Hogeman.

Poem in Honor of Harold Felch, Jr.

The following poem was written by Mrs. Alice Felch of Ridgedale Avenue in Florham Park in memory of her son, Harold Jr., killed in action in Germany:(57)

They are not dead, those boys who paid the fullest price,
We feel them round about us everywhere.
They gave their all; they made the supreme sacrifice;
They died to save the world from dark despair.

We see them all around us in their homes so dear;
A trinket here, a book tucked in a drawer.
The letters that they sent to us from far and near
Will help to keep them with us evermore.

We hear their laughter ringing and their happy song;
We hear their voices speaking to us too.
We'll always seem to see them in the gathering throng
And think of all the things they'd say and do.

They've just passed on a little while before us all
And left sweet memories here on earth below. There in their happy
home no doubts nor fears appall.
They're happier far than mortals here we know.

Some day when all our work on earth is finished here
And you and I pass through the open door,
We'll meet again those boys we've loved and held so dear
And with them dwell with God for evermore.

Local spirit remained high. In September 1943, the *Eagle* printed an advertisement for the Third War Loan, which read in part: "Sure, it'll be tough to dig up that extra money. But we've got to do it—and we will." The advertisement listed several reasons why Americans should contribute and ended with this statement."But mostly, we are right smack in the middle of the biggest, dirtiest war in history. And we're Americans." Patriotism was evident in every quarter.

In Republican-oriented Madison, wartime Democratic President Franklin Delano Roosevelt (FDR) gave townsfolk, and especially business people, much to debate. He had been elected and re-elected since 1932 for an unprecedented four terms. He had survived a panic-inspired bank holiday and created the New Deal and its "alphabet soup agencies." In its early days, the New Deal's Works Progress Administration (WPA) and Civilian Conservation Corps (CCC) fought the Great Depression using public funds to provide jobs for an army of the unemployed (of which Madison received its share).

As the decade progressed, Roosevelt took a number of active steps in response to the growth of totalitarian Nazism and Fascism in Europe, steps that were often referred to as "warmongering" by his detractors. Then came the "date which will live in infamy" in December 1941 when the Japanese bombed Pearl Harbor, and the U.S. entered World War II. Roosevelt then participated in a series of earthshaking conferences with Britain's Winston Churchill, and the Soviet Union's Joseph Stalin that developed a strategy to win the war and create a blueprint for a postwar world.

No other President has ever faced so many staggering crises at home and abroad. One of the most able promoters of his policies was his wife, Anna Eleanor Roosevelt, who was a First Lady in name and deed. She visited Madison on two occasions, the first visit being in March 1945, barely a month before FDR died. The war in Europe was winding down when she spoke to the New Jersey Consumers Cooperative on "Cooperation Essential to a Postwar World." Her stopover here included a tour of Madison Iron Works on Park Avenue,(58) and the MEPCO (Madison Electrical Products Company), both of which produced metal and electrical products for the war effort. On the evening of that visit, she spoke to a packed house in the high school auditorium.

Not long after President Harry S. Truman had made one of civilization's most critical decisions—to drop the atom bomb on two Japanese cities to end the war in the Pacific—Eleanor Roosevelt spoke at Drew University in January 1951. Her topic was "The Struggle for a Peaceful World," a matter of major concern to all in Madison and in a nation recovering from a global upheaval that shattered lives, careers, and hopes for the future. Mrs. Roosevelt headlined a theme that has haunted people ever since—world peace!(59)

"Spirit Of Madison, New Jersey." $125,000 of United States War Bonds purchased by the people of Madison in December 1942 provided "our boys" with this pursuit ship.

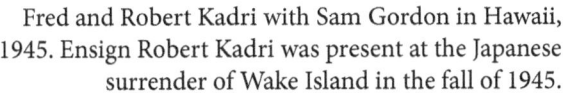
Fred and Robert Kadri with Sam Gordon in Hawaii, 1945. Ensign Robert Kadri was present at the Japanese surrender of Wake Island in the fall of 1945.

D-Day and Madison

"Under the Command of General Eisenhower, Allied na-
val forces, supported by strong air forces, began landing Allied
armies this morning on the northern coast of France."
Press Release, 0933 hours, June 6, 1944 (60)

As told in the remarkable and heroic stories of D-Day survivors, photographs, diaries, recollections of spouses, children, and grandchildren, yearly parades and remembrances, monuments, service medals, and obituaries in the *Madison Eagle*, the horrors and triumphs of that and subsequent days, are kept alive in the local and national consciousness.

In the planning for more than a year, "Operation Overlord" began on June 6, 1944, with 156,000 American, British, and Canadian soldiers landing on five beaches along 50 miles of the Normandy, France coast.(61)

One of the 40 men from Madison who did not return from the battlefields of World War II was Frederick W. Hopping. The *Madison Eagle* of August 10, 1944, briefly noted: "The borough flag has just been at half-mast for another of our Madison boys, who has gone to his reward—a former commuter, Frederick Hopping, who lived on Academy Road. Freddie was a fine type of American. He will be missed by a host of friends in the Green Door Players, where he was always very active."(62)

A young man he was never to meet, Chris Spelker, 75 years later, wrote a touching eulogy for a college class project:

"Fred …enlisted in the U.S. Army … at 35, on May 9, 1942. Fred was assigned to the 29th Infantry Division, 116th Regiment, 1st Battalion, Headquarters Company. Fred would depart England on June 6, 1944, on the SS Empire Javelin, a British troop ship. Fred then left the Empire Javelin, stepped into an LCA, and landed on the Dog Green sector of Omaha Beach at H+40. We'll never know what happened to Frederick Walter Hopping during his assault on the Dog Green Sector. At the end of it all, Frederick Hopping was killed by a gunshot wound to the head, as his unit desperately pushed up the beach past him. He was 37 years old."(63)

Fannie Piano, 96, a life-long resident of Madison and Gold Star Mother (Vietnam), met her husband Ralph under the oddest of circumstances. A neighbor invited her to write letters of appreciation and encouragement to soldiers serving overseas, and she did. One of these soldiers returned in 1945, looked her up, was smitten, and married her the following year. During his service, Ralph Piano fought all over Europe and landed on a murderous Omaha beach with Battery B 462nd Anti-Aircraft Artillery Battalion on June 8, 1944. He earned a Bronze Star Medal and other medals of distinction.(64) Like many returning soldiers then, Ralph was reluctant to talk about this wartime service.

Anthony Cangialosi was another Madisonian who found it difficult to talk about his war experiences. His daughter, Mary Torbali, recalled one of the few stories he told her about the harrowing landing on Omaha Beach, where he was one of the lucky ones who did not drown trying to get ashore in the deep water. With many floating bodies surrounding him, even he was unsure how he managed to make it out of the water to momentary safety. During his service, he was wounded several times and received the Purple Heart medal.

With adoration in her voice, Mary said, "He came home from the war, got on with his life, took care of his family, persevered, and worked hard."(65)

Bronze Star Medal recipient Louis Kenneth Mooney served in the Army's 28th Division. His unit landed on Omaha Beach on July 22 and saw action all over Europe. As explained by his daughter, Sue Ellen LaBelle, he fought his way through the hedgerows in the battles near Saint-Lo and marched in the liberation parade down the Champs-Elysees on August 29, 1944.

A Madison resident who served in the 9th Tactical Air Command, Nicholas A. Sena worked in ordinance and loaded bombs and machine gun munitions onto P-47 fighters. He landed on Omaha Beach on July 8, 1944, and eventually fought his way into Belgium. In 1945, he received the Belgian Fourragere Citation.(66)

Like others who returned from the war, Sena did not tell many stories to his family, but those few he did were harrowing. His son, Michael, related that once, he left his pup tent during the night and sometime later heard a loud explosion. Upon returning, he discovered that a large and lethal piece of shrapnel tore through his pillow, exactly where his head had lain a short time before.

His son spoke of his father's nobility and sense of duty and viewed him as a hero. When he was told he was being nominated for a Bronze Star, he refused to accept it unless all the men in his small crew were awarded one, too.

CHAPTER TWELVE

Rose City Blooms as Affluent Suburb

Spring, Little League baseball, enthusiasm and community spirit!

Postwar America teemed with activity. Americans seemed intent on rebuilding long-neglected roads and bridges, constructing suburban housing developments, housing for returning veterans, and building new superhighways. During the postwar period from the end of World War II through the end of the 1950s, eager New Jerseyites saw the completion of the Garden State Parkway and the New Jersey Turnpike. Travelers could now rapidly move around the State. A suburban housing boom in Madison and elsewhere accelerated the shift of New Jerseyites from urban to suburban lifestyles.(1)

The postwar years found many Madisonians optimistic about the future. One such optimist was Realtor W. Kelton Evans, who constantly prodded the borough council to look forward to the "more ideal Madison facilities, creation of a war memorial, road improvements, the purchasing of new equipment for municipal departments and the establishment of a borough refuse collection system." Evans saw the years ahead as a time when Madison would rapidly expand in population. He recommended the offering of a municipal bond to pay for the expenses of needed improvements. Through an involved system of calculations, Evans estimated that only a nine percent local debt increase could fund the improvements. In the fall of 1945, borough council members listened politely to the realtor's explanation of his plans, thanked him, and assured him that his ideas would be given consideration.

Many council members questioned the amount of money to be spent on the plan, but few could logically quarrel with Evans' assessment of what needed to be done. Bond issue or not, Madison would have to find a way to do most of the suggested projects if it wished to continue to grow and prosper. Eventually, Evans saw many of his ideas usurped by others, and only a few

W. Kelton Evans, popularly known as "Kelly" and a local realtor for 44 years, made a lasting impact on the development and improvement of our community. With his associates, he sponsored and developed Dellwood Park, Cross Gates, Harwood, Woodland Hills, and Knollwood. He contributed his knowledge and experience in civic and local service as a member of the Board of Education, Board of Assessors, Planning Board, 50-year member of Madison Masonic Lodge No. 93, charter member and past president of Madison Rotary Club, and director of local financial institutions.

people gave him due credit. Nonetheless, he clearly had an impact on the thinking of the political leaders, builders, and real-estate developers, who added new sections and improved older areas of Madison in the years following World War II.

Housing remained a focal point as the 1950s drew closer. In 1949, Mayor Norman J. Griffiths called for a committee to study the housing situation in Madison. He hoped that the committee would examine the ways in which low-rent homes could be built and the methods needed to eliminate blighted areas from the borough. This information could then be used by the Committee on the Welfare and Future of Madison to develop a much-needed borough master plan.

The new decade opened amid pressures to expand the amount of available housing, with debate focused on the need for apartments. A 90-unit apartment complex planned for Ridgedale Avenue was at the center of a storm of controversy. The plan was turned down, but ultimately, an apartment complex was built on Ridgedale Avenue.

Postwar Politics

Madison's first postwar leader was Mayor Griffiths, who also doubled as a state assemblyman both during and after World War II. He served as mayor from 1945 to 1951 and proved to be an outspoken politician who did not avoid controversy. Although he frequently received praise in the *Madison Eagle*, Griffiths occasionally got swept along with the popular political currents of the day. The position of the *Madison Eagle* editorial staff was clear: "Yes, Madison is fortunate in having Mayor Griffiths at the helm of its affairs."(2) His strong anti-Communism undoubtedly made some people uneasy in the days just prior to the emergence of Senator Joseph McCarthy and his anti-Communist crusade on the national scene.

The mayor saw no room for compromise on the issue. In March 1948, Griffiths attacked Governor Alfred E. Driscoll for failing to properly investigate "Communistic and un-American activities in New Jersey schools."(3) Driscoll delayed appointing a task force to investigate the possibility that Communists were at work in the schools because of his difficulty in finding people willing to serve. Unswayed by Driscoll's stated reasons for the delay, Griffiths issued the following statement: "Conditions throughout the world, and clearly here in America, indicate that every possible step should be taken to prevent the youth in our schools from being subjected to the insidious teachings of totalitarian ideologies."(4)

Global perspectives seemed to be much in evidence in 1948. Harold E. Stassen, former governor of Minnesota and a presidential candidate, spoke at a Madison home regarding his views on strengthening the United Nations. Stassen called for a major United Nations convention in 1950 to rewrite and strengthen the U.N. Charter. He urged modification of the United Nations by eliminating the single-power veto. To Stassen, the international organization had to be strong enough to monitor the development of atomic energy, which he felt "must be inspected and controlled on a worldwide scope."(5) World affairs had become a topic of conversation in Madison.

Return to War

At the start of the 1950s, television was beginning to make an impact in local homes of those who could afford to make the switch from radio. Increasingly, Americans began hearing and watching newscasts about a faraway land called Korea. By the midpoint of the summer of 1950, the first draft call was issued for the Korean War. Within a few months, Madisonians learned of the first local fatality of that war, Sgt. William Keppel. In October, another name was added to the casualty list when Lt. Samuel Streit Coursen was killed. He posthumously received the Medal of Honor.

Progress seemed to be evident in so many facets of Madison life, yet how sad it was that the town continued to lose young men in war. By February 1951, another local man, Howard R. Smith, became the third resident to die in the Korean "police action," as the war was called. Later in the year, Cpl. William J. O'Donnell joined this sad honor roll.

Lt. Samuel S. Coursen, Madison's Medal of Honor Recipient

On October 12, 1950, The *Madison Eagle's* "About Town" column noted that Mrs. W. Melville Coursen drove Miss Nancy Coursen back to Smith College in Massachusetts.(6)

On that same day, 6,835 miles away in Kaesong, North Korea, in the early months of the Korean Conflict, a 24-year-old Army 1st Lt. of the 5th Cavalry Regiment, C Company, led a platoon of men in the vital battle for Hill 174. In the fog, one of his men entered a concealed enemy emplacement and was shot and trapped. The 1st Lt. immediately jumped into the emplacement, viciously fought the enemy in hand-to-hand combat, and killed seven of them. The trapped soldier was saved, but tragically, 1st Lt. Samuel S. Coursen died in the violent struggle. For his exceptional bravery, "gallantry and intrepidity above and beyond the call of duty," he became the only Madison resident ever to receive the Medal of Honor.(7)

Lt. Coursen received many awards and citations during his brief military career, including the Purple Heart, the National Defense Service Medal, the Korean Service Medal, Republic of Korea Presidential Unit Citation, United Nations Service Medal, Republic of Korea War Service Medal, and the Combat Infantryman Badge.(8) But in a ceremony at the Pentagon, General Omar Bradley, Chairman of the Joint Chiefs of Staff, handed Lt. Samuel Coursen's

Plaque on the monument erected in his memory in James Park.

LT. Coursen received the Bronze and Silver Stars for heroism in Korea and, posthumously, the Medal of Honor. He was memorialized locally by a monument in James Park and by Newark Academy's naming of an athletic field after him. Madison also named Coursen Way for him as another fitting tribute.

greatest award, the Medal of Honor, to his 14-month-old son, Samuel Coursen, Jr.(9)

Needless to say, Samuel Coursen, Jr. did not recall the day's events at the Pentagon in 1951.(10) Yet he spoke poignantly in a telephone interview about the legacy his father left him. The courage, selfless dedication to others, and the striving to achieve and accomplish, all filtered down to young Sam and to his own children. On the wall of his home in Austin, Texas, resides his father's Medal of Honor and a certificate and citation letter signed by President Harry Truman. At a recent Thanksgiving celebration, his son read to the family the section called: "Always with Us," which detailed Lt. Coursen's history and deeds.(11) Sam now has a grandson, Samuel Coursen, III.

Living at Fort Benning, Georgia, at the time of her husband's death, Lt. Coursen's widow, Evangeline Coursen Pouncey, recalled in a phone interview her hearing of the horrific news.(12) A bride of only one year, and with a son only 6 months old, she described him as her "Big, tall, beautiful man, the apple of my eye. I loved him dearly; everyone liked him. He got to see his son only till he was 2 months old."

On that day in Washington in 1951, when her husband's Medal of Honor was awarded, she said that her 14-month-old son cried during the entire trip on an Army plane. Young Sam was fascinated by the flashbulbs used by the photographers and insisted on holding one in his mouth. Just as General Omar Bradley was about to present him with his father's Medal of Honor, his mother quickly pulled it out of his mouth, which made an audible popping sound.(13) No word on General Bradley's reaction.

Born in Madison, Samuel Coursen was schooled at Madison Academy and Newark Academy, excelled at football and boxing, and was class president. He trained at West Point Military Academy, Fort Riley and Fort Benning and is buried at the U.S. Military Academy Cemetery.

Lt. Samuel Coursen's deeds and life are memorialized around the nation. From the NJ Korean War Memorial in Atlantic City to Coursen Memorial Field at Newark Academy, to a plaque at Madison's James Park, to the Baltusrol Coursen Memorial Golf Tournament Trophy, to Fort Benning's Coursen Rifle Range, to a plaque at West Point's Cullum Hall, to Coursen Way in Madison, to memorial signs placed at entrances to Madison on Main St. Madison Ave. and to the Lt. Samuel S. Coursen ferry boat to Governors Island, this son of Madison stands as a role model for the ages.

Housing Improvements

During the winter of 1949-1950, housing once again became as much a topic of discussion as the war when Mayor Griffiths received a statistical report (January 1950) on borough housing prepared by Dr. David Fulcomer and several students at Drew University. Surprisingly, the report found that only 10 out of 143 dwellings surveyed were judged poor in three areas: plumbing, deterioration of the structure, and overcrowded usage. The mayor was hopeful that these few problems could be eliminated.

On March 9, 1950, the *Madison Eagle* ran an editorial that referred to the recent Drew report.

Reflecting the optimism of the postwar era, the editorial cautioned that "good citizenship starts at home, and if standards of citizenship are to be raised, it is essential that housing standards be comparably high, and that is largely the responsibility of those who own the properties."(14) Few would argue with that statement.

Spurred by local editorials that decried the "Suburban Slum" (a vast overstatement of fact), Madisonians were prodded to be more aware of the housing conditions in their community. The newspaper printed editorials relaying the view that otherwise "hard-headed and success-ful" New York businessmen suddenly "leave their practicality in New York" when they return to their homes in suburbia.(15) Again, the newspaper overstated its case to spur citizen action.

Caused in part by deferred maintenance during World War II, the spread of urban poverty in the postwar years alarmed residents. Fears festered in some minds that slums could develop in the suburbs if care was not taken. As an *Eagle* writer put it: "*There is no urgency* in the matter, but certainly a little foresight can do much to prevent grief later on."(16) The improvement of substandard dwellings—no matter how few existed—thus became an important matter in the fight to preserve the character and quality of the borough and to prevent, in the words of the *Eagle*, a "march to ruin."

Graham Macmillan served on Madison's Borough Council for nine years (1953 to 1962) and as its president for several years. A vice president with Prudential Insurance Company, Macmillan bought a home in the Knollwood section of Madison, an area then in need of road repairs. Sensing a need for political action, Macmillan asked to be appointed to a vacant seat on the council, and he was. He then ran for a full term in 1953 and was elected. Quite naturally, he became chairman of the Road Department Committee.

For three years Macmillan and John Artigliere, head of the Road Department, worked to-gether to get the job done—Macmillan in the political realm and Artigliere leading the road crews. Their efforts succeeded, and Madison's streets, including those at Knollwood, were final-ly in decent shape.

School Population Soars

Prosperity has its costs. As Madison's population began to swell in the postwar years, the influx of school-age children taxed the capacity of local schools. In the winter of 1948, a voter referen-dum authorizing the Board of Education to borrow $225,000 to construct two new elementary schools passed by a margin of 2 to 1. WOR Radio announcer John Gambling reportedly urged his Madison listeners to get out the vote in favor of the bond issue. The schools were sorely needed to meet the pressure caused by an increased number of elementary-age children. The bond issue authorized the construction of one school on Green Village Road and another on Kings Road. These were the first new schools built in Madison in two decades. As one letter writer to the *Madison Eagle* wrote: "There is no room in this matter for any further delay, and we cannot assume the responsibility for it."(17)

Approval of the bond issue was extremely important to end 20 years of indecision over the building of new schools. The public finally got the message the school board was trying to give. The *Madison Eagle* reported comments of Board President Earl Reddert who said: "In times of depression financing had been difficult; in time of war building was not permitted and now in time of inflation I was told that we shouldn't build. 'When,' he asked, 'can we build?'"(18)

The projected 1948-1949 Madison school budget was set at $499,981.25, an increase of over $66,000 above the previous year. The budget consisted of the following percentage allocations: 74 salaries, 14 debt service and 12 miscellaneous expenses. Obviously, the largest increase was

Lucy D. Anthony Elementary School, below, at Loveland and East Streets, was built in 1930 in honor of Miss Anthony, a devoted and talented teacher. It closed in 1981 due to declining enrollments and changing program needs. It is now the Kirby Center, owned by the YMCA.

Presently the Madison Junior School, this impressive building was Madison's high school from 1925-1958. Many cultural activities, including the former Colonial Symphony concerts, were held in the school's beautiful auditorium with its fine acoustics for many years.

Green Village Road (closed in 1976) and Kings Road Elementary Schools, identical in design, were dedicated in 1949. The Green Village School was demolished in 2016 in order to make room for the KRE Madison Place Condominium and Rose Hall Apartment development (opened in 2018). In 1930, a dwelling at 198 Kings Road was rented from Joseph Ruzicka for grades K,1, and 2.

for the hiring of additional teachers to meet the demands of the World War II "baby boom."

The new schools were not enough to meet the demands. By 1950, the Madison Board of Education noted that 12 more classrooms would soon be needed. A referendum for a new $450,000 addition to the Central Avenue School was approved by a vote of 980 to 645 in a March 1951 referendum. Some thought enrollment pressures might soon abate when, in 1952, Florham Park announced it would stop sending its students to Madison High School sometime before 1955. Unable to wait for such an indefinite action, the Madison Board of Education, in April 1953, announced it would not take Florham Park students after September 1954. Local residents expressed concern about the overcrowded conditions in local classrooms.

Soaring school costs were also troubling for Madisonians. In one year, 1954 to 1955, enrollment in local schools rose from 2,027 to 2,122. A year later, school enrollment swelled to 2,276. Inevitably, more students meant higher costs and higher taxes. Superintendent David S. McLean and the *Madison Eagle* were highly successful in promoting public acceptance of the higher costs. Typical of the *Eagle* viewpoint was a March 1956 editorial by John B. Ehrhardt: "It would be hard to argue that the drain of the schools is excessive. Indeed, we would suggest that the civilization that consistently spends more on alcohol and tobacco than it does on education is in no position to howl about school costs."(19)

The newspaper's viewpoint proved helpful to community leaders, who were beginning to campaign for the construction of a new high school. A need for the new school was obvious, but less so was its location. In the summer of 1956, the answer came quickly. The heirs to the Twombly fortune donated a 42-acre parcel to the community for use as a site for the high school. As had happened so many times in Madison's history, the community was again assisted by a private benefactor.

The Board of Education unveiled its plan to build a $2-million high school for the borough in February 1956. Carroll B. Merritt, a longtime proponent of the school system and community, helped the movement to grow through his public statements of support. Merritt urged his fellow townspeople to realize that the youth "are our most important asset" and that "it behooves us to give our Madison children the best possible start and in the best possible environment with the best available instructors."(20) In the fall of 1956, Dr. Richard Hough of the Madison School Board startled the community when he announced a projected 50 percent school enrollment increase within the next 10 years. Hough stressed the need for voters to approve a $2,650,000 school construction bond issue scheduled for public vote in December.

The school referendum was closer than many expected. The bond issue was approved by a margin of 258 votes, with 1,938 yes and 1,687 no. The strong opposition vote may have been due to the influence of W. Kelton Evans, who felt the plan was too costly. Surprisingly, the school bond issue divided Madison's two most visionary citizens—Evans and Carroll B. Merritt. Fortunately, in this time of change, the high school was under the guidance of Dr. Ward A. Shoemaker, a principal with a philosophy of diplomacy that served to bring confidence to students, teachers, and parents.

Dr. Ward A. Shoemaker, a rare individual and beloved educator, always ready with a story to illustrate a point, served as Madison High School principal for 27 years until 1960 and 4 additional years as assistant to the superintendent. To him, "The school is a structure, as the outside world is. If youngsters can become accustomed to living within this structure, they will have no trouble later. We try to teach them not only what that structure is but what is behind the curtain that makes it operate. Education should be a living experience, reaching the individual." On the occasion of Dr. Shoemaker's retirement in 1964, Eagle Editor Haynes wrote, "He has contributed more to the general welfare of his community than any community has a right to expect."(21)

Carroll Bradford Merritt, Eagle publisher in the early 1900s, was associated with McGraw-Hill Publishing Co. and retired as Vice President and director of Charles Scribner's Sons at age 75. He was appointed to the State Board of Control, Dept. of Institutions & Agencies and served as president of the Madison Trust Co.; director of the Morris & Essex Kennel Club and Starrett Corp.; chairman of the Shade Tree and Recreation Commissions; fire warden; Mason; councilman; honorary chairman, Ambulance Building Fund Committee.

The years of discussion and planning were over! Noted in the 1959 *Alembic,* "When a building of the size and importance of our Madison High School is completed with such fine results, the outcome is successful thanks to many who had a part in it."

Master Plan Debate

Madison High School Dedicated in 1959.

The winter of 1955, Madison was enlivened by public debate over the recently released master plan for community growth. The controversy grew torrid in January and February 1955. Evans publicly attacked the proposed master plan developed by the Planning Board under the leadership of Harold S. Buttenheim, charging that the plan would "do serious damage to property values here." The plan, titled *The Comprehensive Master Plan for the Development of Madison* (September 1954), did represent some major changes in existing zoning patterns. It proposed that the section of Kings Road facing the railroad be made into a residential zone even though that area contained a large number of commercial establishments. In a guest editorial written for the *Eagle* issue of February 17, 1955, Evans asked the people to be more active in the fight against those who would test planning "schemes" on the town. The realtor argued that the proposed recommendations lacked an "adequate appreciation of Madison as it actually exists, together with its history, growth, potential, and especially, the peculiar interests of numerous neighborhood areas and property owner groups." Among those who supported the Planning Board recommendations was John Hutchinson of Hillside Avenue, then professor of social sciences at Newark State Teachers College (now Kean University), whom the *Eagle* characterized as having "a large political following here." Public sentiment seemed to swing toward Evans' position, and many parts of the proposed master plan were never adopted.(22)

Madison's official planners obviously thought the future would be best served by encouraging greater commercial development. Many local citizens thought that such growth might threaten, rather than increase, the value of their homes. In a June 30, 1955 editorial titled "Madison, the Hub?" *Eagle* editor Ehrhardt said: "Madison's interests have always been residential, rather than commercial." Yet, the newspaper and most local people still felt that Madison was "destined to become more the hub of this section of the country." Whatever the future would hold, it would be determined by careful, rational planning.

A Shared Sanitary Plan

Planners of the 1950s had a brilliant role model to follow in the Madison-Chatham shared plan for sewage disposal known as the Joint Meeting. Farsighted local activists had realized the great importance of this sanitary need as early as 1909. So, they secured an act of the State Legislature to enable the boroughs of Madison and Chatham to construct, own, and jointly operate a sewage-disposal plant. The first plant was put into operation in 1911 on the site of the present installation on North Passaic Avenue on the fringe of the Chatham town line. This joint agreement is likely the oldest shared service agreement in New Jersey.

This Joint Meeting consists of the mayors and borough councils of Madison and Chatham, and the chairmanship of the operation alternates yearly between the two communities.

The joint plant has been enlarged and improved several times to keep pace with population growth and the effluent water quality requirement prior to water being discharged into the

Passaic River. The state has, in the past, put pressure on Madison and Chatham by threatening a $50,000 per day fine if the joint project wastewater plant was not upgraded. This forced Madison to take over $20 million dollars in bond debt in 1990. The subsequent plant addition is able to remove ammonia levels in the effluent from 30 milligrams per liter to less than 2 milligrams per liter. Additionally, the effluent will be dechlorinated to less than 0.1 milligrams per liter of chlorine. The clear waste, which is ultimately routed into the Passaic River, is approximately 95 percent pure with sufficient oxygen to encourage further self-cleansing downstream. It is designed to meet the needs of an area population of 40,000.

The treatment plant is known officially as the "Molitor Water Pollution Control Facility" and is dedicated to three members of the Molitor family who served as superintendent of the facility. The 1971 superintendent was H. Clyde Molitor, who began service in 1940. (The joint plant has been serving Madison and Chatham, and even small pockets of Florham Park and Chatham Township for over 111 years.)

Housing Code Enacted

The growing concern over substandard housing led the borough council in 1956 to establish a housing code. Under that code, action against substandard housing owners could be initiated by the housing officer or any five borough residents. Condemned buildings would be demolished at the owner's expense. In December 1959 Councilman Earl Reddert introduced an ordinance which was to replace the earlier law. The newer law required that a house must have 125 square feet of living space for the first family member and 75 square feet for each additional member over age 10. Children under that age were required to have 50 square feet of housing. The code classifications brought the 1956 law into line with state-mandated regulations. Housing officer Robert S. Deasey saw the future significance of the changes: "We must do our work now instead of allowing matters to stop for another 25 years when we would have much more trouble."(23)

Noblesse Oblige

The old estates continued to dwindle. The death of Florence Vanderbilt Twombly in 1952 was soon followed by an auction at her Florham estate. The two-day event featured the sale of furnishings, antiques, paintings, tapestries, and knickknacks, but most of all, it provided an open house for curious thousands eager for an on-site opportunity to see how "the other half" lived.

Three years later, in July 1955, Madison area residents were saddened to learn of the death of Lloyd Waddell Smith of Florham Park, another estate owner and benefactor. In his lifetime, Smith had been active in promoting many civic and charitable causes. Under his sponsorship, for example, Princeton historians published several volumes of New Jersey history.

Smith's donation of land at Jockey Hollow was of importance in the creation of historic Morristown National Park and the preservation of the Tempe Wick historic house. Smith also donated a parcel of land there to the Morris Area Girl Scouts in 1944. In his will, he gave the Madison Historical Society a trust fund of $1,000, while the Madison Public Library received $2,000. The philanthropist also bequeathed a large sum of money to several area churches, including the Methodist and Presbyterian Churches of Madison. (24)

An ancestor of Smith was Col. Hiram Smith, a member of Gen. Washington's Revolutionary War staff. Lloyd Smith's collection of letters from George Washington was subsequently given to the Morristown Historical Park Library.

Smith represented a remarkable success story. Born into wealth, he was quite young when his family experienced economic ruin and lost their home estate, Boxwood Hall in Florham Park. Smith vowed to regain the property. In 1896, he was admitted to the New Jersey bar as a lawyer, and by 1907, he saved enough money to regain the family home. Later in life, his career interest shifted to the field of investment management, which he conducted until his retirement in 1931. Afterward, Smith assumed the life of a country farmer. Some residents recalled the sight of him, during the early 1950s, driving his 25-year-old Ford on Madison's streets.(25)

The deaths of Twombly and Smith left only Geraldine R. Dodge as a major individual benefactor. At the start of the postwar era in 1948, Mrs. Dodge purchased a new police radio for the Madison police so that they could hook up with the county network. It was one of many civic improvements.

St. Hubert's Opening by Mrs. Dodge

After holding countless huge dog shows at Mr. Dodge's property, she developed another interest by 1958 when she opened St. Hubert's Giralda, a humane society shelter, in a building on her estate. St. Hubert's quickly became well known for its splendid facility, its advanced humane techniques and its educational program, under the direction of Edwin J. Sayres, Sr. St. Hubert's developed a national reputation as one of the finest shelters for homeless dogs. Sayres met Mrs. Dodge in 1935 on the dog-show circuit and soon became one of her most trusted employees, first serving as a dog handler and later as an estate manager.

St. Hubert's Giralda means "small animal orphanage." Hubert was the patron saint of hunters, hounds and small animals. "Giralda" comes from Jerome, patron saint of the orphans. Edwin Sayres, Sr., and Edwin Sayres, Jr., then director, holding resident mascots who were participating in humane education and pet therapy programs. Ding-A-Ling, an eight-year-old Pekingese dog and Sterling, a six-year-old male silver tiger cat, brought happiness wherever they went. Photo citation: 1984 St. Hubert's Giralda

The Lady of Giralda. Mrs. Dodge is shown with some of her own pets. Photo credit: St. Hubert's Giralda

Outside dog runs, half-roofed to provide sunshine as well as protection from inclement weather.
Photo credit: St. Hubert's Giralda

The Shelter • St. Hubert's Giralda's precedent-setting procedures and policies become a landmark in the education field. The shelter receives thousands of calls a year; lost pets are held for owners; the abandoned, injured, and mistreated are professionally treated, restored to health, and placed for adoption. Conferences, seminars and lectures are held in classrooms and the auditorium. Visits are made to schools and institutions. The gallery and library house treasures from Mrs. Dodge's collection. World-famous artists, sculptors and writers are represented there.

Suburbia and the Atomic Age

Like other Americans of the day, Madisonians often shared the uncertainties of the new atomic age. For some, fears of the bomb seemed real. In late April 1957, an air-raid alert emptied the streets for 10 minutes while Civil Defense coordinators planned emergency steps from a control room in the Hartley Dodge Memorial building. Local coordinators of what was then called the Civil Defense RAD-CHEM unit were Drew professors Dr. John Ollum and Dr. Marvin Richards and RAD-CHEM head Donald E. Thomas.(26) In June 1957, Thomas warned local residents that an atomic attack on the Allentown-Bethlehem, Pennsylvania, region would bring substantial radiation to the Madison area. Of small consolation was his assertion that a similar attack on New York City would result in most fallout material being blown out to sea.

College Takes Over Twombly Estate

Peter Sammartino, the multitalented President of Fairleigh Dickinson University, in 1957 announced plans by the university to purchase the 180-acre Twombly estate for $1.5 million to be used as an additional college campus. Existing buildings would be converted into classrooms, residence halls, and offices.(27) One major obstacle remained: three individuals, Joseph and Elizabeth Tomasulo and William Kelly, held an option to buy the Twombly property. After several meetings, the three individuals, represented by local attorney Frank J. Valgenti, Jr., permitted the sale to the university. According to the *Eagle,* they acted in the "best interest" of the community. At the time, approximately 30 firms had placed competing bids for the property. With the college bid accepted, Sammartino announced the institution's plan to have students at the site by September 1958.

Meanwhile, the local housing boom continued through the waning years of the decade. In the summer of 1957, John Horton Evans, son of W. Kelton Evans and also a Madison realtor, purchased the property of the Laura Augusta Home for Girls located between Woodland Road and Garfield Avenue. Unfortunately, the old mansion, once valued at $100,000, was not saved from the wrecker's ball. The property was then subdivided into choice housing plots.

An unnamed *Eagle w*riter lamented the destruction of the landmark, carried out in the name of progress. In a page-one story, the writer called the property "the last remaining parcel of vacant land on the top of the hill in Madison, and [it] comprises approximately 15 acres, several frame buildings, scores of magnificent ornamental and forest trees and a wealth of specimen shrubbery." Alas, what is the price of progress?

Visit of Jackie Robinson

The postwar years were also the time when Jackie Robinson broke the color barrier in major league baseball. In the fall of 1948, Robinson visited Madison to speak in the high school auditorium. Addressing a crowd of approximately 500, he stressed the need for youth to value education. In response to questions from the audience, he told the young people to "Get all the education you can." The Dodger great also predicted that Madison-born pitcher Don Newcombe "should be in the majors soon."(28)

How right he was! By the next year, Newcombe was setting the National League on fire with his pitching. Born on Morris Place, the later Brooklyn Dodger star moved at age five to Elizabeth where he attended school. As a player for the Newark Eagles of the Negro National League, he once appeared—along with future New York Giants and Hall of Famer Monte Irvin—in an exhibition against Manager Gil Lusardi's Colonels at Dodge Field.(25) Then, in

1947, Newcombe was signed to a Brooklyn Dodger contract by Branch Rickey. By 1949, his future was assured, even though he was one of the first Blacks permitted to play in the major leagues. In that year, he won 17 games and pitched 3 consecutive shutouts.

In December 1949, Newcombe returned to the town of his birth. Speaking before a large crowd in the high school auditorium, he urged the audience to practice good sportsmanship and to keep in top physical condition if they had any desire to become a major leaguer. He apparently said little of the difficulty he encountered in breaking the color barrier in professional baseball. The *Eagle* pointedly noted that, although half of the audience consisted of "colored" people and the other half of white people, it was a "friendly evening of entertainment and sociability."(30)

Madison-born, Brooklyn Dodger star pitcher Don Newcombe.

The Boys of Summer

The Madison Colonels, considered by many to be a high-caliber independent baseball team, announced that their catcher, Ed "Duffy" Oswald, would be given a tryout with the Philadelphia Phillies in Clearwater, Florida. The Phillies, in return, allowed Hal Spindell, their catcher of the previous three seasons, to sign a contract for the summer of 1948 with the Colonels. On signing with the local club, Spindell seemed pleased by the change, even though he was leaving the major leagues. "I've been all over the country," he said, "but haven't found anything that impresses me as much as Madison and Dover, where I'll be playing this year."(31)

There was also considerable local talk at the time regarding the possible rebirth of the popular old Lackawanna semi-professional baseball league. World War II had brought a virtual halt to the baseball league which provided so much entertainment and recreation during the previous two decades.

Even in the area of recreation, as in education and housing, there was rising sentiment that the community should do more. In his column "Athletes and Others," *Madison Eagle* sports editor Andy Rickey repeatedly urged the community to provide more and better recreational facilities for local children. His view, which was being increasingly shared by others, was that Dodge Field could not take care of the demand for sports. Rickey suggested the building of more baseball diamonds since they were "very inexpensive" to construct.(32) At the time, Madison was attempting to meet this need by providing softball, volleyball, and baseball leagues at Dodge Field during the summer months.

The important role played by citizens was underscored by Mayor Alfred P. Smith, Jr., in a statement issued in the mid-1950s: "The rapid growth of this community in the past few years has required the concerted effort of not only your mayor, council and paid borough employees, but also requires the time and efforts of those many public-spirited citizens who serve on various boards, commissions, committees and service groups on a purely voluntary basis."(33)

Fluoridation Controversy

The summer of 1955 was marked by a sharp controversy over the proposed fluoridation of local drinking water. Nationally, all eyes were watching for the results of the Newburgh-Kingston,

New York, experiment regarding fluoridation. The *New York Times* suggested that Newburgh children who were drinking fluoridated water had significantly better teeth than the children from Kingston who were drinking non-fluoridated water. Reacting to public concern, Madison Mayor Alfred P. Smith, Jr., said he would urge the borough council to "go slow" on any decision regarding the local water supply until the results of the New York study were fully published and validated. Despite the mayor's hesitation, *Madison Eagle* editor John Ehrhardt, in an article several months earlier, favored the use of fluoride, which he felt was being met with "growing acceptance in the United States."(34) In an earlier editorial he cited the efforts of Mayor Richard J. Daley of Chicago in ordering the fluoridation of that city's water supply for "the good of the children."(35) By November 1955, Councilman Graham Macmillan found himself in the midst of the controversy over fluoridation when he criticized Mayor Smith's slow response to the issue.(36)

While the debate over the fluoridation of water continued until finally resolved negatively, a more significant event occurred with a minimal amount of local publicity: the inoculation of children with the Salk vaccine against crippling poliomyelitis. Health authorities gave the revolutionary vaccine to children in three separate inoculations during an eight-month period.

Transistors, a Nobel Prize, and Madison, Oh My! Madison's Most Controversial Former Resident

"He had the quickest mind I've ever known."
– Dr. Philip Anderson, 1977 Nobel Laureate in Physics

Perhaps no resident of Madison has ever risen to such heights nor fallen to such depths as Dr. William B. Shockley. Living at 45 Maple Ave. and then 22 Academy Rd. in the 1940s and 1950s, he spent his most productive one-and-a-half decades here.

Earlier, as a college student, he attended the California Institute of Technology and was seen as genial and relentlessly competitive. Entertaining friends with parlor tricks and magic, he displayed "infectious energy and a boundless enthusiasm for physics." He earned his Ph.D. in 1936 at MIT.

He then joined Bell Telephone Laboratories, working first in Manhattan and then in Murray Hill. On leave to work for the military during WWII, he made major contributions to anti-submarine warfare.(37) He also authored an important paper on the massive casualties that would result from an invasion of Japan. Shockley's analysis helped persuade President Harry Truman that he should order that the atomic bomb be dropped on Japan in order to quickly end the war.

The Shockley family moved to Madison in 1941, but serious marital problems had already been brewing for some time. Shockley worked fiendishly and traveled a great deal but tried to carve out time for his family. Their children reported that their father, at times, became so enraged that he emotionally tormented them with periodic acts of corporal punishment.(38)

Despite his great emotional turmoil, his work at Bell Labs resulted in one of the greatest inventions of the 20th century. He led the team, including William Brattain and John Bardeen, that created the transistor, an invention that eliminated forever the need for vacuum tubes and opened up a world of speed and miniaturization that reaches into every corner of life today.

Serious dissension soon followed, as Shockley's role in the actual development was suspected by some, and his name was not on the early patents. (39) But Bell Labs insisted that the three scientists share in the discovery. Bardeen and Brattain soon became disenchanted with Shockley and their

Dr. William B. Shockley (center) and Bell Laboratories collaborators John Bardeen (left) and William Brattain (right) won the Nobel Prize for the invention of the transistor.

relationship became quite strained. In 1956, the three men shared the Nobel Prize for physics.

Shockley resigned from Bell Labs in 1955, and his descent appeared to accelerate. He accomplished little of significance and became exceedingly paranoid. He tape-recorded all contacts and calls, alienated most friends, and kept and cataloged all receipts, bills, tickets, and every imaginable record of his life. He started a company in California to make good on his transistor creation, but his employees mutinied because of his ceaseless distrust, quixotic decisions, bizarreness, criticisms, and insistence on taking polygraphs.

But the worst was yet to come. In about 1963, he proposed the "Dysgenics" theory and believed that "the long-term health of the human race was imperiled by the reproductive tendencies of the least intelligent members."(40) Utterly obsessed with genetics and race for the rest of his life, he advocated early on that only superior people should have authority and that a society with democratic decision-making was a liability. Specifically, he believed that certain minorities had lower intelligence, were genetically driven, evolving more slowly, and were largely irremediable. Voluntary sterilization of those less fit was one option he advocated. Frustrated with the lack of support from the broader scientific community, he insisted that cowardly researchers refused to illuminate these issues.

Universal and powerful condemnation obviously followed, and he became a hated pariah. Initially, a promising and brilliant scientist who helped change the world, William Shockley descended into an unrelenting force for bigotry and intolerance. Terminally ill with prostate cancer in 1989, Shockley declined requests to have his children informed of his impending death. They read about it in the *Washington Post*.

The "Quiet Decade"

Some writers have called the 1950s a "quiet decade," but such a view fails to consider how a 10-year period that included war, frequent fear of atomic attack, racial turmoil, and the politics of Senator Joseph McCarthy could be considered quiet. Perhaps it was due to the calm demeanor of President Dwight D. Eisenhower, for eight of those ten years. "Ike" held the confidence of a majority of American people throughout his two terms, and the fact that he inspired trust among people of both political parties did not overshadow his other great attribute of political astuteness.

Madison voters selected Eisenhower twice in the presidential contests of 1952 and 1956. In the latter year, the Eisenhower-Nixon ticket defeated that of Adlai Stevenson-Estes Kefauver by a margin of 5,174 to 1,136 in Madison.

Mayor Tom Taber
at the throttle.

The mid-decade mayor of Madison in 1956 was Thomas Townsend Taber from the Republican-dominated council, where he had served for seven years (1948-1955). He was something of a maverick in political circles, but in a single term, he left his mark on the community, particularly in his efforts to maintain adequate commuter transportation and parking. He was such an avid and knowledgeable railroad buff that he installed vintage signal towers (now with the Smithsonian Institution) at his home property on Hillcrest Road.

As an executive with New York Life Insurance Co., he commuted in the early days and once is said to have obtained permission from the railroad to stoke the steam engine during several daily trips. It was Taber who legislated for Madison's first Planning Board, and later, he served as its chairman from 1962-1967. In his annual mayoral messages, he promoted a law to fix minimum standards for housing, a uniform sidewalk policy, and expansion of borough sewage-pumping stations.

Thomas T. Taber, Jr.'s office at the western end of the railroad platform was a museum, a treasure trove of railroadiana. He often held open houses for passengers waiting for New York trains who shared his enthusiasm for rail transportation. This collection is now in the Railroad Museum at Strasburg, PA.

Preserving the Wetlands

As councilman, Taber spearheaded negotiations with Florham Park early in the 1950s to purchase 83 acres of land between Rosedale Avenue and Spring Garden Brook to protect the wetlands that supplied Madison's drinking water. Taber also wanted to save this splendid wooded sanctuary for wildlife and nature lovers. It was named Memorial Park to honor all those who had served or will serve their country in the Armed Forces.

Following this lead, Mayor William Nordling, in March 1966, created the Memorial Park Advisory Committee and appointed 12 members to devise a master plan for the park. These planners determined that a peripheral area would be zoned for recreation facilities but that the interior would be guarded as a wild and natural area. A rustic central shelter was built beside the skating rink. A wood chip trail, with footbridges to cross two brooks, linked the Rosedale area with the Delbarton Drive playground. Two Little League fields, the community pool, an ice rink, a dog park, and a soccer field remain as parts of the park. The park's interior, featuring a wooded picnic grove named for local nature artist R. Harmer Smith, maintains a natural, wild appearance.

In 1983, Mayor Elizabeth Baumgartner blended the Memorial Park Advisory Committee and the Green Acres Committee into one group called the Parks Advisory Committee, which still advises on the uses for all of Madison's parks.

The Picnic Oak, Memorial Park. R. Harmer Smith's soft-ground etching of the Picnic Oak, and his Woodchip Trail sketch for the cover of a Memorial Park brochure, are only two of his many artistic tributes to his beloved park and Madison. He delighted in the pleasure of picnickers under the spreading arms of the huge Swamp White Oak. By 1970, the oak had died, possibly from drought in the 1960s. As a cross-section of the tree could not be obtained, Sue Hubbard produced a dendrochronology. A portion of her painting (with abbreviated events related to each ring of the tree) appears here. The R. Harmer Smith Picnic Grove was dedicated in June 1981. The plaque, unveiled by his brother, Herbert Smith, is on the forward side of the shelter, gathering place and focal center of the park.

Madison's park system and school diamonds are put to good use by Little League teams and enthusiastic followers. After decades of fine teams and fierce competition, semipro baseball in the area finally declined mostly through lack of funding. For years, Mrs. Dodge supported local teams. 1966 leading hitters of each major league team: Kneeling (L-R) Joe Ubil, North Stars; Leon Orige, Rotary; David Chapin, Kiwanis; Standing: Bill Barry, Forum Club; MikeO'Connor, - Lions; Peter Livesey, Elks.

Soap Box Derbies of the 1940s, as this one on Maple Ave., preceded organized Little League baseball with dedicated supervision of adult volunteers.

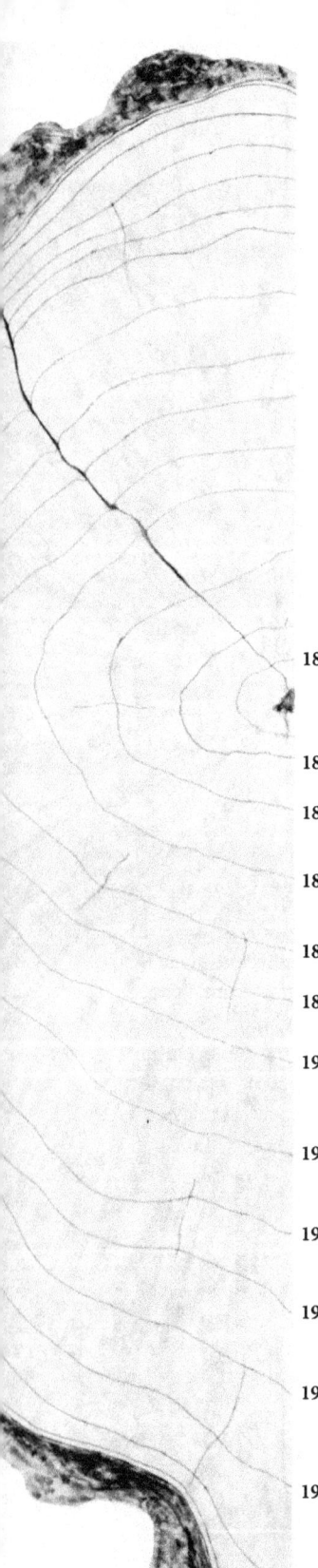

The Memorial Park:
Famous White Oak with Timeline

This swamp white oak lived through
14 decades of Madison's history

1834, Madison was chosen as the official name of the village previously known as Bottle Hill.

1835 — This seedling began to grow on farmland - now Memorial Park • 1837, Morris and Essex R.R. completed to Madison • 1841, Judge Francis S. Lathrop, 1st Commuter • 1842, Madison Iron Works • 1843, Methodist Episcopal Church organized.

1850 — Pop. approx. 600 • 120 houses, 6 stores • 1853, Union Church (later, A.M.E. Church), founded • 1854, Grace Episcopal Church org. • 1856, Seton Hall College founded • 1858, Prospect St.opened but beautiful white oak spared.

1860 — Local men volunteer for Mr. Lincoln's army • 1864 meeting held to raise money for 30 "Volunteers" for Civil War effort • 1867, Drew Theological Seminary founded.

1870 — Bethel A.M.E. Church • Rose Industry • 1871 Property for Niles Park purchased • 1873, YMCA founded in home of James A. Webb • 1st free public school library • 1879, Madison public school built, Green Ave.

1880 — 1881, Fire Dept. organized • Green Ave. School opened • 1882, Madison Eagle started • 1883, 1st telephone (for Dr. Calvin Anderson) • 1888, Great Blizzard • 1889, Madison, a borough - no longer part of Chat., Twp.

1890 — First Borough Council elected • Police Dept., Water and Light Depts. established. • 1891, public water system and electricity installed • 1893, telephone exchange re-established in Burnet bldg. • 1896, First Baptist Church Mission • Thursday Morning Club and Madison Golf Club • 1898, James Park, gift of Daniel Willis James to Madison Borough.

1900 — Pop. 3,756 • Public Library, gift of Mr. James • 1902, most disastrous flood - Spring Garden Brook washes out many burials in Hillside Cemetery • 1907, 1st permanent home, YMCA. • Automobile, a hazard.

1910 — Pop. 4,658 • 1912, 1st Motion picture theater • 1st Trolley car • 1914-1916, Elevation of R.R. tracks and new R.R. Station • 1917, U.S. enters World War I • 1918, Cole Park given to Madison • 1919 1st Girl Scout Troop.

1920 — Pop. 5,523 • 1922, Madison Garden Club • 1923, the newly formed Madison Historical Society moved Madison House from S.E. Cor. Waverly and Main to present site, for its Hdqtrs. changed its name to the Bottle Hill Tavern, a Museum and Tea Room • Rotary Club • Boy Scouts (6 Troops) • 1924, Madison Settlement House dedicated • 1927, Morris and Essex Kennel Club Dog Show at Giralda • Brothers College at Drew, 1928.

1930 — First electric train arrives in Madison. 1935, Hartley Dodge Memorial Building is dedicated.

1940 — Pop. 7,944 • U.S. enters World War II • United Campaign formed in Madison • 1945, World War II ends • 1947, Christmas blizzard • 1948, United Fund of Madison, Florham Park.

1950 — Pop. 10,412 • 1953, Memorial Park created by a borough ordinance (83 acres purchased) • 1954, Madison Volunteer Ambulance Corps organized • 1957, Last Morris and Essex Dog Show at Giralda • Fairleigh Dickinson opened their campus on the former Twombly estate, 1958.

1960 — Pop. 15,122 • Madison Baptist Church organized • 1964, civil rights debates • 1962 Madison Area YMCA • 1966, mayor appoints Advisory Comm. for Memorial Park • 1967, Madison Community Pool • Great Swamp declared a national wildlife refuge • 1969, new Madison Library.

1970 — 1971, Conservation Commission created (now known as Environmental Commission. Apply for "Green Acres" Funds for 26 Acre Park.

The Picnic Oak Dies

Portion of Painting by Sue Hubbard, Photo credit: George Goodwin

Challenging Tradition

Public disaffection with local Republican domination of the political arena often took divisive forms. Usually, the dissidents ran as "Republicans" but took on a slightly different title. For instance, in 1957, Rezin S. Plotz and Sam Gordon ran in the primary election for Madison Borough Council on an "Independent Republican" ticket. They were opposed by party regulars who were known by the usual "Organization Republican" monicker. Plotz and Gordon were pitted against World War II hero Robert Banta of Banta Motors and Paul B. Lee.

Former Mayor Alfred P. Smith, Jr., and Councilman Graham Macmillan endorsed Gordon and Plotz about a month before the April 16th primary.(41) Reminiscent of Thomas Taber's upset victory 10 years earlier, the dissident "Independent Republican" ticket defeated the party regulars in a hard-fought primary. Then, in the fall general election, Gordon and Plotz easily defeated their Democratic opposition. It seemed as though the most heated battles were within the Republican ranks in this one-party town.

Millie and Sam Gordon relaxing at a July 4th block dance on Waverly Place, 1952. Millie worked side by side with her husband for many years.

The statewide governor's race between Malcolm S. Forbes and incumbent Robert B. Meyner in 1957 incited little local interest. Democrat Meyner won handily but dropped the Madison vote to Forbes by a margin of 2,952 to 1,925. Democrats continued to have difficulty in gathering votes in Madison. In the race for mayor, Republican Earl J. Reddert ran unopposed and received 3,358 votes to a single write-in vote for Charles E. Howell.

Despite these impressive election victories, squabbling continued within the Republican ranks. Politics even caused disagreement over logistics for the 1957 annual arrival of Santa Claus in Madison. After extensive discussions, the Republicans finally agreed on the details, and the *Eagle* proclaimed: "Santa to preside at his usual spot: Two groups agree."(42)

Color television also arrived on the scene in time for holiday shoppers. Local merchant Sam Gordon sold the amazing new product to customers in his appliance store and, in an act of public spirit, offered to lend a 21-inch color television to any civic group requesting it.

Gordon's career is a remarkable success story. Starting business in 1941 with the 50-year-old "mom-and-pop" grocery store of Joseph "Uncle Luke" Pierson on Central Avenue, the personable Jewish merchant with a keen sense of flamboyant promotion

"Home Office" • Sam's appliance supermarket on Central Avenue, prior to its opening. It is now a Post Office branch office.

and a sincere regard for the consumer expanded his enterprise into a supermarket and later into a million-dollar chain of appliance stores. Earlier, he helped establish the Madison Chamber of Commerce. The civic-minded Gordon served as a Republican borough councilman and as a member of the local Zoning Board. He also was Rotary Club president.

Rare Talents

Madison had an ample supply of citizens who were achieving so well that they developed national reputations in their fields. One such man was Dr. Emil Schlittler of Green Avenue, a researcher for CIBA Pharmaceutical Corporation of Summit. The Swiss-born Schlittler was best known as the co-discoverer of the tranquilizer Reserpine, a derivative of the Indian snake-root plant.

Similarly, Drew Dean Lynn Harold Hough received many accolades as a speaker and writer. In February 1956, Hough was honored by a London publication as a "brilliant intellect" who was able to deal with problems on "both sides of the Atlantic with equal facility—his mind knows no frontiers."(43)

Madison's distinguished inventor Ralph E. Hersey filed 40 telephone patents during a long career with Bell Telephone Laboratories. His most famous invention was the switching system, which led to direct long-distance dialing. During World War II, Hersey worked on developing ways to protect the telephone system from foreign sabotage.(44)

The twin attractions of greater industry in the suburbs and the location of Drew University in Madison combined to provide a steady stream of scientific, intellectual, and executive talent to the community. Madisonians continued to measure their political and civic leaders by a yardstick that represented high standards of performance.

Community Services Expand

The rapid expansion of the borough during the postwar era brought a desire for greater community services and activities. A group of talented musicians and patrons organized the Colonial Little Symphony (later simply the Colonial Symphony) in 1950,(45) a professional orchestra of 45 members. Season concerts at Madison Junior School featured international guest artists and attracted about 1,000 regular subscribers in the mid-1980s. The orchestra also offered children's concerts on Saturday mornings and in-school music education programs to Madison students at no cost.

Unfortunately, the orchestra entered the 2000s with a declining audience and charitable donations. (Ticket sales covered less than 1/3 of its annual budget.) With the financial crisis of the Great Recession of 2008-2009, contributions from individuals, foundations, corporations, and the New Jersey State Council on the Arts had fallen to the point that the orchestra could no longer balance its budget. And so, after 60 years of bringing quality, award-winning orchestral music to the community, President Robert J. McCoy announced that "the Board of Trustees must act on the knowledge that all reasonable forecasts for the coming season make debt accumulation unavoidable. Therefore, the final curtain must fall."(46)

As the community grew, so did its need for emergency medical services. A major step in

Adele and Joe Corbett, shown here in 1976. In 1954, Adele, then head of Madison-Chatham Red Cross Motor Corps, stressed the need for a separate emergency service. The Corbetts worked tirelessly rallying public-spirited citizens, funds and equipment. The Madison Volunteer Ambulance Corps was formed, and for the price of $1.00, Dr. Robert Schultz, chairman of the Red Cross Chapter, turned over the 1949 Packard ambulance to the new Corps and its president, Joe Corbett. By 1984, over 21,000 calls were answered!

providing them for local citizens was taken in 1954 with the creation of the Madison Volunteer Ambulance Corps. Pivotal in the founding of the corps were Mr. and Mrs. Joseph B. Corbett. Corbett, son of the famed local builder, Sam Gordon, editor John Ehrhardt, and Nona Wiman assembled the necessary equipment. Corbett also served as the first president of the corps. The need immediately became evident. By January 1956, the Ambulance Corps announced that it had just answered its 500th call in less than 18 months of operation. A year later, the corps answered its 1,000th call. In a short period of time, the corps performed an indispensable function for the community.

Early Motor Corps. The Red Cross answered many needs of a growing community.

Prior to the Ambulance Corps, this emergency service was provided by the Madison-Chatham Red Cross Motor Corps. In May 1942, they planned an auction of antiques in James Hall to raise funds for an ambulance to replace their hand-me-down station wagon. On the day of the auction, customers were deterred by a torrential downpour combined with the start of wartime gasoline rationing. The large stock of unsold goods, housed in a Waverly Place store, was constantly augmented by new acquisitions until it became a thrift shop.

So successful was this enterprise that in August 1944, the Motor Corps ladies, whose prime movers were Mrs. Charles Baiter, Mrs. Frank Cusack, and Mrs. J. David Hayes, were able to present an ambulance to the Red Cross chapter, plus $1,000 for maintenance. A new station wagon for ambulatory patients soon followed, then a sedan for the Red Cross staff and administration.

At this time, the founding group withdrew as Red Cross workers and instead incorporated as the "Independent Thrift Shop." A store was then rented at 14 Central Avenue and soon operat-

By 1961, the MVAC needed a headquarters of its own to maintain its outstanding record of community service.

Sketch of proposed headquarters on land given by Mrs. Dodge. Ground was broken in 1962; the building, constructed with 95 percent volunteer labor, was dedicated in May 1963. The Ladies Auxiliary was organized in January 1963 by Mrs. Nona Wiman, who was very active in both the Red Cross and the Corps, and Miss Eleanor Van De Water; Mrs. John Francis served as president.

A call for roofers! Many responded and in less than 24 hours the building was roofed over. Dominic Gareffa, foreground.

ed by volunteers. The Thrift Shop is still doing business today at its current location on Kings Road. The sale of "useful articles at bargain prices"(47) still helps support a long list of local and national charities.

Other community organizations were also active throughout the 1950s. Madison tended to have an organization for every purpose and most were for a good cause, one which would benefit the community. This was another demonstration of the community's exceptional emphasis on civic improvements. In addition, the organizations brought a variety of guest speakers to town. Charles A. Philhower, a well-known authority on the Lenape Indians, spoke to the Nature Club. The daughter of Trygve Lie, the United Nations leader, spoke on being a "Diplomat's Daughter." Guri Lie addressed an afternoon meeting of the Thursday Morning Club at the Settlement House, now the Community House. That same organization also heard John T. Cunningham, a highly respected New Jersey scholar and newspaper writer, lecture on "The Spirit of Jersey." It was becoming very apparent that community organizations were assuming the role played by Chautauqua many years earlier by providing speakers to inspire and excite intellectual curiosity.

Great Swamp Battle: A Hero Emerges: Marcellus Hartley Dodge

On November 3, 1959, the Port Authority of New York and New Jersey, led by Austin Tobin, announced plans to build a ten thousand acre jetport in Morris County's Great Swamp, only a few miles from Madison. The cost was projected to be 220 million dollars. Opposition to the project mounted quickly and led to a meeting in Madison of local and area residents who opposed the planned airport. The citizens had a critical ally from the start of their campaign in Congressman Peter Frelinghuysen, who fought the plan with skill and tenacity. Thanks to his support, the New Jersey Senate voted to oppose the plan. However, Tobin and Port Authority board tenaciously held to their plans for the jetport, even claiming they had a legal right to do so. In reality, the claim was not completely accurate in that the Great Swamp was not in their designated land area under their authority. However, they correctly countered that they could always condemn the private property that was the heart of the swamp.

In a time when there was only a small, but growing, environmental movement in New Jersey and the nation, a debate over the future of the Great Swamp became even more heated as the Port Authority made it clear that it would condemn the swamp area if necessary. New Jersey Governor Robert Meyner, an acknowledged friend of Port Authority Chairman Tobin, refused to take a public stand on the issue by insisting that it needed more study. It was clear to many that the issue would not be resolved easily. Then, in the words of Dodge's godson, Nicolas Platt, someone with the "passion and money" stepped forward with a remarkable plan to save the Great Swamp from destruction. That someone was Geraldine Dodge's husband Marcellus Hartley Dodge. Recognizing that the Port Authority could not confiscate public land, he led a tireless effort to secure private donations of swamp land to the federal government to make its federal preserve. Also playing a key role in the effort was his twenty-nine-year-old attorney George Aguilar. Dodge then set an example by donating his large land holdings there while convincing other landowners to do the same. Fortunately, the federal Department of the Interior was led there by President John F. Kennedy's Secretary of the Interior Stuart Udall, an ardent conservationist, now recognized by many as one of the most effective Interior secretaries of the 20th century.

Mr. Dodge's brilliantly conceived plan worked. The success of that effort was greatly enhanced by the many talented and energetic leaders in the public campaign to "Save the Swamp." (See Cam Cavanaugh: *Saving the Great Swamp.*)(48) Key among these leaders was Helen Fenske, a dynamic organizer who was also the first to suggest that the area be a natural preserve. She became one of the Great Swamp's most ardent defenders.

Interestingly, the often unheralded marriage partner of Mrs. Dodge was an intriguing figure in his own right. He mirrored in his beliefs much of the same love of animals that Mrs. Dodge was, and still is, so known for. This, at first, seems incongruous as he was known as a wildlife hunter. And as the Chairman of the board for Remington Arms Company, which he inherited from his father, of course, produced a great number of weapons for hunting as well as used by the military. At a closer glance, this makes no sense, but Nicolas Platt offers the explanation that his godfather told him that while hunting, he always "shot to miss" the animal.

The photograph here of Mr. Dodge feeding a deer seems to support this view of his true feelings about animals. Indeed his successful efforts to save the Great Swamp is also an act that saved the habitat of thousands of animals. For that alone, the people of Madison, its surrounding communities, and the state owe a special debt of gratitude to this remarkable man.

Looking Ahead

As the postwar period approached in 1959, Madison was a quickly growing community. Most of its remaining large parcels of land were developed into residential housing neighborhoods. The 1950 population of 10,417 climbed to 15,122 by 1960. Nationally, a new era appeared ready to dawn with the election of 43-year-old John Kennedy as President. For Madison, the postwar years were a time of growth and optimism. Who could envision the political traumas the next decade would bring to Madison and to America?

CHAPTER THIRTEEN

Generations Clash in Turbulent Sixties

America in the 1960s, perhaps more than ever, was a land of extremes. For many, it was a time of prosperity: most citizens were generally better off financially and certainly better educated than ever before. Yet, the sixties were also years of dissatisfaction and turmoil as civil-rights protests and opposition to the Vietnam War flared across the nation. Thousands of deeply patriotic Americans voiced concern over the responsiveness of their government and the fairness of their society. It was a decade in which issues were sharply drawn, and passivity on the part of most of the public was not possible. For better or for worse, these would be some of the most volatile times in the nation's history—and in Madison's, for the town was an active witness to the events that shaped this momentous period.

How could it have happened in a "quiet," fashionable, integrated, affluent suburb like Madison, New Jersey?

Death of a President

The first three years of the decade seemed to be a continuation of the stability and prosperity of the 1950s. Few could imagine what would follow when, in November 1963, President John F. Kennedy was assassinated while traveling by motorcade in Dallas, Texas. Madison residents and Americans everywhere could not believe the news of the shooting of the popular President.

Motorists along Main Street tuned in car radios to hear details of the shocking events in Dallas. Some motorists called out to Patrolman Richard French, on duty directing traffic, to tell him of the president's condition. When news of the tragedy was broadcast over the high school public announcement system, several teachers and students immediately broke into tears. According to the *Eagle,* school-crossing guards "said that many of the young children were crying as they rushed to their homes."(1)

Mayor Earl J. Reddert ordered all borough flags flown at half-mast. Public events were canceled, and many businesses closed—as Madison and the nation watched television coverage of the assassination. In characteristic fashion, the *Eagle* editor probed the significance of the shooting and of violence in America in a page one editorial: "Public apathy is the disguised villain who aims the bullet."(2) The newspaper then criticized indifference to human misery as a major cause of social unrest.

Local residents had barely recovered from the shock of the events in Dallas when, on Christmas Day, in 1963, they heard of the death of Marcellus Hartley Dodge. The usual joy of the holiday was mixed with sorrow for those Madisonians who knew Mr. Dodge and for the many who understood his love for the community.

As *Eagle* editor Haynes described this special man in a January 1964 editorial: "His true worth did not stem from his vast fortune. His real distinction came from the fact that he possessed a great heart."(3) Mr. Dodge often remained in the background in the philanthropic endeavors of his wife. His contributions to the welfare of the area, though, were extensive in the field of conservation. He was instrumental in convincing the National Wildlife Federation that the Great Swamp should be preserved as a permanent refuge; 1,000 acres of that unspoiled land was named in his memory. During the last six years of his life he made four gifts of land to the Morris County Park Commission. Mr. Dodge was a board member of the D.L.&W. RR; director of Equitable Life Assurance Society, International Committee of YWCA and Hartley House and a Columbia University trustee for 50 years.

Marcellus Hartley Dodge

After the death of her husband, Mrs. Dodge continued to live in her gabled mansion at Giralda. Although well cared for by her staff, Mrs. Dodge's health steadily deteriorated. Months before her husband's death, Mrs. Dodge had been declared incompetent to handle her own affairs. David H. McAlpin, a friend of the Dodge's, recalled years later that Mrs. Dodge was taken for a ride each day past her late husband's house. McAlpin wrote: "I am told that after his death," she remarked, "There's no use going that way. He's not there anymore.'" Tragically, Mrs. Dodge's condition worsened until she became almost totally noncommunicative. McAlpin recalled visiting her when her doctor was present. To attempt to get her attention, the doctor "flashed an electric torch" in her eyes. Mrs. Dodge continued to stare into the distance and showed no "sign that we were at her bedside."(4)

Martin Luther King, Jr.

While the Dodges represented the best traditions of the old noblesse oblige among the wealthy, societal change was occurring rapidly. The national civil rights movement was emerging as a powerful force, and in 1964, it touched Madison in a significant way when the soon-to-be-called "Barbershop Controversy" erupted. Although the local struggle started over the issue of equal access of all races to a barbershop, the conflict was, in fact, a part of the much larger national effort of Blacks to secure equal rights. That struggle had a dramatic start in Madison when, on February 5,1964, the noted civil rights leader Dr. Martin Luther King, Jr. visited Drew University.

An *Eagle* headline proclaimed, "5,000 Listeners Share in Dr. King's American Dream." Called by the newspaper the "best attended cultural event in the area's history," the lecture of Dr. King at Drew's Baldwin Gymnasium caused quite a stir.(5) King urged his enthusiastic listeners representing college students, townspeople, and outsiders—to strive to overcome inequality in American life. King spoke for nearly one hour to the packed house and to those who, unable to gain admission, listened to the speech by way of loudspeakers placed in other rooms and on the lawn outside.

King was one of the most inspiring speakers of his time. With a dramatic delivery, he declared to the crowd that, "I am proud to be maladjusted to segregation and discrimination. There is a great need for creative maladjustment." Inside the gymnasium, King received a tumultuous welcome, but outside the building, a few protestors put right-wing literature under windshield

Dr. Martin Luther King, Jr., with Dr. George Kelsey, Drew
University President Dr. Robert Oxnam, and Mrs. Kelsey.

wipers of parked automobiles. The literature branded King as a Communist.

Future Madison Mayor Gary Ruckelshaus was in the audience that night. He remembered it this way: "I was in the gym that night to hear Dr. King, and one thing that always stuck with me was his ability to speak without notes for more than an hour and captivate an excited and sometimes boisterous crowd. It was inspiring and thrilling."(6) As Thomas P. Sellers, Jr., a major figure in subsequent Madison civil rights activities, also recalled later: "I was in awe of his ability to speak and to move people."(7) The *Eagle* reporter who covered the event was also impressed by King's "quiet but forceful style." Few at the time knew just how persuasive King had been on that crisp winter's night. By the advent of spring, they would find out.

Dr. George Kelsey: Madison's Master Theologian And Teacher

"Racism is so diffused in the atmosphere that those who sincerely will to be healthy are obliged to breathe in a poisonous environment."
– Dr. George Kelsey, 1965(8)

What do Martin Luther King, Jr., Christian Existentialist theologian Paul Tillich, Protestant Reformed theologians H. Richard, Reinhold Niebuhr, and Baptist educator and civil rights leader Benjamin E. Mays have in common? These theological and civil rights luminaries were all, at various times, in the orbit of Dr. George D. Kelsey, professor of Christian Ethics in the theological and graduate schools of Drew University from 1951 to 1976.(9)

Born in 1910 in Columbus, Georgia, he was the valedictorian of his all-Black Cabin Creek High School class. Many years later, he deplored this racist system in which "The poorest segments of the population had to attend private schools which…they had to build and maintain."(10) In 1946, he earned his Ph.D. from Yale University.

Teaching at Morehouse College, Kelsey gave a young sociology student attending one of his Bible classes the only "A" grade the student received during his Morehouse years. Kelsey saw something exceptional in him. The student wanted to become a doctor or lawyer. Yet, Kelsey and Morehouse President Benjamin Mays helped persuade the young Martin Luther King, Jr. that the ministry would allow him to synthesize his burgeoning socio-political views with Kelsey's social gospel approach and the great truths from the Bible. He saw that King "stood out in class not simply academically, but in the sense that he absorbed Jesus' teachings with his whole being." King never forgot Kelsey's life-altering mentorship.

Less than a decade later, during the Montgomery Bus Boycott, Kelsey wrote to King, "Congratulations on the great leadership which you are providing to our deprived people in Montgomery. I have always been proud of you as one of my students and as a friend. You surely can imagine my present feelings." In King's letter accompanying his draft manuscript on the Montgomery Boycott, he beseeched Kelsey for guidance. He took his advice to "stress Christianity as the motivating force behind the Montgomery protest," adopting a sentence Kelsey wrote in the margins: "Christ furnished the spirit and motivation, while Gandhi furnished the method."(11)

Following a guest lecture and leading a seminar course at Drew University in 1950, George Kelsey was invited to join the faculty as an associate professor of Christian Ethics.

In his youth and young adulthood in the South, and even after being hired by Drew University, Kelsey knew the humiliating experience of discrimination and labeled it as apartheid. In preparation for his move to Madison, and before meeting the realtor, a list of highly desirable homes was suggested that he was sure to love. However, when meeting the realtor, whose mouth must have dropped to the floor upon seeing the new clients, the couple was immediately steered to a different and more "compatible section" of Madison.(12)

He certainly had this episode on his mind in a lecture to the United Methodist Church in Madison when he said, "The six-figure black…when he wishes to buy the home of his choice in the suburbs knows that racism is alive in America."(13) The Kelseys lived at 5 Cedar St. in Madison until their deaths.

In 1979, George Kelsey was honored by delivering the convening prayer at the 96th Congress of the U.S. Senate. He died at the King James Care Center in Chatham Township (now Chatham Hills Subacute Care Center) on April 3, 1995.(14)

Barbershop Beginnings

On a warm April day in 1964, Tom Sellers stood on the sidewalk across the street from a small barbershop in Madison. He knew what he had to do; there was no turning back. As a man, as a Black, as a husband and father, as an American, Sellers felt he had to muster the courage to cross that street and enter.

The barbershop, which looked so small in the afternoon sun, took on more importance the longer Sellers looked at it. The place was Italian-owned, like five of the town's six other barbershops. For a fee of $1.75, the barber would gladly cut someone's hair—if that someone were white and had "normal" hair. The knowledge was an insult to Sellers, who made a good living for himself and his family as an interior decorator. What was it he had heard that Dr. King had said 10 weeks earlier? He said: "Nonviolent protest will require dedication if it is to succeed!" It was time for someone to take a stand in Madison, create controversy, and show that even the Rose City could not be exempt from a call for justice.

A year earlier, Sellers remembered that the *Eagle* reported that some Blacks were unable to secure haircuts in local barbershops. Sellers remembered this account as he walked to the barbershop, opened the door and received the stare he knew was coming. When the barber told him he would not cut his hair because he did not know how, Sellers marched through the door and across the street once again. This time, he was full of determination. He knew he had to be ready to do what he felt was necessary: report to his supporters, be asked for comments by newspaper reporters, file a formal complaint with the State Division of Civil Rights, and escort his wife to a dramatic civil-rights vigil outside the White House. Later, even his teenage son Tommy would become involved in the controversy.(15)

For Sellers, the aftermath of the incident was a hard time indeed. Few persons agreed with his contention that he was simply in need of a haircut that day. He received threats by telephone and mail. There were demonstrations of support, too, from churches and groups local and afar. The aspect that seemed to bother some Madison residents the most, however, was the vocal support coming from Drew University.

Borough Council: Hands Off

Owners of the barbershops were not alone in resisting suggested changes in haircutting policy, although it was the barber, through his trade association, who fought the rights issue by hiring lawyers. Customers tried to shout down a group of protesters and became angry when four men demanded haircuts. Donations were made to a special legal expenses fund set up by the beleaguered barbers.

To the dismay of Sellers and his supporters, the Morris County Prosecutor's Office commended the Madison police for "restraint" in handling crowds and picket lines. An attempt to step up the controversy fizzled when two Africans from Drew's student body were denied haircuts with the explanation that they had arrived too near closing time. To the press, the barbers pointed out that they were not meant to be part of the state's Public Accommodations Law and that they had the experience and knowledge to cut the hair of whites only.

Members of the borough council put the matter to a vote when it drafted a resolution underscoring the need for impartiality and noninvolvement. It was approved, and Mayor Earl Reddert said he was in agreement.(16) Other local statements also provoked the ire of the protesters. The Rev. Lawrence Callaghan, pastor of St. Vincent's Church, said university students "know nothing of the past relations of our colored and white people"(17) and that there had been true racial harmony through the years. The comment was no doubt made sincerely but must have sounded incongruous in light of recent events.

Pickets and Placards

Throughout 1964, the barbershop controversy was chronicled in the *Madison Eagle*, the *Morris County Daily Record*, the statewide *Newark Evening News* (now defunct) and the *New York Times*. Legal ramifications were obvious; related causes were inextricably linked.

"Students to Picket 5 Madison Barbers," exclaimed a headline on May 5 in the *Newark Evening News*, which detailed how undergraduates were about to set up picket lines and man them. Students at Upsala College in nearby East Orange demonstrated outside two barber shops near their campus for the same reason. A group in Madison, meanwhile, called itself "Barbers Association for the Protection of Civil Rights" and announced that it reserved the right to serve whomever it wished.

Ironically, and unknown by most people, the Dalena barber shop had been quietly cutting the hair of Black students for years, always after the shop was closed and with the shades down. A person from Drew University had requested that John Dalena accommodate the students since they were unable to obtain haircuts elsewhere in town. As recounted by his son John years later during a Zoom call, his father was a quiet and welcoming man performing a courageous act. Yet, despite concerns about repercussions from some people in town and other barbers if they knew, he persisted. And so, his father was surprised when his shop was picketed.(18)

Bonnie Barrow, teacher and homemaker, won state recognition for her civil-rights column in the *Madison Eagle.*

The picketing of Madison barbers continued in May when such groups as the Madison-Florham Park Human Relations Council and the Civil Rights Action Committee of Madison both voted to be active participants. Placards included messages such as: "This is Madison, Mississippi?" and "Race Has No Place in American Life or Law, Said President John F. Kennedy." Former Mayor Gary Ruckelshaus, in a 2023 personal interview, remembered seeing at least one news van from (New York) Channel 2 News covering the picketing.

CITIZENS OF MADISON SUPPORT
OPEN BARBERSHOPS

ON MAY 5, 1964, THE MINISTERS OF MADISON AND FLORHAM PARK CALLED A CONFERENCE OF THOSE CONCERNED OVER RACIAL DISCRIMINATION IN CERTAIN BARBER SHOPS. THE CONFERENCE VOTED OVERWHELMINGLY TO SUPPORT THOSE SHOPS WHICH DO NOT DISCRIMINATE BECAUSE OF RACE. THE CONFERENCE WAS COMPOSED OF CONCERNED CITIZENS OF MADISON AND FLORHAM PARK AND REPRESENTATIVES OF THE FOLLOWING ORGANIZATIONS:

THE HUMAN RELATIONS COUNCIL OF MADISON AND FLORHAM PARK, THE MADISON AREA MINISTERIAL ASSOCIATION, THE CIVIL RIGHTS ACTION COMMITTEE OF MADISON AND THE MORRIS COUNTY NAACP.

(Citizens of Madison Support....)
Photo citation: *Madison Eagle,*
May 14, 1964.

As the controversy dragged on, the Madison Chamber of Commerce issued a statement on May 12 that was hardly calculated to please the civil rights demonstrators. It announced that "small businesses should have the right to determine whether or not they will practice discrimination."(19) A week later, the Chamber's president, James Baumgartner, backed off from its previous position, stating: "The Chamber of Commerce does NOT believe that racial discrimination should be practiced by *any* business in Madison."(20)

At the same time, some barbers were calling for strong action by Drew President Dr. Robert F. Oxnam to stop the picketing by university students. Acting in the age-old tradition of academic freedom, Oxnam replied that "I would strongly oppose measures to restrict the freedom of a faculty member or a student to express his own belief, or to witness as his conscience calls."(21) In response to charges that nonresident students should stay out of local affairs, Oxnam replied: "This is their country and what happens or does not happen here does affect them."

The controversy took on the proportions of a crisis on May 13 when the Rev. James Sessions, a Drew chaplain, and three Drew students were arrested on disorderly persons charges. They had attempted to get a haircut at Dalena's Barber Shop located on Park Avenue and were each held on $50 bail for trial. Hundreds of onlookers milled about in front of the barbershop at the time of the incident. Some customers began yelling, "Throw them out!" when the four men appeared. One letter to the editor in the *Madison Eagle* of May 14 summarized the situation well. In part, the writer said, "The longer the delay in this dispute, the more ill will is bound to grow, so perhaps it is now time to consider the possible dire consequences. No Madison citizen wants a seething Madison."(22)

Through these early days of crisis in the community, Kenneth Haynes, editor and publisher of the *Madison Eagle*, took a leadership role in attempting to air the issues in the best tradition of journalism. As a public service, a page in the May 14 issue of the *Eagle* was devoted to statements, both pro and con, regarding the situation.

Bombs and Firecrackers

In an apparently connected incident, there was a bomb scare, causing the Drew University administration building to be evacuated by local police, who later reported that they found no explosives. Pickets, meanwhile, continued to patrol in front of the Dalena barbershop, but now they were being increasingly met by counterpickets, many of whom were students from Fairleigh Dickinson University's campus. Police spent part of the afternoon dispersing small crowds in James Park who were arguing the issue.

The Human Relations Council met that evening to discuss ways of relieving tension. While council members were meeting, firecrackers were set off in six of their cars parked outside the building. None of the cars were extensively damaged. Moving quickly because of the strained atmosphere, the state Division on Civil Rights (DCR) announced it had found probable cause to support the charge of Thomas Sellers of racial discrimination in the initial incident. George S. Pfaus of that state agency asked Madison residents to remain calm while the "due process of law" was followed. Despite such requests, the situation continued to deteriorate. On May 15, a bomb scare emptied Central Avenue School, and on May 16, the Morris County Chapter of the NAACP urged the county prosecutor to restrain the actions of the Madison Police Department for allegedly aiding the barbers.(23) Less than 24 hours earlier, the police guarded barbers while two Blacks were refused haircuts. Across the street in James Park, demonstrators sang the hymn of the civil rights movement, "We Shall Overcome."(24) It was clear to many people from other communities that the issues being tested in Madison stemmed from broad, national concerns. More than local tradition was being tested here, and the eyes of the nation continued to watch for the outcome.

Twelve members of the NAACP were refused haircuts on May 16. At the same time, one local barber said he would no longer cut the hair of any Drew students because they were "fomenting trouble."

Bethel A.M.E. Church held a meeting on June 28 regarding the barbershop controversy. In a typewritten flier distributed earlier, the church leadership said: "You may never want to enter a 'white barbershop,' but you do want to be considered a human being." The flier asked the question: "Why must every Negro in Madison join the fight to open all barbershops?" Four answers were then posed as reasons why all Blacks should join the fight.

In its newsletter of August 1964, the Morris County Fair Housing Council ran a short description of the picketing titled "Dateline Madison." It read in part:

> At first one may fear picketing: it is a new and strange experience for many . . . and one originating from a lonely decision (as true decisions necessarily are). No one can picket for you. In the long run no one can mold a better world and hand it to you. One has to participate in some way to feel a part of the struggle for a better world.(25)

One handbill distributed to people at the time of the picketing was titled: "Now Your Town

Can Have a Professional Riot—No More Amateur Demonstrations."(26) The satirical document claimed to offer the services of professional demonstrators for any cause: "Everybody's Fighting Something...Why Aren't You?" Services offered—with tongue in cheek—included chants designed for any occasion, extra sheriffs' badges, trained cats "to decoy police dogs," and banner painters who "can misspell anything." Picketing continued on a weekly basis through the summer of 1964.

Civil-Rights Seesaw

The New Jersey Board of Barber Examiners notified the state's 11,000 barbers on August 5 that they were required to serve anyone who sought a haircut—regardless of race. The board threatened to revoke the license of any barber who refused "to cut or shave the hair of non-white persons on the ground that he does not know how to do so."

Undaunted by the board's decision, the Barbers Association greatly expanded its membership during the waning days of summer while awaiting a decision on the Sellers complaint from the State Division of Civil Rights. Membership in the association grew to 2,500 barbers representing more than 1,000 New Jersey barber shops. Members held a mass rally on August 26 at the Berkeley-Carteret Hotel in Elizabeth to show their support for the legal effort started by Madison barbers. They also planned a campaign to pressure the State Board of Barber Examiners to reverse its recent decision.(27)

Dr. George Lassiter, chairman of the Concerned Citizens of Madison, called the decision by the Barbers Board "most welcome at a time when confusion is surpassed only by frustration." Lassiter saw the national as well as local significance of this action when he also commented that "the announcement by the State has the effect of assuring members of the Negro community that the law is colorblind."

September 1964 was not as difficult as the barbers expected. Picketing remained infrequent as the activists seemed to be waiting for a decision from the State Civil Rights Division. John Greco, a 20-year-old spokesman for the Civil Rights Action Committee, indicated in an article in the *Morris County Daily Record* that his group was satisfied that the long-awaited Civil Rights Division decision would vindicate the actions taken against the barbers.

Roses Do Have Thorns! "Our thin line of civilized living and culture is based on due process of law. If due process is violated, we defeat none but ourselves." – Theodore N. Turner

Illustration citation: *Madison Eagle*, May 21, 1964.

Although unheralded, key public citizens also labored mightily to settle the controversy through peaceful discussions. Since the mayor and council provided very little guidance in the controversy, the *Madison Eagle* proved to be the key vehicle in shaping public opinion. This was increasingly the case in the fall of 1964 as editor Haynes continued his journalistic mission. This editor, who frequently wore a bow tie, proved indispensable to the community during the crisis. Haynes forced the reading public to deal with the real questions behind the tension and bravado. As a result, the community was better able to understand the complex maze of legal and moral issues.

An End to Picketing

By October 20, both the Civil Rights Action Committee (CRAC) of Drew University and the Concerned Citizens of Madison agreed to cease the picketing of local barbershops until a ruling was received from the state DCR. In a statement distributed to its members, CRAC expressed "our hope that the local barbershop problem can be solved peaceably through the legal channels of the State government, but this need not diminish our active concern." The committee still recommended that its followers patronize only the two local barber shops willing to serve nonwhites: Modern Barbershop and Fritz's Barbershop. To emphasize its continuing commitment, CRAC held a meeting on October 28 at the University Center to discuss future plans and to see a film taken of the arrests of Sessions, the Drew chaplain, and the three students on May 13.

Madison barbers received a setback in November. Their request for an investigation of the State Board of Barber Examiners was denied by the Office of the New Jersey Attorney General. Toward the end of the month, one barber, previously intransigent on the issue, announced that he had given a Black man a haircut. The logjam of inflexible positions was beginning to break.

Then, on December 16, 1964, the long-awaited decision from the DCR was received, ruling that barbershop discrimination against Blacks must end.(28) Although the decision specifically answered a complaint against a Madison barber, DCR Director George S. Pfaus said, "Its intent applies to every barbershop practicing discrimination."

Despite the clear-cut ruling, some Madison barbers still refused to allow nonwhites to receive haircuts in their shops. Their spokesman claimed that they would appeal the decision through the courts, and one barber said he would close rather than obey the ruling.

Reginald Barrow of Florham Park, a party to one of the original complaints filed with the Division of Civil Rights, attempted to test the ruling by showing up for a haircut from the same barber who refused him months earlier. The barber again refused with the statement that "he has many barber shops which he can patronize but it seems that I am his favorite barber." It was subsequently learned that the barber had cut Barrow's hair seven years earlier while employed at another local shop.

As the legal imbroglio continued throughout December 1964, John P. Ramos of Madison penned a letter to the editor of the *Madison Eagle*. To Ramos, "People all over the world may be asking, 'What is Madison, New Jersey like?' Also, local citizens may ask the same question. The answer is not clear." Through his question, Ramos touched a sensitive nerve for Madison residents. Later in his letter, he cut beneath the legal tangle to state that "surely some quiet, white citizens are humiliated when Madison's worldwide voice is saying 'No . . . because you are not white like me'?"(29)

The cool weather of January 1965 seemed to put a damper on the street action. The only slight spark to break the sudden quiet was when the local Barbers Association announced that the price of haircuts was going up to $2.00 effective February 15, 1965. A barber spokesman said the rate increase was due to cost-of-living factors and because of the civil-rights litigation. Some people objected to the extra cost of a haircut to fund litigation aimed at defying the decision of the Civil Rights Commission. To the Rev. Robert Goodwin, pastor of Madison Methodist Church, "The continuing practice of some of the shops is detrimental to the life of our community. Rather than creating a oneness among our citizens, it is breaking the community into segments, standing man against man, neighbor against neighbor; it is divisive and destructive."

A Civil Rights March

The Madison barbershop controversy was not the only focus for civil rights activists. With the civil rights struggle heating up in the South, Dr. George Lassiter of the Morris County Fair Housing Council charged county realtors with "ducking their responsibility" to provide fair housing opportunities for Blacks. In pointing to a natural preoccupation of easterners with the civil rights struggle in the South, Lassiter asked, "What good is it to be concerned with discrimination in Alabama if we are not able to tackle it here?"

On a chilly afternoon on March 14, 1965, approximately 400 marchers paraded from Central Avenue School to the steps of Hartley Dodge Memorial. An additional 250 demonstrators walked from Morristown Green to Madison, giving added support. As this banner-bedecked contingent came within sight of the borough hall, a great cheer arose from those already waiting there. According to a *Madison Eagle* report: "The emotional impact was so great that many spectators wept." (30) Among those walking from Morristown were Mayor E. Marco Stirone and about 35 nuns from the College of Saint Elizabeth (now University) led by Sister Hildegarde Marie, President. The Master of ceremonies for the rally was the Rev. Theodore Goyins, pastor of Bethel A.M.E. Church. Speakers included Father Paul Knauer of St. Vincent's Parish and the Rev. Robert Goodwin. As Ken Haynes, the *Eagle* editor, phrased it, the march to the Dodge Memorial "was a big step in a town where the public, as shortly ago as last summer, had been more upset over the disturbed quiet on their Main Street than they were over the issues raised between the barbers and their Negro neighbors, who wanted equal rights in the barber's chair."(31)

A program of songs and speeches prevailed at this dramatic demonstration in a community previously wracked by ugly disagreement.

Vietnam Protest

In the fall of 1965, another local controversy pushed the barbershop issue out of the headlines for a few months. On September 30, Drew political science instructor James Mellen spoke at a Rutgers University *teach-in* organized to protest the Vietnam War. Objections to the conflict were gaining momentum in 1965, and the nation was bitterly divided over the proper course of action. Mellen, who called himself a "professed Marxist and a Socialist," said what came to be considered as treasonous by many: "I stand with my colleague from Rutgers. I don't fear a Viet Cong victory in Vietnam, I welcome it."(32)

In making his unpopular statement, Mellen was allying himself with the position of Rutgers University Professor Eugene Genovese, who caused a storm of controversy the previous April with similar remarks.

Political leaders and many others expressed outrage over Mellen's statement, with some urging his dismissal from Drew University. Drew President Robert Oxnam, always a voice of reason, called Mellen's comment irresponsible but defended the instructor's right to express his viewpoint. An *Eagle* editorial expressed the viewpoint of most townspeople: "Mellen may be brilliant at teaching political science, but his maturity and his wisdom are minimal if he thinks that his conscience obliges him to utter every thought that comes into his head."(33)

Both the Mellen and Genovese statements became campaign issues in the 1965 election for governor. The candidates that year were incumbent Democrat Richard Hughes and Republican State Senator Wayne Dumont. A week after the Drew "teach-in," Dumont visited the university and spoke to Drew's students. In reference to Genovese and Mellen, Dumont said, "...they can say what they want but not on platforms provided by the government or by the educational system."(34) The state senator felt that the Genovese incident was even more regrettable because Rutgers was a state-owned institution. He felt private institutions, including Drew had more latitude in such matters. Still, Dumont and many Madisonians remained upset by what they considered to be the apparent treason in Mellen's statement. Indeed, the Drew Board of Trustees did not renew Mellen's contract, a move praised by former Vice President Richard Nixon. Nixon, who spoke before the Florham Park Republican Club a week after Dumont's appearance at Drew, urged Rutgers to act in a similar fashion toward Professor Genovese.

Dumont's position may have helped him in gathering the local vote for governor in November. Although he lost the statewide election, the Republicans carried Madison by 3,260 to 2,544 for Hughes. Gradually, the Mellen incident faded from the news, but the tension between Madison townspeople and the university caused by the barbershop issue was only heightened by the Mellen statement.

Jungle Conflict

While the nation and town debated the merits of the Vietnamese involvement, some of Madison's young were being sent to the jungle conflict. SP4 John Sabatini, Jr., was stationed at Cantho in the middle of the Mekong Delta. He was fortunate, for his platoon, early in 1968, was under constant Viet Cong rocket fire, yet miraculously none were killed. In an *Eagle* article, Sabatini expressed dismay over those protesters who burned their draft cards and thereby lowered the morale of fighting men. He had praise for those conscientious objectors who served in battle areas as medics.(35)

Elsewhere in the jungle, Sgt. Thomas P. McDermott of Glendale Road was wounded three times in the fighting. McDermott, who served as a medic with the 4th Battalion, 42nd Artillery and with the 4th Infantry Division, was subsequently awarded the Bronze Star, the Army Commendation Medal and three Purple Hearts.

By war's end, five Madison young men had sacrificed their lives in the conflict: Lt. John T. Coll, Jr., P.F.C. Ralph Piano, Jr., SP4 William A. Meister, SP4 Douglas J. Markovich and Russell Engel. Vietnam veteran Peter Torrani died of leukemia shortly after returning home.

A President Steps Down

President Lyndon B. Johnson was generally blamed for prolonging the "impossible war," and in April 1968, he announced that he would not seek reelection. Anti-war activists felt relief at the decision. Madison's Democratic Committee Chairwoman, Mrs. Jeannette Balber of Hoyt Street, expressed the feeling well: "He has put country above partisan policies and has provided the Democratic Party with an opportunity to renew itself."

Ronald C. Eisele, Woodland Road, a coordinator of the Volunteers for McCarthy organization, which supported anti-war candidate Senator Eugene McCarthy of Minnesota, was hopeful that Johnson's action would "save some lives" by shortening the war.(36) Eisele and many other Americans were concerned with the mounting costs of the war in dollars and lives.

The "Hippie House"

Even Madison had its Hippies—as some of the protesters were called—and its anti-war demonstrations. While most demonstrations involved Drew students, local Hippies were not always collegians but simply rebellious young people. Some lived in a house at 47

These memorial tablets on the walls of Madison High School (a portion of each shown here) honor three graduates who lost their lives in combat. The specific military action, citation, and their interests and contributions to school life are recorded, as well as the annual award recipients most representing their ideals. Photo credit: Dean Michaels Studio.

Madison Avenue, which soon became known as "Hippie House." Some Madisonians felt that the "far-out" crowd who lived there followed a communal lifestyle that contrasted unacceptably with the local norm.

Public pressure against the Hippies led to a series of police crackdowns culminating in a raid in late September 1968. The raid was based on apparent health code violations, although the American Civil Liberties Union soon joined the fray and accused the police of harassment. On October 11, the Morristown District Court approved the Madison borough government's request to have the Hippies evicted for code violations.

One Hippie plaintively asked: "Why do they hate us so much?" Editor Kenneth Haynes responded in a poignant column. In part, he wrote, "It seems to this observer that the question is worth investigating. The answer could help us to find ourselves as a community."(37) Once again, Haynes and the medium of the *Madison Eagle* played effective roles in serving as a community conscience. Although there were no printed responses to the question, its impact was surely felt. The problems associated with rebelling youth were being experienced in varying degrees all over America. Madison's confrontation was the reflection of a national phenomenon in an age of public unrest.

Drew University, Madison, and Rock Music

When Elton John sang, "I remember when Rock was young, me and Susie had so much fun," he could have been describing the music scenes in Drew University's Baldwin Gym in the late 1960s and early 1970s. Students and Madisonians were in the right place at the right time when "College campuses across the country were essential for the growth of popular music, and of rock music in particular."(38) Many bands and solo performers of different genres, before they became famous and expensive, made their way to Drew University to play in the poor acoustics and uncomfortable seating at the 1500 seat gym.(39)

In the late 60s, rock music reflected the counterculture of those turbulent times.(40) Beginning with concerts such as Chad and Jeremy in September 1966, organized by Social Committee chair student Glenn Redbord, Drew hosted many musicians during Rock's heady college campus days. There followed, among others, the Young Rascals (February 1967), The Animals (March 1967), Lovin' Spoonful (May 1967), Judy Collins (September 1967), and the Four Tops (November 1967).

Subsequent years through 1971 saw campus concerts by The Who, Iron Butterfly, Blood Sweat and Tears, Chuck Berry, Mountain, Allman Brothers, Carly Simon, The Byrds, The Flying Burrito Brothers, Frank Zappa and the Mothers of Invention, Pete Seeger, Jefferson Airplane, Van Morrison, Livingston Taylor, Richie Havens, and Gordon Lightfoot.

After 1971, rock concerts by future Rock and Roll Hall of Famers slowed way down, though some luminaries of other genres still appeared on campus. These included Billy Preston, John Sebastian, Southside Johnny and the Asbury Jukes, Harry Chapin, Eddie Rabbit and R.E.M.(41) Eventually, even Bob Dylan couldn't resist a visit in April 1996, and B.B. King came two years later. These concerts took place in the Simon Forum and Athletic Center, which opened in 1994. Remarkably, at least 15 of the performers who played at Drew were ultimately inducted into the Rock & Roll Hall of Fame in Cleveland.(42).

One of the more interesting appearances that tied Madison and the performers together occurred between Jefferson Airplane (the band), the Jefferson Airplane replica of an airplane, and Madison's notorious Hippie House. In 1968, when the band appeared at the Fillmore East concert hall in Greenwich Village, the fire marshall ordered them to remove their life-size replica of a WWI fighter biplane, which had served as a publicity gimmick outside the theater. The enterprising residents of the Hippie House, attending the concert and knowing a good deal when they saw one, brought the psychedelic-colored plane home to Madison. It proudly sat on the front lawn of the house until it was burned by vandals.

When Jefferson Airplane held their concert at Drew in October, Grace Slick herself, "announced their [the Hippies] plight to the audience and passed the basket to help out with their legal troubles. The effort apparently raised a couple of hundred dollars," ultimately to no avail.(43)

Bob Dylan's concert in 1996 brought a large legion of Drew graduates, his "older generation of fans," from far and wide. He played in the recently opened Simon Forum and Athletic Center to 4,500 adoring fans who paid $12 a ticket and whose comments afterward included, "He is a god," "A visionary," and "Dylan rules."(44)

Before rock performers filled large venues and arenas, they played the college circuit, ironically sowing the seeds of a new business model that soon shut the colleges out. Small venues closed, consolidated music companies gained control of concerts, and costs skyrocketed. While college campuses once played a central role in the evolution of rock music and culture, as Dr. James Carter, Drew University history professor summed it up, "...the business of rock music had changed, and this altered rock music culture in significant ways. But during those few years, the college campus provided the social and physical space for the growth and evolution of rock music culture."(38) And Drew University in Madison, NJ was right in there.

Supreme Court Rules

On January 25,1966, the New Jersey Supreme Court considered an appeal by Philip Gatti, operator of Phil's Barber Shop, 39 Main Street, to overturn the Division of Civil Rights ruling that barbers must cut the hair of all individuals. Through his lawyers, Albert F. Dalena of Madison and Paul Colvin of Dover, Gatti maintained that the Public Accommodations Act of the State Civil Rights Law did not specifically mention barbers. The barber's lawyers further argued that requiring barbers to cut the hair of all customers amounted to involuntary servitude and, as such, violated the Thirteenth Amendment of the Federal Constitution, which abolished slavery.

Legal arguments aside, the Supreme Court session was a difficult one for Bonnie Barrow, *Madison Eagle* columnist and the wife of Reginald G. Barrow, a major participant in the case. She later wrote of the contention in court that barbers should not have to touch people who are "unclean and undesirable." "In the courtroom," she wrote, "I looked at Mr. Thomas Sellers and my husband, both of whom are clean-cut and well-dressed men. I must admit that the statement appeared humorous. At the same time, it was annoying to hear a statement of that nature."(46)

No Appeal from Barbers

The participants in the landmark State Supreme Court case waited in suspense for almost a month before the court ruled on the appeal. On Monday morning, February 21, 1966, the court rendered its unanimous decision that a barbershop is a place of public accommodation, and as such, it must provide service to all people. In writing the court decision, Associate Justice John J. Francis said the granting of a state license signified that a barber is qualified to cut "not just Caucasian hair" but the hair "on the head of any human being." In a front-page story headlined "Barbers curbed on bias in New Jersey," *New York Times* correspondent Walter H. Waggoner reported that Paul Colvin, one of Gatti"s lawyers, said that "the civil rights division would have to bring a proceeding to compel Mr. Gatti to obey the law, and then file a criminal suit if he continued to refuse to do so."(47) He then indicated Mr. Gatti would fight the case "every step of the way."

Those who hoped the controversy would end with this decision were disappointed by the comments of Colvin. Within 24 hours, Reginald Barrow asked the State Division on Civil Rights how they planned to implement the court decision. Some townsfolk believed that the state Division on Civil Rights could not implement the decision if there were to be an appeal to the United States Supreme Court. Nevertheless, DCR Director Pfaus said Gatti had 10 days to comply with the original division order, which was again being invoked.

Finally, on February 24, Peter Triolo said, "We're throwing in the towel." With that statement, Triolo, on behalf of the 2,500-member Barbers Association, announced that there would be no appeal to the United States Supreme Court. Gatti also conceded: "As far as I'm concerned, the fight is over."(48)

In an extensive editorial in the March 3, 1966 edition of the *Madison Eagle*, editor Haynes assessed the impact of the two-year stand-off on the community. In his judgment, the "viewpoint of many a belligerent resident" had mellowed since the start of the controversy. The crisis, when viewed from "a local standpoint," made some residents "permanently aware of what being a Christian American really entails."

Drew University President Dr. Robert Oxnam, urged townspeople not to view the local crisis as only an example of ethnic conflict between Italians and Blacks. In a statement issued on May 12, 1964, the educator stated: "Those who would involve the parentage of men are badly misled. It is not a matter of where or in what condition our grandfathers were born, but rather the travail of America in 1964."(49)

An important question remained when the controversy ended: Were the results worth all the anguish, energy and money spent on the crisis? Tom Sellers said "Yes," and he felt the community has been much improved. The barbers seemed to want to forget the whole thing. One barber carefully avoided comment so he would not "stir this up again." It does seem as though Madison had gained much from this bitter struggle. No longer are Madison's Blacks viewed as silent partners in the community.

A Democrat Comes Close

Earl J. Reddert had the difficult duty of being the mayor of Madison during the tumultuous time of the barbershop controversy. Reddert, who served from 1960 to 1965, was succeeded by William G. Nordling, also a Republican. In the 1965 contest for mayor, Nordling beat Democrat Herman A. Lingerman by 3,476 to 2,343. The council vote was much closer that year. Before absentee ballots were counted, it seemed as though Democrat John P. Snyder had pulled off an upset, but after the count came the familiar result: the Republicans won both seats in the council. Prall Culviner had 3,009 votes while fellow Republican Ludwig Clifton had 2,984, only 5 votes more than Snyder. Alan King had a total of 2,778 to finish fourth.

Nordling immediately galvanized the Republicans into action. Shortly after the election, he announced his plan to implement more off-street parking, develop Memorial Park, and resolve the issue of whether to build a new public library. In response to criticism that the Republicans were not supportive of community interest in sponsoring a swimming pool, Nordling said he would consider such a venture if it were run by a private corporation. Although the Democrats did not win the election, they did seem to succeed in softening the Republican Party's position on the need for a community pool.

Candidates Night

At the time of council elections in the fall of 1967, things again heated up in Madison politics. The Jaycees and the League of Women Voters sponsored their joint annual Candidates Night in the Central Avenue School auditorium. Five candidates, including incumbent Mayor Nordling, each spoke for approximately 10 minutes on the question: "What do you consider to be Madison's most pressing problems, and how would you solve them?" Led by Nordling, Republicans emphasized the quality of government then being provided to the community by—you guessed it—the Republicans. The GOP candidates did, however, allow that there were still a few "voids that require filling before we can rest our case." Republican council candidate W. Alan Raffensperger felt that rising prices and inflation posed the greatest single problem. His running mate John Halgren agreed.

On the other hand, the Democratic candidates saw a need for more fundamental change. Ralph Engelsman, Jr. argued that there was a need to stabilize Madison's tax rate and to develop a new industrial park. He also urged a better advertising campaign to lure industry to the suburbs. Another Democrat, Joseph Stockert, urged the development of better zoning ordinances, improved recreational facilities and a code of ethics for municipal employees.(50)

The challenge by Democrats to end the long-standing Republican domination of Madison's government provided a great deal of drama. *Eagle* editor Haynes warned readers of the tendency of Candidates Nights to turn into verbal free-for-alls. The audience was even known to get into the fracas on some occasions. Haynes lamented that some candidates planted belligerent "hatchets" in the audience to ask questions "not designed so much to test the sincerity of an opposition candidate as to shame, maim and disqualify him before the voters."(51) Things could get rough in suburbia.

In the November election, incumbent William G. Nordling, running unopposed, led all candidates with 3,644 votes. Republicans also swept the race for council with victories by Raffensperger and Halgren, although the latter candidate only narrowly defeated Democrat Engelsman. Twenty years later, Engelsman was elected mayor.

Expansion of the Suburbs

While politics proved a lively fall activity for Madisonians, the quiet but steady process of suburban growth continued throughout the 1960s. Slowly, the community's past was being altered. The pressure of suburban housing continued to cause land values to skyrocket to unheard-of heights. The property formerly used for growing roses or farming was now more valuable as housing developers sought land.

At the midpoint of the decade, Alphonse Troianello sold his extensive rose-growing range to Parmar Homes, Inc. Troianello's two large greenhouses were dismantled and sold to the Julius Roehrs Company in Freehold. The former Troianello land was soon transformed into a 25-home development along Avon Drive named Yardley Village.

Another important local site became a focal point of the building boom in the late 1960s when the farm of Dr. and Mrs. William C. Terhune was sold to the developers of John Marshall Village. The Terhune farm (Marshall Lane off Greenwood Avenue) was well-known in Madison for its herd of sheep. In 1968, the builder projected that 13 new homes would soon be built on the former Terhune property. He promised that the Terhune farmhouse, over 100 years old, would not be destroyed. It still stands in the midst of the development.

The Terhune farmhouse is surrounded by John Marshall Village. In addition to sheep, Dr. and Mrs. Terhune raised exotic peacocks. At one time the original farmhouse had been separated and the center portion added.

Railroad Troubles

Madison's commuters received a jolt in the winter of 1966 when the Erie Lackawanna Railroad asked the Public Utilities Commission for permission to end its passenger service. The public outcry was loud in opposition. Among the most effective of the business and political pro-testers was Mayor Nordling. At a Public Utilities hearing in Newark, Nordling reminded the commissioners of the earlier town contribution of $159,000 to build the train station and to the many other local investments in the maintenance of the rail line. Nordling also estimated that 2,000 people used the Madison station each day. Persuaded by the testimony, the Commission ruled that the passenger line should continue in operation.

New School, New Leader

In April 1967, School Superintendent David S. McLean retired. He had seen the need to build new schools to meet the rising number of children in Madison. In 1966, McLean correctly forecasted that "new housing developments in Madison will push elementary facilities to the limit."(52). His successor, Dr. John J. McKenna, was a former Madison school teacher who also knew the problems associated with rapid suburban development.

By the spring of 1970, the new superintendent had a facility open on Woodland Road, the Torey J. Sabatini School, named after a well-known local Italian American civic leader, builder, and 27-year Board of Education member. McKenna also took the lead in asking that teachers develop a sex education program for local schools. The program would be integrated into the framework of existing courses, and it was to stress the family as a basic unit.

Local residents expressed some shock when a March 21, 1968, *Madison Eagle* news story

Torey J. Sabatini was elected to the Board of Education in 1941 on a write-in vote and served nine terms. His extensive knowledge of building construction contributed to the building of the Kings Road and Green Village Road schools, the new high school, the Ambulance Corps building, as well as additions to the elementary and high schools.

A school named in his honor is testimony to one so dedicated to his community. He was past president of the Forum Club and past chairman of the club's Naturalization Committee, has been active in his church, and was a member of Madison Auxiliary Police during World War II, past president of Rotary Club, director of United Campaign, and Chamber of Commerce member.

claimed that the number of marijuana users in the high school might be as high as 70 percent. Nevertheless, the main areas of local concern were those dealing with a rising school budget and the fear of spiraling taxes. From 1967 to 1968, the local school-age population grew by 48 students (from 3,246 in 1967 to 3,294 in 1968).

Building a New Library

The same suburban growth pressures that created a demand for new schools also brought about a heightened citizen awareness of the need for a new community library. The James Library was, and remains, an acknowledged architectural gem, but it was too small to meet the needs of an expanded population. Fortunately, Madison had the civic leadership necessary to mount the effort to build a new library. Important figures in the movement were Robert W. Nichols, of rose-growing fame, who served as president of the Library Board of Trustees during the mid-1960s, and Burr L. Chase, a councilman who served briefly as acting mayor.

The library's children's room was opened in 1913 across the street in the James Building.

Nichols and Chase spearheaded a local effort to expand the size and services of the Madison Library. In April 1965, both signed an agreement with Martin S. Buchner, President of the Florham Park Library Board of Trustees, to permit residents of Florham Park to use the Madison facility. Chase signed the agreement in his capacity as acting mayor. The two local activists were aided by the provisions of the will of Warren H.

Madison Public Library, dedicated May 25, 1969.

Barton, former library board member and president of the First National Bank of Madison. The will, probated years earlier in 1957, stipulated that $75,000 would be given to a children's library department when established in a new library building. The department was to be named after his wife, Florence N. Barton. When Mrs. Barton died seven years later, another $500,000 in stocks and bonds were given to the local library.

Plans were soon developed for a new facility off Keep Street. Under the leadership of Mayor Nordling, financing was arranged for the construction by municipal ordinance. In March 1968, the beneficent Mr. Chase donated $71,000 for the erection of an auditorium on the library site. The auditorium was to be dedicated to the memory of his late wife, Helen Whitney Chase. By December of that year, the Quirk Moving Company of Englewood began packing the books and materials to be moved to the beautiful contemporary new library. Simultaneously, Library Director Elizabeth Budell started a drive to enroll all of Madison's 6,000 families as library users.

With the 1969 opening of the new library, the community gained a facility that contained a quiet reading room, a children's wing, and a large stack area. Equally important, the library represented a coordinated community effort that was funded largely by municipal funding.

The Madison Public Library continues to be a haven for informational, recreational, educational, and cultural pursuits for all ages. It offers books, digital media, computer services, historical, and consumer information. In addition, for children, story hours, summer reading programs, year-round movies, filmstrips, and entertaining programs. The Chase Auditorium hosts concerts, films, lectures, and classes.

Later that year, a committee headed by Chase suggested to the mayor and council that the old James Library be converted to use as a cultural center or museum. The committee's proposed cultural use for that fine building was then realized with its conversion to the unique Museum of Early Trades and Crafts created by Director Edgar Law Land in 1970.(53) The Museum preserves, researches and exhibits the development of life in the home, farm and shop from the late 1600s to the mid-1800s. An extensive collection of tools of the craftsmen and products they produced are housed here. The nonprofit museum relies on public funds, private gifts and contributions.

Edgar Law Land at work in the barrel maker's shop.

Tools were prized and passed from father to son.

YMCA Expansion

The Lackawanna freight station site between Keep Street and the railroad was designated as the future location of the YMCA as early as 1959. At that time, Mrs. Geraldine Dodge donated $40,000 to purchase the 6.3-acre property from the railroad. By 1959, the YMCA membership had swollen to 1,037 active and 577 sustaining members. When the previous YMCA building on Main Street was erected in 1908, membership was only 133 active and 36 sustaining. As Madison continued to grow, the need for the new facility became evident. W. Alan Raffensperger, President of the YMCA Board of Trustees, and General Secretary William Arthur proved to be the catalysts needed for the new building. Under their leadership, the board approved plans for a $1,115,000 structure on the newly acquired property. The proposed facility would feature a full-sized gym, swimming pool, exercise room, locker rooms, and meeting rooms and was to be designed with the possibility of future additions in mind. Raffensperger stated that it would "represent a tremendous investment in the future... one from which all will benefit and of which all will be mighty proud."(54) His prediction proved accurate. By the summer of 1961, Raffensperger, Arthur, and Mrs. Ralph Stoddard broke ground at the new site on Keep Street. Popular New Jersey historian John T. Cunningham spoke at the ceremony on the development of the project.

The project was delayed through part of 1962 by the bankruptcy of the contracting firm of Clifford S. Evans. During the year of construction, Madison Area YMCA President Raffensperger announced that the YMCAs of both Chatham and Madison had decided to

The new YMCA under construction. View from Keep Street early in 1962.

October 28, 1962. W. Alan Raffensperger and Bill Arthur laying the cornerstone.

YMCA pioneers present on the scene in 1907 witness the 1962 opening of the cornerstone of the Main Street building. L-R Ralph Stoddard, Kenneth MacDougall, Arthur Buttenheim, Mrs. Stoddard, Roy Genung, Charles Foster, and Carroll Merritt. W. Alan Raffensperger, board president, stands beneath the shovel.

merge into a single unit in order to better serve the needs of area youth. Then, on January 7, 1963, it finally happened. The spanking new YMCA opened for business, and the old YMCA on Main Street closed after 54 years of service. The generosity of yet another Madison benefactor, Charles L. Benjamin, made this new addition possible.

The new building was formally dedicated on February 10. Especially significant was previously mentioned inclusion of the old railroad freight station into the architectural design of the rear of the complex. The former freight storage area was converted into modern offices.

In January 1963, the *Eagle* ran an editorial that aptly summed up the YMCA expansion: "The most satisfying and longest lasting new year gift Madison, Chatham, Florham Park is likely to receive is the new YMCA Family Center."(55) Two years after its opening the YMCA leadership announced plans for a new wing. Fund Chairman Raffensperger tirelessly headed the successful drive to raise the necessary $500,000. Although only two years old, the YMCA building was then operating at 100 percent capacity. In October 1966, R.W. Stickel, then President of the

Bill Hopping, fundraiser. His annual Madison Central RR shows, started in 1965 to support the YMCA building fund, attracted 12,000 visitors and raised over $36,000 by 1984. Hopping called the layout, set on an 18 x 25-foot stage, "One of the most elaborate privately-owned Lionel displays in the U.S."

The 90-minute show had 22 trains operating on a timetable. Set in a model New Jersey village, it enveloped a full day and night, a storm, recorded sound effects, and a circus. The show was governed by a Seth Thomas railroad clock, a gift of George Marr from the Milburn, N.J. freight house.

Madison Area YMCA, presided at the dedication of the new wing. Once again, citizens were willing to contribute the necessary funds to provide for the area youth of the community.

Building a Pool

Successful efforts to build a new YMCA and a modern public library led to heightened citizen concerns about other unmet local needs. Chief among these was the desirability of creating a community pool. The movement to build a pool was a remarkable example of civic spirit and the hard work of volunteers. During a 14-month planning period, a specially appointed committee discussed plans and developed financial projections. They attempted to do all this with the future interests of borough residents in mind. By April 1968, ground was broken for a pool estimated to cost $250,000. As the *Madison Eagle* described the committee's efforts in a May 1968 editorial: "Those in any suburban community who dream of realizing new civic goals would do well to study the remarkable progress of Madison's Community Pool Committee."(56) Also noteworthy is the fact that the pool was open to all people of Madison regardless of race or nationality. Soon, the symbol of "Rose, the Madison Mermaid," became known to all in town.

April 1968 Groundbreaking!
Mayor Nordling and Tom Walsh
share the ceremonial shovel.

Children eagerly awaiting a Fourth of July dip!

Pressure for Change

Perhaps the issue that generated the most controversy was the question of *charter change*. For several years, some local residents questioned the efficiency of the borough government. While many thought a change in the type of government was necessary, others felt that local problems were due to the political dominance of the Republicans. Whatever the varying motivations, popular sentiment appeared to favor a study of charter change. Former Mayor Thomas T. Taber, in July 1968, reflected the view of the traditional powers in town when he wrote that there was "no present need to consider changing the form of government presently existing in Madison."(57) Mayor William G. Nordling also rejected the need for charter study and, by implication, any need for a change in the form of government. However, 1,697 Madisonians signed a petition which called for a vote on the question.

The issue reached the ballot during the 1968 presidential election between Richard M. Nixon and Hubert H. Humphrey. The carefully worded question posed the creation of a special Charter Study Commission. The impressive turnout for the vote was 86 percent of Madison's total registered voter population of 8,194. By more than a three-to-one margin, voters approved the call for a charter study. In the presidential contest, Nixon defeated Humphrey by 4,060 to 2,673. Also on the ballot were contestants for seats on the Charter Study Commission itself. Elected were Ralph Maione, Frank Benedict, E.G. Stanley Baker, Frank H. Campbell, and Robert E. Knowlton. When the Charter Commission Study got under way, Maione served as chairman and Baker as secretary for the group.

The Charter Commission issued a report dated July 30, 1969, which recommended that voters approve the Mayor-Council form of government available under the Optional Municipal Charter Law. The proposed form of government provided for a division of the municipality into four wards, each represented by a councilman. Three other councilmen would be elected at large from the entire community. The commission also stated in its report that a "popularly elected mayor is necessary for the proper operation of the municipal government" and that this practice should remain. In addition, the new form of government provided for an administrator to give a high level of full-time service, which would result in financial savings to the community.(58)

Pros and Cons of Wards

The commission included in its summary a statement that it did not attempt "to grade the past but to assure governmental success in the future." Nevertheless, some local citizens expressed dissatisfaction with the way the municipal government had been operated during the past decade.

Opposition to the charter change recommendation surfaced in Madison during the fall of 1969. Opponents generally charged that the proposed system of political wards would be a divisive influence in the community and too radical a change from the then-existing form of government. In October 1969, some members of the commission issued a statement to rebut criticism of their report, arguing that wards would "encourage diversity" on the council, which would match the diversity of the people of Madison.(59) Undoubtedly, the ward system would have permitted greater representation of ethnic groups living in certain well-defined neighborhoods. Existing at-large voting tended to diffuse the balloting strength of ethnic groups.

Despite the apparent logic of the commission's arguments, the charter change recommendations suffered a November defeat at the polls by a margin of two to one. Those who voted against the change were swayed by the arguments of Mayor Nordling and others that the ward system was somehow akin to big-city machine politics.

Despite the decisive charter change defeat, the movement had a definite impact on the community. The political tug-of-war between Republicans, who generally opposed the change and Democrats, who frequently pushed for the new system, did result in several important developments. Shortly after the battle was over, the Republican mayor authorized the hiring of a borough administrator, one of the major recommendations of the commission. The mayor's term of office was also changed from two years to four years. Glenn O. Head was the first mayor to serve a four-year term. Proponents of reform could take some consolation in these improvements.

A Time of Tragedy

The nationwide trauma of the 1960s was not over. In 1968, two of America's charismatic leaders were cut down by assassins' bullets, Martin Luther King, Jr. and Robert F. Kennedy, brother of the martyred President.

Since it is generally conceded that Madison's barbershop controversy grew out of Dr. King's call to action here, his assassination in Memphis, Tennessee, was particularly poignant. Praise for the slain leader came from many quarters.

Albert F. Dalena, attorney for the barbers in 1964, called King's death "a real tragedy."(60) He felt that the nation had lost "a truly great American and a great leader of his people."

In 1965, Mabel Jackson Robinson was selected New Jersey's Mother of the Year, chosen for her years of religious and civic activities, for traits highly regarded in mothers and for the achievements of her children: a Washington lawyer, now a Federal judge, District of Columbia; a veterinarian; an aircraft firm manager; and a teacher. She was a charter member of the local NAACP chapter, member of the National Council of Negro Women, Morris County Urban League, and Madison-Florham Park Human Relations Council. In 1979, she wrote, "There are too many weaknesses in our structure, causing our foundations to crumble in some areas." She took years to change others, and she has regarded as her mission the eradication of racial segregation in all areas of education, employment and housing throughout Morris County.

Mrs. Mabel Jackson Robinson, matriarch of an illustrious Madison family, called the King assassination "one of the most tragic things that has ever happened in our country."(61) As one of the area's best-known leaders, Mrs. Robinson had been selected New Jersey's "Mother of the Year" in 1965.

King's longtime friend was Drew Professor Dr. George D. Kelsey. (See Kelsey Sidebar) Upon hearing of the death of his former student (at Morehouse College, Atlanta, Georgia), Kelsey summed up the leadership of the man who had made such an impact on Madison and on the nation: "Many people are now asking who will fill the void that King's death leaves in Negro leadership. The fact is, King was not a Negro leader in the strict sense of the term. He was an American leader. His message was directed to the hearts and minds of all the people, and his goal was the America of the American creed."(62)

Special services were held in Madison—a town once deeply divided over the question of "equal rights." Blacks and whites from all strata of the community sat shoulder to shoulder at the memorial service in Grace Episcopal Church with the entire governing body in the front pew. Madison had come a long way since the winter of 1964.

In June 1968, when Senator Robert Kennedy, yet another American leader, was killed, local people had good reason to pause and reflect on the direction of their turbulent world. A long moment of silent contemplation was observed in Kennedy's honor at a Madison High School awards assembly. In Madison churches, special prayers again were offered in the name of a departed leader.

Scholars, politicians and sociologists would spend a long time evaluating the perplexing decade of the 1960s.

CHAPTER FOURTEEN

The End of an Era as Madison Faces New Challenges

The turbulence and turmoil of the 1960s did not end with the dawn of a new decade. Concerns over the continuance of the Vietnam War and the May 1970 bombing of Cambodia stirred public unrest throughout the nation. When four students at Kent State University in Ohio were killed while demonstrating against the perceived invasion of Cambodia, college campuses everywhere erupted in protest. In Madison, Drew University students and faculty vocally protested President Richard M. Nixon's decision to order the bombing of North Vietnamese Army positions along the Ho Chi Minh Trail in Cambodia.

Two years later, local residents were also increasingly mesmerized by the growing media coverage of the break-in of the Democratic Party headquarters in the Watergate Hotel in Washington, D.C. Televised hearings of the Senate Watergate Committee led by Sen. Sam Ervin uncovered the burglary's connections which led investigators all the way to the Office of the President of the United States.

These proceedings ultimately led to articles of impeachment against the president being brought by the House Judiciary Committee. Like so much of the country, Madisonians were split over the issue of removal of the president from office. The release of some of the so-called Watergate tapes sealed the President's fate. Nixon then resigned, and Vice President Gerald Ford became president. Soon thereafter, he pardoned Nixon of all crimes.

As if all of this national political trauma didn't bring enough stress, Madisonians also had to deal with many challenging community issues in the 1970s and 80s. The passing of Geraldine R. Dodge, the much beloved local benefactor, greatly saddened many in the community. To some, her death appeared to mark the end of the era of great community benefactors of "Millionaire's Row," who helped shape Madison's future in ways that greatly benefited its growth as an exceptional and successful community.

Death of Geraldine R. Dodge, Her Will, Giralda Farms, and the Birth of the Geraldine R. Dodge Foundation

Following a debilitating illness from a form of arteriosclerosis that left her bedridden and uncommunicative for much of her last decade, Geraldine Rockefeller Dodge died on August 3, 1973. Funeral services were held at Grace Episcopal Church, and her ashes were interred in the Rockefeller family vault at the Sleepy Hollow (New York) Cemetery.

Although a very private person, she had been the subject of local legend for many years, and her passing was acknowledged as the end of an era. Mrs. Dodge considered Madison to be her hometown, and the generosity of her and her husband spanned four decades, from the purchase of the Ahrens Fox fire engine in May of 1921, to building a new municipal building in 1935, and granting the use of land she owned on Prospect Street for the construction of the Ambulance Corps building in 1961. Under the provisions of her will, the Prospect Street land was donated to the borough.

This record of generosity fueled speculation about the provisions of her will. What would become of the beautiful park-like 345-acre estate? Might it become a borough or county park? Would it be developed and thereby remain on the tax rolls? These were possibilities that could profoundly alter the character of Madison. Speculation ended on September 24, 1973, when the will, dated October 29, 1962, was made public. For Madison, the will had two critical provisions. Her estate, Giralda Farms, "shall be sold to private owners…that it shall continue to remain subject to assessment for real estate taxes…"(1). With few exceptions, all her other properties and personal possessions were to be sold, and the monies used to establish the Geraldine R. Dodge Foundation. St. Hubert's Giralda, created to benefit animals, was to receive the proceeds from the sale of all art with animal subjects. St. Hubert's still maintains her strong commitment to helping animals.

Animal artwork and dog show trophies from Mrs. Dodge's collection.

"The Sale of the Century"(2)

Sotheby Parke Bernet was selected to hold sales and auctions to dispose of Mrs. Dodge's extensive art collections as well as personal and household possessions. Her art collections had been appraised at five million dollars before her death; the auction catalog ran to some 1,800 pages. The five-day sale at Giralda Farms included household items, such as linens, clothing and books, which were sold at a two-day pre-auction tag sale held in one of the barns. The auction included animal bronzes, paintings, oriental rugs, farm equipment, and a 1930 mint condition Ford with 9,000 original miles; in all, a total of some 2,000 items. With gross receipts of about $25,000, the tag sale may have been "the poshest tag sale ever held."(3) Collections of jewelry and marble were auctioned in New York in sales from mid-October into December 1975.

Spectators during three days waited in line to enter the "inner sanctum" of the Matriarch of Madison's Golden Era.

The mansion, not visible from any public road, had been an object of curiosity and even mystery. More than 60,000 people lined up to enter the estate, tour the house and grounds, and attend the pre-auction tag sale and auction. As a student at Drew University, Robert Woolley had often wondered what lay beyond the gatehouse on Loantaka Way. His curiosity was captured by the *New York Times*: "Time stopped here around World War I," observed Robert C. Woolley, the Sotheby's executive who organized such house sales. "Everything here evokes turn-of-the-century tastes."(4)

The auction took on aspects of celebrity. Some items sold for much more than the pre-sale estimate; the provenance enhancing the perceived value. As the *Wall Street Journal* observed: "The auction goers not only have money to blow, they are also willing to lay it out for artifacts that appear to have no conceivable use and little aesthetic value. It is difficult enough figuring out what some of the things are."(5) St. Hubert's Giralda did realize $2.85 million from the probate process, along with some 160 works of art not included in the auction.

Giralda, A Mansion in May 1976

Following the house sale and auction, The Woman's Association of Morristown Memorial Hospital (now Morristown Medical Center) asked the estate executor, Fidelity Union Trust, for permission to use Giralda Farms as the site for their second decorator showcase, a major fundraiser for the hospital. Cognizant of Mrs. Dodge's long-time loyal support of the hospital, Fidelity Union granted permission. The mystique of the mansion and the estate, coupled with fascination with Mrs. Dodge, ensured a large turnout. Some 55,000 people attended during the month-long event, including First Lady Betty Ford, accompanied by New Jersey Congresswoman Millicent Fenwick, and Jackie Kennedy Onassis. More than $270,000 was raised.(6)

A view of the Dodge estate mansion. Originally constructed by Daniel Willis James in 1893, it was ill-suited to modern corporate needs.

Demolition of the Dodge mansion.

Demolition

Very few expected the mansion and other buildings to be saved. The mansion did not represent the work of a noted architect, and its mechanical systems had not been upgraded in many years. PIC Realty (a division of the Prudential Insurance Company) then exercised its option to purchase the estate in May 1978, and demolition began on Friday, June 6, 1978. As Kathleen O'Brien reported in the *Daily Record*, "When wreckers started demolishing the main buildings Friday, they were destroying not a palace, but a rather plain, large house already stripped of its finery."(7) The carriage house and the gatehouse on Loantaka Way were saved; the carriage house was to serve as a realty office for PIC Realty.

It was the end of an era. Jean Jenkins, writing in the *Madison Eagle* in June 1978, considered the great estates that were now gone and their important and lasting impact on both the history and future of Madison:

The huge estates spanning the years from the 1890s to this mid-century required thousands of workers to keep the very rich comfortable in perfect and luxurious settings. The big estates drew to this area a variety of ethnic people—the Scotch, the Irish, the blacks, and the Italians. Some were highly-trained specialists, artisans, craftsmen and landscapers...it took the talents and dedication of hundreds of housekeepers, maids, cooks, butlers, footmen, gardeners, carpenters, masons, etc. to produce an estate worthy of a multi-millionaire.

The real gift of the very rich to Madison was something they never anticipated—a local population of hardworking, industrious, intelligent people whose forebears, with no monuments commemorating their names, left this priceless human heritage to the community.(8)

The Geraldine R. Dodge Foundation

The Geraldine R. Dodge Foundation was established in 1974 with an endowment of approximately $30 million, which, with additional distributions from the Dodge Estate, had increased the total to $62.6 million by 1978. The charter trustees, several of whom continued in office for many years, established five major areas of philanthropy: secondary education, the arts, critical issues and the public interest, animal welfare, and local projects. The foundation's guidelines specifically excluded from the application process higher education, health, religion, and international projects. Proposals for capital projects (bricks and mortar), endowment funds, and deficit operations would "ordinarily not be considered."(9) In 1977, local projects were defined as support for "organizations located in the immediate area taking into account Mrs. Dodge's will, the guidelines, the intrinsic merit of the project, and its anticipated impact."(10)

An entire subsection of the will deals with Geraldine Dodge's desire to provide funds for the construction of a Madison Health Center. The will states: "I have for some time had under consideration the providing of suitable facilities for a Madison Health Center and have had this under discussion with representatives of the Borough of Madison."(11) In fact, those discussions had progressed sufficiently that the borough purchased an adjacent lot to allow for expansion of the existing health department. Applications were submitted by the borough but never funded by the foundation.

Mrs. Dodge had also suggested the establishment of a museum, perhaps to be known as Giralda Museum, to contain portions of her art collections, especially paintings and bronzes. Such a museum might be located in Madison, perhaps in the vicinity of the Hartley Dodge Memorial, in which case it should be designed and constructed with materials "harmonious" with that building. Howard G. Wachenfeld, attorney for Fidelity Union Trust, reported to Judge Robert Muir, Jr. of New Jersey's Superior Court that each trustee of the foundation was familiar with the will and Mrs. Dodge's suggestion that a museum be built to house her art. Ultimately, the trustees decided to donate $250,000 and 11 pieces of art valued at $179,500 to the Morris Museum of Arts and Sciences (The Morris Museum was renamed in 1985).(12) Some of those funds were used by the museum to establish a permanent memorial to Geraldine Dodge containing the donated art.

Dodge Foundation Awards First Grants

The first local grants for the 1977-1978 year were announced in the summer of 1978. Madison received grants totaling $141,000 including real estate valued at $81,000: the borough parking lots between Prospect Street and Maple Avenue, the house and lot at 10 Maple Avenue, and the small greensward at the intersection of Kings Road and Green Avenue. Volunteers converted this land into a pocket park with roses, perennial plantings, and benches. Subtracting the value of the real estate, Madison's grants amounted to $60,000. Four other Morris County organizations received a total of $334,575, excluding the value of the art given to the Morris Museum.

Madison's disappointment was palpable. After the will was published in 1973, *Eagle* editor Kenneth Haynes reassured readers, "Mrs. Dodge states and reiterates in the will that her legacy is to the people of the area for their best interests."(13) In the summer of 1979, Mayor Roger Vernon challenged the foundation's distribution of funds and suggested that a committee be formed to monitor decisions made by Fidelity Union Trust and the trustees of the foundation. Vernon also accused the executor and trustees of an "apparent pattern of turning its back on Madison."(14) With authorization from the borough council, Vernon formed a 15-member Citizens Review Committee consisting of representatives of the Madison organizations mentioned in the will. Morristown attorney and Madison resident George L. Mahr was appointed counsel to the committee.

Mahr began his task with enthusiasm, unrelenting for many years, but to no avail. He continually sought delays to the execution of the will, until a final ruling by the Superior Court cited that he and the Citizens Review Committee lacked standing in the matter.

Geraldine Rockefeller Dodge, by virtue of her wealth and philanthropy, had a great deal of power, especially in Madison, where the borough council and residents would make every effort to implement her suggestions. Is it possible that she assumed that would also apply to the foundation? This cannot be known, but it does provide an explanation of the ongoing belief, still shared by some in Madison, that the foundation had not honored all her wishes. Barbara J. Mitnick, in her outstanding biography of Geraldine Dodge, offers another explanation. In 1962, Mrs. Dodge fell twice, breaking her wrist and then her hip. Following this, "she was often confused and unable to handle her affairs." Concerned about her mental and physical deterioration, her husband, Marcellus Dodge, began the process of becoming her legal guardian, which was formally accomplished in June 1963. Given the short time span from the broken hip, Mrs. Dodge's frequent confusion, and the date of the will, October 9, 1962, Mitnick concluded it is likely that Marcellus and her attorney, Ralph Lum, "provided appropriate guidance concerning the formation of its provisions...It is reasonable to assume he [Marcellus] would have wanted his wife's estate (be) put to what he considered the highest purposes."(15)

By 2019, the Geraldine R. Dodge Foundation was one of the largest in New Jersey awarding in that year $8.5 million in grants, all to New Jersey organizations. The grants provided support for the arts, education, environment, informed communities, and Morris County projects. With its motto: "Imagine a Better New Jersey," the foundation has become a force for good in the state, becoming Mrs. Dodge's greatest legacy. As for a Madison health center, the trustees have adhered to their "no bricks and mortar" policy.

Giralda Farms Becomes a Corporate Park

High property taxes have always weighed heavily on New Jersey homeowners and did so in the aftermath of Geraldine Rockefeller Dodge's death in 1973 when the Madison Borough Council rezoned her huge estate for single-family development. Although the ordinance was a 'holding action' until borough officials learned what the estate's executors had in mind, residents adamantly called for tax relief, objecting to any development that would add extra tax burdens, such as investments in education.

Their voices were heard as local officials negotiating with the estate executors lent open ears to the concept of a high-end corporate park, as proposed by the estate's new owners, PIC Realty.

That was in 1976, and for the next 16 months, the borough and PIC Realty hammered out an agreement that would permit the development of only 15 percent of each parcel of land; the remainder would be private parkland. Even environmentalists, who preferred the estate to remain an open space, came on board, offering their voice on ecological matters. Satisfaction grew as the company hammered out the details of the site, with size restrictions, underground garages, and new impervious coverage that would retain natural water flow. The company also retained an allée of trees planted by Mrs. Dodge after her 1916 move into the property, and the main entrance on Madison Avenue featured an old well house that was to elegantly display the heirs' name, Giralda Farms. Madison would show New Jersey how it could accommodate revenue-producing corporations into their bucolic setting.

Gatehouse at the main entrance to Giralda Farms off Madison Avenue is derived from a 91-year-old well house in use when the property was known as the James estate.

It was a long and tedious venture, but the property sale to PIC Realty was finalized in 1978. As they began to make the needed improvements, their sales department began to entice area corporations with the benefits of settling in their new Giralda Farms. First to come on board was Schering-Plough Corporation, the Kenilworth, NJ pharmaceutical company that enthusiastically built its world headquarters there in 1984. Soon afterward, the park began to welcome new purchasers: Atlantic Mutual Insurance Corporation constructed a four-story office building, followed by A.J. Moeller, under the trade name of its shipping division, Maersk, opened its building in 1988. In 1992, American Home Products became the largest facility with nearly 500,000 sq. ft. of interior space. Additionally, the company converted a former carriage house into a corporate dining area and, in 1993 built a child development center available to its employees.

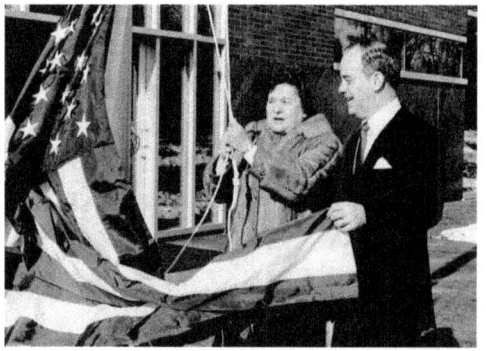

Mayor Elizabeth 'Betty' Baumgartner raises the American Flag at the 1984 dedication of Schering-Plough's new world headquarters at Giralda Farms.

The borough's amicable relationship with PIC Realty proved worthwhile. In 1998, the company donated $150,000 towards a fire truck and underwrote the construction of a bike path that went around three sides of Giralda Farms. It also paid for the much-needed widening of Woodland Road and Madison Avenue. By 1985, increasing electrical needs at Giralda Farms required a new transformer at the James Park substation. PIC funded the project through a no-interest loan to be repaid by a 15% yearly deduction on its utility bill. Without this loan, the borough's only recourse would have been to issue capital bonds. Further burnishing its image among residents, in 1984, PIC, in conjunction with Schering Plough and Giralda Farms, sponsored a Summer Pops Concert by the New Jersey Symphony with 2,500 attendees. The concert, now called the Giralda Music and Arts Festival, continues to be held every June.

For a brief time in the early 1990s, the planners' vision of a corporate office park for the headquarters of Fortune 500 companies appeared to be achieved. The companies had become part of Madison, while they and their employees supported local philanthropic and arts organizations. Their employees also supported downtown merchants and restaurants. Everyone was happy, but the second half of the 1990s and the first two decades of the 21st century were to see many changes.

American Home Products divested its interest in consumer products to focus on its medical division. In 2002, the firm took on a new name, Wyeth, from its major Wyeth-Aayerst Pharmaceuticals division, but not many years later, that firm was purchased by Pfizer. Before then, Wyeth was the borough's largest taxpayer and employer, with one thousand employees. But in the mid-2000s, Pfizer, its new owner, spun off its divisions and sent all but a small contingent

The most recent tenant at Giralda Farms, Atlantic Rehabilitation Institute.

from Giralda Farms to other New Jersey sites. Allergan Pharmaceuticals, the last corporation to consolidate its New Jersey offices to Giralda Farms, leased the former Pfizer building for three years until the company was purchased by AbbVie in 2020.

Changing times, the COVID-19 pandemic, economic downturn, acquisitions, spin-offs and mergers greatly affected Giralda Farms, leaving only one new owner, Atlantic Rehabilitation Institute, as a projected long-term proprietor. Their new facility changes the private office park concept since the rehabilitation center is a public health service facility and, therefore, accommodates a larger number of regional clients.

Giralda Farms was an uncertain entity in 1973 and for nearly a decade afterward. With the arrival of Schering-Plough, it seemed that a solution had been found. In the mid-2020s, it still remains uncertain as overall property taxes never decreased during the past forty years. However, without the revenue to the borough from Giralda Farms property tax payments, home property taxes would likely be much higher. The site itself remains as beautiful to onlookers as it did when it was inhabited by Marcellus and Geraldine Rockefeller Dodge.

The Renovation and Restoration of Madison's Dowtown: Business Owners Call for Improvement

Downtown Main Streets had much to worry about in the mid-1970s, and among them was Madison's dilapidated downtown shopping district. With the appearance of three malls within a ten-mile radius, shop owners worried aloud about the newest threat that was raging throughout the country: shiny new malls that glittered on the inside and sprawled over acres and acres of paved parking lots. As shopping malls fed the country's appetite for modernism, style, comfort, and endless fun, traditional downtown Madison's shop owners huddled over doom-filled forecasts for America's Main Streets. They then looked out their windows and saw broken curbs, irregular and cracked sidewalks, and an ugly asphalt-patched state highway running through the town.

They complained to one another, to their council representatives, and to the mayor to no avail. "Look at your own buildings," they were told, which were just as unattractive, with layer upon layer of man-made material covering the original brick facades. So, empowered by their Chamber of Commerce, they sought relief and modernization. They finally found an ear in the new editor of the *Madison Eagle*, Louise Easton, who herself said, "We had just moved to town and were greatly impressed by the viability of the downtown district, but when we saw the ugly streetscape, we worried about its existence against the malls."(16)

On the editorial page, Editor Easton wrote of a new fad taking hold in America, "downtown restoration," while pointing to successes in both rural and older suburban communities. In private, she brought the conditions to Mayor Glenn Head, who rejected any possible governmental interest in underwriting new sidewalks on privately owned property. "Governments provide services only," the mayor said. But the property owners persisted, willing to pay their share of the costs. They were looking for continuity, and that became only possible if the borough did the sidewalks and then billed every property owner. They were fortunate in November 1974 when Roger Vernon was elected to the borough council. He immediately became their ally and very quickly an advocate for the complete renovation of the downtown district.

Getting the Ball Rolling

Vernon started the ball rolling by pushing the borough council to place the electric utility's wiring underground in the main parts of the downtown shopping district. In April 1977, the council approved the first phase of the controversial endeavor. While the mayor noted it would only cost taxpayers an additional $5 per year, some citizens objected to public funds being used for what they considered was helping private commerce.(17) In response, Council President Carl Fruehling described the underground wiring as "an important part of the sequential plan for improving Madison's electric system."(18) Thus began the 20-year odyssey that turned a new sidewalk campaign into an innovative public-private partnership that not only created a beautiful Main Street, but one integrating its historic background, its shopper-friendly atmosphere, and innovative community events that led to Madison topping *New Jersey Monthly* magazine's list of Best Places to Live in 2019.

It took a few years to complete the wiring. In the meantime, property owners formed a special Downtown Committee of the Madison Chamber of Commerce. In a personal interview, Pat Luciano, the chamber president at the time, recalled that: "the property owners worked hard just years before to provide good parking for our customers by donating land behind our stores to the borough. When we finally got that, we began getting complaints from customers about how ugly Main Street was. They stumbled over broken sidewalks and curbs, complained about the trucks since Main Street was also Route 24, a state highway, and began finding their way to the malls."(19)

While concerns and conflicts mounted over the public improvements, the property owners moved ahead. It started with Joseph Falco, proprietor of Rose City Jewelers/ Gemologists and owner of one of the most historic buildings in downtown Madison, which sat at the corner of Waverly Place and Main Street. He contracted with architectural consultant Robert Guter to choose its new color scheme, awning design and sign. Then, they contacted Carmen Toto, Jr. to paint the building. Soon,

Falco building with its new color scheme, awning design, and signage.

the Luciano family, which owned two buildings across the street and operated The Locker Room, a men's specialty clothing store, followed suit. Other property owners followed, and the glow for renovation never left. "Madison has a bright future and a most important history," Falco said, "and we're happy to be part of its new beginning."(20)

Opposition and Founding of the Downtown Development Committee

In the meantime, dissenters appeared immediately and so ferociously during those ensuing years in the seventies that by 1980, when Roger Vernon was defeated by Elizabeth Baumgartner for a second term as mayor, the borough administrator resigned. Some criticized the cost of undertaking the underground wiring project, and more objected to the choice and design of the architectural firm hired to design and implement the construction of the sidewalks. Property owners also successfully challenged the design, which bypassed traditional concrete for unanchored pavers.

While critics were tearing apart local architect Harry Weaver's sidewalk design, the Geraldine R. Dodge Foundation offered a grant to the Project for Public Spaces, a New York urban redevelopment firm that undertook a study of the use of public spaces and integration with community events. The results of their study encouraged both elected officials and private property owners to see Madison's uniqueness as both a historic space and an extremely popular venue for residents. The community soon came on board and was able to unite most everyone by developing a Downtown Development Commission (DDC).

Created in 1981, the DDC consisted of 26 members, representatives of the various constituencies: merchants, property owners, residents, universities, public employees, the governing body, civic organizations, communications, recreation, and social service groups. Their mission, clearly developed and written, was to play an important role in integrating the entire community into the downtown hub, recognizing the value of early planners' decisions in physically creating streetscapes and spaces that easily encouraged and then accommodated community togetherness.

Jerry Stevenson, its first chairman, effectively represented the residential community. He also praised the leadership of Mayor Baumgartner. "The borough had nothing to guide us, only a mayor in Baumgartner who recognized a need to bring people together, to move forward regardless of controversy. I think she feared, like most of us, that the project was dangerously close to collapsing under the weight of the controversy." Stevenson was among those who advocated for splitting the project into three sections, which is eventually what happened. "It gave everyone an opportunity to focus on one project at a time." This lessened the earlier confusion about the project.(21)

It still took two years for the DDC to gather information, study the plans, and continue to find its role amidst a field of conflicting opinions and many professional voices. In 1983, they hired Donald Smartt to a newly created position as downtown manager. Smartt first brought the property owners on board, encouraging and guiding them to professional consultants for the renovation of their buildings. He then coordinated a greater number of community activities, all leading to seeking historic status for the downtown.

Finalizing the Design Of The Sidewalks

John Hatley, who served a later term as DDC chair, credited Mayor Baumgartner for "her wisdom and in keeping the community focused."(22) Owner of a local engineering company, Hatley was among the many volunteers who assisted the borough engineering department in keeping the many plans before them complete and accurate.

But it was not until 1986, that Hatley coordinated the actual finalization of the project with then Councilman Gary Ruckelshaus. Ruckelshaus, agitated by the long delay, sat with Hatley and together they steered the project to completion. According to Ruckelshaus, the pair worked with the architect to develop a sidewalk design that most everyone would accept. Construction drawings were then prepared, and the bond issue funded. Parking, sidewalks, stormwater control, lighting, relocation of an electrical transformer vault, drainage, and the types and location of trees all became primary concerns, as well as the required public space for events and sidewalk access for merchants' basements.(23) The project was completed on time and within budget. Finally, Mayor Ralph Engelsman and members of the council proudly cut the ribbon in 1990!

It was worth the long wait, for, in true Madison style of community participation, the Garden Club of Madison offered to beautify the downtown with hanging baskets along Main Street from Green Village Road to Waverly Place. Over the years, the beautiful baskets have been extended to the entire downtown area.

The Need for Open Space – Green Acres and the Creation of Summerhill Park

Years earlier, in the spring of 1971, the New Jersey legislature approved a referendum question that would authorize bonding $80 million for the purchase of open space for "Green Acres."(24) Of the $80 million, $40 million would be for state land acquisition and development and $40 million would be for municipal and county land acquisitions.

The need for additional open space was appreciated by Madison Councilman John Hubbard, who submitted a letter to the editor of the *Madison Eagle* just prior to the general election calling for the protection of additional open space in town. Hubbard argued that Madison was 80 acres short of "meeting even our minimal requirements" for recreational and parkland.(25) Madison voters seemed to agree, supporting the successful state referendum by a nearly five-to-one majority.(26)

The following March, Mayor Glenn Head submitted a list of eight undeveloped properties in the borough to the New Jersey Green Acres Assistance Program that were potential candidates for purchase and Green Acres matching grants. Prominent among them were vacant properties located between Central and Ridgedale Avenues, that now comprise Madison's Summerhill Park. As only one site could be considered at a time for Green Acres' grants and one of those vacant properties, the Nelson Dane property (located toward the south side of what is now the current park), was an immediate candidate for development. This stretch of land became the mayor's top priority for acquisition.(27)

At his 1973 New Year's Day annual address, Mayor Head declared parks and recreation as the borough's greatest need. A week later, the council approved two resolutions: One authorized the engagement of consultants to aid in the preparation and handling of applications for state Green Acres grants. The second called for the professional appraisal of properties for park and recreational purposes.(28)

In addition to wanting to satisfy Madison's need for additional parkland and protection of the underground Buried Valley Aquifer, the council was also concerned that residential development of the Dane property would have a negative impact on Madison's taxpayers. In a private interview, then Councilwoman Connie Stober stated: "I think both reasons favoring the acquisition were pretty much equal. In my memory, Madison has always favored park space and the argument against residential development was always present, citing services and additional school costs."(29)

On December 8, 1973, the *Madison Eagle* reported that nearly all purchase arrangements had been completed for the approximately twenty-four-acre parcel that included a portion, but not all of the Dane property, the former Villa Lorraine estate of Theodore Washington Stemmler, and a number of smaller parcels. On September 3, 1974, the borough council officially accepted state reimbursement of $253,650 for 50% of the cost of acquisition.(30)

As with most significant initiatives, the borough's purchase of the property was not without opposition—from adjacent property owners and residents concerned about costs. The borough government was also split.

The parkland was referred to as the "Green Acres Park" for the next twelve years. Then in 1986, the Parks Advisory Committee proposed a contest to choose a permanent name for the parkland. According to Chairwoman Cathie Coultas, over 400 names were submitted from which the committee chose eight for submission to the borough council. The council selected the name "Summerhill Park,"(31) which had been suggested by former resident Marguerite Roberts Krantz, whose father, Stanley Roberts, had owned a house and greenhouses located near the Stemmler greenhouses. Roberts

The Luke Miller Forge, a 21st Century addition to Summerhill Park.

referred to his business as "Summerhill Greenhouses."(32) An additional 1.21 acres were added to the park with the sale of the Luke Miller property in 2005.

More recently, in the 2018 – 2019 timeframe, the Open Space, Recreation, and Historic Preservation Advisory Committee took a new interest in the park, and plans were put in place to create 1.5 miles of hiking trails that would provide walking connections to downtown Madison, other borough parks and recreational facilities and two schools. The construction of the new trails was paid for with a grant award from the county and a $10,600 matching contribution from the borough. Future plans call for the creation of two additional trail segments and an arboretum.

Growing Diversity in Government During the 1970s

Madison residents saw two changes to their borough's political landscape during the 1970s—one was significant and long lasting, and the other was unprecedented but transitory.

The latter represented local fallout from national politics and specifically, the Watergate scandal that ultimately led to President Richard Nixon's resignation. Reflecting the evolving national disgust with the Republican administration and its supporters, Democratic candidates at the state, county, and local level enjoyed great successes that election year. Democrat Brendan Byrne defeated Republican Congressman Charles Sandman for Governor of New Jersey in a landslide victory that carried Democratic candidates to substantial majorities in both the State Assembly and Senate. In the 23rd NJ Legislative District, that included Madison at that time, Democrat Stephen Wiley was elected to the State Senate and Democrats Gordon MacInnes and

Rosemarie Totaro were elected to the State Assembly.

Locally, Democrats Frank Benedict and Elizabeth Baumgartner were both elected to the Madison Borough Council, creating a four-to-two Democratic majority in a town that had a two-to-one Republican majority in registered voters. At the county level, Democrat Douglas Romaine was elected to the Morris County Board of Chosen Freeholders (now Commissioners) along with Republicans Peter Burkhart and Dean Gallo.(33) Except for Governor Byrne and Ms. Baumgartner, all the Democrats elected that year served but a single term and no Democrat has ever been elected again to a commissioner seat in Morris County. It was a substantial, one-time victory for the Democrats, but it proved to be only a short blip on the long-range political radar.

What was significant and long-lasting was that the Madison government had become more diverse and was no longer a white male bastion. In November

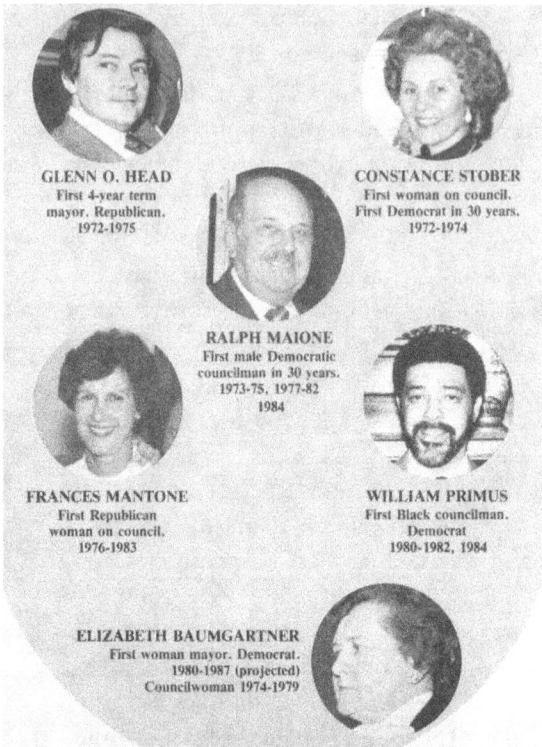

GLENN O. HEAD
First 4-year term
mayor. Republican.
1972-1975

CONSTANCE STOBER
First woman on council.
First Democrat in 30 years.
1972-1974

RALPH MAIONE
First male Democratic
councilman in 30 years.
1973-75, 1977-82
1984

FRANCES MANTONE
First Republican
woman on council.
1976-1983

WILLIAM PRIMUS
First Black councilman.
Democrat
1980-1982, 1984

ELIZABETH BAUMGARTNER
First woman mayor. Democrat.
1980-1987 (projected)
Councilwoman 1974-1979

These candidates made history in Madison.

1971, Democrat Constance "Connie" Stober became the first woman elected to the Madison Borough Council.

Why then? And why Connie Stober? It could have been that it was just time for a woman to be elected to the borough council. But as she pointed out, Connie Stober had worked very hard to get elected. The 1971 election was her second try for a council seat. A founding member of the Madison Community Pool Board of Trustees, she was already well-known in the community.(34) Whatever it was, she became the first of what would become many women in borough government.

Stober's election was followed shortly by Ms. Baumgartner's election to the council two years later. In 1976, Republican Frances Mantone was elected to the first of her three terms on the council.(35) She was then joined by Republican Beverly Graeber in 1982.

In 1974, Elizabeth Baumgartner became the first woman to be elected Mayor of Madison, serving two terms. There would not be another two-term mayor in Madison until Robert Conley was re-elected in 2015 and then again in 2019 and 2023. The first Republican female mayor was Mary-Anna Holden, who was elected in 2007.

It was also during this era that William Primus became the first (and only) African American to be elected to the Madison Borough Council. He was first elected in 1979 and then again in 1984.

Frances Mantone(36)

Frances Mantone loves Madison. She also loves her Italian heritage. The North Street native says that together, they have inspired her life as a mother, businesswoman, and public servant.

Family history records Mantone's grandparents, 1903 immigrants Madeline and Anthony Pico, settled on North St. Mr. Pico worked as a gardener on the Florham Park Twombly estate. Their daughter, Rose, remained on North St. after she married Peter Cattano of Morristown (they met at a dance at The Thursday Morning Club's Community House). Peter Cattano opened a barber shop first on Park Ave., then Main St., and eventually Waverly Pl. They raised their three children on North St, until they purchased a house on Grove St., when Frances was 13.

In those early years, Frances Mantone's entire life centered around relatives and friends in her one-square block Italian neighborhood where, she recalls, "life was good, and I was happy and secure." That sense of comfort and well-being became her voice for people in later years. But first, she met and married Sam "Jiggs" Mantone in 1956, who had an eye out for her whenever she passed Main Street's Mantone's Gas Station and Repair Shop, where he worked with his father.

Sam and Frances lived on Baker Avenue, raising three sons, as Sam and his brother, Louis, opened an auto repair and service shop on Kings Road. The business flourished as the community grew, and in the 1970s, Frances began representing the company as a member of the Chamber of Commerce.

"It was an exciting time to become involved," she recalled. "Our downtown was in the midst of a major restoration, where issues came up that were new and, at times, controversial." Her daily contact with people from all sections of Madison gave her insight into different viewpoints, and she soon found her voice in speaking for many people beyond the business community: those who were unheard and those underprivileged who needed public assistance. It was not long before she served as Chamber of Commerce president.

By the early 1980s, Mantone was asked to run for a vacant borough council seat on the Republican ticket. She won easily and was re-elected, spending seven years speaking up for a broader population whose voices were seldom heard. She left the post content that this public service and her later years as an appointed planning board member (where she served as chair) cemented her belief that she had represented everyone in her beloved Madison.

In her personal life, Frances Mantone was a proud friend and mentor to an expansive group of Italian women, encouraging their involvement with St. Vincent's parish duties, socialization, and charitable work. When Msgr. Vincent Puma, a former pastor of St. Vincent's, opened a kitchen in a tiny Paterson convent basement to feed its hungry people, Frances mobilized her friends to prepare food, and together they celebrated annually in her home. The 50 guests would together travel to feed 250 families once a week for many years to come.

She extended her own outreach by heading the Madison Eagle Christmas Fund for five years and then with the Women's Auxiliary of Madison Ambulance Corp, where she also served as president. Her greatest honor came when then-Mayor Gary Ruckelshaus asked her to chair the Millennium Ball at the Hartley Dodge Memorial on January 1, 2000, to conclude the yearlong celebration as the new century arrived.

"I've known no other place in the world except Madison," she said. "It was where I was born, loved, and educated. The town has given much to me, and my wish was only to help those who needed it most. I was fortunate in doing that with the respect and help of all Madison citizens." The ball, which was attended by 400 people, epitomized her long and loving relationship with the people of Madison.

As Frances Mantone retired from public service, husband Sam ran and won a seat on the borough council. His easy win helped a conflicted town and government to complete an embattled sidewalk renovation plan on Waverly Place. He was preparing a run for his second term, when he died suddenly on Father's Day in 2010.

She continues to live in her Woodland Avenue home, while two of her sons, Jerry and Sam, along with their families, live in Madison. Her middle son, Michael, lives in Macungie, Pennsylvania.

Dr. Saul Cooperman, Educator Extraordinaire

Madison's well-deserved reputation as a community with excellent schools and talented teachers and administrators has been recognized as such for decades. In the 20th century, Madison was fortunate to have as Superintendent Saul Cooperman, a man who would show in his career an amazing ability to bring about improvement in many key aspects of education. As Madison's Superintendent of Schools from 1974 to 1982, he focused on curricular innovation, parental involvement, and the concept that all students could succeed in life if encouraged by their teachers and parents.

When Cooperman arrived in Madison as Superintendent of Schools, he immediately took to the streets and neighborhoods in order to get to know the community and to introduce himself. He immediately also began scheduling regular meetings with teachers, administrators and parents. He listened carefully and began to articulate his most often used question that soon became his trademark and mantra during his long and significant career at the highest levels in education: "Is it good for the kids?"

In Madison, Cooperman immediately faced declining enrollments, resulting in badly underutilized school buildings. He dealt with the issue head-on and developed a master plan that closed some schools. "The decisions were difficult, but they were the right ones," he said. He felt the process worked because "we focused on kids and not non-educational issues."

When, in 1982, Cooperman was named New Jersey's Commissioner of

Education by Governor Thomas H. Kean, he took this strategy to the state level. As a change agent, he proposed an "alternate route" to teaching certification that could be achieved by someone who took required certification coursework while already employed as a teacher. After considerable public discussion and some revision, the plan was approved by the state. The "Career and Technical Educator (CTE) alternate route program," as it was soon being called, became a useful way to alleviate teacher shortages and bring liberal arts college graduates into the teaching profession.

Without a doubt, Madison helped shape the achievements of this gifted educator, and both the community and the state benefited greatly from his extraordinary leadership.

Community Newspapers and the *Madison Eagle*

Community newspapering came into its own in the 1960s and 1970s, when the dramatic physical and cultural changes to suburban communities created new opportunities for weekly newspapers to help shape the community. The *Madison Eagle* recognized its role as a strong stakeholder in Madison from its inception in 1882, carrying its strong voice in major issues, from those of economic, political, and civil liberties. Indeed, its reporting was so thorough that much of this history book is based on articles printed in the newspaper.

The infamous Barber Shop case in the 1960s brought fame to the newspaper, as publisher Ken Haynes kept the story alive and forcefully helped the community face the dark side of bigotry. (See Chapter 13.) On the business side, he developed a unique way to face off the competition from the 'free circulation' newspapers, which were luring advertisers away from paid newspapers, by giving each of his circulation communities their own pages and combining news of area interest.

By 1973, the *Madison Eagle* writers were describing Madison's uniqueness with its thriving downtown business district, its diversity and universities, possessing its own electrical utility, and a paid fire department. But it also had problems: the downtown's crumbling sidewalks and neglected buildings (including housing rental units) were immediately obvious, as was the need for low-income housing. As we note in these pages, the *Eagle* also titled the popular Christmas Walk (which preceded the Christmas parade), Bottle Hill Day (with Mayor Baumgartner), and the Madison Eagle Christmas Fund (with Barbara Valk). Most important to the time, the *Eagle* served as a place for ideas and opinions, as it continues to do today.

The Decline in Print Journalism

However economically successful the prize-winning newspaper was when William and Louise Easton sold it to the sister-brother team of Elizabeth and Steve Parker in 1991, the newspaper could not withstand the devastating effects of the national economic downturn in 2008. Like all print journalism, their respected media group, which had accumulated a total of 14 local newspapers in central New Jersey during its rise over the previous 15 years, became a victim to the forces of innovative electronic media capturing both readers and advertisers.

By 2020, the need to provide New Jersey citizens with local news became so great that The Corporation for New Jersey Local Media was formed as a nonprofit organization to build strong communities through journalism and civic engagement.(37) It set out to raise private funds and purchase newspapers, the first being the Parkers' 14 local newspapers called New Jersey Hills Media Group, which it purchased on March 3, 2022.(38) It remains the largest independent weekly newsgroup in the state. Nonprofit newspapers may be a new model of operation, but the *Madison Eagle* is flourishing under it, continuing to publish faithfully every Thursday, as it has since 1882.

The Need for Affordable Housing

If the tumultuous 1960s and 1970s exposed a shortage of affordable housing in Madison, as it did in all suburban New Jersey, it also prompted churches, organizations, and Drew University to actively join hands with the Morris County Fair Housing Council to protest racial discrimination, the proliferation of substandard rental units, and the lack of affordable housing. This began an arduous journey that led Madison to become one of the most outstanding providers of affordable housing in the state.

While the first federally funded construction of low-income housing was authorized in 1934, it was the Housing Act of 1949 that established the national housing policy entitling "a decent home and a suitable living environment for every American family."

In the late 1940s, a study by College of Saint Elizabeth students revealed that the borough had several substandard housing units. In response to increasing pressure from clergy and citizens, Mayor Norman Griffiths appointed a committee to establish low-rental housing. Members of the committee included all local clergy, real estate brokers, and a representative of the local American Legion chapter. Its charge was to investigate ways of providing private low-income housing. Simultaneously, the *Eagle* was running a front-page story of the horrific living conditions in an Oak St. apartment house.

From that modest start, a number of bodies were created to deal with the problem. In 1961, the Human Relations Council of Madison and Florham Park was created and met with less than stellar success. The council did create the nonprofit corporation called Madison Community Homes, which was formed jointly with Bethel A.M.E.Church to construct eight duplex homes on borough-owned Floyd Street property. They, too, failed to get the required support for the project.

Ordinance Approved in 1970

Eventually, the ordinance passed on November 9, 1970. The authority was chaired by Rexford Tucker, with fellow members Joseph Imbriacco, Lillian Tuttle, William Primas, Alex Peterson, and John Erikson named its first Commissioners. But they could not act until the state Department of Community Affairs would name a commissioner to serve as the governor's appointee. With much pressure on state representatives, the state moved Primus, an African American Madison resident, into that position.

The Tumult Begins

In contrast to urban housing, which failed to deliver safe, clean, and diverse neighborhoods, the authority decided to build on several different sites. This was in line with what Mayor William Nordling had earlier called "checkerboard housing."(40) But for the next nine years, the authority bogged down in bureaucratic details, unsuccessfully sought scattered sites, and had to deal with vocal objections from community residents. The authority finally got moving, and it did so on a property on Belmont Ave. One of the most contentious moments came when the authority, through its power of eminent domain, voted to tear down a house owned by Mr. and Mrs. Norman Robinson, who for years vacillated on a prospective sale to the authority. The authority was about to finalize its plan to develop 20 units of scattered site housing. More than 70 protesters made it to the meeting, including a newly formed Madison Citizens for Quality Housing. Angry residents did not hold back. They came prepared with their own plans to develop housing and a list of sites that were not in their neighborhood. That became the mantra at future hearings on each of the sites that were eventually chosen.(41)

Authority Chairman William Primus tried to quell the audience with facts: that the mayor and council would not even consider selling them other sites for the project until—and unless—they acquired the Belmont Avenue site. The citizens were furious, distrustful, and certain that Madison would be infiltrated with "unsavory people who would bring crime to their town" and, mostly, lower their booming property values. None of this ever proved to be true.

While their action set in motion the Authority's present development of its 30-unit housing on Community Place, John Avenue, Park Avenue, and Belmont, it did not come easily. George Zipfel, the leader of the Citizens for Quality Madison Housing had been appointed as a Madison Housing Authority Commissioner by Mayor Roger Vernon.

In 1980, the housing authority appointed Louis Riccio as its executive director, who remained in the position for almost 40 years. Mr. Riccio, in a 2019 interview, credits the ultimate success of that first Madison affordable housing project as well as ones in later years to having two powerful Republicans, Barbara Valk, and Irving Valkys, as Madison Housing Authority Commissioners. Ms. Valk served for almost 40 years before her death in 2012, while Mr. Valkys served nearly 30 years until his death soon afterward.

Mayor Elizabeth "Betty" Baumgartner

The Republicans held majority power on the borough council for many of those years, even while Elizabeth Baumgartner, a popular Democrat, served as mayor. Mr. Riccio noted how the three—Valk, Valkys, and Baumgartner—worked together both publicly and behind the scenes to keep dissenters, both elected officials and appointed authority members, from destroying the projects. There were many authority members purposely appointed to the housing authority as "watchdog" members, for they represented the part of the Madison Republican Party that was convinced that Mr. Riccio had a personal motive to create a more diverse community. As much as they tried, these illegitimate rumors never became public, and one by one, these recalcitrant members either gave up their seats on the authority or were not re-appointed. In fact, one member reluctantly complimented Mr. Riccio on his departure. "I may not agree with what you are doing, but I have to admire you for what you are doing," Mr. Riccio later recalled in his interview.(42)

Senior Citizens Housing

When she first joined Borough Council after her historic election victory in 1973, Elizabeth Baumgartner was an advocate for senior citizens. She immediately called for the creation of a Senior Advisory Committee to keep elected officials abreast of its growing population, as well as their physical, housing, and financial needs. Her words went hollow within the GOP-controlled council until Roger Vernon, a Republican, was elected and supported her cause.

By 1980, support for senior housing grew within the community, and in an editorial on Feb. 14, 1980, the *Madison Eagle* noted that the federal government had allocated substantial funds for public assistance housing in the metropolitan New Jersey area and called for municipalities to submit applications. "There is no reason why the borough can't have two applications before the U.S. Department of Housing and Urban Development (HUD) at the same time," the editorial noted as the housing authority continued with construction of its scattered site projects. (43) The borough agreed to set aside a portion of its Floyd Street property for senior housing and to also conduct a feasibility study to determine interest in the housing.

HUD at the time informed the housing authority that while there were funds available to construct senior citizen housing, unless they applied for, and eventually constructed family housing first, they would not receive any funds for senior housing. The authority began the construction of its first affordable housing in 1981-82 and simultaneously applied for a grant to build senior citizen affordable housing.

The authority's persistence paid off. In September 1981, the borough received notice from Congresswoman Millicent Fenwick's office that it had received a $6.1 million federal grant to construct 80 units of senior housing.(44) However, it was not as easy as it appeared. The housing authority felt forced to abandon its plan to use the Floyd Street site, was denied use of the Green Village School site (their favored location), and could not afford to purchase a Main Street property that was ultimately developed as a strip mall. With approval from the borough council, it found the most suitable site to be Belleau Avenue at the corner of Chateau Thierry Avenue.

Once again, the story of overwhelming acceptance changed when Belleau Avenue residents combined forces with the newly developed Madison Commons, a 208-unit private development across the street. The residents objected—and eventually sued, charging that a former mayor, Glenn O. Head, had promised the site as parkland.

The federal government stepped in and warned that if plans for the new housing were not approved before Feb. 6, 1984, it would rescind its funds. While Madison Housing Authority Chairman James Roberts told its members, "It's time we take the gloves off and fight,"(45) they would appeal to a reluctant borough council for support, even while one of its own members, well-known Republican dissident Robert Jones, objected to the authority sending a letter to residents asking for their support. Jones said he had not "seen a groundswell of support...I

Rexford Tucker Senior Housing.

have not seen the people banging down our doors...where are the people?" he asked.(46) In a scurry of activity over the next few months, including the rejection of yet another alternate site (the Green Acres Park on Central Avenue), the authority placed pressure on the borough council to accommodate the housing. An irate Mayor Elizabeth Baumgartner made a swift plea to Congressman Joseph Minish and successfully had him intercede with HUD not to remove the project from its priority list because of the pending suits and the slow court action. Less than one week later, approval was granted just as Mayor Baumgartner was re-elected to a second term.

The 80-unit Rexford Tucker Senior Housing was completed in 1986 and named after the man who first raised Madison's conscience to the need for subsidized housing and worked personally to garner support from Madison clergy and community residents to correct what he considered an injustice to lower-income people no longer able to afford to live in Madison.

A Unique Partnership with Drew University

In 1985, just as the community was building the Rexford Tucker Senior Housing, Drew University President Paul Hardin presented a plan to the mayor and council. The university proposed to donate a parcel of land they received from the Geraldine Rockefeller Dodge estate for the construction of public housing in return for permission to construct moderate-income faculty housing on a seven-acre tract bordering Loantaka Way and Madison Avenue. The unique plan was the university's way of meeting an acute need for moderate-income housing for its junior faculty. The faculty housing would be sold at below-market value costs with a deed restriction, so owners would never be able to sell homes at market value. That plan did not come to fruition exactly as proposed, as Drew University ended up having to purchase the faculty parcel from the Geraldine R. Dodge Foundation at full market value.

Drew University faculty housing located off of Loantaka Way.

As soon as the concept was made public, residents from the nearby neighborhood appeared before the borough council in opposition to the plan. Their argument was that the combination of the 12 units of affordable public housing and the 46 faculty units would be too dense for the site.(47)

For more than a year, residents spoke in opposition to the plan before the Madison Planning Board, which would have to approve the site plan. Their complaints were varied, but mostly, they were concerned about the value of their homes. At the same time envi-

Near-by Madison affordable housing units.

ronmental anxieties appeared, especially since the housing would abut an arboretum named for beloved Drew botany professors Drs. Florence and Robert Zuck. In spite of these pleas and concerns, the plan was approved by the board on September 16, 1986, and a unique relationship between housing and the university was given to the town. The housing was constructed with little or no impact on the neighborhood property values. The Zuck Arboretum remains part of the Drew Preserve and is an outstanding woodland retreat for students and visitors.

As before, Madison's citizens and newly emerging political leaders showed the will and the civic pride to be able to resolve the difficult challenges they faced in the 1970s and early 1980s. As former mayor Elizabeth Baumgartner might say today, "Geraldine Dodge is very proud of the community she so loved."

Madison Affordable Housing Corporation and More Senior Housing in the 1990s

The last of the federally subsidized housing units were built in 1996, eight two-bedroom units at 80 Park Avenue next to the previously constructed units several homes away. In the 1990s, the federal government ended its long-standing commitment to underwrite low-income housing throughout the country. Instead, it paved the way for housing authorities to earn their own income for the maintenance of the present structures and the construction of new ones. This led Madison to create not only a unique but the first-ever such organization in the county. The Madison Affordable Housing Corporation incorporated as an independent nonprofit organization with its own volunteer trustees. The corporation (now HQM, Inc.) obtains financial grants and subsidies leveraging privately financed construction loans to purchase property and construct housing wherever it chooses. It assists neighboring communities and private organizations, such as Habitat for Humanity, to build on lower-income homeownership programs, and provides organizational assistance and training to housing authorities. Amazingly, it gets no subsidies from either the federal or local governments.

Bottle Hill Day – A Beloved Madison Tradition

It all began with a May 1974 proposal to the Madison Borough Council from the Board of Health for a municipal fair to be held in the fall. The presentation was made by Councilwoman Elizabeth Baumgartner, who was the board's council liaison.(48) According to the *Madison Eagle* editor and steering committee member Louise Easton, the original plan was to hold a healthcare exhibition sponsored by the board; however, Easton was able to convince Ms. Baumgartner that a "hometown fair" that celebrated Madison and its history would have a much broader appeal to Madison residents.

The council approved the concept, and a steering committee led by co-chairs Baumgartner and Philip Del Guidice of the Madison Health Department began developing plans for the event to be held on September 28.

Built around the theme of Bottle Hill, the small rural village that grew to become modern Madison, the objective was to expose residents to the historic Madison and the Madison of 1974. With that in mind, the event, which received joint sponsorship by the borough government, the Madison Chamber of Commerce, and numerous civic organizations, was quickly given the name that it continues to have nearly a half-century later as "Bottle Hill Day."(49)

Bottle Hill Day has continued to grow over the years. Events for children began to be offered at Dodge Field beginning in

Bottle Hill Day in Madison.
Photo Credit: Judi Whiting.

1988, and a "mammoth auto show featuring new, classic and antique automobiles" sponsored by the Madison Chamber of Commerce and the Madison PBA took place on Central Avenue in 1989.(50)

Following a dozen years of being a mid-September event, the current tradition of holding Bottle Hill Day on the first Saturday in October started in 1992. That day saw the dedication of a plaque honoring Bottle Hill Day founder Elizabeth Baumgartner, who sadly had lost her battle with cancer in January. The other events included the dedication of the sundial and park next to the Museum of Early Trades and Crafts and a commemoration of the 500th anniversary of Columbus's voyage to the New World.

By the end of the second decade of the 2000s, Madison's Bottle Hill Day had fully evolved into a huge "family, entertainment, and community celebration" that annually attracts as many as 20,000 celebrants from the town and surrounding communities.(51)

Madison Celebrates National and Local Anniversaries

Madison residents love public celebrations, especially when there are parades, picnics, balls, and fireworks. The 1970s and 1980s saw a host of anniversary celebrations marking significant events in the town's (and the nation's) history. These included the Madison Public Library's 75th Anniversary, celebrated on Bottle Hill Day in 1975, the Centennial of the first issue of the *Madison Eagle* in 1977, and the Madison Fire Department's Centennial in 1981. But by far, the most extensive celebration of the era was the borough's multi-year celebration of the Bicentennial of the American Revolution.

Bicentennial Celebration

Four lasting legacies of the bicentennial celebration were the creation of the Bicentennial Quilt, which remains on display at the Madison Public Library, the distribution of historical markers for extant eighteenth-century Madison houses, the library's *Madison Eagle* Index, and the publication of the first edition of this book, as *The Madison Heritage Trail*, in 1985.

Madison's planning for the bicentennial celebration started early. Madison Councilman Anthony Donato was named Chairman of Madison's American Revolution Bicentennial Committee by Mayor Glenn Head in May 1973.(52) The first public meeting of the Bicentennial Committee took place in November of that year.

Madison's
Bicentennial banner.

By May 1974, plans had been put in place to identify eighteenth-century historical sites in the borough, raise the necessary funds to help defray the costs of the celebration, develop a master calendar of events, create a collection of historic photographs, and write a new history of the town.(53)

The plans to raise money to support the many planned activities were developed by finance chairs Elmer Branch and James E. Burnet III. Limited edition one-pint pewter tankards and six-inch silver plate place pieces, each engraved with the bicentennial logo—designed by Jean Ann Hayes and announced in October 1974—were offered for sale along with bicentennial pins and 1975 appointment calendars that featured Madison photos and associated commentary.(54)

A New History of Madison

The bicentennial goal of publishing a comprehensive history of the town was established early in the committee's planning. Fairleigh Dickinson professors John Fritz and Walter Savage were named Chairmen of the Madison History Subcommittee in February. The committee quickly recognized that before anyone could do much writing, a lot of research would have to be performed. To do that effectively, an index of all the relevant articles published in the *Madison Eagle* since its inception would first have to be created.(55)

The indexing project took five years and the efforts of 20 volunteers, a professional indexer/editor, and a part-time typist. Funding came from Ken Haynes, the borough, the Bicentennial Committee, and CETA (Comprehensive Employment Training Act) grants. The fruits of the team's labor: the complete typed index card file that still resides for patron use in the library.

The index served the book's author and the researchers well, and the Bicentennial Committee objective was achieved with the 1985 publication of *The Madison Heritage Trail: An Intimate History of a Community in Transition.* A large number of individuals, companies and corporations also contributed to the cost of the publishing project.

Markers for Historic Madison Homes

The Bicentennial Committee charged its Historic Sites Subcommittee, chaired by Sandra Fulda, with the task of identifying Madison homes that were verifiably constructed during the eighteenth century. Verified homes received bronze plaques marking their historic status, which were mounted by the borough.

The authenticated houses were the Josiah-Luke Miller house at 105 Ridgedale Avenue, the Joseph Miller house at 81 Ridgedale Avenue, the Sayre House at 31 Ridgedale Avenue, the Aaron Carter house at 12 Woodland Road, the Joseph Wingate Farm at 91 Woodland Road (demolished in 2023), the Daniel Burnet house at 100 Rosedale Avenue (demolished in 2020), the Benjamin Bruen house at 242 Kings Road (which currently appears to be headed for demolition), the Isaac Cory House at 216 Greenwood Avenue, and the John Russell house at 192 Loantaka Way. Two sites, the site of the original Presbyterian Church on Kings Road and the site of the original Bottle Hill Tavern, were also recognized.(56)

The first homeowners to receive a Historic House Project plaque with the date their house was built were Jim and Kate Malcolm, the President of the Historical Society, Susan Simon, and the Chair of the committee, Virginia Laughlin. Over 100 Madison residents proudly placed the plaque on their homes.

Forty-three years later and with a seed money grant from the Madison Elks, the Madison Historical Society conducted a new Historic House Plaque project. Utilizing Madison property tax records and other corroborating research, the society identified over 250 homes that were constructed between the town's founding ca.1730 and 1900. Like the Bicentennial project, the program called attention to the rich historic character of Madison, gave recognition to the community's architectural origins, and encouraged the appreciation and preservation of its unique heritage.

Bicentennial Events

The first major event sponsored by the Bicentennial Committee was a May 7, 1975, town-wide picnic held on the Drew University athletic field. The day included performances by the Madison High School Band and the Morris County Junior Militia Fife and Drum Corps, a mounted drill by the Chester Calvary, a demonstration of cannons and flintlock rifles by the Chatham Colonial Rifles, and a free tethered balloon ride. Food and drinks were available from the Drew University food service, and a beer garden was managed by the Madison Jaycees.(57)

Another was the February 7, 1976, borough-sponsored Bicentennial Ball held at the Hartley Dodge Memorial. A five-piece orchestra for dancing and a bar were set up in the east wing meeting room, and a piano for those seeking quieter entertainment in the west wing meeting room. The council chambers were set up as a social lounge. Both hot and cold hors d'oeuvres were served. In keeping with the Bicentennial theme, attendees were encouraged to dress in the style of the period, and a number did.(58)

The main event took place on August 28 of that year with the joint Bottle Hill Day-Bicentennial celebration that featured a huge parade that started at the Madison Plaza and ran up Main Street and Madison Avenue to the Drew athletic field. Invited dignitaries included Mayor Glenn Head and borough council members, U.S. Senator Harrison A. Williams, Congresswoman Millicent Fenwick, State Assemblymen John Dorsey and James Barry, and Freeholder Director Leanna Brown. The parade was followed by a picnic with crafts and games for all.(59)

December Holidays in Downtown Madison

Madison has had a long history of public Christmas celebrations. Both Santa and the famed Christmas tree were occupying space on Waverly Place as far back as the 1940s. The tree, reportedly, existed as early as 1946 in the *Madison Eagle*.(60)

But Santa was alive and well even before that, arriving as far back as 1877, albeit in the local churches and organizations. In a review of Christmas festivities, the *Madison Journal* reported that "the appearance of Santa himself was not only novel in itself but proved a source of merriment for the little ones."(61) He appeared at The Presbyterian Church's children's celebration.

Santa's visit always created much enthusiasm, and more so once his arrival on Waverly Place became firmly planted. In 1953, the *Madison Eagle* proudly displayed photos of its largest crowd ever. "Santa and His Reindeer Bring Christmas Greetings to 5,000 Madisonians," the paper's headline beamed across its front page.

With such a welcoming history, it's no wonder that Madison greeted more than 10,000 visitors to its 2019 Christmas Parade and Santa visit. In recent history, three individuals, Carmine Toto, Jr., Rose Ferdinand, and Carmela Vitale, were instrumental in creating the Waverly Place wonderland. Rose Ferdinand was the first of the trio, having been involved with the Madison Christmas Committee since it first began collecting donations from the public for Christmas decorations in 1965.

Ms. Ferdinand retired as treasurer of the committee in 2019. She was always the guiding light for those who were responsible for Santa's arrival and the festivities that preceded his visit with the children.

In the meantime, other activities were being presented to attract Madisonians to prepare for Christmas. In 1974, the new owners of the *Madison Eagle* sponsored a Christmas Walk on the Friday after Thanksgiving downtown. Publisher Bill Easton enlisted an eager Chamber of Commerce to provide a pre-Christmas social hour before Santa's arrival. And the residents came, happy to personally meet their shop owners.

Carmen Toto, Jr stands beside Santa's new house.

Everyone loved the parade and a new Santa house constructed by Carmine Toto, Jr. By 1980, Carmela Vitale, working with the Christmas Committee, was given the responsibility of organizing and extending the parade's march along Main Street. More so, she created the idea of having a theme each year and started planning during the summer months by obtaining floats, organizations, and bands to march. Carmine Toto, Jr. credits Carmela Vitale with "forming the parade as you see it today."(62)

Carmine Jr., who died in 2021, also recalled visiting Santa's house when it was located at the corner of Kings Road and Green Avenue. In 1980, he and his family built the new Santa house, placing it on the Kings Road railroad station lawn, and then began adding Santa's Village. He replaced that house with a shining replica in 2018. Toto's Christmas Village was all these years, lacking a menorah, the traditional Hanukkah celebration for those of Jewish faith.

Regardless of attempts by Madison's beloved Jewish family, Sam and Mildred Gordon, there was little effort to have one installed within the community to commemorate the holiday until 1999, when the Rabbinical College of America-Lubavitch, based in Morris Township, arranged to have a menorah installed adjacent to Santa's Village. Mayor Gary Ruckelshaus attended their "Festival of Lights" celebration, along with many Madison residents. Among them were Marcia and Rick Brous, daughter and son-in-law of the Gordons, who stated: "It's wonderful to know that the town of Madison has begun to acknowledge the diversity within the community in recognizing other religions at this holiday time."(63)

The history would not be complete without the mention of Santa Claus, who for 35 years was local resident, Bill Odell, whose magical touch delighted children from 1978 to 2013. Mrs. Claus came along in the guise of former Mayor Elizabeth Baumgartner during the 1980s, who turned over the reins to Carmela Del Guidice in 1990.

In 2015, the Christmas Committee and its noted volunteers were recognized by Mayor Robert H. Conley at its January 26 meeting, with a proclamation thanking them for bringing joy to the community, recognizing "their dedication in helping to make Madison such a special town." And, in return, the Christmas Committee welcomed residents and visitors to see the longest parade ever in 2019, along with clocking 3800 children visiting with Santa. Madison's Santa parade has now become a tradition in north-central New Jersey.

The Madison Eagle Christmas Fund (MECF)

Madison doesn't just know how to celebrate the festivities of the holidays; it also understands the spirit of giving that distinguishes the holidays. That spirit of sharing with those most in need has been manifested by the nearly 50 years of the Madison Eagle Christmas Fund (MECF).

Barbara Valk – A Champion of the Poor

Barbara and Don Valk's gift to their 5-year-old son Chris in 1970 was the opportunity to make an impoverished Madison family happy at Christmas and to develop a budding social conscience about the unseen families who lived somewhere in the community. He was the son of financially privileged parents. His mother, for many years, kept her conscience focused on the families living in substandard housing because she understood they went without the luxuries her family enjoyed at Christmas and all year long.

Ms. Valk began a one-woman campaign, casually soliciting her well-to-do but skeptical friends at cocktail parties and Republican political and social events. The donation enabled her to purchase gifts for a few people she had encountered. She was, at the time, and for many years afterward, chair of the Madison Republican Committee.

In 1973, when she learned that the *Madison Eagle* had new owners, Ms. Valk took advantage of her introductory luncheon with co-owner and editor Louise Easton to make a proposition. She described the need to the surprised newcomer and ended with one question, "Will the newspaper help me out?" Not only did she get approval, she also got a partner.(64)

By the following year, the pair had launched the Madison Eagle Christmas Fund, raising $1,300 through articles in the newspaper. With the same passion, they elicited help from their friends to shop for and deliver gifts and food to 60 people, including children and senior citizens. Those who helped and remained active with them for many years included Eleanore and Alan Goetze, Nancy and Bob Megargel, and Carmela and Pat De Biasse.

"That first year was an exciting one for us and our children, who were all adolescents and were, like Chris Valk, being indoctrinated into social service. They went along on the delivery runs, and when finished, we gathered at the Goetze's home for fun and frolic, sharing stories of our happy experiences. "A new world opened to us all," said Louise Easton, who is the lone survivor of the original group.(65) The volunteer families continued this tradition of shopping, delivery, and partying for many years. Years later, the memories were still alive and expressed by Chris Valk, in a eulogy at his mother's funeral in 2012. "Some of the earliest memories were of sight, sounds, and smells of poverty," he said, "all of which were very transformative."

The Fund Grows Over the Years

Thanks to the borough's social service department and the public-school social worker, the list of needy families grew. The fund also grew from donations by merchants and church organizations. Volunteers came from churches, schools, and members of many other community organizations.

Of great value was the acknowledgment and support of the borough's governing body and administration. Linda Durney, the social services liaison, served the fund for 37 years, stepping down after 2018. She recalled the fund's assistance to the needy beyond the Christmas season. "What is so extraordinary are the times when the fund also assisted in the off-season with emergencies, whether for medical expenses, utility/rent payments, or special programs for a child," she said. Mrs. Durney served under four chairs, "each one of them very dedicated to addressing the identified needs in Madison."

Within ten years, the fund was boasting help from at least 70 volunteers to shop and deliver to more than 250 residents. Donations reached a peak after the first few years when the Committee decided to acknowledge donors through the newspaper rather than send out handwritten notes.

Organizational Changes

All was not well with the organization in the years before and after 2010 when two new co-chairs, who had taken the reins from a high profile, creative, and efficient chair named Julie Carlson, decided they would dissolve the organization. Already retired from the organization and literally on her sick bed, Ms. Valk once again called in her volunteer friends for help. Gary Ruckelshaus, who had been mayor of Madison from 1996 - 1999, answered the call, immediately volunteering to take over as chair. That was 2012, the year Ms. Valk died. Louise Easton came out of retirement to assist. Along with other retirees, they kept the organization going. In 2015, they sent out an appeal for volunteers in the newspaper. A small group of volunteers responded to the appeal, and many continue to be active in the organization to this day.

Ruckelshaus retired in 2016, and leadership of the fund was assumed by co-chairs, Stacey Smollen and Jen Boyer. Ruckelshaus observed that "dinosaurs like me are leaving it in good hands." With its new leadership and signature name, the MECF has concentrated on reaching out to families through school-based programs such as Free & Reduced Lunch and to senior citizens through the Madison Housing Authority and Pine Acres Nursing Home. Instead of the wrapped gifts offered in its earliest days, the MECF now offers gift cards from local Madison shops so that residents themselves can select what they most need. This new approach has also boosted the Madison business community. In 2022, the fund's annual collection had exceeded $80,000.(65) It spread its gift card donations that "brought relief and care to over 500 residents" among over 30 Madison shops and restaurants.(66) The rich history of the MECF continues to evolve, but the support of the *Madison Eagle* newspaper remains strong.

Coach Theodore "Ted" Monica

Madison has had many standout teachers, counselors, pastors, and coaches. But none can rival Madison High School Football coach Theodore (Ted) Monica, renowned throughout the state for his leadership, unique teaching and coaching skills, and unyielding friend and mentorship to hundreds of high school students and coaching assistants. Unpretentiously known as "Coach," Monica served Madison from 1955 until his retirement in 1999, leaving a legacy unparalleled in both local and state sports.

His career began in 1954 as a recent veteran of the United States Marine Corps, with a position as the assistant football coach at Jonathan Dayton Regional High School in Springfield, NJ. Within a year, his unique leadership skills gained respect and admiration as he brought the team significant success and himself a new position as a physical education teacher and head football coach at Madison High School.

At Madison High School, he quickly established high standards for its football players, quickly creating a local football power. Additionally, he consistently elevated the game of each player on his team. Monica's motto: "Deal in results. Try to make something happen by working hard," spurred his players to become champions.

Winners they were, they took nine state championships, nine Suburban

League championships, and produced a record 38-game winning streak. Monica was particularly proud of the 1979 team, which was ranked the top high school team in the State of New Jersey by *The Star Ledger* newspaper.(67)

Coach Monica received the highest honor available when he was named "all-time winningest coach" in the State of New Jersey with a record of 177-50-4, a title he held for many years. While he retired from coaching in 1981 to become Director of Athletics, he remained active in Madison High School football for the remainder of his life. In 2007, the Madison High School football stadium was named the Ted Monica Stadium at Twombly Field.

Along with the venerable Coach Vince Lombardi, Monica ran the NFL draft day for the Green Bay Packers throughout the 1960s. Later, he traveled countrywide with Lombardi, jointly speaking at football coaching clinics. He also scouted for the Cleveland Browns. At the same time, he was instrumental in overseeing the Madison Recreation Department, where he took immense pride in ensuring that children of all ages had extracurricular sports and recreation available to them year-round.

Coach Monica remains in the hearts of almost five decades of students and athletes that he taught, motivated, and mentored. Former students credit him with their success, not only in sports but throughout life.

Although Coach Monica had retired from coaching the high school team by the time he joined the team, future NFL Super Bowl quarterback Neal O'Donnell displayed a talent that Monica could not ignore. O'Donnell said, "On his own time, the Coach personally worked with me for an hour at six am every Sunday morning in the high school gym. He prepared me for major college and professional football and his values prepared me for life after football."(68)

Madison's All-State football star and the University of Alabama running back, Peter Jilleba, also became an undefeated, two-time New Jersey Heavyweight State Wrestling Champion after Monica encouraged him to "try wrestling instead of basketball" as an off-season sport.(69) "Coach Monica was always more of a father figure than a coach. He was always there for me."(70) Tony Gero, a Florida State alum, feels sure that Monica changed his life. He said, "I would never have gone to college if it wasn't for the Coach."(71) Mississippi State quarterback Steve Natale, who worked as an assistant coach under Monica for five years, said, "He taught us life experience, sacrifice, preparation, attention to details, and to always work harder than your opponent."(72)

Coach Monica followed his students' careers well into their adult years, proud of their success stories and their shared values. They were there to salute him at his funeral when he died at the age of 90 on March 3, 2020.

A Time of Transition

The end of the 1960s decade, its transition to the 1970s, and later to the 1980s, brought significant changes to Madison, not unlike what other communities were facing. Political upheaval was still brewing from the conflicts of the 60s, as were higher expectations for women, minorities, and the poor. In Madison, this led to the emergence of women such as Cathie Coultas,

Louise Easton, Fran Mantone, Connie Stober, Barbara Valk, and the amazing Mayor Elizabeth Baumgartner, all of whom played significant roles in the positive growth of Madison in the post-'60s era.

Concern for the protection of the natural environment also came to the forefront of national and local activism. In Madison, efforts were made to protect available park land and, wherever possible, to acquire new parks for the future. Concerned citizens worked closely with many very talented mayors and members of the council to preserve lands that were being targeted for development. Their successes struck at the heart of what Madison was all about: the maintenance of an exceptionally beautiful American community through positive leadership and broad citizen participation. It also helped that Madison's elected leaders had a remarkable ability to work with state and federal officials to solve difficult issues such as low-income housing and the highway construction of a new Rt. 24, and the over-development of the borough.

Similarly, the challenging issue of how to provide low-income housing in what was perceived as a high-income community was handled with leaders addressing the issue with fairness and constructive solutions. The successful resolution of the issue was led by local leaders such as Robert Burroughs, Louis A. Riccio, Mayors Roger Vernon, Gary Ruckelshaus, and William Primus, all of whom played key roles.

While those years began with the loss of two extraordinary benefactors for Madison, beginning with Geraldine Rockefeller Dodge and her husband, Marcellus Hartley Dodge, other benefactors stepped up to the plate. It was those citizens working together that established the "Rose City" as a beacon to other cities and towns attempting to address similar challenges as the end of the 20th century grew ever closer.

CHAPTER FIFTEEN

Community Action in the 1980s and 1990s in Order to Preserve a Unique Madison

The period of Madison's history, dating from the mid-1980s to the new millennium, revealed the continued development of a rare quality not found in many American communities. Madisonians believed that their community was an exceptional place in which to live, and that inspired community action to solve even extremely serious challenges.

Those years prior to the dawn of the new 21st century were also marked by the emergence of highly effective mayors of both major political parties and other community leaders who were able to resolve difficult issues in a way that continued to move the community forward. It was also a time when women increasingly began to exercise political power. It would take this combination of community involvement and strong leadership to meet the many challenges the community faced.

The James Library (Museum of Early Trades and Crafts)

It took a single comment by a borough councilman to save the crown jewel of downtown Madison, the iconic 1900 James Library, from its loss in the 1990s. The Green Village Road building, the architectural legacy of philanthropist D. Willis James, had been long neglected and was feeling the pain of age and the disinterest of officials around essential investments in its upkeep.

From its opening in September 1970, the Museum of Early Trades and Crafts (METC) was a public success. By 1973, the museum had the seventh-highest public attendance of all of New Jersey's 63 museums.(1) Two years later, its rank had risen to sixth place, with a projected 75,000 annual total attendees.(2) But finances and the physical condition of the building were serious issues that would linger for years to come.

In 1968, when the committee led by Burr L. Chase was still investigating what the borough should do with the historic building, Madison realtor W. Kelton Evans advocated that "the 'Old Library' should be modernized and made even more useful than in the past—a quarter million dollar asset must never be allowed to deteriorate, regardless of changing times and lack of so-called practical usefulness." He went on to write that "The few thousand

Museum of Early Trades and Crafts.

dollars needed for modernization (after nearly 70 years) will require only a nominal expenditure of taxpayers' money to preserve and enhance the usefulness of one of Madison's most unique and beautiful structures."(3) History would show that it would take a lot more than what Evans estimated as a "few thousand dollars."

In March 1973, the *Eagle* reported that the "four-inch stone veneer of the turn-of-the-century building is bulging, pried from the structural terra cotta building blocks by expanding ice that found its way through the roof." Projected repairs would "probably run to several thousand dollars."(4).

That year, the final year of its initial three-year lease agreement with the borough, the museum's monthly rent had risen to $150. The museum did receive a $3,600 annual appropriation from the borough and a first-time grant of $5,000 from the county. But, as it did not charge an entrance fee, its operations and the care of the historic building were very much dependent on public and private support.

In July 1973, the borough council approved a ten-year lease agreement with the museum (retroactive to November 1972) for a token one dollar a year rent, but with the museum responsible for "all maintenance of the building." Under the previous lease, the borough had been responsible for major maintenance and repair of the building (like the recent bulging wall).(5)

But the questions of how to repair and maintain, and who was responsible for what, would not go away. In 1976, Princeton University rejected Madison's request that the university underwrite repairs to the building. (James' will stipulated that ownership of the building would go to Princeton if the borough did not use it for educational purposes.)

In February 1983, when the museum's lease was up for renewal, the debate flared up again. Museum Director Edgar Land declared that he would "move out" if he were required to make repairs to the aging building. He stated that the museum had undertaken normal maintenance of the building, including the repair of the gutters, painting the building, and making ceiling repairs, "...but what you want us to do is make repairs on a building that have come about because of 80 years of neglect by the borough." He stated that "the building was in bad shape when we took it over."(6)

The museum's lease was ultimately renewed, but the issues regarding the state of the building did not go away.(7) Later that year, the council appropriated $10,000 for an architect to evaluate structural defects that had continued to plague the building.(8)

The previously unthinkable idea of selling the building emerged when the lease again came up for renewal in the early 1990s. According to then-Councilman Gary Ruckelshaus, the borough council informally took sides—should it be sold, or should the council invest $2 million of taxpayers' dollars for major renovations, including compliance with the federal government's Americans with Disabilities Act (ADA).(9) Although the specific issue of selling the building was never formally introduced as a work session item, a straw poll of the six council members showed that there were two votes to sell, three votes to retain, and one undecided. In the case of a tie, Mayor Donald Capen would be called upon to break the tie, and he had made it known that he would vote to sell.

Torn by his own personal love for the building where he spent his childhood in the library and his role on the council as the steward of taxpayer monies, Ruckelshaus weighed the options for several weeks. It was a casual conversation with his fellow councilman and close friend, Dennis Mullins, who noted that "the building is part of the fabric of Madison."(10) That rang true, and so, Ruckelshaus moved to settle the issue. The borough would retain the building, and the council would offer the museum a new lease that stipulated that the two bodies jointly undertake the renovations, including the mandated compliance with the ADA requirements.

Mullin's comment had saved the day—and the beautiful building. The formal vote to renew the lease was passed with only a single dissenting vote (11)

The question of how to raise two million dollars without burdening the taxpayers remained foremost in the councilmembers' minds, as it also did to the museum's new board chairman, Stanley Brown of Chatham. Chairman Brown presented his plan to Ruckelshaus, suggesting that the borough offer $80,000 in support through a challenge grant that would give one dollar of borough funds for every two dollars raised by the museum's trustees. The council eagerly approved the plan and stood by as the museum trustees set out to raise $160,000. Amazingly, the trustees instead raised nearly $1.8 million, and the borough contributed $200,000.

The borough not only saved the building, but the museum remains firmly in the collective hearts of Madison. Governor Christine Todd Whitman and then-Mayor Gary Ruckelshaus proudly presided over a ribbon-cutting ceremony for the completed renovation on Bottle Hill Day, October 4, 1997.(12) Looking back two years later, Ruckelshaus described it as "the day I was proudest of Madison and of being mayor."(13) A year later, the renovation project garnered the museum one of eight New Jersey Historic Preservation Awards announced that year.(14)

Crafting a Historic Preservation Ordinance

Historic preservation, particularly of the downtown and several distinctly significant neighborhoods, had become an important public need in the late 1980s and 1990s. The saving of the James Library was one important example.

To help protect the integrity of the borough's newly renovated Downtown Historic District, the district was placed on the State and National Registers of Historic Places in 1989 and 1991, respectively, but the borough still did not have its own historic preservation commission or a historic preservation ordinance.

The Madison Borough Council established the Madison Historic Preservation Commission (HPC) in 1993 with the purpose of encouraging and advancing the protection, enhancement, and perpetuation of noteworthy examples of elements of the borough's cultural, social, economic, and architectural history.

"Among the duties of the five-member commission will be preparation of a survey of Madison's historic sites. The commission will also advise the Planning Board on planning decisions regarding the borough's historic sites," reported the *Madison Eagle*. (15)

To further that effort, Mayor Ruckelshaus convened a forum of over 100 stakeholders and interested Madison residents in March 1996. Historic Preservation Commission Chair Joe Falco, Jr., perhaps Madison's earliest preservationist, served as its master of ceremonies.(16) Keynote speaker, lawyer Michele Donato, described alternative legal approaches to preservation, what it is intended to accomplish, and what it would take to make it work. She argued that "historic preservation would protect property values and enhance the community."(17) Other forum experts, including Madison architectural historian and future HPC chair Janet Foster, discussed the benefits and the pitfalls and how towns like Madison have benefitted from historic preservation ordinances.

From that point on, public hearings were held on various versions of a municipal historic preservation ordinance. Strong feelings on both sides were discussed and debated, with some property owners favoring a strong ordinance that would help retain the "turn of the century" character of Madison, while many others rejected the idea of the town having the power to "dictate" what could and could not be done with their private property. After four years of starts and stops and many versions of an ordinance, the council finally approved one in

December 1999.(18)

Subsequently, in 2005, the portion of the Ridgedale Avenue residential neighborhood from Park Avenue to the Luke Miller House joined the Madison Downtown Historic District on the National Register of Historic Places. The newly named Bottle Hill Historic District was added to the list of designated "historic sites and districts" in the Madison Borough Code in 2008. In 2022, the borough adopted detailed *Madison Historic Design Guidelines* that had been prepared by the Madison Historic Preservation Commission the previous year.

Tropical Storm Doria and the Spring Garden Brook Project

Tropical Storm Doria smacked into northern New Jersey on August 27 and 28, 1971. The consequential damage to Madison occurred over a few short hours. The fixes took over twenty years.

The *Madison Eagle* reported that the 1971 storm dumped over 10 inches of rain on Madison and surrounding New Jersey communities in a short span of time during the early morning hours of April 28. All that concentrated rainfall resulted in record flooding on several small streams in eastern Pennsylvania and New Jersey, including Spring Garden Brook and Black Creek in Madison.

The underground culverts that carry the waters of Spring Garden Brook across Main Street could not handle the deluge. The result was serious flooding that made the road impassable between Greenwood and Alexander Avenues and just east of Rosedale Avenue. Stormwater from the Alexander Avenue-Main Street flooding reached the first-floor level of the nearby New Jersey Bell (now Verizon) switching office. Water poured into the building through a ground-level air vent, damaging exposed electronics, cable connections, and the emergency power supply (batteries) in the basement, putting 10,000 Madison subscriber lines out of service for 30 hours. New Jersey Bell took emergency measures to quickly restore service. The company estimated that the cost of repairs would come to $250,000 (or about $1.6 million in 2024 dollars).

Storm runoff flowing down the hill from Pomeroy Road also entered the library, ruining the carpeting and padding in the building's adult wing. The library had to close for a week. Additional flooding also occurred on Elm Street at the railroad underpass and in the Loveland Street-Anthony Drive neighborhood, where storm sewers feeding the Black Creek system were overwhelmed.(19)

This was the second serious flooding event with the brook system in less than a month. And so, in December 1972, Mayor Glenn Head presented an ambitious reconstruction project that would give the system the capacity to withstand a "100-year storm" without flooding.(20) The plan was quickly and unanimously approved by the borough council. However, when Madison applied for a federal grant to help pay for the project, Madison's downstream municipal neighbor, Florham Park, successfully argued that the proposed project would increase flooding within its borders. What followed were nearly ten years of negotiation, and it was not until 1982 that an agreement was finally reached between the neighboring communities, and work could begin on what would become a ten-year construction program.(21)

Initial project phases focused on improving the capacity of Spring Garden Brook downstream from Cross Street. The second phase, which took place in the 1985 timeframe, involved the construction of a three-sided concrete culvert over the channel bed in the Dean Street area and armoring adjoining portions of the streambed upstream to the Main Street culvert and downstream from Trail Place with layers of rock ("rip-rapping"). Phase II was completed with the installation of a new culvert under Main Street east of Cross Street by the spring of 1986.(22)

The borough addressed issues with the system upstream between Greenwood Avenue and Cross Street in the 1991 -1992 timeframe. The project involved regrading and reshaping the channel, construction of the open culvert that runs over the stream bed behind portions of the Rosedale Manor Apartments, through the Hillside Cemetery, and terminating at the underground tunnel under Main Street and rip-rapping the streambed between the Cross Street and the open culvert.(23)

Dean Street Culvert for the Spring Garden Brook.

The last phase of the project was the final construction of the 115-foot-long concrete tunnel under and across Main Street in the Alexander—Greenwood Avenue area. This was the most complex part of the project as it required digging up Main Street and rerouting water mains and New Jersey Bell telephone cables. Main Street had to be closed between Greenwood Avenue and Rosedale Avenue for over three months. With the reopening of Main Street in late spring 1992, almost 21 years after Hurricane Doria, the flood control program for Spring Garden Brook was finally completed.

Spring Garden Brook under Dean Street.

Demolition of the Bottle Hill Tavern

Unfortunately, the difficulties in maintaining a profitable restaurant in the historic Bottle Hill Tavern played havoc on the desires of community residents to preserve the building as an important part of Madison's history. As the site of Lafayette's visit in 1825 on his return to America (as described in Chapter 4) when it was known as the Madison House, it was rightly venerated as important to local and national history. Mario Torrani was among the owners who tried to successfully operate the property as a restaurant after it was moved from Waverly Place to Main Street.(24)

After Mr. Torrani died in 1959, his wife Mary continued to run the tavern for a short while, but by December of that year, she had sold it to prominent Morristown restaurateur Henry Lam. Mr. Lam announced his plans to make extensive renovations to the historic building and to rename it "The Bottle Hill Restaurant." In subsequent years, the business went through sev-

Bottle Hill Inn (as the Widow Brown's Inn) before it was demolished

eral different proprietors, bankruptcies, and at least one temporary closing. In 1967, the then proprietor, Frank Baldan, gave it an altogether new name: Widow Brown's Inn, which it kept until 1986 when the business was renamed Bottle Hill Inn by new owner Bob Mueller.(25)

Unfortunately, Mr. Mueller's stewardship ended quickly, and by January 1988, the Inn's doors were closed for good. A plan to renovate the structure for use as a bank proved unprofitable, and sadly, the landmark building was demolished in 1991.(26) A new bank building that recalls the look of the old tavern but with a drive-up window and ATM was then constructed on the site. The new bank opened as the Summit Trust Company on December 23, 1993. It is now a branch office of The Bank of America.

Great Mead Hall Fire

On Thursday, August 24, 1989, one of Madison's most historic and iconic buildings was swept by a fire so intense that it burned for 23 hours, required 2.3 million gallons of water to extinguish, and involved the deployment of more than 200 firefighters from Madison and thirteen surrounding communities. Drew University was subject to nothing less than a traumatic event: Mead Hall, the university's main administration building, was devastated by fire.(27)

Mead Hall was more than just an administration building with an expansive office for its president. It had enormous historical importance and architectural distinction, having earned places on both state and federal registers of historic sites in 1976. Built in 1823 by the Gibbons family, the name Mead Hall honors Roxanna Mead Drew, the wife of philanthropist and Drew patron Daniel Drew (see Chapter 5). It is a superb example of the Greek Revival style of architecture, which blossomed in the first half of the 19th century, pre-Civil War period.

The fire was started by sparks from a painter's torch being used to remove old paint on the first floor, which then traveled up the building's hollow outside walls—a common method of keeping early 19th-century buildings cool in the summer heat. The 1989 fire did considerable damage to the interior of the building and the

Mead Hall Fire on the Drew University Campus.

roof had to be removed by crane to finally extinguish the flames. But, due to its design and sturdy construction, the walls remained. A considerable number of valuable works of art, furniture, and chandeliers were saved by fast-thinking faculty, administrators, and students who rushed into the building and grabbed what they could. As the fire burned, Dr. Robert Bull led a group to retrieve valuable artwork and mirrors. One valuable painting was saved when a piece of oilcloth from the ceiling fell over it, protecting it from both flame and water.

Drew University Executive Vice President and Chief Operating Officer W. Scott McDonald, at the time Drew's interim president, saved computer discs from the basement computer center. The discs contained some of Drew's most important records. Computer tapes and paper files from the university computer center did not burn but were totally waterlogged from the relentless water from the fire hoses. The paper that was retrieved had to be placed in refrigerated trucks to be freeze-dried. The computer tapes were sent to technicians in hopes of salvage. Student employee checks were spread out on the ground to dry them out in the sunlight.

Drew had a substantial insurance policy on the building that would not only cover all the damages but was broad enough to begin an immediate rebuilding and restoration program under the leadership of its new president, former New Jersey Governor Thomas Kean. During the process, great care was taken to stay historically true to the building's 19th-century roots. The restoration took over three years, and Mead Hall was finally rededicated in December 1992.(28)

The fire occurred only days before the registration of new students. The computer was destroyed. At a welcoming assembly for new students, many of their parents were concerned about how the fire would impact the registration process. Interim president Scott McDonald told assembled parents that there were worse things. Many of them had registered similarly with paper and pen when years ago they had enrolled in college.

Open Space and the Environment – The Loantaka Moraine

Challenges to Madison's long-standing protection of open spaces appeared in the late 1980s, sparking action that became more crucial during the next decade. The first occurred soon after PIC Realty purchased the former Dodge Estate, which included an undeveloped parcel of 26 acres bordered by Woodland Road, and Loantaka Way, known as the Loantaka Moraine. The community began to worry when the company announced that the land was ecologically unsuitable for office space but would be appropriate for single-family homes.

The site was believed to have been created by the southern leading edge of the Wisconsin glacier that spread over the area approximately 11,000 years ago. (See Chapter 1). Geologists describe it as a terminal moraine, noting that the lovely, wooded expanse is a significant recharge area for the underground aquifer, which supplies Madison and its surrounding communities with drinking water through artesian wells. This fact made any development highly inappropriate.

When PIC Realty presented a plan to construct 26 homes on the property, neighbors protested to the borough council and then applauded their decision to explore the possibility of purchasing the land for open space. Councilman Gary Ruckelshaus led a long investigation into the availability of grants and loans to cover the property acquisition costs, but in time, it was deemed too expensive for the borough to acquire it alone.

Ruckelshaus persevered, initiating discussions with the Morris County Parks Commission, that eventually agreed to acquire the entire property, adding it to its adjacent Loantaka Park Reservation by using all of its four-year allocation of state Green Acres funds. A huge win for Madison!(29)

Another PIC Realty acquisition that came with their purchase of the Dodge Estate was a three-acre parcel bordering Gibbons Place, Woodland Road and Loantaka Way. According to then-Councilman Gary Ruckelshaus(30), a representative of the company proposed to Mayor Donald Capen that it would donate the lovely, flat piece of land for a park. When PIC Realty management subsequently changed, this was forgotten, and the company sold the property in 1997 to a local developer, Joseph DeMarzo. Local neighbors became alarmed and contacted Ruckelshaus, who was by then the mayor, to intercede. An immediate meeting with Mr. DeMarzo ended amicably. DeMarzo's conditions that the sale price cover all his costs to date and that the deal be consummated within 60 days were quickly approved by the borough council.

Ruckelshaus then set out to obtain funds from the state Green Acres program for an emergency grant and the Morris Land Conservancy (now The Land Conservatory of New Jersey) for a donation and asked that they hold the property until the borough could take title. Unfortunately, neither group had adequate funds to make the purchase. Ruckelshaus then

brought a Conservancy representative and a local bank official together to secure a loan, which was quickly approved, and the may-
or's action was accepted by the borough council. When the final
arrangements fell into place, Mr. DeMarzo's costs were covered,
and Madison had a new park at a net cost to the borough of less
than $40,000. Today, that lovely tree-lined property is known as
Gibbons Pines Park and is used for neighborhood recreation.(31)

Additionally, the borough officially designated two sites as parkland that had never been previously approved. The largest was
the 27-acre site between Ridgedale and Central Avenues, known
as Summerhill Park. (See Chapter 14). The second was a 2.5-acre
wooded parcel bordered by Belleau Avenue and Chateau Thierry
Ave. In the early 1970s, then-Mayor Glenn Head told neighboring

Gibbons Pines Park

residents that the borough-owned parcel would be designated a park. But it was never consummated, and in 1995, the property was being considered for sale. This possibility brought nearby
residents to the borough council. Council President Ruckelshaus took on an investigation and,
after poring over many borough council minutes, discovered the words that echoed in the residents' minds, it was to be a park! Ruckelshaus took action again by informing Mayor Donald
Capen and the borough council of the past promise. The mayor and council members agreed,
and Belleau Woods Park was created, much to its neighbors' delight.(32)

The Friends of Madison Shade Trees

The borough has long been blessed with residents who sincerely care about the beauty and importance of trees and plantings. To further that effort, Judy Mullins organized and founded the
Friends of Madison Shade Trees (FMST)(33), and Madison is much better for it. Considered
Madison's own Johnny Appleseed, Mullins has led the FMST, through donations and grants,
in planting hundreds of trees and plants, with emphasis, of course, on rose bushes throughout
the town. Of primary significance are the Rose Garden Park at the intersection of Kings Road
and Green Avenue;(34) the dramatic and historically correct re-landscaping of the Madison
Train Station; the plantings in and around the commuter parking lots; the trees lining the
Greenwood Avenue side of Cole Park; and the magnificent 900-foot long Burning Bush hedge
from Prospect Street to the train line trestle.(35)

In 2004, FMST partnered with Madison's Affordable Housing Corporation at its first-time
homeowner project on Elm Street to provide appropriate property trees and foundation screen-
ings for the new housing units.

Ornamental tree replacements were made at both the Niles Park and Central Green neighborhood passive parks that had suffered from a combination of drought and deer destruction.
FMST has supported deer enclosures at Central Green and on the campus of Drew University
to extensively study forest floor re-growth to gain insight into deer destruction and develop
strategies for prevention.

A 2005 National Tree Trust grant provided over $11,000 for 31 flowering pear trees to be
planted along the borough right-of-way, running the length of Madison's east business district
to the Chatham border.(36) This continued the central business district's flowering red spire
pear tree theme, unifying and expanding a sense of place when entering Madison.

Partnering with the Shade Tree Management Board and the newly formed Madison
Playground Committee in 2005, FMST assisted in providing shaded recreation areas for

Madison's children. Over a dozen October Glory maples from a former FMST project (the site of the ca. 2008 municipal Public Safety Building) were professionally moved to Dodge Field. (37) Resurrecting Madison's roots, a rose propagation project is now underway to create young offshoots from the Rose Garden Park's Rotary Red Rose (*Mirepoix*).

The clearing of deadwood and dangerous trees at the Chateau Thierry Park also strengthened FMST's partnership with Madison's Downtown Development Commission.

Another collaboration of FMST with The Rotary Club of Madison, local master gardeners, and the County Agriculture Extension Office was the development of garden plots at the Rexford Tucker Senior Citizen Facility, as were new walking paths.(38) Recently, the Rotary Club launched a project to plant 100 trees around town in honor of its 100th anniversary. The first phase, consisting of 52 trees, was completed in the fall of 2023.(39)

Judy Mullins

A mature female holly tree, blossoming proudly at the Madison train station, bears a plaque thanking Judy Mullins for the "Greening of Madison." The well-deserved acclamation credits this 'super' volunteer for her quiet, unrelenting beautification efforts throughout the community.

Arriving in Madison in 1980 as an early environmentalist with a head filled with knowledge regarding the importance of shade trees, she single-handedly created a borough-wide canopy of appropriate, colorful, and environmentally friendly greenery. She co-founded the Madison Shade Tree Authority (now the Madison Shade Tree Management Board) and, almost simultaneously, the Friends of Madison Shade Trees. It was apparent that the success of her "Green Madison" vision depended on public interest and funds to offset the borough's limited tax-dollar budget.

Judy Mullins' knowledge of appropriate trees for a downtown area gave the Madison Historic District a graceful arch of branches and dappled shade. Her leadership and energy have led Madison to plant scores of saplings along residential streets visibly contributing to Madison being declared a Tree City USA. Judy's leadership also created many cooperative projects involving Madison's Parks Committee and the Garden Club of Madison where hundreds of new trees have been planted and old trees properly pruned and preserved. To support these efforts, she raised hundreds of thousands of dollars in grants and donations with endless patience and attention to detail. Without Judy Mullins, Madison would simply not be the warm and welcoming picturesque small town where people want to live and raise their families.

The Legendary Tuttle Oak

The FMST organization took the Tuttle Oak as a symbol of the value Madison has historically placed on trees and also kept the local folklore/legend/myth alive about General George Washington having tied his horse to the Tuttle oak. The true history is that in the summer

Sketch of the Tuttle Oak from an original soft-ground etching by the late R. Harmer Smith.

of 1858, Rev. Samuel L. Tuttle opened Prospect St. to run through his estate, through the property of Henry Keep, and then to Kings Road. When Rev. Tuttle came upon workmen preparing to cut down a large oak tree standing nearly in the center of the planned street right-of-way, he stopped them, saying that "it was too splendid a tree to destroy."(40) The tree stayed and remained in the streetway until November 1996, when it was fatally damaged in a truck accident. (41) A cut of the tree is on display in the Madison Public Library.

In addition to its designation as a Tree City USA, Madison has also been recognized by the Arbor Day Foundation and the National Association of State Foresters because the borough met its four major requirements: To have a tree board or department, a tree care ordinance, a community forestry program with an annual budget of at least two dollar per capita, and hold an annual Arbor Day Observance.(42)

During the 1990s, several Madison Council members also participated in the Ten Towns Commission, which was concerned about the preservation and long-term health of the Great Swamp National Preserve. This commission led to land use changes in the ten towns to limit run-off and prevent pollution from finding its way into the Great Swamp.

The Illuminating Story of Madison's Own Electric Utility

As it entered the early decades of the twentieth century, the borough's locally owned electric utility faced some serious challenges. The *Madison Eagle* documented endless squabbles over the purpose, structure, ownership, rates, surplus, wholesale vs. home-grown electricity, and even the raison d'etre of the electric utility. "The early debates became enmeshed with the equally sticky debate over the municipal ownership of the electric company, which was a concept of independence held dear to the hearts of Madisonians."(43)

Everything came to a head in September 1923 when the borough council voted—without any public input—to buy power from Jersey Central Power and Light Co. (JCP&L), leaving the utility to be either sold or gradually die off. *Eagle* Editor John Clarey strongly disagreed with the council consensus and led a campaign to resist the change. Clarey spent the subsequent months running for mayor on a platform stating that he would remove the Water and Light Committee chairman, Frank Waters, and secure an injunction to prevent the contract with JCP&L from becoming operative. He charged his opponent with the "gradual scrapping of most of the utility's assets..."(44). The voters of Madison seemed to agree with Mr. Carey, and he won handily. And the utility was never sold.

Consumption of electricity climbed steadily during the following decades, and the Madison Electric Utility continued to deliver exceptional service to its commercial and residential customers. A post-WW II boom in electricity usage necessitated the construction of two new power sub-stations, the first on Kings Road in 1954 and the second at James Park in 1970.

In 1956, the borough established a policy to track the rate structure charged by JCP&L in the surrounding towns, but typically with somewhat lower rates. This rate structure covered the costs of the purchased power as well as all personnel and capital costs and still produced a modest surplus. The surplus came to about $550,000 annually, a portion of which was transferred to the borough budget, reducing the municipal tax levy.

However, issues with the utility arose again during the 1970s and 1980s when JCP&L significantly raised its rates due to the era's dramatic rise in fuel costs. When Madison and four other municipalities lost a 1979 court challenge to resist the increase, the borough was subject to a substantial increase in its costs. This forced the borough council to raise the municipal tax rate by 3%.(45)

With this rise and another increase in commercial rates, the borough council was overwhelmed with complaints, notably from the H.P. Higgs Co. The company challenged the legality of the utility's yearly transfer of surplus funds to the borough's general operating fund.(46) Mr. Higgs also argued the electric rates should be based on the cost of services and not on the rates of other privately owned utilities.

The borough initially lost the case in superior court, but the appellate division reversed the ruling in 1983. The appellate court decision legalized Madison's approach to rates and surplus, allowing it to bill the utility "in lieu of franchise and gross receipts taxes, and generating a surplus both of which are transferred to the borough..."(47). This was a big win for the borough and other municipal-owned utilities in the state.

The rules of the game then changed on October 24, 1992, when the federal government deregulated the wholesale price of electricity. The Energy Policy Act of 1992 created the outline for a competitive wholesale electricity generation market.

As an annual purchaser of over 100 million KWH, Madison found itself in the enviable position of soliciting competitive prices from wholesale suppliers and watching the prices go down. After receiving several bids, Madison selected Pennsylvania Electric Company (Penelec) as the supplier. According to Borough Administrator James Allison, the selection would save the borough about $2.6 million in its power supply budget, and residential customers would receive rate reductions of about 15%. The net effect was that the borough could sell more electricity at lower rates *and* produce a larger surplus.(48)

Subsequent fixed-rate contracts were negotiated at extremely competitive rates, and annual surpluses of approximately $5 million were available to be transferred to the borough budget to defray taxes.

Although a small amount of the electricity that the borough purchased came from hydroelectric plants in New York, the source of most purchased by the borough was closely tied to the world price of oil. Accordingly, the cost to Madison of wholesale power would be seriously affected if oil prices changed significantly.

A dramatic July 2008 peak oil price of $147 per barrel led the Madison Electric Utility Committee to recommend that the borough not adopt a managed wholesale power purchase agreement.(49) The borough council consequently entered into a fixed-rate contract for five years. The timing of the contract proved extremely unfortunate as the price was fixed so high that any chance of a surplus was destroyed and serious losses would be incurred if there were no hefty rate increases.

Electric rates, which had been consistently less than those of JCP&L, increased by 8% in 2007, 15% in 2008 and 24.5% in 2009. Ratepayers were stunned at the price hikes, and the borough had to seriously cut back its capital expenditures for the term of the fixed-rate contract.

Learning from the error of their 2008 decision, the borough moved to a managed approach for all further contracts. Retaining the rate level, the utility returned to the substantial surpluses, instituted a dividend to be paid back to the ratepayers, and reduced rates for lower-income seniors.

Available records show that for the 41 years since 1976, the Madison Electric Utility provided over $150,000 million in revenues to the borough, which reduced property taxes by an average of 42%.

Financial Implication of Maintaining a Clean Environment

As a result of the State of New Jersey threatening Madison and Chatham with a $50,000-per-day fine if their jointly owned-and-operated wastewater treatment plant was not upgraded, Madison was forced to take on over $20 million in unanticipated bonded debt in 1990. The action caused Madison's bonded debt to jump from approximately $9 million to over $29 million.

After lengthy discussions, Councilmen Joseph Verbaro and Gary Ruckelshaus recognized the impact of such a debt load and led the council to adopt a "pay-as-you-go" policy (meaning no bonding; capital projects would only be funded out of existing cash assets) that was strictly observed throughout the 1990s. This policy led to stable taxes and no property tax increases for seven straight years, a record for which Madison was recognized in a citation from then-Governor Christine Todd Whitman. During the decade of the 1990s, by strictly adhering to pay-as-you-go, Madison's bonded debt was driven down from over $23 million to under $10 million by the turn of the century, while at the same time, the borough's electric utility was successfully providing its residents and businesses with inexpensive and dependable power.(50) (51) (52)

In 2019, the borough council was again faced with the need to approve a bond ordinance for $1,272,000 to help finance Madison's share of an anticipated $7.2 million project to upgrade the Madison Chatham Joint Meeting. Borough Administrator Raymond Codey explained that the project was required to meet recently enacted Federal Environmental Protection Agency (EPA) standards for phosphorus discharges by replacing aging equipment and increasing the capacity of the plant to address anticipated demand.(53)

The pay-as-you-go policy, as well as the extraordinary electric utility performance, together with a 20-year capital plan that anticipated and provided for large capital expenditures, led to Madison's ranking in Standard & Poor's and Moody's Bond ratings being increased to AAA. As quoted in the *Bond Buyer,* "The outlook [for Madison] is stable based on the expectation that financial management bolstered by pay-as-you-go funding of capital improvements and a strong local economy."(54)

New Route 24

The state-chartered Morris Turnpike of 1804 had become a very congested Route 24 in Madison and Chatham a century and a half later. As the eminent New Jersey historian John Cunningham wrote in his forward-looking addendum to the original *Madison Heritage Trail*: "The 'new' Route 24 was planned in the 1950s. 'Old' Route 24 began to be replaced by a well-engineered, limited access superhighway, paid for with State funds." Connecting to the new Interstate Route 78 in Springfield Township, "it would link with Interstate 287 north of Morristown, then swing around the county seat to open the way westward to Mendham and Chester."(55)

The link between I-78 and John F. Kennedy Parkway was completed in 1976. As Mr. Cunningham noted: "The new road (then) came to a screeching halt—often literally in peak traffic hours—at Chatham. Traffic dumped off Route 24 crawled through Chatham, Madison and on to Morristown."(56)

In the late 1970s and early 1980s, officials and residents in Chatham and Madison actively lobbied the state to complete the five-mile missing link in the expressway from John F. Kennedy Parkway to I-287. They argued forcibly that the current configuration was creating intolerable volumes of traffic onto Main Street and side streets in residential neighborhoods.(57)

In 1980, state officials offered three alternative route configurations for the missing link, but the mayors of Madison, Florham Park, and Chatham stated that they would only accept a route that followed the original freeway design for which the state purchased right-of-way 20 years earlier. "Alternate 1 (the original design) is not an alternate; it is the highway," stated Chatham Mayor John Bennett.(58)

The real issue was the location and number of access roads to the new highway. One would be at Columbia Turnpike near Morristown Airport, which was not controversial and exists today. The other two were controversial. One was planned for construction at the Madison-Chatham border near Brooklake Road and the PSE&G power lines. Referred to as Triborough Road by the state, it was actively opposed by residents in the impacted neighborhoods(59) and by Florham Park Mayor Ralph Loveys.(60) The second connector would run parallel to Danforth Road and across what was then the Exxon property and was also opposed.

The state would continue to argue that both connectors were necessary, and residents in the impacted neighborhoods would continue to object to their construction.(61) In any case, Florham Park Mayor Ralph Loveys and Madison Mayor Elizabeth Baumgartner stated "they will not consider any feeder roads until the freeway is completed to Rt. 287."(62) Construction of the "missing link" would begin in 1988(63) and was completed in November 1992. Even then, the state would argue that the disputed connectors were needed(64). They were never constructed. And the "swing around the county seat westward to Mendham and Chester" was also long ago shelved by the state, and the "old Route 24" was renamed Route 124.

The Railroad: Electrification, NJ TRANSIT, and Midtown Direct Service

By the 1970s, the once proud railroad that made Madison's rose industry possible and enabled the town's twentieth-century evolution into a suburban bedroom commuter community had earned the derogatory sobriquet: "The Weary Erie." The railroad corporation was essentially bankrupt, and the green, circa 1929-1930 "Lackawanna Electrics" with their uncomfortable rattan seats, poor lighting, and lack of air conditioning, were universally despised. They were certainly obsolete by post-war standards, as was the railroad's 3,000-volt direct current electrification that powered them.(65)

In 1976, the railroad formally petitioned to join the recently created government-sponsored Consolidated Rail Corporation (Conrail). After Congress ordered Conrail to cease all of its remaining passenger operations, the railroad, which had been operating the former Erie Lackawanna commuter lines under contract from the New Jersey Department of Transportation, turned over operations responsibility to the recently formed rail subsidiary NJ Transit Rail Operations, Inc. in 1983.(66)

With the change, NJ Transit (NJT) retired the existing direct current power distribution system on the Morris and Essex Division in August 1984 and replaced it with a 25,000-volt alternating current system. With the re-electrification, the old Lackawanna Electrics were replaced with modern, stainless steel, air-conditioned Arrow III MU cars. (67)

In 1996, NJT introduced the "Midtown Direct" service, a one-seat ride to New York Penn Station on the Morris & Essex Lines. Before Midtown Direct, the Morris & Essex trains terminated in Hoboken, where Manhattan-bound commuters had to transfer to PATH (Port Authority Trans-Hudson) trains to cross the Hudson River. The $70 million state-funded project included five miles of new track, a 350-foot-long bridge, and modifications to the track system. The expanded service cut the overall travel time to Manhattan by 20 minutes and led directly to an increase in commercial and residential real estate development around many of the towns, like Madison, with stations on the line.(68)

In the mid-2000s, NJT introduced new Bombardier Multilevel Coaches on the Morristown Line. These new coaches increased per-car capacity by 15 to 30% and eliminated the unpopular middle seat of the Arrow III's 3-2 seat configuration.

In a 2015 report, NJT stated that the Madison Train Station had an average of 1505 weekday train boardings in 2011.(69)

Attending the September 1984 dedication of new electrification of trains: Assemblyman R. Frelinghuysen, Mayor E. Baumgartner, Assemblyman D. Gallo, and Senator L. Brown.

New Arrow IIIs take over. All-new air-conditioned modern passenger cars, faster running times, flexibility in schedule, and more comfort.

Renovation of the Madison Train Station

The stately gem that is the Madison Train Station was opened in 1916 and is on the National Register of Historic Places (See Chapter 11). By the mid-1990s, however, it had fallen into a deplorable state with boarded-up windows, permanently closed restrooms, and a coating of dirt and grime on its exterior—to the despair and alarm of many in Madison. In 1996, new mayor Gary Ruckelshaus sent a letter to NJT requesting that the building be "cleaned up and repaired." This letter triggered a succession of events that no one anticipated.(70)

NJT initially responded by setting up a meeting with NJT people to tour the facility. The mayor invited interested Madison residents to join the tour, and the groups spent half a day roaming around the buildings and grounds, taking notes and making comments. As a follow-up to that meeting, two members of the Historic Preservation Commission, Ronald Poeter and Mary-Anna Holden, performed a detailed review of the building, which pointed out the extent of its decline.

For the next few years, NJT worked with the not-for-profit organization known as the Friends of the Madison Train Station, founded in 1996 by Gary Ruckelshaus and Joeseph Falco. (71) This public-private partnership led to a fundraiser, conceived by preservationist Richard Romano, for the sale of engraved pavers at the station, which raised $135,000 for building repairs, new curbs, and new lighting; a $100,000 Department of Transportation grant for landscaping thanks to the Friends of Madison Shade Trees; and nearly $15 million spent by NJT in repairs, renovations, and ADA required improvements (including an elevator, ramps, and raised platforms). Once again, positive community action led to great improvements.(72)

The Friends of the Madison Train Station became (and remains) the operator of the on-site parking at the station and uses the parking fees to maintain the grounds, clear snow, and make modest repairs to the building.(73) The multimillion-dollar restoration and renovation brought a NJ State Historic Preservation Award to New Jersey Transit in 2007, accepted on behalf of the project team who patiently worked hard on the 11-year project, including Madisonians Gary Ruckelshaus, Richard Romano, Ronald Poeter, and Mary-Anna Holden.(74)

Dedication of the renovation of Madison Train Station.

Visit of President George H. W. Bush

President George H. W. Bush, the only sitting president ever to visit Madison, spoke to a rally on the steps of the Hartley Dodge Memorial Building on November 2,1992 at 8:00 am. It was his last day of campaigning before the presidential election. Bush explained that for him, it was also "The last day I will ever campaign for myself for president of the United States or anything else."(75)

Madison Borough Administrator James Allison, Mayor Capen, and Council President Ruckelshaus met daily with members of the FBI, Secret Service, and the President's staff prior to the visit. On the morning of the speech, the entire governing body met privately with the president in the council chambers, where he was shown some of the historic artifacts located there. These included the Rodin bust of Napoleon, (which was subsequently sold by the Hartley Dodge Foundation to an unnamed collector for an undisclosed sum in 2019) (76) and

the nine-foot-tall oil painting of Abraham Lincoln painted by W. F. Travers (which is now on loan to the National Portrait Gallery in Washington, D.C.). As soon as President Bush saw the portrait, he quipped, "I have one of those where I live too."(77)

The President made a rousing speech to the crowd of 5,000 (including future N.J. Governor Chris Christie) on the steps of the Hartley Dodge Memorial; the Madison High School Band was behind him.(78) Security was high, with armed Secret Service and FBI agents strategically placed around the building.

President George H.W. Bush with Council President Gary Ruckelshaus.

Although President Bush lost the national election and New Jersey to Democrat Bill Clinton, Madison gave him the victory he hoped for on that cold November morning. On Election Day, he carried Madison.

Vibrant Local Culture: The Shakespeare Theatre of New Jersey

In 1879, *Madison Journal* reader Mrs. Sallie Battey, writing from New York City, bitterly complained that pedestrian tastes in staged plays abound, "while the legitimate temple of the muses is almost deserted...and even Shakespeare is disappearing before the change of thought and the revolution in taste."(79) How utterly delighted she would have been almost 100 years later, when the New Jersey Shakespeare Festival came to, and then permanently settled, in Madison!

The Festival's reincarnation, as The Shakespeare Theatre of New Jersey (STNJ), is now one of America's largest and most respected classical theaters. Its origins go back to 1963 as a humble summer stock company in the resort town of Cape May, New Jersey. Founded by the veteran actor and director Paul Barry, he named the company The New Jersey Shakespeare Festival. Barry's real love was the stage, and he was committed to bringing the classics to New Jersey. Unfortunately, the company's home, the deteriorated Cape May Playhouse built in 1902, was demolished by 1968, and the hapless Shakespeare Festival was left homeless and in debt. One of the many alums from that period was well-known actor Christopher Lloyd of *Back to the Future* fame.(80)

Relief came in 1972 with a phone call from the head of Drew University's Theatre Department, inquiring as to whether Barry's company was interested in taking on some Drew student interns. Being that the company was homeless, he asked if Drew would be interested in housing them. He met with University President Robert Oxnam, and an hour later, they had a deal. The New Jersey Shakespeare Festival found a home in Drew's old Bowne Gymnasium.(81)

The company proved to be a great success, with brisk ticket sales, a 23-week season, and a 100th production birthday party hosted by Governor Brendan Byrne. In the first seven years at Drew, it earned 27 awards for excellence from the New Jersey Drama Critics Association, and remarkably, in the decade of the 1980s, Paul Barry became the first American to have directed Shakespeare's entire canon.(82)

Success continued through the early 1980s, but things were quietly shifting on the national theater scene. Funding issues, competition with at-home entertainment activities, a quickly deteriorating performance space, and management differences all began presenting problems. Unfortunately, tensions between the Trustees and the Barry team led to Barry's resignation in 1990. The Theatre's future was in doubt. The Trustees were determined to save it. To address the issues, a nationwide search began for a new Artistic Director. In October 1990, 34-year-old Bonnie J. Monte, who had served as the Associate Artistic Director of the famed Williamstown Theater Festival in Massachusetts, after 17 interviews, was hired as the new Artistic Director.(83).

Under Monte's effective leadership, momentum built through the early 1990s and much good work was accomplished both onstage and behind the scenes. During her first season, 1991, she eliminated the prior repertory system and created a major reform, a system of "three week-runs of five shows opening back-to-back." Also notable was the tremendous expansion of the educational initiatives as both in-school and on-site programs at the theater flourished. That first season finished with an all-star flurry of *Twelfth Night*, with Elizabeth McGovern, Laila Robins, Paul Mullins, and Edward Herrmann. And a budget surplus. However, it became clear that productions were limited by the deteriorating facility and the lack of viable technical systems. With a strong record of excellence in productions and fiscal responsibility under Monte's guiding hand, discussions began in 1993 for a major capital campaign to create a state-of-the-art performance space.(84)

Two incidents occurred thereafter that helped create unanimous board recognition of the urgent need for a new space. One of the most distressing problems with the nearly 100-year-old Bowne Gym building was its lack of handicap accessibility. After actor Christopher Reeve's ("*Superman*") horse riding accident in 1995, he was no longer able to attend shows at the festival to see his wife Dana perform. The building was virtually inaccessible for wheelchair patrons.

Dana and Chris became vocal advocates for the creation of a facility that would accommodate patrons with all types of accessibility issues. Then in 1996, a huge summer storm hit during a performance of *Richard III*. A particularly strong thunderclap provided the tipping point, and a portion of the roof above the audience started to disintegrate. This alarming occurrence aided the full and strong support for a campaign that was essentially already underway.(85)

With a dedicated and active board, a determined staff, and the tremendous help of Drew's President at the time, former Governor Thomas H. Kean, as well as many loyal patrons, NJSF engaged in a highly successful $7.5 million campaign led by Board President Margaret Domber to expand and completely renovate the old Bowne Theater.

Bringing the renovation in on time and on budget was a major accomplishment, and in June 1998, The F.M. Kirby Shakespeare Theatre, a state-of-the-art jewel of an intimate 308-seat performance space, opened to great fanfare and provided a massive sea change for the institution.(86)

"The new F.M. Kirby Shakespeare Theatre allowed for a significant expansion of the performance season into the fall and early winter months. The company was able to produce as many as seven Main Stage shows, and by 1998, the theatre's annual budget had quadrupled from the 1991 figure of $500,000 to $2.0 million." By 2002, an agreement was reached with nearby Saint Elizabeth University to use their outdoor Greek amphitheater for several productions and it has become quite popular, its audience quadrupling over 20 years. A year later, the staff and board decided

F.M. Kirby ShakespeareTheater after renovation of Bowne Gymnasium.

to change the name of the institution to dispel the widespread misperceptions caused by the word "festival" in the theater's name, and it officially became The Shakespeare Theatre of New Jersey.(87)

In 2011, the theatre acquired and began renovation on an old valve factory located in nearby Florham Park. The facility was to be used to centralize all of the institution's behind-the-scenes operations. In 2019, the facility was officially named the Thomas H. Kean Theatre Factory.(88)

After 34 years at the helm, Bonnie Monte retired at the end of the 2023 season. She retained the title of Artistic Director Emerita and all agree that she transformed the Shakespeare Theatre "into one of the nation's most celebrated professional classic theater companies with first-class indoor and outdoor space, an expansive education program and an outreach program that brought Shakespeare into schools." Former Governor Thomas Kean said of her: "During her tenure, Bonnie Monte has taken the Shakespeare Theatre to new heights. She is one of New Jersey's arts leaders. She will be succeeded but never replaced."(89) She is succeeded as Artistic Director by Brian Crowe.

Perhaps in our dreams, we might see a very (very) old woman, Mrs. Sallie Battey, bouncing along on NJ Transit, returning to Madison to give Bonnie Monte a heartfelt hug and a thank you for avoiding those pedestrian tastes and rightfully restoring Shakespeare on his pedestal, at least in Madison.

May Day Cleanup

When Assistant Borough Administrator James E. Burnet IV came up with the idea of having a townwide spring beautification day, he turned to his fellow Downtown Development Commissioners (DDC) for assistance. His goal was to "remind residents of a shared need to maintain our downtown and public spaces."(90) They heartily endorsed the idea, as did a later audience of the governing body. Then, in true Madison style, the citizens responded to the call for a DDC-sponsored May Day on May 2, 1998.

More than 250 volunteers spent their morning cleaning up the downtown on that first May Day. They responded enthusiastically to the organizing committee that included the Downtown Manager Anthony Donato, representatives of several community organizations, and other resident volunteers. The following year, the volunteer May Day squad grew to 500, and since then, 800 to 1,000 people have come out annually to the event held on the first Saturday in May, now known as Madison Clean and Green Day.

One resident, Mary Kay Krowkowski, was instrumental in encouraging children, especially scout troops, to participate in the event. As a result, half the volunteers are under the age of 18.

May Day volunteers ready to beautify Madison.

May Day volunteers cleaning up the flower beds.

As it has since its incorporation in the late 1870s, the *Madison Eagle,* under the banner of editor Garry Herzog, kept citizens up to date on the committee's activities and the day's schedule. Mayor Gary Ruckelshaus and the borough council's commendation set an example for future governing officials who have endorsed the spirit of the day as a true reflection of Madison residents' historic community unity in service. Burnet accepts credit for initiating the project, but is quick to credit the people who chaired the event in later years, Mara Johnson and Lisa Ellis and the DDC.

Memorial Day in Madison

Madison's long history of annual Memorial Day Parades continued to be part of Madison's tradition and grew in attendance during the 1990s. Former Mayor Jack Dunne worked tirelessly to create respectful tributes to Madison's veterans in several ways, by planting trees in James Park, and posting veterans' names who gave their lives in combat on the street signs where they lived. In later years, he organized and created an engraved paver plaza surrounding Madison's World War I Memorial.

Celebrating the New Century

While the world anticipated the arrival of the year 2000, Madison residents prepared for its longest and largest celebration of the event. Meticulously choreographed by old-timers and chaired by former councilwoman Jo Renee Formicola, the entirety of 1999 and the early days of 2000 were devoted to organizing the events that would ignite a commemorative collective by creating mementos that would keep them alive forever.(91)

Madison native and businessman Jack Morris and his wife Pat brought together a creative team to develop the Rose City 2000 logo that appeared on newspaper articles, posters, and stationery throughout the year (92), while former Councilwoman Frances Mantone sold miniature replica Millennium Clocks for the Downtown Development Commission to help offset the cost of the events.

By mid-year, they were ready to celebrate and did so with a huge picnic called "A Celebration of Time"(93) where, on a picture-perfect June 5, more than 2,000 residents and friends gathered at Madison's Memorial Park. Planned as an old-fashioned, family-oriented get-together, the picnic featured an "all you can eat" barbeque, sports, games, and musical entertainment. It was the largest picnic ever held in Madison. Honored were Madison's oldest resident, 103-year-old Portia Stallings, and long-time Madison businessman and former Councilman Sam Gordon.(94)

Not to be outdone, Madison High School alumni gathered for an "all class" reunion held on the school's hockey field, chaired by Chaz Ricci. The happy event was attended by nearly 800 alums, including 1929 graduate Delight Lewis!(95)

The burial of a time capsule, conceived and chaired by longtime resident and retired police officer Frank Sena, captured the attention of attendees and onlookers as it was buried in the front plaza of the Hartley Dodge Memorial Building, where it is marked by a bronze plaque noting the capsule is to be opened in 2049. It contains a proclamation by then-Mayor Gary Ruckelshaus to future residents and a significant sample of documents detailing Madison's history through its then-current clubs and organizations (96).

The burial of the Millennium time capsule for 2000 on the steps of the Hartley Dodge Memorial Building.

Capping off the events was a New Year's Eve countdown to the year 2000 party on Waverly Place. Organized by Madison natives Janice Piccolo, Frances Mantone, and Carmela Vitale, more than 1,000 folks awaited the countdown to the new millennium with live music, dancing, and singing. The final countdown was led by Mayor Gary Ruckelshaus. The party, running from 11 pm to 1 am, was livened with the continuous showing of Carmine Toto's movies of notable past Madison celebrations.(97)

To keep the memories alive, the Millenium Committee appointed longtime resident Peggy Merrick to head a Quilting Committee, and she, along with fifteen other members, met monthly to design and create a quilt Illustrating important Madison events from 1900 through 2000, using the design of the recently installed Millennium Clock on Waverly Place. With the planning and intricate work, it took approximately two years to complete the work, which hangs in the Children's Section of the Madison Public Library.(98)

A Final Touch – The Millenium Clock

Madison's landmark "Millennium Clock" was the finishing touch to the downtown renovation that began in the 1970s (see Chapter 14) and is a lasting reminder of the town's Millennium celebration. As one of the originally considered accessories to the renovation, it was not included in the final plan due to its cost, which was $20,000. That sum did not include the installation, a paver plaza, benches, light poles, bollards, brick planters, and landscaping.

A fundraiser for the clock project was established in the spring of 1998 by Mayor Gary Ruckelshaus with the objective of a Bottle Hill Day-1999 dedication. The dedication would be a highlight of the planned year's events welcoming the new Millennium. True to the town's character and spirit, many of Madison's generous corporate residents, its two colleges, and its many civic organizations contributed more than $30,000 within only a few weeks. With such overwhelming support and the word-of-mouth excitement of Madison residents for the proposed clock, it was decided to attempt to advance the dedication by a year to the 1998 Bottle Hill Day.

Things worked so smoothly that the clock was purchased, and the aggressive installation date was met. The 16-foot Seth Thomas 1880s-style clock was placed at the north end of Waverly Place, the very center of downtown Madison. The borough's electric utility and public works department coordinated and performed all phases of its installation. With its four faces, the clock can be seen by traffic moving in all directions. The design allowed room for the annual Christmas tree to keep its traditional spot.

Congressman Rodney Frelinghuysen presided over the dedication on Bottle Hill Day, October 3, 1998. An impressive bust of President James Madison was later added to the clock plaza in 2003. This community-based effort resulted in a highly successful beautification of the downtown area.

Martell Foundation Created

The T.J. Martell Foundation for Leukemia, Cancer & AIDS Research was founded in 1975 by Madison resident Tony Martell in memory of his son, "T.J.," who died of leukemia that same year. A record company executive who worked with many of the biggest recording stars of the era, he used his vast contacts to make the foundation the music industry's favorite philanthropic organization for cancer research. Despite offices in several major cities raising money for research, Tony wanted his hometown to become a part of the effort.

In 1995, the first T.J. Martell Foundation Walkathon was held with the assistance and cooperation of the Madison Area YMCA. For the next 20 years, the Walkathon was an annual event. Then, in 2015, it was replaced by the first Vicky and Tony Martell Evening of Jazz at Madison's Shanghai Jazz Restaurant.(99) Over 25 years, through these two events, T.J. Martell's hometown of Madison, raised over $2 million of the nearly $300 million raised by the foundation for cancer research.(100)

Madison Enters the Information Age

As the 21st century approached, a man with an eye toward the future stepped forward with a vision for making Madison relevant as a leading community in the "Information Age." That person was future Madison Mayor and then AT&T Vice President of Technology and Infrastructure Ellwood "Woody" Kerkeslager. His unique vision was to "provide community access to the critical information and communications technologies underlying the transition to the information age." He believed the way to do it was to "allow people of all ages and

incomes to obtain shared access to learn to use those technologies…" and to "develop a community network with full community involvement…" that would "also create a virtual space for all
parts of the community to utilize…."101)

It also took an institutional partner: the Madison Public Library,
led by Director Nancy Vernon (Adamczyk) which had long been
the "community center for Madison" and was "traditionally the
center of information in a town".(102) The library had some experience in the digital information age. As early as the fall of
1982, library staff could access the MAIN (Morris Automated
Information Network) database with a view of the collections of
all participating libraries from a terminal on the library's reference desk.

Mayor Ellwood
"Woody" Kerkeslager

The vision of a coordinated Madison community network be-
gan to take shape during the summer and fall of 1995.(103) Through a series of meetings—initially between Kerkeslager, Director Vernon, Board President Donald Valk, and Mayor Gary
Ruckelshaus—to address the need for public computers in the library.(104) The meetings
quickly expanded to a discussion of Kerkeslager's vision for a community network project, and
by the end of the year, the basic elements of the project were established. A broad proposal
was submitted for consideration by the borough council in March of 1996. Six months later,
the network had a name, RoseNet, a mission statement, and a detailed plan. As stated in the
November-December edition of the Library Newsletter:

> The project will advance Madison into the information age, enhance the sense of
> community spirit by allowing us to share activities and information, provide access to
> information and communications technologies throughout the world, and increase
> the life-long learning resources for Madison residents by giving them access to PCs in
> the Library.

AT&T and other local corporations committed substantial contributions of equipment and
services to help realize the RoseNet vision. By March 1998, Kerkeslager was able to report
that the total value of the services and equipment donated by contributors AT&T, Cabletron
Systems, and Lucent Technologies came to nearly $1 million.

RoseNet made its formal introduction to the community at the April 1997 *Mayor's Conference*
held at the Hamilton Park Executive Conference Center in Florham Park. Clearly, there was
great interest in the conference, as witnessed by a capacity crowd of 125 borough business owners, educators, residents, and officials.(105)

In his welcoming address, Mayor Ruckelshaus observed that Madison would be the first New
Jersey municipality, and one of the first in the nation, to integrate all aspects of community life
through a town-wide network. He predicted that more than 800 businesses, about 100 non-
profits, and government agencies would ultimately participate in the RoseNet project.(106) As
its project leader and conference organizer, Kerkeslager was the conference keynote speaker.
He began his presentation by stating that the tools of the information age are (and will continue
to be) digital technologies and that the role of RoseNet would be to bring "the digital technology tools of the future to the entire community, utilizing the structure of community network-
ing in new and exciting ways."

By the summer of 1998, the library's newsletter was able to report that all the library's facilities were fully installed and functioning, with the link to the AT&T Labs to be in place in July.
The RoseNet website was available by Bottle Hill Day 1998 with the library's and the borough's

websites functional. Fiber connections to all twenty-two borough buildings were in place by the end of the year, with the library, borough hall, and Madison High School to be in service by year's end, with five more in service in September 1999. The entire borough code and land use ordinances were accessible on RoseNet. By August 2000, the borough engineer was also using the RoseNet Geographic Information System (GIS).

A Model for Community Networks Worldwide

The RoseNet vision went beyond Madison. Kerkeslager viewed RoseNet as a template for what has been described in the literature as a "Third Generation Community Network," one that "uses community development processes and techniques that engage leaders and organizations in a community to speed up the diffusion and adoption of information technology across all sectors of the community."

In November 1998, Kerkeslager invited Mayor Gary Ruckelshaus to attend an international conference of Mayors, part of the Global Forum, an internationally recognized think-tank of which Kerkeslager was an organizing member. Mayor Ruckelshaus presented the RoseNet story to this assembly held in the chambers of the French Senate in Paris. As Kerkeslager observed, "It was clear that Madison was seen by the attendees as a leading community, filled with the energy of private enterprise and brimming over with potential."(107).

Even in an international context, it was obvious that Madison's leaders had created a model for citizen involvement in technology that inspired other communities to develop similar initiatives. Madison's unique community-wide action prepared its citizens for the dramatic technological innovations that would follow in the new millennium.

CHAPTER SIXTEEN

The New Millenium

M ost Madison residents looked forward with high hopes for the dawn of a new century in the year 2000. However, there was a widespread fear throughout the country that the advent of the new century would bring about a serious problem with the calibration of time, as the old system might not be able to handle the change to a new system. Fortunately, the existing system held up with few problems emerging. Local residents were relieved when they looked up at the Millennium Clocks on Waverly Place. All should be well, or so it seemed at the time.

Madison residents could look back with pride at the community's long and eventful history. From the American Revolution, through several wars, a worldwide depression, and an ongoing technological revolution featuring cellphones, laptops, and the advent of self-driving automobiles, local residents, and all Americans, had much to be proud of. However, no one had prepared for the evil from the sky that was to be among the worst tragedies the nation has had to endure.

Madison's Millennium Clock.
Photo credit: Judi Whiting

09-11-2001 – The Attack on America

The first decade of the new millennium saw three national catastrophes: the September 11, 2001 ("9/11") Al-Qaeda terrorist attacks, the endless wars in Iraq and Afghanistan, and the "Great Recession" of 2008–2009. All impacted Americans to a greater or lesser degree, but with Madison's proximity to New York City, the 9/11 attacks on the World Trade Center (WTC) struck the borough and its citizens in a very personal and devastating way.

It was at 8:46 AM EDT on Tuesday, September 11, that the hijacked American Airlines Flight 11 crashed into the North Tower of the WTC. Seventeen minutes later, United Airlines Flight 175 struck the South Tower. With the second crash, it became clear that the first strike was not an accident. America was under attack, but no one yet knew by whom. Then, as we watched our television sets in horror, we saw the South Tower collapse into rubble at 9:59 AM. The North Tower came down 29 minutes later. By then, many in town were desperately trying to contact friends and loved ones who lived or worked in downtown Manhattan. What we found out later was that much of the landline and cellular service into and out of the downtown had been taken out by the attack.

Looking back, Madison Superintendent of Schools Arthur Travlos stated that the administration had "an absolutely crazy" day on September 11.(1) Working with all the schools, the administration wanted to make sure that no child was being sent to a home with no parents there. "Our first concern was our children. What do we tell them? How do we get them home, knowing that parents may be caught in the city, unable to get home? The bridges were closed, the tunnels were closed," stated Travlos.(2) Contingency arrangements were made to care for any children whose parents could not be contacted at the borough hall. Gratefully, the borough's preparations were not necessary, as school administrators were able to contact relatives or neighbors of all the children.

By the end of what was a very long day, borough officials were still unable to account for at least nine residents who were believed to be at or near the World Trade Center at the time of the attack.(3) Ultimately, it was determined that three Madison residents lost their lives in its aftermath. Those tragically lost were James Crawford Jr., Tim Hughes, and Patrick McGuire. In addition, two former residents, Jean and Donald Peterson, were on United Airlines Flight 93, which crashed in a field near Shanksville, Pennsylvania. Peter West, who had grown up in Madison but lived in Tewksbury Township, was also a WTC 9/11 victim.(4) A monument to honor the memories of these six Madison residents was dedicated at James Park on May 18, 2002. The monument includes a portion of a stressed steel beam recovered from the rubble.

Madison's 9-11 memorial located in James Park.

Madison Responds to the Horrific Acts

Mayor Jack Dunne called for a "Madison Day of Mourning and Hope" to be held on September 20 on the steps of the Hartley Dodge Memorial. In announcing the service, Mayor Dunne stated: "As the aftermath of this horrific act of terrorism unfolds before us, I mourn the loss of the gallant police and rescue workers who have died. I mourn the loss of the members of our community and of all who are unaccounted for. They have all made the supreme sacrifice."(5)

Hundreds of Madison residents filled the Hartley Dodge Memorial plaza that Thursday. The crowd was reported to stretch around both ends of the Hartley Dodge Memorial; it also crossed Kings Road to the slope of the Madison Train Station. Most of the attendees were huddled under umbrellas, as there was a light but steady rain. "The heavens are crying with us tonight," observed Mayor Dunne.(6)

Three days after the terrorist attacks, Madison's central business district was transformed into a display of sympathy and unity. As reported in the *Madison Eagle*, "Main Street was lined with American flags, and lampposts were decorated with ribbons of red, white, and blue on a black background. Merchants hung American flags from their building facades or displayed them in their windows, as did countless residents."(7)

Coordinating with the Southeast Morris Chapter of the American Red Cross, the Madison-Florham Park Interfaith Council, and Grace Counseling Center, the Madison YMCA served as a clearinghouse for information about blood drives, church services, and free counseling, and provided a help hotline and advice for talking with children about tragedy and war. Blood drives were also scheduled by local Red Cross chapters to meet the mounting need in New York City.

On November 29, the *Madison Eagle* announced that Madison Mayor Dunne had established a "Madison 911 Family Assistance Fund" to benefit the three Madison families who lost husbands and fathers in the attack. When the books were closed on the fund in October 2002, a total of $101,197 had been contributed by 400 residential, business, and corporate donors.(8)

Madison at Ground Zero

Madison also made its presence felt at "Ground Zero." Madison Police Sergeant and volunteer firefighter D.J. Brightly and Madison Fire Captain (later Fire Chief) Louie DeRosa were first deployed at the site Wednesday evening as members of New Jersey Task Force One.(9) According to Chief DeRosa, their personal pagers first went off at 9:15 AM on the 11th. They arrived at the Javits Center on 11th Avenue, where they set up their base of operations. Working on separate teams, Brightly and DeRosa remained there for nine straight days.

Each Task Force team consisted of 250 highly trained specialists in different aspects of a rescue operation. Brightly was a rigging specialist trained in stabilizing damaged or collapsed structures to prevent any further loss of life during search and rescue operations. DeRosa was a technical search specialist. Unfortunately, with all the devastation, the searchers went from looking for survivors during their first days to looking for any human remains. DeRosa stated, "With all the dust, you would go into a room, and everything was gray. It was like you were on the moon." His overall impression was that the scene was "the closest thing to Hell that he could imagine. The smoke. The fires. The blackness."(10)

DeRosa and Brightly finally returned to Madison just in time to join the Day of Mourning ceremony at Hartley Dodge Memorial, where they were greeted with a "thunderous ovation" from the attendees.

Other Madison residents who also labored at the site were Port Authority Policeman Gerald Colligan and Newark Fire Captains Anthony Perniciaro and Robert Rohemmihs. Along with DeRosa and Brightly, they were later presented with Valor and Heroism Medals by the American Legion Post 43 of Madison and Florham Park.

Confronting a False and Ugly Rumor

One unfortunate outcome was an ugly rumor that circulated through Madison and Chatham. It alleged that employees at a Madison fast-food business applauded or cheered during the attack. To his great credit, Mayor Dunne quickly and forcefully addressed the issue. At the October 10 borough council meeting, the mayor declared that he and the Madison Police Department had thoroughly investigated the rumor and determined that it was a "complete fabrication." He described the affair as "a disturbing situation that is not only upsetting to me as mayor but also is a poor reflection on our community."(11)

Despite the false rumors by a few, in all other ways, Madison responded well to a terrible local and national tragedy. As the editor of the *Madison Eagle* concluded:

> … we consider all that has happened in Madison in the days since Sept. 11. And we understand what is special about this town; its solidarity of the human spirit, supported by countless helping hands. It is this sense of community that makes Madison great, and in turn makes America great.(12)

The 9/11 Commission Comes to Madison

The National Commission on Terrorist Attacks Upon the United States, commonly known as the 9/11 Commission, was established on November 27, 2002, by President George W. Bush and the Congress of the United States. On December 15, President Bush appointed former Governor of New Jersey and then President of Drew University Thomas Kean to head the commission.

Governor Kean brought the commission to Drew's Baldwin Gymnasium for its fifth public hearing, which addressed "Private/Public Sector Partnerships for Emergency Preparedness," on November 19, 2003. In his opening remarks, Kean stated: "One of the lessons learned from 9/11 is that private sector preparedness remains critical to our national security. The commission is charged with recommending ways to improve emergency preparedness in the aftermath of September 11th."(13). After interviewing over 1,200 people in 10 countries and reviewing over two and a half million pages of documents, the commission issued its final report, *The 9/11 Commission Report*, on July 22, 2004.

Changing Fabric of the Madison Community

Throughout the years, the majority racial/ethnic composition of Madison's population has reflected that of Morris County as a whole—very white. However, Madison had consistently attracted a more diverse population than most towns in Morris County, a trend that continued into the new millennium with some notable shifts in its minority composition.

The 1970 and 1980 U.S. censuses showed that Madison had the fourth largest African American population in the county, behind only Morristown, Morris Township, and Parsippany.(14) But the numbers were small. In 1980, Madison's Black population represented only 3.9% of the borough's total. County-wide, the percentage was 2.5%. Since then, families have come and gone, but the numbers have been relatively constant. In 1990, there were 704 African Americans living in Madison, representing 4.5% of the population.(15) Thirty-one years later, in 2021, the number was 631, representing 3.8% of the population.

What has changed the most is the marked increase in Madison's Asian and Hispanic/Latino populations. In 1990, the number of residents self-identified as being of Asian descent was 454 (2.8%); it was 1,206 (7.2%) in 2021. As a percent of the population, the Hispanic/Latino community was the borough's fastest growing, going from 445 (2.8%) in 1990 to 2,237 (13.2%) in 2021. And just as late 20th century Madison had Morris County's fourth largest Black population, early 21st century Madison had the county's fourth largest Hispanic population, behind only Dover, Morristown, and Wharton.(16)

Madison's African American Community

Although still representing a modest percentage of the population, the borough's African American residents have continued to play a vital role in the community, making substantial contributions to life in Madison. Dr. Charles Robinson served 9 years as President of the Madison Board of Health in the 1970s and 80s. He also served on the Florham Park/Madison Human Relations Commission and was a local Red Cross volunteer.(17) William Primus, Madison's first African American firefighter and councilman, and Robert Burroughs led the fight for affordable housing during that same timeframe. Primus later assumed the position of Chairman and CEO of the Urban League of Morris County(18). Robert's brother, George Burroughs, served as Director of the Madison Community House for 26 years until his death in 1994, and George Martin served three terms on the Madison Board of Education from 2003 to 2010. Martin then followed Primus to the Morris Urban League, where he serves as its Chairman of the Board.(19)

The Senior Pastor of Madison's First Baptist Church, Rev. Dr. A. Craig Dunn, currently serves as chaplain for the Madison Police Department and has played a leadership role in building a positive relationship between the police and Madison's African American community. And in 2020-2021, resident Kenisha Tucker founded the Hidden Figures project that reminds the town of the many contributions that have been made and continue to be made by Madison's Black community.

One of Rev. Dunn's primary missions has been to minimize the chance that the Madison police and the minority residents in town will have to struggle with the terrible police/minority confrontations that have plagued other towns and cities in New Jersey and in the rest of the country. The immediate impetus for Rev. Dunn's work with the department was the August 2014 fatal shooting of Michael Brown Jr., an 18-year-old Black man, by a white Ferguson, Missouri police officer. This horrific event sparked protests around the country and motivated Rev. Dunn to meet with Madison Police Chief Darren Dachisen and his leadership team to discuss how the First Baptist Church might support the police department. As an outcome, Rev. Dunn organized meetings at the church with police, residents, council members, college presidents, other religious leaders, and interested citizens, which became known as the "Beloved Community Conversations." He wanted each community member to know and be known by Madison police officers. "You are less likely to hurt someone you know," he noted.

From block party barbecues with police, clergy, and community leaders, to meetings like Beloved Community Conversations, and peace marches (planned with the police department), to Meet the Muslims Next Door get-togethers, his approach has been relentlessly relational. June 2020 saw a peaceful gathering of many people at Dodge Field, including police chiefs from surrounding towns, following the death of a Black man, George Floyd, on May 25, 2020, at the hands of Minneapolis police officers. Reverend Dunn's goal has been strong community building. Rev. Dunn consistently lauds the police chiefs in Madison as progressive and helpful.(20)

Kenisha Tucker had first conceived of the "Hidden Figures" project after attending several Community Conversations meetings organized by Mayor Robert Conley and Councilwoman Debra Coen and speaking with her sister, Sharela Coon-Bonfield, about racial inequality and its impact on the community. Ms. Tucker observed the gaps in the town's Black history and the stories from the community that had never been told or had been forgotten. Working with others, she began collecting these stories, many of which were ultimately captured in banners of individual and family names that lined the streets of downtown Madison during the summer of 2021 (and in subsequent summers). "I was able to find out about so many individuals and stories that are noteworthy and of historical importance," she stated.(21).

Hidden Figures banner, one of many that lined the streets of downtown Madison.

The contributions of some of the Hidden Figures have already been described in previous chapters of this book. Others include Officer Bill Hagens, who was the first Black officer and sergeant in the Madison Police Department, Charlotte Nebres who was the first Black ballerina to play Marie in the New York City Ballet's production of *The Nutcracker*, and Beresford

Russell, Jr., who founded Madison's Russell Electric, an electrical contracting company, and who volunteered as a scoutmaster and coach for the Madison recreation track program.(22) These projects reflected Madison's exceptionally positive approach to improving racial and ethnic relations.

Madison's Growing Asian Community

One long-time Madison Asian family that left an indelible mark in Madison was the family of Darwin Chang and his second wife, Yen Ma Chang. Mr. Chang had been forced to flee China in December 1944 during the World War II Japanese occupation. Yen Ma Chang was born in Beijing, China. Darwin and Yen Ma married in 1961 and moved to Madison from Maplewood in 1969. In 1976, they purchased and restored the landmark Gee Building on the corner of Main Street and Central Avenue.

After a 20-year engineering career at PSE&G in Newark, Darwin, together with Yen Ma, established the borough's first Chinese take-out restaurant, the Four Seas Cuisines of China, on Central Avenue. After several more Chinese restaurants opened in the area, the couple decided to expand their business to being a full-service restaurant with the same name at a new location at 24 Main St.(23) Darwin's daughter Martha and her husband, David Niu, later took over the business. While continuing to offer gourmet Chinese cuisine, they also made it into the go-to spot for live jazz enthusiasts in New Jersey. In 2011, *DownBeat Magazine* included their renamed Shanghai Jazz Restaurant & Bar on the magazine's international list of 150 "Great Jazz Rooms."(24)

In 2020, another prominent Asian immigrant announced his intention to make his mark on the map of Madison. Waseem Chaudhary purchased the former Drew University Alumni House at the southwest corner of Madison Avenue and Vinal Place, demolishing the house with the intention of constructing a 14,300-square-foot mosque on the property. In his testimony to the Madison Planning Board, Mr. Chaudhary stated that the mosque would be used for his extended family but "would be open to all who wish to pray there." Chaudhary told the Planning Board, "I am building this for the community...." He observed that currently the closest mosque to Madison is in Boonton.(25)

Waseem Chaudhary's life personified the American dream. He first came to this country from Rawalpindi, Pakistan, in 1988. His first job in the U.S. was as a cashier at the Dunkin' Donuts shop on Madison's Main Street. With a strong work ethic, he quickly moved up to assistant manager and, not long after, was made a manager in 1990. In 1996, he changed directions and purchased the Shell station at the corner of Main Street and Prospect Street and a second station in Dover. By the spring of 2021, his company, Waseem Petroleum Group, had grown to be a major wholesaler and retailer of petroleum products in the metropolitan area. At the time of this writing, the company has over 200 employees and owns or leases more than 100 service stations.

After several months of hearings, the Madison Planning Board unanimously voted in October 2021 to grant Mr. Chaudhary preliminary and final site plan approvals for the construction of the proposed mosque. As Planning Board Chairman Steve Tombalakan observed, "We're hearing that Mr. Chaudhary wants to build this to say thank you to his God for giving him the success he's had in life, and he wants to do it by providing the town with some impressive architecture. And I'm thinking: 100-something years ago, a rich man named Mr. Webb [was] in town who felt the same way, providing a chapel that we still look at as one of the most beautiful buildings in town."(26) Groundbreaking for the construction of the mosque took place in late 2023.

Madison's Growing Latino Community

So, how did Madison also become the home of the fourth-largest Latino community in Morris County? It all started when a small group from Filandia, Quindío, in Colombia, arrived initially in New York and eventually made their way west to settle in Madison. In the ensuing decades, the large majority of Latinos in Madison can trace their roots to this little town in Colombia. One such immigrant, Dora Ramirez, reflected on some of the many positive impacts the Latino community has had on Madison: "We've helped create a fusional culture, where we learn and grow from each other. We Colombians are more loud and out there, with a positive energy that creates a noticeable diversity as people walk around town." While there can be a language barrier between the Latino and white populations, Ms. Ramirez spoke of the "spirit of give and take," where the majority-white residents can learn and benefit from exposure to the Colombian culture and people.(27)

The local Colombian community developed several social clubs and community groups over time, including the *Quindianos Unidos por Colombia* (Quindianos United for Colombia), *El Club de los 100* (The Club of the 100), and *Unidos por Nuestros Niños* (United for our Children). These clubs meet at the North Star Club, which was originally founded as a social club for Italian immigrants. The community's new social clubs provide both a connection to the past–to families and friends left behind and to the present culture that is the minority here–and also serve as a support framework for people to survive and thrive in Madison. Ms. Ramirez said that "there is a balance between integrating with a new community and holding onto and surrounding yourself with people like you."(28)

The Latino community in Madison has received support from many different groups and organizations, including the immigrant advocacy group Wind of the Spirit, the Morris County Organization for Hispanic Affairs, and St. Vincent Martyr Church (SVM). In response to the previously unknown need for this community, in 2006, the first ad hoc Spanish-language masses were held at St. Vincent's with guest priests from the Newark Diocese. St. Vincent's Pastoral Associate Jan Figenshu reflected, "We expected maybe 30-40 people and were amazed when more than 150 people showed up at the first Spanish mass." Even if the children spoke English, there was a desire to pray together in Spanish. "People like to pray in their native language". There were also new *migrant* young men, mostly undocumented, who worked in local restaurants and sat at the back of the church during mass.(29)

Spanish-language masses began to be held more regularly at St. Vincent's, usually around major religious holidays and then moved to monthly services by 2007. When Monsignor George Hundt arrived at St. Vincent's in 2009, he requested that the Paterson Diocese assign a Spanish-speaking priest to SVM. Father Antonio Gaviria arrived soon thereafter. Father Antonio was from Colombia and had served in Paterson and Dover prior to arriving at St. Vincent's. His background made him a great advocate for blending the white community with their Spanish-speaking fellow parishioners.

Members of the church even held English classes in their homes and assisted with documentation related to the proposed Development, Relief, and Education for Alien Minors (DREAM) Act and for the Deferred Action for Childhood Arrivals (DACA) program, along with other legal and medical support arranged through the church.

There was a concerted effort by St. Vincent's to build trust within this community, where many, at first, didn't even want to officially register as parishioners. It is notable that at this same time, trust was being built in the broader Madison community through the efforts of Rev. Dunn and the Beloved Community. By 2019, there was regular attendance at the weekly Spanish mass of 100-125 people. Today, the weekly church bulletin and website are in Spanish and English, a signal to all parishioners of the size and importance of the Spanish-speaking community to St. Vincent Martyr Church.

It appears that Latinos in Madison now felt welcomed and supported. Ms. Ramirez reflected that, "We always felt welcomed and safe. The Madison police made their presence obvious but in a good way. In Madison, the police know who you are, where you live, and where you come from. They're there to protect us."(30) The Welcoming Community Resolution, passed in 2017 by the Madison Borough Council, offered support to the immigrant community and helped alleviate tensions in Madison.

Political Changes

And just as Madison's ethnic complexion changed in the first two decades of the 21st century, so did its politics. Going back to the founding of the borough in 1889, its first mayor, James Albright and its first woman mayor, Elizabeth Baumgartner, were Democrats, but they were infrequent exceptions to the norm. For most of its history, Madison was predominantly–even overwhelmingly–a Republican town. Years, even decades, would go by when there was no Democrat in any elected office in Madison. This changed dramatically in the second decade of the new century when Democrat Robert Conley was elected mayor in 2011, and in 2012, Democrats captured a voting majority on the council. Following the 2019 election and through the most recent 2024 election, no Republican has been elected to the Madison Borough Council.

In a town where Republicans had historically outnumbered Democrats by as much as two to one, by March of 2022, registered Democrats in Madison outnumbered registered Republicans by over 1,000 voters, according to voter registration data published by the Office of the Morris County Clerk. As to whether the shift from a "red" to "blue" Madison will last or whether it is a temporary reaction to national politics as it was briefly in the early 1970s, only time will tell.

Major Changes in Madison Public Infrastructure

Madison saw an unprecedented number of capital projects in the late 1990s that continued into the new century. A prime catalyst was the 1990 federal Americans with Disabilities Act (ADA). A long planning period preceded each project as governing bodies reviewed deferred maintenance issues, space needs for 21st-century services and new technology requirements.

In 2008, the borough government completed its first major construction project in 70 years: a new Public Safety Complex on the corner of Kings Road and Prospect Street. The Madison Public Library dedicated two new additions in 1993, one being the Local History Center shared with the Madison Historical Society. The borough government and the Museum of Early Trades and Crafts jointly funded improvements to the James Library building that were completed in 2017 with substantial grant support from the Morris County Historic Preservation Trust Fund.

The new century also saw the creation of a center for community activities–the Madison Civic Center–at 28 Walnut Street. The Civic Center would house the Senior Center, Teen Center, and Madison Health Department in the former Forum Club building. But this proved to be a temporary addition as the borough council announced plans in 2020 to demolish the building to make way for 30 affordable housing units to be constructed on the site.(31) The Health Department subsequently moved to the first floor of the Hartley Dodge Memorial, and the Senior Center will move to the former Masonic Lodge at 170 Main Street. Once the necessary renovations to the building are complete, the Senior Center will occupy the first floor and will be named the Peggy Heller Senior Center of Madison.

In 2005, borough residents approved a referendum for a $34.8 million bond issue to expand and renovate all five public schools. The total project cost was $45.9 million designated for the first major schools' renovation program in 40 years. A subsequent bond referendum for $79.4 million to fund various infrastructure, safety, and security upgrades, increased accessibility and interior renovations for the schools was approved by Madison voters in December 2024.

Local nonprofit organizations also undertook significant building improvements. The Thursday Morning Club dedicated a major addition to the Community House located on Cook Avenue in 2009, and the Madison Area YMCA expanded its family center in early 2002 and then again in 2021.

Recent community-supported projects include the $1.3 million reconstruction of the Hartley Dodge Memorial outdoor plaza and stairs, which was completed in early 2022 to be followed by a planned renovation of the building's east wing in 2025 that will ultimately house a Madison History Museum. Borough funds were also allocated for roof restoration for the Madison Public Library building. The new roof was the first phase of a major library renovation project. This project, which will be completed in early 2025, will provide ADA improvements to the library entrance and restrooms, asbestos abatement, new lighting and ceilings, new furniture, and internal configuration changes to create a new teen area and study and conference rooms. Funding is shared between the borough, the library, the Friends of the Madison Public Library, and a $914,000 state matching grant through the New Jersey Library Bond Construction Act of 2017.(32)

Hartley Dodge Memorial Renovation and Public Safety Complex

The long and winding road to the renovation of the Hartley Dodge Memorial and the construction of the new Public Safety Complex began in the early 1990s. The layout of Madison's town hall presented serious challenges to satisfying ADA accessibility requirements. The primary needs were an elevator that could service the entire building and handicapped-accessible restrooms.

As the planning process for the mandated upgrades progressed, other pressing needs were identified. In April 2001, Council President Mary-Anna Holden stated she could not foresee the police department remaining in its present quarters for much longer because it was considered substandard, crowded and without much-needed storage space.(33) Then, in July 2002, Superior Court Judge Reginald Stanton warned Mayor Jack Dunne that the municipal court, located on the first floor of the east wing, needed to be moved to a different venue because "The crowded conditions make it impossible to conduct court sessions with reasonable efficiency and with the required dignity and decorum."(34) A facilities committee chaired by Councilman George Hayman was then appointed to review all the space needs

Madison's new Public Safety building.

at the borough hall. In their November 2002 report, the committee recommended that the court remain in town and that the police department move out of Hartley Dodge Memorial. Chairman Hayman observed "there were only five police officers when the headquarters was built as part of the Hartley Dodge Memorial in 1935."(35) Then, in February 2004, architect Robert Russell identified one more major need: "new fire equipment, which the department says it is mandated to purchase, won't fit into the Hartley Dodge bays." Consequently, the decision was made to construct a new Public Safety Complex on the west end of the commuter parking lot on Kings Road.(36)

Once the Public Safety Complex was completed and opened, plans for renovating the Hartley Dodge Memorial could move forward. Work began in late May 2008 with preparations for asbestos removal. Eighteen months later, borough employees were able to return to a renovated Hartley Dodge Memorial from their temporary quarters in the old Bayley-Ellard High School. The construction of the new, up-to-date courtroom, located in the old fire department bays, led to a shared services agreement for a joint court to handle the cases from Madison, Chatham Borough, Chatham Township, and Harding Township as of February 1, 2011. Morris Township joined as the fifth town in 2014.

More Affordable Housing in the New Millennium

Although conflicting views and directives from the state government on the need for mandated affordable housing continued to bring a drought of construction in suburban communities, Madison's Affordable Housing Corporation (now HQM, Inc.) continued to build housing whenever the opportunity arose. It did so in 2014 when it applied its experience in building homes in outlying communities to help three Madison families construct their resident homes on Strickland Place. The project was applauded for converting the land into an environmentally safe location for housing for hometown families. This was a first in Madison!(37)

Because the state's Council on Affordable Housing failed to enforce its construction mandates, the state Supreme Court, in 2015, ruled that state judges would take over the regulation of affordable housing. Madison, with its excellent supply of affordable housing and lack of new land for further development, successfully settled for 147 units through new and existing construction. The signed agreement of April 22, 2021, initiated the development of 44 units, 30 of which are under construction at the site of what had been the Madison Civic Center on Walnut Street and another 14 across three buildings on a parcel off of Community Place.

The Madison Area YMCA Grows to Serve the Community

In 1987, the YMCA had nearly 7,000 members, and its Campaign '87 raised $1.6 million for improvements to the Family Center, the Wellness Child Care Center (renamed the F. M. Kirby Children's Center in 1992), and an increase to the YMCA Endowment Fund. Serving the residents of Madison, the Chathams, Florham Park, Harding Township, Convent Station, East Hanover, and Passaic Township, membership had increased by 50% between 1981 and 1987.(38)

The new millennium ushered in another major campaign, aptly named Plan 2000. Chairpersons Helen and Michael Caulfield led the way in securing capital for the $4.8 million project, which included a much-needed 14,000-square-foot addition to the Family Center. The original freight station corner of the complex was demolished to make way for the new building, and the former fitness center became "Kids Central," fully compliant with ADA and fire regulations.

Hometown favorite Neil O'Donnell, Madison quarterback legend and NFL star, and his wife Leslie were instrumental in giving back to the community. Their gift of $200,000 to Plan 2000 allowed Madison to qualify for a $350,000 challenge grant from the Kresge Foundation. The O'Donnell Fitness Center was, and remains, a highlight of Y membership.(39) The grand opening was held on June 8, 2002.

The year 2010 saw the retirement of YMCA President and CEO Barry Kroll who was followed by Diane Mann assuming the position. The following year, 2011, the Madison Area YMCA partnered with 50 other NJ YMCA locations in the My Y is Every Y program that allowed members to freely use the services and facilities of all the other partnered YMCAs.

Included in the Y's long-range plans for more than 30 years was a larger pool and expanded recreation space at the Family Center. In 2018, the YMCA launched the Our Community, Our Future fundraising campaign, which by the spring of 2021 had resulted in a total giving of $10.5 million from more than 1000 donors.(40)

The charitable support, combined with Y reserves, enabled the Y to construct a 28,865-square-foot expansion that included an eight-lane, 25-yard competitive pool with a spectator balcony and 8,500-square-foot gymnasium and sports center, as well as an expanded fitness center. Groundbreaking for the new facilities occurred in August 2019, and construction was completed in the second half of 2021.(41)

The Madison Area YMCA has a history of looking to the future. The words John T. Cunningham wrote in 1990, looking back,

2021 addition to the Madison YMCA.

still ring true. "The years roll on. They have been good years for the Y, good enough to serve a community and an area well."(42)

Renovation of the Madison Community House

In February 2007, the Thursday Morning Club Board of Trustees approved a proposal to raze and rebuild the gym/auditorium and Rose Wing portions of the Madison Community House. Serious structural issues needed to be addressed in the gym and the understructure of the Rose

The new addition to the Madison Community House features a new gymnasium, catering kitchen, and two classrooms.

Wing. Compliance with ADA and state nursery school regulations was important to the final plan. The reconstruction/expansion included an ADA-compliant ground-level entry, ADA-compliant restrooms, a commercial catering kitchen, two secured preschool classrooms, a gymnasium, and the Rose Wing meeting space.

Initial funding was available from a generous bequest from Mary Louise Carlson, but the club still needed to raise a substantial amount. Bernadette Grohol and Olga Soriano spearheaded the project. Club members, the Community House "family," community organizations, foundations, and corporations were successfully solicited.

J.R. Prisco, Inc. was selected to be the project's prime contractor. This was a special project for J.R. Prisco as his father, James Prisco, Sr., had grown up in the Cook Avenue neighborhood before founding the company. Demolition and then reconstruction began in June 2008.(43)

The project is best summarized in the club history written by member Michal Sherer Holzman when she reported: "Over 65% of Thursday Morning Club members pledged a donation along with 240 individuals from the public, 33 foundations and organizations and 14 corporations and businesses. This project was completed without a mortgage ahead of schedule and on budget."(44) An opening celebration was held on January 25, 2009.

Madison's Open Space, Recreation, and Historic Preservation Trust Fund

In 1971, New Jersey became the second state in the nation to adopt state funding for open space preservation when it approved its first Green Acres Bond Act. Madison took advantage of it when it created Summerhill Park (described in Chapter 14), but by 1997, the state's conservation community realized that they needed a more reliable source of funding and successfully put a ballot question before the citizens to provide stable funding for the next decade. New Jersey voters overwhelmingly agreed, and thus, the Garden State Preservation Trust (GSPT) was born. It was so successful that the fund was depleted within seven years. After each of the 13 Green Acres Acts, the legislature had to write legislation to allocate the funds. In November 2014, it approved state funding for preservation by dedicating 4 percent of corporate business tax to preservation and environmental programs through 2019 and then dedicated an additional 2 percent of existing corporate business tax revenues from fiscal year 2020 going forward. By March 2020, it amounted to $146 million per year.

Madison was quick to get on board in 2002, thanks to newly elected Council Members Astri Baillie and Donald Bowen, who convinced the borough council to establish an ad hoc Open Space Committee. The committee immediately devised a referendum asking voters to approve open space, recreation, and a historic preservation tax of two cents on every $100 of assessed property tax value. It was passed the following November. "By establishing a dedicated open space trust fund, we were able to generate funding from other sources, including the County Open Space and Farmland Preservation Trust, Green Acres and other private and public entities," Baillie wrote in her own history of the fund.(45) By 2004, Madison had a permanent Open Space, Recreation, and Historic Preservation Committee to advise the mayor and council on land acquisitions, the use of the funding, and grant possibilities. Baillie and the committee saw the fund as a mechanism to:

- Expand recreation facilities, fields and parks.
- Protect drinking water quality.
- Protect historic treasures.
- Enhance property values and quality of life.
- Maintain a beautiful community.

The first use of funds was in 2004-2005, when the borough purchased the Luke Miller property on Ridgedale Avenue, which included its historic house that was scheduled for demolition. The borough subdivided the property so that the house sat on only 0.59 acres, making it compatible with the area zoning. The house, with a historic easement, was then sold at auction for more than the borough's purchase price. The remaining 1.21 acres of the property were sold to the borough, which then added them to the adjacent Summerhill Park. It was a tribute to the citizens willing to keep this important property in the newly created Bottle Hill Historic District.(46).

Saving the Drew Forest

Throughout the school's history, the 53-acre Drew Forest Preserve has become an outsized feature of Drew University's unique dedication to the study of ecology, ecosystems, and wildlife. Seen as a bountiful natural laboratory in a suburban setting for students, faculty, visitors, wanderers, and scientists, it includes the Zuck Arboretum and Hepburn Woods. "At least 120 different bird species have been observed, including spring and fall migrants, nesting birds, and raptors. Both herons and human visitors are attracted by two ponds, ecosystems rich in amphibians, turtles, dragonflies, and more."(47) In addition, its physical features allow for the study of geological and glacial processes, highlighted by the large kettle formed by the retreat of the Wisconsin Glacier about 15,000 years ago.(48)

In recent years, the university has unfortunately suffered from difficult financial constraints and loss of enrollment, and in 2022, it decided to do what was previously thought unthinkable: sell the Drew Forest for residential development. In opposition to this plan, a grassroots organization, the Friends of the Drew Forest, led the fight for a conservation sale of the property. The group highlighted the forest's ecological value to the community and its critical role as a recharge zone for the Buried Valley Aquifer system, the source of drinking water for Madison and 25 other municipalities in northern New Jersey (49). Two years of legal battles and intense negotiations followed, involving many area municipalities and local and state political leaders.

In November 2024, Madison and Drew University announced a non-binding agreement in which the borough agreed to purchase the forest for about $65 million with grant monies from federal, state, and county sources and the borough's Open Space, Recreation and Historic Preservation Trust Fund. The total also included the value of land on other parts of the campus that could be used to build multi-family, inclusionary residential housing.(50) While the community now awaits a final resolution of the sale, the forest yielded one more piece of evidence of its worth when an eagle-eyed Drew student recently photographed a rarely seen barred owl.(51)

"Geraldine" Returns to Madison

Madison residents celebrated Mrs. Dodge's 1921 gift of a state-of-the-art Ahrens-Fox Model P-4 fire engine in 1921. The Ahrens-Fox has been described as the "Rolls Royce" of fire engines at that time; it served Madison for more than 40 years. It then suffered a parts failure while fighting a fire at St. Vincent's Church in 1954, causing it to be considered so unreliable that it was sold to a Pennsylvania fire department for parade duty. It was subsequently sold to Harrah's Casino and Hotel in Las Vegas for display at an antique automobile collection, and in 1980, it was purchased by a private collector.

When Fire Chief Louie DeRosa learned in 2012 that the Ahrens-Fox was in a private collection in Ware, Massachusetts, he traveled to there in September and returned with "Geraldine"

Christmas 2020 with Geraldine and Santa driving the streets of Madison.

on a one-year loan with the understanding that it could be purchased for $150,000. Organized by Madison firefighters, volunteer citizens, and other supporters, The Friends of Geraldine set out to raise the needed purchase price. By July of 2013, the *Madison Eagle* was able to report that "with the $93,000 raised through donations and a historic preservation grant from the Morris County Freeholders (now Commissioners), Geraldine will remain in Madison."(52) Mrs. Dodge's 1921 gift now lives at its own bay at the Madison Public Safety Complex. After some needed engine repairs, Geraldine has become a regular favorite in the Madison parades. It remains an endearing symbol of the community's spirit and love for its history.

The Last Picture Show

Unfortunately, not all historic symbols can be saved. As owners and proprietors changed over the years, Lyon's theater's name also changed formally and informally. Lyon's Madison Theatre, Lyon's New Madison Theatre, the New Madison Theatre, Roth's Madison Theatre, Madison Theater, Madison Cinema 4, Clearview Madison Cinemas, and Madison Bow-Tie Cinema. At some point, it became a "theater" (rather than a "theatre").(53)

Equipment continued to be upgraded over the years, with Cinemascope arriving in 1954. But the view of the theater as Morris County's finest began to fade in the last quarter of the 20th century, with limited showing of first-run movies. By 1981, the large, single screen in the theater was divided into separate smaller screens, first as a triplex and then as a quad. The building began to look tired and outdated. Needless to say, the beauty of its dome and chandelier and painted frescoes had become things of the distant past.

After acquiring Clearview Cinemas from Cablevision in 2013, Bow-Tie Cinemas became the final operator of the theater. They installed upgraded digital projectors and stadium seating. When the Garibaldi Group sold the theater to Saxum Real Estate for $1.7 million in February 2017, after a year on the market, Bow-Tie Cinemas maintained a month-to-month lease on the space and continued to show movies. Many residents were, therefore, shocked when Bow-Tie Cinemas suddenly terminated its lease and moved out on May 30, 2017.

Saxum Real Estate presented plans to the Planning Board to build a mixed-use, multi-story residential and commercial structure on the theater site. Some borough residents noted that the theater had dwindling patronage and had lost its importance. Others lamented the cultural and historic loss to the town and formed a grassroots organization, Save Madison Theater, Inc. Sandy Kolakowski, a founding member along with former mayor Woody Kerkeslager, helped the organization collect more than 2,100 petition signatures in support, with the intent of creating a non-profit entity to purchase and manage a low-cost theater. However, Kolakowski noted that the biggest impediment to their plans was the lack of a willing seller.(54)

Saxum Real Estate then went to the Historic Preservation Commission where discussion revolved around the costs and wisdom of making major structural repairs to the aged building.

The Commission expressed concerns about the proposed replacement building's limited consistency with the architecture of the historic district. Ultimately, the commission approved the demolition of the building due to its poor state. The Board of Adjustment then later granted approval for the construction of the proposed building, which was completed in 2024.

Supporting the Arts, Education, and Culture in Madison

The arts have long been prominent in Madison with the Colonial Symphony, the Shakespeare Theatre of New Jersey, the Museum of Early Trades and Crafts (METC), the Playwrights Theatre, Shanghai Jazz, the Harmonium Choral Society, and the Baroque Orchestra of New Jersey, being major contributors to the cultural life of Madison. As the *Madison Eagle* noted in a September 2004 editorial: "Madison has become a center for the arts and culture without anyone really saying so in so many words, or nurturing connections among the diverse arts venues, or promoting the image of Madison as an arts destination."(55)

The Madison Arts and Culture Alliance (MACA)

With the objective of "making our local scene as vibrant an arts venue as possible," a small group of Madison arts and culture advocates began meeting weekly at the Nautilus Diner in January 2004.(56) The group referred to themselves as the Madison Roundtable on Arts and Culture. The Roundtable quickly grew to have representatives from over a dozen organizations. Together, they agreed that Madison needed a permanent advocate organization for the arts and culture. And so, the Roundtable became the Madison Arts and Culture Alliance (MACA) with the stated purpose: "to promote and expand the arts as a whole in the borough, and to function as facilitators and consultants to the community."(57)

The Alliance quickly made its presence known. Members participated in the 2004 Memorial Day performances, and they also teamed up with the Madison Chamber of Commerce to provide Thursday night shoppers with a series of jazz and pop performances on stage in the shopping district that summer. Working with the Madison Downtown Development Commission (DDC), a committee of MACA members arranged for the music and dance offerings for that year's Bottle Hill Day, a function that it has continued to perform.

From the beginning, MACA wanted a physical home, and it proposed that the borough purchase the former Green Village School building to be that home. The borough council declined to do so. The property was ultimately sold to Kushner Real Estate in 2015, and the Rose Hall Apartments and Madison House Condominium now stand there. However, as part of the sale, a 3,000 square foot facility fronting Kings Road, equipped with restrooms, dressing rooms, a ticket booth area and a large performance space, which opens out to a large patio area with an outdoor stage, has been leased for 30 years to the borough for a dollar a year. It is now known as the Madison Community Arts

Rose Hall Apartments, which includes the Madison Community Arts Center.

Center. Madison's arts and cultural community now has a permanent home, and it represents an exceptional community effort to expand the arts in Madison.

Dr. Robert Butts and the Baroque Orchestra of New Jersey

This early history of arts institutions is often intertwined with the lives and passions of their founders. Madison's examples include: the Museum of Early Trades and Crafts (METC) and antique tool collector Edgar Law Land and the Shakespeare Theatre of New Jersey and actor/director Paul Barry. The 1996 founding of the Baroque Orchestra of New Jersey (BONJ) by Maestro Dr. Robert Butts is another.(58)

In 1996, Dr. Butts met with the owner of the historic Darress Theatre in Boonton, who wanted to have an orchestra in residence at the theater. In response, Butts established a new orchestra that would perform music of the Baroque and Classical periods–the 17th and 18th centuries. The Baroque Orchestra of Boonton performed its first concert at the Darress in November 1996.

In the spring of 2002, Anne Matlack, conductor of the Harmonium Choral Society and Director of Music at Madison's Grace Episcopal Church, suggested that Dr. Butts bring the (now) Baroque Orchestra of New Jersey to the church as part of its music program. In November, the BONJ presented its first concert at Grace Church, featuring the music of Bach and Handel.

In August 2006, the orchestra presented the first of what was to be an annual Summer Music Festival. The festival has always featured an orchestra concert, chamber music concerts, a cabaret or theater evening, and an opera concert. It has also featured international as well as New Jersey artists and world premieres by local and international composers and has collaborated for special events with other arts organizations in the community.

Due to renovation work at Grace Church, the orchestra moved to the newly completed Dolan Hall on the campus of Saint Elizabeth University for its 2007-2008 season. Since then, it has divided its performances between Dolan Hall and Grace Church.

In response to the COVID-19 pandemic, the orchestra produced its first Virtual Summer Music Festival in August and September of 2020. With the artists recorded individually, four concerts were created and broadcast virtually on Sunday evenings.

Maestro Dr. Robert Butts conducting the Baroque Orchestra of New Jersey at St. Elizabeth University's Dolan Hall.

Grace Community Music Series and the Harmonium Choral Society

The Grace Community Music (GCM) series was established in 1996 by Dr. Anne Matlack, the Organist/Choirmaster at Grace Episcopal Church, and her husband, Jabez Van Cleef. The couple envisioned GCM as a series "dedicated to enriching the cultural life of the Madison area by presenting high-quality concerts throughout the year and with related events intended to build a stronger sense of community." As it developed over the years, several performers and groups became GCM staples.(59)

Prominent among them is the Harmonium Choral Society, the other group for which Dr. Matlack is the artistic director. Founded in 1979 and based in Morris County, the 100-voice Choral Society has been recognized widely for its musical excellence, innovative programming, commissioning of new choral works, and community partnerships. The Harmonium annual June concert takes place at Grace Church, as does the spring Chamber Singers Concerts.

In November 2006, Grace Church became an important venue for the First Annual Madison Holiday Arts Festival, sponsored by the Madison Arts and Cultural Alliance (MACA). Dr. Matlack was a MACA board member at the time.

GCM's relationship with the Baroque Orchestra of NJ has long been a productive one. Dr. Matlack has played harpsichord and organ with the ensemble and started a series of lunch-time organ recitals for the orchestra's Summer Music Festival. The choirs have participated in the Baroque Orchestra (holiday) Wassail Concerts and Family Concerts to the enrichment of both groups.

Madison's own world-class harpist, Merynda Adams, often performed in GCM and MACA Holiday Arts concerts and beginning in 2017, her Chamber Music for Charity programs have become an annual part of the series. As it approaches its nearly 25th anniversary, GCM remains a Madison arts mainstay, achieving its goal of enriching the community's cultural life.

Madison Education Foundation (MEF)

The following quote from a Madison STEM (Science, Technology, Engineering, and Math) teacher captures the essence of MEF's purpose, which is to fund teachers' great ideas that energize and enrich the experiences of Madison public school students: "With this grant money, I will ensure that our program continues to grow its role as an intellectual, creative and social outlet for our students.—a Madison teacher."

The foundation began in 2003 as the Madison High School Educational Foundation (MHSEF), launched under the leadership of parent volunteers Donna Dughi and Sarah Levine. The impetus for establishing the foundation came from the high school's goal to start fundraising for educational purposes, efforts that were already thriving at the elementary and junior schools. The founders' vision was to provide teachers with a direct, timely source of funds for enrichment ideas that align with district goals but go beyond its budget.(60) As word spread and teachers became more comfortable submitting requests, the pipeline of proposals grew. In its first three years, MHSEF awarded 18 grants across 11 departments totaling $80,000.

As the foundation continued to grow, so did the needs of Madison's schools. With state funding and regulations further squeezing the budget, the administration asked the foundation leaders to consider serving the entire district. On July 1, 2010, MHSEF officially became the Madison Education Foundation (MEF), opening grant eligibility to educators at all Madison public schools. The foundation's core mission remained the same: to fund teacher-initiated enrichment programs that did not fit within the district budget. In its first year as a district-wide foundation, MEF awarded 45 grants totaling $67,000.

With ongoing community support, MEF has been able to grow, adapt, and consistently deliver on its mission. In the words of a school principal:

> Today, as the school day ended, I had countless teachers literally jumping in joy about all of the grants that were approved…I cannot explain or truly write how much MEF means to our school, to the teachers, to the students, and to this learning community.

As of 2022, MEF had awarded more than 500 grants totaling over $1.7 million across all grade levels and curriculum areas.(61) This exceptional achievement reflects the depth of Madison's community spirit and its strong support of education.

Something Wicked This Way Comes: Recent Natural Disasters, Near Disasters, and Major Storms

Madison is known for its community spirit, resiliency, and willingness to pitch in to help others. This was admirably demonstrated in the greatest traffic jam to hit Madison and Morris County in anyone's memory. On January 29, 1987, the *Madison Eagle* reported that the previous week's 12-inch snowstorm stranded cars for 8 hours along Route 24 and Park Avenue from Morristown down to Route 78. Traveling on Main Street to Delbarton Drive took one resident 4 hours–and she was one of the lucky ones. An out-of-towner, in apparent desperation, phoned the Madison Police Department, crying that her car had broken down on Kings Road and that she had no way of getting to her destination. At the same time, in another part of town, a local high school student, Carlson Bull, spent three hours digging out 25 cars in a municipal parking lot. He was offered payment but declined it.(62) He was Madison's superhero that day.

Other "Storms of the Century" Followed

On March 6, 1993, Madison was hit by the Storm of the Century (history shows there can somehow be many storms of the century in the same century). The fast-moving storm originated in the Caribbean due to extremely low barometric pressure. Frenzied weather forecasters predicted great devastation along the Eastern seaboard. Madison was hunkered down. With gusts of 50 mph and 13 inches of snow, Madison fared well and missed the brunt of the storm. The *Madison Eagle* called the storm the hyped equivalent of the hyped "Comet Kohoutek's 'Light Show of the Generation' in the late 1970s."(63)

A week after New Year's Eve, the "Blizzard of '96," another "Storm of the Century" dumped 25 inches of snow on Madison. DPW crews worked for 35 hours straight in the blinding storm, laying 50 tons of salt on roads. Schools were closed on Monday and Tuesday. Romanelli's Pizza and Bagel Chateau remained open with adjusted hours, and some customers arrived on skis. Dominick Romanelli explained, "I must be out of my mind" [to stay open].(64) President Clinton declared New Jersey a snow disaster area. The parking lot at the Madison Community Pool became a snow dump, filled with 15-foot snow mounds. James Allison, borough administrator, estimated the storm cost Madison $90,000, triple the amount spent for snow removal the entire previous year.

After a summer of drought, Tropical Storm Floyd generously compensated for the lack of water by dumping 9 inches of rain onto Madison on September 16, 1999. Municipal services managed to contain the damage, respond to emergencies, repair downed electric cables and leaking gas lines, and trim fallen branches and trees.

Tropical Storm Irene and the Halloween Snowstorm

Although later surpassed, what was then the costliest disaster in New Jersey history began on August 28, 2011, when yet another 100-year storm, Tropical Storm Irene, slammed into Little Egg Inlet with winds of 65-70 mph and 10 inches of rain. In Madison, the storm wreaked havoc with trees, toppling them and blocking Kings Road and Midwood Terrace, demolished homes on Barnsdale Road and Sinclair Terrace, blacked out electric power to the public library, and flooded many basements. Manhole covers popped, power outages were caused by fallen trees, and many sump pumps were inoperative as a result. On the first day of the storm alone, the Madison Fire Department pumped out 110 basements, 135 calls for help went to first responders, and 170 calls to the Police Department. Mayor Mary-Anna Holden asked residents to help by each family adopting storm drains and clearing them of debris.(65)

The names "Halloween Nor'Easter," "Snowtober," "Shocktober," "Storm Alfred," and "White October" bring back disturbing memories for residents of Madison, not to mention those along the East Coast of the US, from the Carolinas to the Canadian Maritimes. On October 29, 2011, a rare fall snowstorm swooped down and created havoc with high winds, piling record amounts of heavy, wet snow onto trees that still had leaves.

Meanwhile, in Madison, the Police Department closed all major roads, and a number of streets had live wires down. The Volunteer Ambulance Corps opened a warming shelter, and the Public Safety Complex provided charging stations.

Madison public schools were closed for two days, and Drew University's closure lasted three days. Due to ongoing safety issues concerning downed wires and trees, Halloween trick-or-treating was postponed until November 4. Phone and internet connections remained problematic until midweek.

Superstorm Sandy

While 2011's Tropical Storm Irene was terrible, 2012's Hurricane/Superstorm Sandy (officially Post-Tropical Cyclone Sandy when it reached Madison) was horrific. In New Jersey, high tide, a full moon, and the storm surge made for record storm tide heights. Rainfall was nearly 12 inches in some areas, with wind gusts of 90 mph along the shore. Twelve fatalities were recorded, 2.6 million people lost electricity, and a federal disaster area was declared. NJ Transit and Amtrak shut down, gasoline rationing ensued, and total economic losses were $30 billion.(66)

Despite being hard hit with sustained winds of 40 mph, Madison fared better than many towns, again because of its preparedness (Mayor Robert Conley had already issued an emer-

Damage from Superstorm Sandy at
the corner of Brittin and Rosedale.

Cleanup following the storm.

gency declaration two days before the storm's arrival) and having its own electric utility.

National Public Radio reported on Madison and Summit, comparing how the two neighbors handled the restoration of power differently. While Summit relied on JCP&L to restore power fully, it was unable to do so for 12 very long days. Madison was blacked out but up and running in some sections within two days and in most of the rest of the town within five days–despite initially losing its two JCP&L feeder lines, 30 utility poles broken, and more than 100 homes damaged by fallen trees.(67) Devastation across the borough totaled $20 million, exacerbated by a fuel crisis, very long gas lines, live wires on the ground, blocked roads, and limited NJ Transit service. The borough arranged for bus service into New York City for two weeks. Yet, there were no deaths or injuries, and Madison was able to hold its general election on November 6. Despite the major disruptions, Madison children were allowed to celebrate Halloween Trick or Treating on November 3.(68)

Madison had the spirit to help its own, but exceptionally, also to look beyond its own borders to help other towns that were even more severely damaged. Madison adopted the small coastal town of Union Beach, a town nearly wiped off the map by the storm. Under the impetus of Mayor Robert Conley and Councilman Robert Landrigan, the entire Public Works Department arrived in Union Beach to spend thousands of hours in cleanup and construction, donating truckloads of material and support.(69)

The Y2K Bug

The year 1999 saw the emergence of a new kind of threat; under the 20-20 hindsight category of "Much ado about nothing," Madison, and indeed the rest of the world, were preparing for a great potential cataclysmic event, "The Millennium Bug" (or more colloquially, "Y2K Bug.") Due to software/hardware programming shortcuts made decades earlier that recorded a year with only the last two digits, most of the world's computers were unprepared for dates that, on January 1, 2000, might now be read as 1900. Dire warnings were made that software programs and hardware would fail in areas such as banking, utilities, medical, and governmental records and that insurance companies and banks would be especially hard hit. Some predicted that the panic leading up to the fateful date, even September 9, 1999, might also lead to chaos as many programmers had used 9999 to mark the end of a software program.

With an impending crisis, Madison was not a town to sit on its hands. Under Mayor Gary Ruckelshaus, Administrator James Allison, and the borough council, preparations were made well in advance, and the electric utility was declared ready. Madison replaced 33 of its computers, and all others were deemed ready. Two generators that provided emergency power for communications as well as power to sewer and water pumping stations were replaced. The police department's alarm board was replaced, and all photocopiers and mail machines were Y2K compliant. And what was the outcome of all this? Very little of any consequence happened around the world, but Madison could point to its ability to prepare for potential disasters, even if they failed to show up. Also, the upgrade in systems, software, and hardware helped to modernize Madison and bring it into the new millennium.(70)

COVID -19 Pandemic 2020-2021 – Madison Responds

A little over a century after the 1918 "Spanish Flu" pandemic (see Chapter 11), the world experienced another catastrophic pandemic. In early 2020, a new viral infection known as COVID-19 arrived in the U.S. The pandemic's first Madison case was recorded on March 17, and its first death was reported on April 2. On March 9, New Jersey Governor Phil Murphy declared a state of emergency. All schools were closed on March 10, and stay-at-home restrictions were imposed on March 24. People who were considered "nonessential workers" were asked to work from home, and school children could only receive remote, virtual instruction via the Internet. Madison quickly became a "ghost town" as there were no cars on the roads and no pedestrians on the sidewalks. All but essential businesses were closed.

By mid-May 2020, there were 123 cases of the virus reported in Madison, with 14 deaths. About half the deaths were elderly persons residing at the assisted living facility and the nursing home in town. Grocery stores remained open but with restrictions. Only one person per family was allowed in, and the wearing of a mask was mandatory. As time went on, more restrictions were put in place, with special early morning shopping hours established for seniors, one-way aisles delineated, and 'social distancing' imposed.

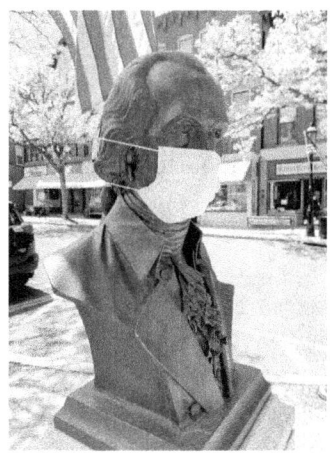

Waverly Place's statue of James Madison with COVID-19 face mask. Photo credit: Herman Huber

Madison residents quickly became adept at using computers or other smart devices to hold meetings, and communicate with family, friends, work, and school. Group gatherings were not allowed; this included school graduations, birthday parties, weddings, and holiday get-togethers. For Easter, the Easter Bunny rode the historic "Geraldine" fire engine around town, and if a young person had a birthday, both the police and the fire departments, followed by friends in cars, had a parade by the house wishing the child a happy birthday.

As these and other "stop-the-spread" restrictions imposed serious economic hardships on many local workers and businesses, the Madison Borough Council enacted a series of measures that the mayor called the "COVID-19 Crisis Response Toolkit" in late March and early April. Residents who were recently furloughed or whose jobs were terminated due to COVID-19 received a $200 rebate on their electric bill. Businesses that had to close because they provided "non-essential services" and other businesses that had major downturns in revenues due to the restrictions received a $400 rebate. In addition, all interest and penalties for non-payment of property taxes (for balances under $10,000) and utility bills were waived for three months. Utility disconnects for non-payment were also waived.(71)

As the pandemic progressed, it became very clear that business owners in town needed more assistance if they were going to survive, so the community came together to help them financially via the Madison Main Street Foundation and community donations. In partnership with the Madison Area Chamber of Commerce, businesses were awarded grants through the Small Business Recovery Grant Program. As of mid-November 2020, a total of $192,000 had been distributed across two payments, one in mid-June and the second in August. "Madison Strong" was launched to help support the project by selling lawn signs and magnets.

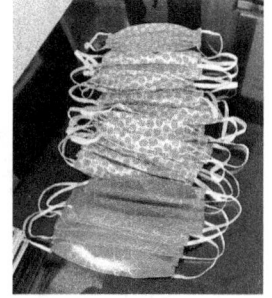

Masks created by the Front Line Sewing Angels.

Madison's creativity, spirit of cooperation, and community involvement produced new volunteer groups that continued to solve the serious local problems created by the pandemic. One of the first groups was the Front Line Sewing Angels. The hospitals were experiencing a shortage of masks needed by the staff. The

Sewing Angels not only made masks but eventually produced scrub caps. The leader of this group from Madison was Christine Preston. By summer, they were making masks for the deaf with a clear plastic insert for reading lips and sending the masks and scrub caps around the country.(72)

A high school student from Chatham started making plastic shields covering the face and neck using a 3-D printer.(73) Soon, the 3-D printers at the high school were taken home by some of the teachers and were being used to make face shields. Jason Erdreich, a Madison Junior School teacher, set up 15 3-D printers from the school district in his home and produced over 12,000 badly needed protective devices for front-line workers. For this, he was recognized nationally by the Mazda Heroes Program in the late fall.

The Madison High School Interact Club supported the First Baptist Church of Madison by collecting donated food for the church's food pantry program, and the Madison Senior Shopping Network provided support to local seniors for groceries and other supplies. The Madison Rotary Club helped by granting the Network $1,000 to supplement the cost of groceries for seniors.(74) Working with the Foodbank of New Jersey and Seashore Fruit and Produce Co., Inc., the Madison Area YMCA had distributed more than 1,300 food boxes to families needing help by October 2020.(75)

Residents Alix Jennings and Barbara Hughes led a community effort to provide weekend meals for Madison students in need. They raised more than $83,000 in donations. The Grace Episcopal Church sold yard signs with the inscription, "Keep your spirits up, Madison," with the money going to the food project. Even though the schools were physically closed, the Madison school district prepared lunches for the free lunch program. Bag lunches were picked up at the high school as the program continued throughout the summer. By the spring of 2021, Barbara Hughes was still organizing the collections for "Food for Friends" at Grace Episcopal Church every Saturday morning. The food was then delivered to various food banks across New Jersey. The First Baptist Church food pantry also participated in this program.

In response to the pandemic and its hard-hitting impact on both Madison residents and businesses, the Madison Eagle Christmas Fund (MECF) undertook a Pandemic Outreach in February of 2021. To address food insecurity among the town's most at-risk residents, the charity offered $50 Stop & Shop gift cards to all senior citizens living in Madison Housing Authority residences and remote sites. These cards were packaged in gift bags with Valentine's candy by a Madison HS senior. For 90 MECF families in financial need, the MECF provided a $200 Stop & Shop gift card and then $300 in gift cards to 35 coffee shops, lunch places, and restaurants

Covid Trick or Treat. Trick-or-treaters could safely pick up their treats without fear of infection; treats were placed creatively at curbs and at the ends of driveways.

in Madison. With the purchase of $27,000 in gift cards to food establishments, the charity was able to give immediate support to not only families but to the town's businesses.(76)

A program known as FLAG (Front-Line Appreciation Group) was established in partnership with local restaurants. This area-wide group collected money to help restaurant workers prepare meals for hospital workers. FLAG eventually expanded across the country in 26 states with over 117 groups.

Boxcar was a New Jersey Parking App based in Chatham. After the pandemic hit, Boxcar was transformed into a grocery delivery app. In April, residents could pick up boxes of food ordered through the app at the Madison train station parking lot. Residents never had to get out of their car; volunteers would load the box into the car. An anonymous donor pledged $100,000 to help feed vulnerable families through this program.(77)

With the coming of warm weather, the rate of the virus infection began to slow down, and Madison cautiously began to reopen. By the end of May 2020, people were able to visit the parks, small gatherings were allowed outside with masks worn, and social distancing rules were observed. Madison High School was able to hold an outdoor graduation ceremony on the Ted Monica Field. The Madison Community Pool opened; retail stores were allowed to have indoor shopping; the Farmer's Market opened at Dodge Field; and the outdoor METC summertime concerts started. Residents were also able to visit beauty salons, barber shops, and restaurants that set up outdoor dining facilities. Areas on Waverly Place were set aside for dining, as well as areas on the sidewalks of Main Street and Central Avenue and in some parking lots. The Madison Public Library offered outdoor pickup of borrowed books in the courtyard. Eventually, patrons were able to make appointments to browse inside the library building and access the public computers. Residents adopted many pets, especially cats and dogs; people commented they had never seen so many dogs being walked around town before.

However, in the fall months, a second wave of the virus arrived. By October 20th, Madison had reported a total of 197 cases. With 13 new cases between November 1 and November 9, a total of 231 people were recorded as having had the virus. In response, Governor Murphy announced that some previously rescinded restrictions had to be reinstituted. At the beginning of the 2020-2021 school year, Madison schools had been put on a hybrid schedule with half the students in school (wearing masks) and half attending virtually on specified days of the week in order to facilitate social distancing in the classrooms.

The second wave also forced the cancellation of the annual Christmas parade, so Santa Claus toured every street in Madison, riding in the Geraldine fire engine, followed by police cars and other fire trucks with sirens blaring. Treats were distributed to children at the curb. Holiday joy was spread with MACA presenting free musical events on various virtual platforms around town.(78) Families were also able to use the Boxcar App to set up appointments to visit Santa Claus in front of his house located on the Maple Avenue parking lot.

With the first doses of the vaccines finally arriving in mid-December 2020, some restrictions could slowly be eased. First responders and healthcare workers were in the first group to receive the vaccines. The next group eligible (in early 2021) for the vaccinations were those 65 and older. By May, everyone aged 16 and above could be vaccinated, and in the late fall of 2021, the eligibility age was dropped to 12 and above. Booster shots were available for those over the age of 50.

New Jersey loosened restrictions on indoor and outdoor gatherings as the weather became warmer and more people were fully vaccinated. Students were able to have their proms as well as graduation ceremonies. Many activities were still limited in numbers to allow for social distancing. The 2021-2022 school year started with the wearing of masks and in-person instruction. The schools were outfitted with unit ventilators and rooftop unit systems that provided fresh air throughout the buildings. Social distancing of three feet was implemented in the classrooms and hallways.

By December 2021, the highly infectious Omicron variant of the virus had arrived in Madison, resulting in an uptick in the number of cases. As of that time, there had been 27 total deaths in Madison due to COVID-19, and approximately 2,000 residents had been reported to have had the virus. Although the virus continued with no end in sight, newer means of fighting it have continued to be marketed. By 2023, the benefits and risks of new vaccines continued to be debated in Madison and the nation.

Madison Responds to the Challenge of Climate Change

As the COVID-19 plague moved from a pandemic to an endemic, life in Madison and the world returned pretty much to normal–or at least to a "new normal." In 2022 and 2023, the Madison community moved to a new challenge: the rapidly accelerating impacts of worldwide climate change.(79)

In March of 2023, the United Nations Intergovernmental Panel on Climate Change warned that global climate change was rapidly leading to catastrophe. The report noted that as humans have continued to use heat-trapping fossil fuels, including coal, oil, and natural gas, and as trapped carbon dioxide continues to heat the planet, the world will approach a tipping point during the 21st century. The consequences would be catastrophic droughts, storms, fires, flooding, food shortages, and disease–unless major interventions were shortly initiated.(80)

To underscore the immediacy of the panel's projections, three months after the report was issued, the *New York Times* reported in an opinion piece that "Phoenix has had 15 straight days of 110-degree temperatures. At the same time, a punishing heat dome has pressed down on Texas. Wildfire smoke from Canada obscured the Chicago skyline, setting off a spike in asthma hospital admissions in New York and Washington D.C. On Sunday, eight inches of rain fell in a few hours near West Point, N.Y.–a 'once in a thousand years' event–even as an entirely different band of violent storms buried the Oklahoma City area in floodwaters, too."(81)

But New Jersey, and in particular Madison(82), had not been idly resting on its laurels. With its long shoreline and many rivers, the state is particularly vulnerable to the consequences of climate change. Acknowledging an annual temperature increase since 1895 of 3.5 degrees Fahrenheit, the state passed the Global Warming Response Act of 2007(GWRA) and the NJ Energy Master Plan in 2019. The target was to reduce emissions to 80% of 2006 levels by 2050 (known as the "80x50 Target"). Subsequent amendments to the GWRA included a goal of 100% of electricity sold in the state to be derived from clean sources of electricity by 2035 and a policy to reduce greenhouse gas emissions to 50% below 2006 levels by 2030. Three key strategies emerged: Replace internal combustion engine vehicles with electric ones, convert space and water heating units in residential and commercial buildings to electric heat, and replace fossil fuels with renewable energy sources.(83)

Madison embraced the urgency to deal with these problems. Madison's January 2023 Climate Action Resolution provided for implementation of the 2022 Climate Action pilot program (developed by the borough's Climate Action Ad Hoc Committee (84), whose goals were to create "the framework for a recurring Climate Action Process and identify near-term climate actions that the borough can consider to reduce greenhouse gas emission and improve resiliency,"(85) thus supporting NJ state goals requiring municipal level climate action. By incorporating energy efficiency, sustainability, and resiliency into Madison's 2020 Master Plan, the borough was already on the path toward renewable energy. By January 2023, it had installed public EV chargers, smart metering, support for solar energy for public power generation, and invested in infrastructure for its electric utility.

A major step forward came with the Madison 2022 Climate Action Report, which set out specific and measurable energy-related goals for the borough. These included:

Decrease the total carbon footprint by 80% from 140,000 tons in 2018 to 28,000 tons by 2050 (the major sources being fossil fuels in buildings and vehicles).

Plug-in electric vehicles to provide 25% of total non-emergency light-duty municipal vehicle mileage by 2025 and 100% by 2035.

Have 1200 town-wide plug-in electric vehicles by 2025 (there were 282 as of June 2022).

Have 1,000 residences with rooftop solar power by 2050 (currently less than 100).

Generate 5% of electricity by 2050 from in-town municipal, school, and commercial solar assets by, for example, creating municipal solar power carports.

Continue to meet or exceed state standards for the renewable content of purchased power.

Maintain/enhance the electric grid and anticipate increased demand.

By 2050, reduce fossil fuel use for space and water heating by 90%.

Increase resiliency by managing increased precipitation and stormwater, mitigating increased temperatures (e.g., shade trees, etc.), and addressing social vulnerabilities in pursuing health equity.

In addition to these goals, the Climate Action Process recommended an annual cycle that would assess measured progress toward goals, develop new or adjusted actions, and present to the borough council these new or modified actions for consideration and adoption.(86)

The June 2023, Climate Action Annual Report showed good progress. As but one measurable example, 9% of light-duty non-emergency vehicle mileage by the municipal fleet was electric, up from 0% the previous year. This placed Madison on course to meet the short-term goal of 25% by 2025.

Other progress included offering discounted energy audits for residents, a $20,000 award for green infrastructure planning and implementation, the planned renovation of the Cook Avenue parking lot with green improvements such as rain gardens for stormwater recharge, and maintaining the excellent record of low downtime for the electric grid compared to other neighboring utilities.(87)

In addition, the 44-unit affordable housing project, which broke ground at Walnut Street and Community Place in November 2023, was designed to be highly energy efficient. The project will be built to "passive house" net-zero energy standards that include solar panels, heat pumps, and other features designed for energy efficiency. When the application was approved in 2022, borough planner Dr. Susan Blickstein described the passive energy design as being "groundbreaking" for this type of project.(88)

Despite some goals being decades away, Madison had acted in the early 2020s as a community to deal with major issues that affect it and, indeed, the rest of the world.

EPILOGUE

Madison's Exceptionality

Madison's long history, stretching out for over four centuries, is an admirable model to look at for what works best in creating and maintaining excellent, well-functioning communities. One key aspect for the application of the concept of "exceptionalism" is the ability of a community to adapt to change and to also maintain allegiance to the basic fundamental beliefs that led to the founding of the United States. Among these are a fair application of laws and a similar response to handling disputes in the courts. Our American values also call for welcoming immigrants in a manner that gives them an opportunity to join us under the conditions primarily set by the federal government. Many communities, such as Madison, have welcomed and supported immigrants, even though the process of adjustment by all parties has taken some time.

In Madison, community organizations that have been created for the benefit of all citizens have also been an extremely powerful force throughout its history. The ongoing success of these organizations has been highly significant in making Madison known today as one of the most desirable communities in which to live. (*New Jersey Monthly Magazine* named Madison #1 in Best Places to Live in NJ in August 2019, and Livability.com rated Madison 24th in the top 100 Best Small Towns in the U.S. in 2015.)

This is not to suggest that Madison is the only exceptional township, borough, or city in the nation. It is, however, one that has met significant challenges in a history that has included a Revolutionary War invasion by the British that came close to Bottle Hill/Madison's borders, the impact of two worldwide epidemics, and several major fires, floods, and other disasters.

And while politics and political party identity have usually been formidable in Madison, those characteristics are frequently tempered by a belief that even difficult issues can be resolved by goodwill and creative solutions. Madison has also benefited from a long line of effective mayors of both major political parties who believed the good of the community was paramount in their efforts.

What is truly amazing about Madison is the belief of its residents that people working together can accomplish virtually anything. From winning a battle to secure more housing for low-income residents to the creation of its own utility and computer network systems, Madison citizens and their leaders have consistently solved key challenges.

In detailing Madison's exceptionality as an American community, we find all the characteristics that distinguish this community: belief in the human rights of all individuals, faith in the fundamentally good nature of most people, and a desire to help others in need by providing opportunities for improving their economic status, as well as a strong belief that people can peacefully pursue their own spiritual/religious paths. Madison is a clear reflection of how such a principled community can achieve remarkable results.

Today, Madison faces the same frequently difficult challenges being encountered by all American communities: environmental issues, population growth, increasing diversity, and local funding matters, including rising taxes and unstable world affairs. If its history provides a clear vision of what Madison's future will be, we can be confident that it will continue to be an exceptional place to live. This is also a living testament to the durability of the powerful principles and daring plans of America's founding fathers and mothers that have resulted in both an exceptional America and an equally exceptional place called Madison, New Jersey.

Frank J. Esposito
And the Madison History Committee

ABOUT THE AUTHOR

F rank J. Esposito received a B.A. in Social Studies and an M.A. in History from Glassboro State College (now Rowan University) in 1965 and 1969, respectively, and a Ph.D. in American History from Rutgers University in 1976. From 1970 to 2021, he taught history at Kean University, where he served at various times as a Dean, Vice President for Academic Affairs, University Ombudsman and Interim President. He was also awarded a Kean Presidential Award for Distinguished Teaching in 1995 and an Award for Distinguished Service by School Leadership Team 1 of Newark, NJ Public Schools. Also in 1995, he played a principal role in the development of legislation leading to the passage of New Jersey's Charter School law. In 2009, Esposito was a candidate for New Jersey Lt. Governor on the Independent ticket with gubernatorial candidate Chris Daggett.

Dr. Esposito is the author of nine books, and over 100 newspaper and journal articles. His published books include *Travelling New Jersey* (1978); *The Madison Heritage Trail: An Intimate History of a Community in Transition* (1984); *Public School Choice: National Trends and Initiatives,* NJ Department of Education, 1988; *Victorian New Jersey* (2005) with Donald Lokuta; *Images of America: Ocean City, NJ* (Vol.1, 1996, Vol. 2, 1998); with Robert J. Esposito; *Manhattan's Musical Heritage* (2005), with Tara Esposito; *Kean University* (2017) with Erin Alghandoor, Elizabeth Hyde, and Jonathan Mercantini; and *The Secret History of the Jersey Devil* with Brian Regal.

He and his wife, Sherry, live in Ocean Township, New Jersey.

ACKNOWLEDGMENTS

After having written several books on the various aspects of the history of New Jersey, I was intrigued when, in 1981, the Madison Bicentennial Heritage Committee contacted me to write a comprehensive account of the history of Madison. And so, an exciting adventure began...the publication in 1985 of *The Madison Heritage Trail: An Intimate History of a Community in Transition*. Then, years later, in 2016, a new Madison leadership committee embarked on a new book. The new committee, which was created to update, revise, and expand the research based on the earlier book, asked if I would again join them.

This new effort to create a committee for a revised and enhanced study of Madison's history began with the leadership of Nancy Adamczyk, the retired longtime Director of the Madison Public Library and Susan L. Simon, a past president of the Madison Historical Society and an award-winning teacher, who holds a Master's Degree in Interdisciplinary Studies: Teaching Mathematics.

Nancy Adamczyk had served as Chair of the Madison Bicentennial Heritage Committee, which published the original *Madison Heritage Trail* in 1985. She would go on to apply her excellent research skills to the development of this book.

Susan Simon proved to be an accurate chronicler of the COVID-19 pandemic in Madison and an expert in selecting vintage and contemporary photographs for the book.

Committee appointments soon included the then-president of the Madison Historical Society, Dr. Linda E. Connors, who agreed to serve as chair of the committee. Connors holds a Ph.D. in Modern European History, specializing in nineteenth-century British history. Much of her professional career was spent as a university librarian with responsibility for acquisitions and collection development.

Louise Easton and her late husband William were co-owners of the *Madison Eagle* newspaper for 25 years. Louise, an award-winning journalist and writer, wrote many excellent articles while also serving as editor of the newspaper. She remains today as one of Madison's local treasures and contributed significant historical stories and insights into Madison's history.

Another gifted member of the committee is Herman Huber, who holds a Ph.D. in Clinical Psychology from Rutgers University. He had been on the faculty at Drew University in Madison, New Jersey, and was later chair of the Psychology Department at the College of St. Elizabeth, where he taught graduate and undergraduate courses and advised thesis students. He also happens to be a marvelous writer.

Another committee member is David Luber, who holds a Ph.D. in Systems Engineering from the University of Pennsylvania. He retired in 2008 after a 35-year career at Bell Laboratories and Telcordia Technologies. Dave played a key role in the committee's intense process of researching past events and in editing and reorganizing the new chapters. He is also a superb writer.

The committee was also most fortunate to have as a member Gary Ruckelshaus, a former Madison council member and mayor, who was able to provide first-hand accounts of how and why important decisions were made in Madison government during the 1990s. It was also a stunning revelation when he recently found out that he is a descendant of Reverend Azariah Horton, an important founding father of Madison who died of smallpox while treating American Revolutionary soldiers.

Maria Slabaugh, who joined us just after our work started, proved to be our computer expert, who also kept us aware of the growing diversity of Madison residents. Both roles have proven critical to our research.

The committee also received help from the following area residents, who contributed material that appears in sections of the book: Astri Baillie, James E. Burnet IV, Dr. Robert Butts, Janet Foster, Dr. Anne Matlack Hicks, Dr. Brian Regal, Dr. Douglas Simon, and Joanne Spigner.

The encouragement and assistance of fellow scholars Dr. Frederick Herrmann, Dr. Mark E. Lender, the late Dr. Peter M. Kalellis, and the late Dr. Saul Cooperman were immeasurable. A sincere debt of gratitude is also given for the tireless secretarial support of Tejal Sarbaugh.

Our editor, Celeste Chin of Creative License Publishing, proved invaluable in bringing order to the text. She continually challenged us to deliver a readable and authoritative document with an economy of words. Any remaining errors or other shortcomings are those of the authors. Ms Chin's partner, Madison's own Kris Pfeifer of Pfeifer Design, brought her considerable design skills to the book's layout and attractive cover. American Society of Indexing member, Molly Hall, provided the comprehensive index that follows.

To my four young muses... Alexandra, Ella, Henry, and George, who, with their curiosity, interest in history and countless queries, always inspire me.

Frank J. Esposito

BIBLIOGRAPHY

Barber, John W., and Henry Howe. *Historical Collections of the State of New Jersey.* New York: S. Tuttle, 1847.

Bardon, Fred B. *A Historical Recapitulation: The Public Schools of Madison, N.J.,* Madison: 1910.

Barnes, Valerie. *Behind the Scenes at Giralda Farms.* Bernardsville: Bernardsville Book Company, 1976.

Becker, Carl M. *The Village: A History of Germantown, Ohio, 1804-1976.* Germantown: Historical Society of Germantown, 1981.

Beers, F.W. *Atlas of Morris County, New Jersey.* New York: Beers, Ellis, and Soule, 1868.

Biographical and Genealogical History of Morris County, New Jersey. New York: Lewis Publication Company, 1899.

Boyd, W. Andrew. *Morris County Directory for 1883-84.* Paterson: Press Printing and Publishing Company, 1883.

Brydon, Norman F. *The Passaic River: Past, Present; Future.* New Brunswick: Rutgers University Press, 1974.

Carlevale, Joseph William. *Americans of Italian Descent in New Jersey.* Clifton: North Jersey Press, 1950.

Cavanaugh, Cam. *Saving the Great Swamp.* Frenchtown: Columbia Publishing Company, 1978.

Christianson, Scott. Interactive by Chris Heller. "When the Empire State Building Was Just an Architect's Sketch; How the World's Most Famous Skyscraper was Built." Smithsonian.com, November 10, 2015.

Clark, Joseph. "Diary of Joseph Clark," New Jersey Historical Society, *Proceedings* First Series vii (1853 - 1855).

Cooperman, Saul. Interview by Frank J. Esposito, Counterpoint television show, CTN Network, 1980's. Kean University Archives, Union, N.J.

The Contents of Giralda: From the Collection of the Late Geraldine Rockefeller Dodge. Sale catalog, New York, Sotheby Parke Bernet, Inc., 1975.

Cunningham, John T. *Chatham: At the Crossing of the Fishawack.* Chatham: Chatham Historical Society, 1967.

_____. *Images of America: Madison.* Dover, NH: Arcadia Publishing, 1998.

_____. *University in the Forest: The Story of Drew University.* Florham Park: Afton Publishing Company, 1972.

_____. *University in the Forest: The Story of Drew University.* 2nd. ed. [n.p.], Phoenix Color Corporation, 2002.

Dauenhauer, John J., Rt. Rev. *A Brief Sketch of Saint Vincent's 1805-1939.* Paterson: 1939.

Dover Index. May 1879, in Barden's Ledger Book, Madison Free Public Library, Madison, NJ.

Ecker, Richard E. *Korean Battle Chronology: Unit by Unit, United States Casualty Figures and Medal of Honor,* Jefferson, NC: McFarland and Co, 2005.

Eckhertz, Holger. *D DAY Through German Eyes - The Hidden Story of June 6th 1944.* DTZ History Publications. Kindle Ed.

Esposito, Frank J. *Travelling New Jersey.* Union City, NJ: Wm H. Wise, 1978

_____. *The Madison Heritage Trail; An Intimate History of a Community in Transition.* Madison, NJ, The Madison Bicentennial Heritage Committee,1985.

_____ and Donald Lokula. *Victorian New Jersey.* Union, NJ: Kean University, 2005.

_____ and Brian Regal. *The Secret History of the Jersey Devil.* Baltimore: Johns Hopkins Press, 2018.

Fitzpatrick, John C. *The Writings of George Washington.* Washington: U.S. Government Printing Office, 1932.

Fleming, Thomas. *New Jersey: A Bicentennial History.* New York: W.W. Norton, 1977.

_____. *The Forgotten Victory.* New York: Reader's Digest Press, 1973.

Gerlach, Larry R. *New Jersey in the American Revolution 1763-1783; A Documentary History.* Trenton: Historical Commission, 1975.

Gertner, Jon. *The Idea Factory: Bell Labs and the Great Age of American Innovation.* New York: Penguin Press, 2013.

Gilligan, Thomas W., Editor. *American Exceptionalism in a New Era.* Stanford: Hoover Institution Press, 2017.

Gordon, Thomas F. *History and Gazetteer of the State of New Jersey.* Trenton: Daniel Fenton, 1834.

"The History of the Madison Golf Club 1896-1972." *NJSGA Golf Magazine,* Spring, 2011 and *Golf.Com Magazine* Sept.-Oct. 2020.

History of Morris County, New Jersey. New York: W.W. Munsell, 1882.

Hodgson, Godfrey. *The Myth of American Exceptionalism.* New Haven: Yale University Press, 2009.

Hulbert, Archer B. *The Paths of Inland Commerce.* New Haven: Yale University Press, 1920.

Kachewski, Marjorie. *The Quiet Millionaires.* Morristown: Morris County Daily Record, 1970.

Kelsey, George. *Racism and the Christian Understanding of Man.* New York: Charles Scribner's Sons, 1965.

Kemble, Stephen. *Journals.* New York: New York Historical Society, 1884.

Kirkbride, Stacy B., Jr. *Kirkbride's New Jersey Business Directory for 1850-1851.* Trenton: 1850.

Klamkin, Marian. *The Return of Lafayette 1824-1825.* New York: Charles Scribner's Sons, 1975.

Kraft, Herbert C. *A Delaware Indian Symposium.* Anthropological Series, Number 4. Harrisburg: Pennsylvania Historical and Museum Commission, 1974.

Kramer, John, ed. *North American Suburbs: Politics, Diversity and Change.* Berkeley: Glendessary Press, 1972.

Lane, Wheaton J. *From Indian Trail to Iron Horse: Travel and Transportation in New Jersey, 1620-1860.* Princeton: Princeton University Press, 1939.

Lemann, Nicholas. *American Democracy.* (Library of America) New York: W. W. Norton, 2020.

Lender, Mark E., and James Kirby Martin. *Drinking in America: A History.* New York: Free Press, 1982.

Lipset, Seymour Martin. *American Exceptionalism: A Double-Edged Sword.* New York: W.W. Norton, 1996.

Madison, Borough of. *Master Plan: Comprehensive Revision, 1975.* Madison: 1976.

Madison Environmental Commission and H2M Associates, Inc, *Madison Borough Environmental Resource Inventory,* 2011. https://www.rosenet.org/DocumentCenter/View/1572/Environmental-Resource-Inventory-PDF

Madison's Heritage: An Historical Account Collected During October,1964. Madison: 1964.

Malone, Linda L., *Morris County Census Trends,1970 to 1980.* Trenton: Department of Labor, Division of Planning and Research, Office of Demographic and Economic Analysis, 1986.

McCormick, Richard P. *New Jersey: From Colony to State.* Princeton: D. Van Nostrand, 1964.

McEniry, Sister Blanche Marie. *Woman of Decision: The Life of Mother Mary Xavier Mehegan.* New York: McMullen Books, 1953.

Mitnick, Barbara J. *Geraldine Rockefeller Dodge.* Morristown: Geraldine R. Dodge Foundation, 2000.

Munn, David C. *Battles and Skirmishes in New Jersey.* Trenton: Department of Environmental Protection, 1976.

O'Gorman, Edith. *Convent Life Unveiled or the Trials and Persecutions of Miss Edith O'Gorman of St. Joseph's Convent, Hudson City, New Jersey.* Hartford: Connecticut Publishing

Co., 1871.

Parker, Barbara. *Tours of Historic Madison*. Madison: Madison Historical Society 1983.

Pilch, Henry. *Madison Fire Department — 100th Anniversary*. Madison: 1981.

Preston, John Hyde. A *Gentleman Rebel; The Exploits of Anthony Wayne*. New York: Farrar and Rinehart, 1930.

Rae, John W., and John W. Rae, Jr. *Morristown's Forgotten Past; "The Gilded Age."* Morristown: John W. Rae, 1979.

Redmond, William F. II. *Growing Up in The Rose City: The Past Pleasantly Remembered*. Friendship, Maine: The Will Redmond Foundation, 1987.

Sammartino, Peter. A *History of Higher Education in New Jersey*. Cranbury: A.S. Barnes, 1978.

_____. *The President of a Small College*. Rutherford: Fairleigh Dickinson Press, 1954.

Seely, Sylvanus. Unpublished Diary. Lloyd W. Smith Collection, Morristown: Morristown National Historical Park.

Sewell, Alan. *The Diary of American Exceptionalism: Pivotal Events in American History 1783-2023*. New HavebL New Ideas Publishing, 2023.

Shaw, Viola, and Barbara Parker. An *Intimate History of the Presbyterian Church of Madison, N.J. 1747 to 1862 from the Journal of Samuel L. Tuttle*. Madison: Arbee Co., 1980.

Sherman, Andrew M. *Historic Morristown New Jersey: The Story of Its First Century*. Morristown: Howard Publishing Company, 1905.

Shurkin, Joel. *Broken Genius: The Rise and Fall of William Shockley, Creator of the Electronic Age*. New York: Macmillan, 2006.

Smith, Samuel. *The History of the Colony of Nova-Caesaria, or New Jersey*. Burlington: James Parker, 1764; reprinted, Trenton: William S. Sharp, 1890.

Smith, Samuel Stelle. *Winter at Morristown 1779-80: The Darkest Hour*. Monmouth Beach: Freneau Press, 1979.

Sitterly, Charles Fremont. *The Building of Drew University*. New York: Methodist Book Concern, 1938.

Snyder, John P. *The Story of New Jersey's Civil Boundaries*. Trenton: Bureau of Geology and Topography, 1969.

Southworth, George C. *Post-Revolution Chatham*. Chatham: 1966.

Stockton, Frank R. *Stories of New Jersey*. New York: American Book Company, 1896.

Stoddard, William O., Jr. *On the Old Frontier*. New York: D. Appleton, 1924.

Stryker, William, ed. New Jersey Archives, Vols. I and III.Trenton: John L. Murphy, 1901; 1906.

Thatcher, James. *Military Journal of the American Revolution*. Hartford: 1862.

Tuttle, Samuel L. A *History of the Presbyterian Church, Madison, N.J.* New York: M.W. Dodd, 1855.

Tuttle, William Parkhurst. *Bottle Hill and Madison; Glimpses and Reminiscences from Its Earliest Settlement to the Civil War*. Madison: Madison Eagle Press, 1917.

Vanderpoel, Ambrose Ely, comp. *History of Madison Lodge No. 93 of Free and Accepted Masons, Madison, N.J.* New York: Charles Francis Press, 1934.

_____. *History of Chatham, New Jersey*. Chatham: Chatham Historical Society, 1959.

Vecoli, Rudolph J. *The People of New Jersey*. Princeton: D. Van Nostrand, 1964.

Wacker, Peter. *Land and People: A Cultural Geography of Preindustrial New Jersey: Origins and Settlement Patterns*. New Brunswick: Rutgers University Press, 1975.

Weslager, C.A. *The Delaware Indians: A History*. New Brunswick: Rutgers University Press, 1972.

White, Bouck. *The Book of Daniel Drew*. New York: Doran, 1910.

Whyte, William H. *The Organization Man*. New York: Simon and Schuster, 1956.

Widmer, Kemble. *The Geology and Geography of New Jersey*. Princeton: D. Van Nostrand, 1964.

Wilsey, John D. *American Exceptionalism and Civil Religion*. Downer's Grove, IL: IVP Academic, 2015.

Woodward, W.E. *Lafayette*. New York: Farrar and Rinehart, 1938.

Wright, William C., and Paul A. Stellhorn. *Directory of New Jersey Newspapers, 1765-1970*. Trenton: N.J. Historical Commission, 1977.

NOTES

CHAPTER 1: From Violence: Serenity

1. William Hartwell Ludlow, "Why Is Madison Where It Is?" *Madison Eagle*, May 25, 1934, p. 7, and reprinted in *Madison Eagle*, December 30, 1954, p. 2.

2. Madison Environmental Commission and H2M Associates, Inc, *Madison Borough Environmental Resource Inventory*, p.17.

3. In this historical study the authors will use both terms, "Native American" or "Indian", as interchangeable depending on the context. The name "Indian" is based on a geographic misperception started by Christopher Columbus who thought he was in the "Indies." However, many Indian tribes, including the Lenape Delaware, still use it as part of their tribal name. Many scholars also still use the name "Indian" in their published writings.

4. Sometimes the name Lenni-Lenape is used by historians, and others, erroneously to describe the Indians of New Jersey. I believe, as does the late preeminent archeologist Herbert C. Kraft, that Lenni-Lenape is a redundancy in the Lenape language: therefore the name Lenape is more accurate. See Herbert C Kraft, A *Delaware Indian Symposium*, Anthropological Series Number 4 (Harrisburg: Pennsylvania Historical and Museum Commission,1974), p. 2.

5. See C.A. Weslager, *The Delaware Indians: A History*, (New Brunswick: Rutgers University Press, 1972), pp. 41-42; and Frank J. Esposito "Indian-White Relations in New Jersey, 1609-1802," Ph.D dissertation, Rutgers University, 1976, p. 1.

6. This amazing archeological find was described in "4,000-Year-Old Bowl Discovered in Swamp," *Madison Eagle*, October 30, 1969, p. 1.

7. Mary Smith, quoted in John W. Barber and Henry Howe, *Historical Collections of the State of New Jersey* (New York: S. Tuttle, 1847), p. 90.

CHAPTER 2: The Mystery of the Beginning

1. See Viola Shaw and Barbara Parker, *An Intimate History of the Presbyterian Church of Madison, N.J. 1747 to 1862 From the Journal of Samuel L. Tuttle* (Madison: Arbee Co., 1980).

2. and 6. Ibid., p. 15.

3. See Ambrose Ely Vanderpoel, *History of Chatham, New Jersey* (Chatham, N.J.: Chatham Historical Society, 1959).

4. Ibid., pp. 30-33.

5. and 7. Shaw and Parker, op.cit., p. 14.

6. Ibid., p.15.

8. "Petition of Elizabethtown People, 1696" in William A. Whitehead, *New Jersey Archives*. First Series, Vol. II (Newark: Daily Advertiser, 1881), p. 128.

9. "Minutes of Essex County Court at a meeting held at Elizabethtown Relating to Samuel Carter," Ibid., pp. 313-314.

10. "Copy of the Journal of John Reading," in *Proceedings of the New Jersey Historical Society*,

January-October, 1955, p. 91.

11. Shaw and Parker, op.cit., p. 2.

12. Ibid., p. 3.

13. For details regarding the 1883 fire at the home of Frank Budd, see Vanderpoel, *History of Chatham, New Jersey* (Chatham, N.J.: Chatham Historical Society, 1959).

14. Email communication from Janet Foster to David Luber (September 16, 2024). She noted in her email that trees needed to be cut and brought to the site, the wood needed to be fully dried (which could take up to two years) before it could be worked into beams and joists, shingles, and clapboards cut, hinges and nails fabricated, foundations and chimneys constructed, etc. She also noted that recent research has suggested that the earliest dwellings in the original colonies were built with palisades, or slender trees roughly trimmed and placed vertically into the ground. Closely spaced, the wooden poles would then be covered with "daub", a mixture of mud and grasses. The finished structure if you can call it that, had a space for a fire and usually a chimney built of horizontally stacked logs covered with daub. (A definite fire hazard.) This could then house the family for the couple of years required before a more permanent frame dwelling could be constructed. (See: https://www.academia.edu/6728054/Rich_Man Poor_Man_Pioneer_Thief_Rethinking_Earthfast_Architecture_in_New_Jersey)

15. Edgar Law Land, interview, Museum of Early Trades and Crafts, Main Street and Green Village Road, Madison, N.J.

16. Shaw and Parker, op.cit., p.14.

17. and 18. Ibid., p. 17.

19. Ibid., p.16.

20. and 23. Ibid., p. 22.

21. Ibid., p. 24.

22. Ibid., p. 26

24. Ibid., p. 37

25. A 2019 survey of surviving tavern licenses in the New Jersey State Library Archives failed to locate any pre-1753 tavern licenses for Bottle Hill.

CHAPTER 3: Bottle Hill: In the Midst of Revolution

1. https://www.hanovertownship.com/DocumentCenter/View/573/Whippany-Burying-Yard---Walking-Tour-Pamphlet-PDF

2. https://digitalcommons.providence.edu/cgi/viewcontent cgi?referer=&httpsredir=1&article=1002&context=primary

3. Thomas Paine, *The American Crisis, Number 1* (Philadelphia: Cist, 1776), p. 1.

4. Morris County Remonstrances, 1776. (Newark: New Jersey Historical Society)

5. Shaw and Parker, op.cit., p. 46.

6. Barbara S. Parker. *Tours of Historical Madison* (Madison Historical Society, 1983), pp. 19-20: See also Andrew Sherman, "*Washington's Army in Lowantica Valley,* Morris County, New Jersey, winter of 1776-77," *American Historical Magazine,* (Volume III January 1908-November 1908) (New York: The Americana Society, 1908) pp. 581-596.

7. Ibid., p.47; Also see Richard Veit statement in Di Ionno, Mark, "Digging for History," *The*

Star-Ledger, May 18, 2016, p. 1

8. The Loantaka encampment has been the subject of much discussion and investigation in recent years. In the manuscript titled "Damages by the Americans in New Jersey, 1776-1782" in the Archives, State Library, Trenton, N.J., are entries which clearly suggest damages by troops encamped nearby. Also important are two other highly significant pieces of evidence: The *Greenman Diary* and a *New Jersey Journal* advertisement, n.d.

9. Shaw and Parker, op.cit., p.46.

10. and 11. Ibid., p. 47.

12. Ibid., pp. 45-46.

13. John C. Fitzpatrick, ed., *Writings of Washington, VII* (Washington: U.S. Government Printing Office,1932). pp.34-35.

14. Ibid., p. 14.

15. Ibid., p. 105.

16. Shaw and Parker, op.cit., p. 39.

17. The sidebar is based on an October 2020 interview of former mayor Gary Ruckelshaus by Louise Easton.

18. Tench Tilghman, Letter, February 7, 1777, Newark: New Jersey Historical Society.

19. Fitzpatrick, op.cit. p.395.

20. Joseph Clark, "Diary of Joseph Clark," *Proceedings of the New Jersey Historical Society*, First Series, VII (1853-1855), p. 96.

21. James Thatcher, *Military Journal of the American Revolution* (Hartford: 1862), quoted in Larry R. Gerlach, ed., *New Jersey in the American Revolution 1763-1783* (Trenton: New Jersey Historical Commission, 1975), p. 347.

22. Sylvanus Seeley, Unpublished Diary, Lloyd W. Smith Collection, Morristown National Historical Park, Morristown, N.J.

23. Fleming, Thomas, *The Forgotten Victory: The Battle for New Jersey-1780* (Pleasantville, NY; Reader's Digest Press, 1973).

24. Samuel Tuttle, quoted in William Parkhurst Tuttle, *Bottle Hill and Madison* (Madison: Madison Eagle Press, 1917*)*, p.83.

25. *New Jersey Journal*, Sept. 18,1782, p. 2.

26.. William Stryker, ed., *New Jersey Archives, I* (Trenton: John L. Murphy, 1901), p. 195

27. William Nelson, ed., *New Jersey Archives, III* (Trenton: John L. Murphy, 1906), p. 36.

28. *New Jersey Journal*, Nov. 15, 1780, in Austin Scott, ed., *New Jersey Archives, V* (Trenton: State Gazette, 1917), p. 111.

29. Ibid., p. 111.

CHAPTER 4: From Bottle Hill to Madison

1. See "Old Turnpike Roads," *Madison Eagle*, April 1, 1899, p. 1, for an account of early road construction.

2. John T. Cunningham, *Chatham: At the Crossing of the Fishawak*, p. 56.

3. For one of the best descriptions of transportation networks in New Jersey, see Wheaton

J. Lane, *From Indian Trail to Iron Horse: Travel and Transportation in New Jersey 1620-1860* (Princeton: University Press, 1939). For a description of rail travel on the Lackawanna, see John T. Cunningham, *Railroading in New Jersey*, and Thomas T. Taber, *Commuter Railroad*.

4. "Sussex Wagons" are described in "Communicated," *Madison Eagle*, November 8, 1889, p. 3.

5. Fred B. Bardon, *A Historical Recapitulation: The Public Schools of Madison, N.J.* (Madison: 1910), p. 27.

6. William Parkhurst Tuttle, *Bottle Hill and Madison: Glimpses and Reminiscences from Its Earliest Settlement to the Civil War* (Madison: Madison Eagle Press, 1917), p. 154.

7. Viola Shaw and Barbara S. Parker, *An Intimate History of the Presbyterian Church 1747-1862*, p. 111.

8. John T. Cunningham, *University in the Forest* (Florham Park: Afton Press, 1972), pp. 46-48.

9. "Francis M. Bruen Reaches 81 Years," *Madison Eagle*, January 9, 1920, p. 1.

10. Thomas F. Gordon, *History and Gazetteer of the State of New Jersey* (Trenton: Daniel Fenton, 1834), p. 107.

11. Lane, *From Indian Trail to Iron Horse*, p. 293.

CHAPTER 5: The Impact of Immigration and the Civil War

1. "Miss Burnet's," *Madison Eagle*, July 1, 1937, p. 7. This is a continuation of a longer page 1 article entitled "Miss Burnet's History of Postal Department A Dedication Feature."

2. "Madison's Hospitality," *Madison Eagle*, October 8, 1897, p. 1.

3. See "The Man Who Looks and Listens," *Madison Eagle*, March 3, 1911, pp. 1, 5, for an informative account of John Waters.

4. Ibid., pp. 1, 5.

5. "Isaac Gordon Found Dead in Shack Where He Lived," *Madison Eagle*, April 13, 1917, p. 12.

6. George Helm Yeaman. Wikipedia, July 27, 2018, http://ea.wikipedia.org/George-Helm-Yeaman

7. Tom Eblem, "In 'Lincoln', Forgotten Kentucky congressman plays pivotal role." *Herald-Leader*, Nov. 25, 2012. http://www.kentucky.com/entertainment.movies-news-reviewsw/article 44390847.htm/

8. For a printed interview with the then 76-year-old Stoddard, see *Madison Eagle*, February 10, 1911, p. 1.

9. "March 4, 1861-1908: A Reminiscence," *Madison Eagle*, March 6, 1908, p. 8.

10. Stacy B. Kirkbride, Jr., *Kirkbride's New Jersey Business Directory for 1850-1851* (Trenton: 1850), in Special Collections, Alexander Library, Rutgers University, New Brunswick, N.J.

11. F.W. Beers, *Atlas of Morris County, New Jersey* (New York: Beers, Ellis and Soule, 1868).

12. Robert W. Carver, "Thomas Who? -- Gibbons!." A short write-up covering a collection of Gibbons papers located at The Museum of American Financial History, New York City, New York. November 5, 1996. pp. 1-5.

13. John T. Cunningham, *University in the Forest* (Florham Park: Afton Publishing Company, 1972).

CHAPTER 6: Emergence of Small Town Madison

1. "Madison", *Madison Eagle*, November 11, 1882, p. 2.

2. *History of Madison Lodge, No. 93*, p. 25.

3. "Fire! Fire!," *Madison Journal,* vol. 1, no. 18, October 27, 1877, p. 1.

4. Ibid., p.1.

5. "Our Fire Company," *Madison Eagle*, November 18, 1882, p. 2.

6. "Madison," *Madison Eagle*, November 11, 1882, p. 2.

7. W. Andrew Boyd, *Morris County Directory for 1883-84* (Paterson: Press Printing and Publishing Company, 1883). Also helpful is *New Jersey State Gazetteer and Business Directory*, 1888.

8. "O'Hara & Hanlon; Practical Horseshoers," *Madison Eagle*, June 15, 1888, p. 2.

9. Henry Pilch, *Madison Fire Department —100th Anniversary* (Madison, 1981).

10. For a fascinating account of Madison's past, see "Anderson B. Gee Reminisces" in *Madison Eagle*, November 20, 1947, pp. 7-8.

11. *Newark Daily Journal*, October 1877, clipping in Bardon Ledger Book, Madison Public Library, Madison, N.J.

12. "Collector G. E. Bardon," *Madison Eagle*, March 17, 1899, p. 1.

13. See John T. Cunningham, *Chatham: At the Crossing of the Fishawack* (Chatham Historical Society, 1967), pp. 108-110 for a description of the coal-freighting business and the role played by Chatham.

14. "Notes About Town," *Madison Eagle*, January 27, 1883, p. 3.

15. The Visual Capitalist (https://www.visualcapitalist.com/worlds-most-populous-cities-500-years-history/) ranked New York as the second in world population behind only London in 1895. And the term "urban centers" is really good wording since NYC was only consolidated in 1898 and in London, the "city" is only a small part (1 square mile) of the greater London.

16. "Injustice," *Madison Eagle*, June 23, 1883, p. 2.

17. For a full reading of these fascinating editorials, see William P. Tuttle, "The Future of Madison," *Madison Eagle*, January 22, 1897, p. 2.

18. "Dissolution of Partnership," *Madison Eagle*, February 24, 1883, p. 1.

19. "Change of Ownership," *Madison Eagle*, January 16, 1903, p. 2.

20. "We Wish to Explain," *Madison Eagle*, February 10, 1883, p. 2.

21. *Dover Index*, May 1879, in Bardon Ledger Book, Madison Public Library, Madison, N.J.

22. *Morris County Chronicle*, July 1881, in Bardon Ledger Book, Madison Public Library, Madison, N.J.

23. Ibid., June 24, 1880.

24 *Morristown True Democratic Banner*, January 1880. Morristown-Morris Twp. Library, Morristown, N.J.

25. "Eagle Feathers," *Madison Eagle*, August 16, 1889, p. 3.

26. For a fascinating account of Madison's past, see "Anderson B. Gee Reminisces," *Madison Eagle*, November 20, 1947, pp. 7-8.

27. "The Corner Store Robbed," *Madison Eagle*, November 25, 1887, p. 3.

28. O'Gorman, Edith. *Convent Life Unveiled or the trials and persecutions of Miss Edith O'Gorman of St. Joseph's Convent, Hudson City, New Jersey.* (Hartford: Connecticut Publishing Co.,1871.)

29. The difference between nuns and sisters is that nuns live a truly cloistered life while sisters go out into the world to do good works.

30. "Eagle Feathers," *Madison Eagle*, September 6, 1889, p. 3.

31. "Eagle Feathers," *Madison Eagle*, June 14, 1889, p. 3.

32. See "A Warning" *Madison Eagle*, March 29, 1989, p. 2; "Water," *Madison Eagle*, April 26, 1889, p. 2.; and "Water! Water!," *Madison Eagle*, May 17, 1889, p. 2.

33. "It Is Mayor Albright," *Madison Eagle*, January 17, 1890, p. 2.

34. "The Borough Election," *Madison Eagle*, March 15, 1895, p. 2.

35 "Let there be light: How Madison Became Illuminated," *Madison Eagle*, May 17, 1984, p. 1 and July 4, 2002, p. 1.

36. "Let there be light – part II: Madison Electric Co. then and now" *Madison Eagle*, May 24, 1984, p. 15.

CHAPTER 7: The Age of Roses and Great Estates

1. The descriptions of rose growing in Madison were largely culled from back issues of the *Madison Eagle*. Especially useful are "Madison Greenhouses Grow Millions of Roses Annually," May 16, 1930, p.4; "A Flower Once Made Our Area Famous," September 11, 1980, p. 15; "Was A Pioneer Rose Grower," Louis M. Noe obituary, March 26, 1909, p. 1; "Big Shipment Easter Roses," April 12, 1901, p. 1; "Madison Roses," April 26, 1884, p.3; "Christmas Roses," January 3, 1890, p. 3.

2. James Robert Littlejohn, Diary, unpublished manuscript (on microfilm), Chatham Public Library, Chatham, NJ.

3. Joseph Ruzicka and Wilma Ruzicka Nichols, "Rose Reminiscing with Joseph Ruzicka," typewritten manuscript, n.d., Madison Public Library, Madison, NJ. The manuscript was printed by the *Madison Eagle* in three parts on May 20, 1948, p.1; May 27, 1948, s. 2, p. 1; June 10, 1948, p. 1. See also Robert Nichols, tape recorded interview with Frank J. Esposito, July 15, 1981, Madison Public Library, Madison, NJ.

4. "Ridgefield Park Era, 1889," news clipping, in Fred Bardon's notebook, Madison Public Library, Madison, NJ.

5. In his speech, Ruzicka also stated his belief that the rose industry suffered from over-expansion. See "Million Rose Plants Under Glass in Madison, J.F. Ruzicka Tells Rotarians," *Madison Eagle*, October 21, 1932, p. 6.

6. "Rose Reminiscing with Ruzicka," *Madison Eagle,* June 24, 1948, pp. 2,4.

7. "Rose Reminiscing," *Madison Eagle,* June 17, 1948, p. 4.

8." About Roses," *Madison Eagle*, August 20, 1886, p. 2.

9. "Ruzickas Celebrate 55th Anniversary," *Madison Eagle*, September 5, 1957, p. 1.

10. "About Roses," *Madison Eagle*, August 20, 1886, p. 1.

11. "Madison Roses to Take Spotlight In Big Festival Planned for June," *Madison Eagle*, May 6, 1948, p.1.

12. For an excellent treatment of the great estates of Morris County, see John W. Rae, and John W. Rae, Jr., *Morristown's Forgotten Past, "The Gilded Age."* (Morristown: John W. Rae 1979). See also, George Danco "The Way They Were," *Morristown Daily Record.* May 24, 1981, pp.4-6.

13. Ibid., p. 57

14. Ibid., p. 58

15. Frank R. Stockton, *Stories of New Jersey* (New York: American Book Company, 1896).

CHAPTER 8: Ethnic Vigor Diversifies the Community

1. From a private interview by Frank J. Esposito with the Corbett sisters, Helen and Lucile, March 30, 1982.

2. Ibid.

3. A good overview history of the Madison Italian community, including the Maione and Valgenti families, is provided in "Italians give Madison an Ethnic Glow," *Madison Eagle*, July 1, 1976, p. 13. The story of both families is from that article, in addition to a personal interview on March 6, 1981, of Frank Valgenti, Jr. by Frank J. Esposito.

4. "Manual Training," *Madison Eagle*, February 6, 1903, p. 1.

5. "The Italian Immigrant," *Madison Eagle*, May 8, 1903, p. 3.

6. "Madison Stands Alone in Americanization Work," *Madison Eagle*, May 13, 1921, p. 5.

7. "Civil Leaders Turn Out for Dedication of Hall," *Madison Eagle*, February 24, 1955, p. 1.

8. An obituary of Rev. Rebecca Prout Lassiter appeared on p. 14 of the November 6, 1978 edition of the *Madison Eagle*.

9. "Testimonial Tea to Honor The Rev. Rebecca Lassiter," *Madison Eagle*, November 14, 1967, p. 3.

10. White Brothers advertisement, *Madison Eagle*, December 23, 1943, p. 9.

11. White Brothers advertisement, *Madison Eagle*, March 11, 1927, p. 4. The White Brothers Taxi Service did not advertise or have any presence in the *Madison Eagle* until that date. Richard White, Jr., was married in 1922, and so may have been working in some way with cars or taxis even before 1927.

12. William 0. Stoddard, "A Plea From Lincoln's Friend to the Colored Voters of Madison," *Madison Eagle*, September 2, 1910, p. 6.

13. For a full list of Black family names in 1910 Madison, see *Madison Eagle*, November 15, 1910, p. 1.

CHAPTER 9: Benefactors Create a Modern Madison

1. See "Benefactors' Foresight Guided Latter Day Growth of Madison," *Newark Evening News*, November 17, 1923, for a discussion of early benefactors.

2. *Biographical and Genealogical History of Morris County, N.J.*, (N.Y.: Lewis Pub. Co. 1899), p. 3.

3. The History of the Madison Golf Club 1896-1972; NJSGA Golf Magazine, Spring, 2011 and Golf.com Magazine Sept.-Oct. 2020)

4. "D. Willis James Dies After Short Illness," *Madison Eagle,* September 9, 1907, p. 1.

5. A good overview of the uses of James Hall can be found in "James Hall Has Filled Important Role in Social, Civic Life of this Community," *Madison Eagle*, April 20, 1939, p. 1.

6. One immigrant helped by James was the nephew of Major-General Simon Bernard of Napoleon's army. These accounts are in "He Nobly Helped the Destitute Jew," *Madison Eagle*, September 27, 1907, pp.1, 4.

7. Ibid., pp. 1,4.

8. "James Park Dedicated," *Madison Eagle*, July 8, 1898, p. 1.

9. For a full description of the impact of James' death on Madison, see "Madison Pays Tribute to Mr. James," *Madison Eagle*, October 4, 1907, p. 1.

10. "The True Measure of Success," *Madison Eagle*, June 12, 1903, p. 6.

11. "Editorial Review," *Madison Eagle*, June 21, 1907, p. 2.

12. *The Eagle* article was titled "Did They Kill 1,700 Wild Ducks?" The total the *Eagle* claimed killed for the season was 1,300 ducks, but the 1,700 ducks figure quoted by the *New York World* allegedly represented only a three-week period. See *Madison Eagle*, December 2, 1910, p. 1.

13. In 1939, Giralda Farms announced it had found the "perfect dog" in "Sieger, Ferry Rauchfelser," a Doberman Pinscher. McClure Halley, Kennel Manager, traveled 8,000 miles around the world to find the dog for Mrs. Dodge. See "Giralda Farms Secures World Famous Pinscher," *Madison Eagle*. January 12, 1939, p. 6.

14. "Tax Board Allows Reduction of $46,415 in Borough Assesments," *Madison Eagle*, August 25, 1922, p. 1.

15. Internal email from architectural historian Janet Foster to Herman Huber dated November 12, 2019.

CHAPTER 10: Memories of "The Old Boys"

1. "Charles C. Force Passes Away," *Madison Eagle*, March 16, 1906, p. 1. In the obituary an unknown writer stated that the "Old Boys Club of Bottle Hill" once numbered 18 members. Fred B. Bardon identified the "Old Boys"—he thought 17 in number — as David Pierson, B. Warren Burnet, William J. Brittin, Dr. Lewis A. Sayre, Dr. John L. Munn, Flavel W. Day, Henry P. Day, Elijah D. Burnet, William T. Budd, Henry R. Burnet, E. Nelson Samson, Charles C. Force, Frank S. Freeman, Pierson A. Freeman, J. Frank Burnet, Arthur N. Bonnel and Hudson Minton. See Fred B. Bardon, *A Historical Recapitulation: The Public Schools of Madison*, N.J. (Madison, 1910), p. 31.

2. "Communicated," *Madison Eagle*, October 31, 1895, p. 3.

3. See "The 'Old Boys' Meet," *Madison Eagle*, May 6, 1898, p. 1; the article contains several fascinating stories about the coming of the railroad to Bottle Hill.

4. For further information, see "Lewis Albert Sayre, A Biography of the Well-known Physician and Surgeon," *Madison Eagle*, July 20, 1898, p. 3; "A Native of Morris County," *Madison Eagle*, August 14, 1891, p. 3; and "A Bottle Hill Boy," *Madison Eagle*, March 10, 1899, p. 8; "Death of Dr. L. A. Sayre," *Madison Eagle*, September 28, 1900.

5. For W.J. Brittin's obituary, see "William Jackson Brittin," *Madison Eagle*, September 17, 1897, p. 1.

6. For B. Warren Burnet's obituary, see "Madison Loses Venerable Citizen," *Madison Eagle*,

February 19, 1909, pp. 1, 10.

7. The Madison Tuttles and Bruens also intermarried with the well-known Lum family of Chatham. See "Death of Mrs. Tuttle," *Madison Eagle*, May 5, 1911, p. 1.

8. The destruction at the Hillside Cemetery and train derailment at Seaman's Crossing as a consequence of the 1902 storm were reported in the article: "Havoc Caused by Cloud Burst," *Madison Eagle*, August 15, 1902, p. 1.

9. Ibid, p. 1.

10. "The MacDougalls of Madison: if they can't do it, nobody can." *Madison Eagle*, March 19, 1881, p. 15.

11. Ibid., p. 15..

12. "Albright Elected," *Madison Eagle*, March 13, 1903, p. 1.

13. "Editorial," *Madison Eagle*, April 17, 1903, p. 4.

14. Albright's speech is quoted in "Albright Nominated," *Madison Eagle*, March 6, 1903, p. 1.

15. "News of the Madison Fire Department," *Madison Eagle*, June 19, 1903, p. 1.

16. "Largely Attended," *Madison Eagle*, March 20, 1903, p. 1.

17. "The Things That Are Caesar's," *Madison Eagle*, February 3, 1905, p. 4.

18. "Editorial," *Madison Eagle*, March 16, 1906, p. 4.

19. While Madison was part of Chatham Township, the local option vote was taken frequently, sometimes with strange results. See Kenneth Haynes and Dorothy Fredrickson, "Madison Heritage Tales: Prohibition," in *Madison Eagle*, March 15, 1979, p. 17.

20. "Trolley on Way Here," *Madison Eagle*, Feb 2, 1912, p. 3.

21. "Trolleys in Operation," *Madison Eagle*, Feb 9, 1912, p. 1.

22. "Trolley Wanted in Madison Under Certain Conditions," *Madison Eagle*, May 17, 1910, p. 7.

23. "1928 Marked Improvements In All Boro Departments," *Madison Eagle*, December 18, 1928, p. 1.

24. "End of Trolley Tracks Recalls No Man's Land," *Madison Eagle*, July 21, 1933, p. 1.

CHAPTER 11: Prosperity, Prohibition and the World at War

1. "Successful Democratic Rally," *Madison Eagle*, October 20, 1911, p. 10.

2. "A Record of Things to Be Accomplished," *Madison Eagle*, October 8, 1909, p. 1.

3. "Madison and its Attractions," *Madison Eagle*, March 25, 1921, p. 1.

4. "Anderson B. Gee Reminisces," *Madison Eagle*, November 20, 1947, pp. 7,8.

5. "End of All Wars in Sight--Bryan," *Madison Eagle*, December 2, 1921, pp. 1,7,8.

6. "'Think Clever Dog Was Much Sought Milk Thief," *Madison Eagle*, August 19, 1910, p .7.

7. From an advertisement for the Madison Academy, *Madison Eagle*, September 12, 1912, p. 1.

8. "Prof. Marcellus Oakey Dies Suddenly," *Madison Eagle*, May 10, 1912, p. 1.

9. "New Principal's Views," *Madison Eagle*, June 28, 1912, p. 1.

10. An article on Stoddard appeared in the *Madison Eagle*, April 7, 1916, p. 6.

11. "An Artist With an International Reputation," *Madison Eagle*, June 8, 1917, p. 7.

12. See "Ordinance," *Madison Eagle*, October 23, 1914, p. 8, which describes the entire project as approved by the Madison Borough Council.

13. "Here is the First Picture of the New Station," *Madison Eagle*, Jan 29, 1915, p. 1.

14. For the full text of Doug Simon's article "America and Madison prior to World War I," see *Madison Historical Society Newsletter*, November, 2016, pp. 1-3.

15. "Peace Service on Sunday Evening," *Madison Eagle*, October 2, 1914, p. 1.

16. "Benefit Concert for Red Cross," *Madison Eagle*, October 2, 1914, p. 1.

17. "Dr. MacQueen Speaks of Europe's Battlefields," *Madison Eagle*, October 23, 1914, p. 1 and "President Tipple Tells of War Experiences," *Madison Eagle*, November 6, 1914, p. 2.

18. "Camp Fire Girls to Aid War Orphans," *Madison Eagle*, March 1, 1916, p. 1.

19. "Many Attend Reception to Organize National Women's Peace Party," *Madison Eagle*, May 26, 1916, p. 1.

20. "United States Must Prepare," *Madison Eagle*, June 2, 1916, p. 1.

21. "Fighting Fourth Liberty Loan Campaign Is Going Through With a Regular Whoop," *Madison Eagle*, March 2, 1917, p. 1.

22 "A Patriotic Appeal to All Citizens," *Madison Eagle*, March 2, 1917, p. 1.

23. "Military Company and Rifle Company Formed at Meeting in James Hall," *Madison Eagle*, March 30, 2017, p. 1.

24. "Plant Beans and Be Patriotic Says William O. Stoddard Jr.," *Madison Eagle*, March 30, 2017, p. 1.

25. "Isn't Pacifism Passivism?" *Madison Eagle*, March 30, 2017, p. 4.

26. "Ex-President Taft and Wayland Ayer Raised $5,000 for Y.M.C.A. At Front, *Madison Eagle*, June 1, 1917, p. 1.

27. *New York Tribune*, February 27, 1918, p. 8.

28. LePan, Nichcolas, "Visualizing the History of Pandemic," Visual Capitalist. [Online] March 14, 2020. https://www.visualcapitalist.com/history-of-pandemics-deadliest/.

29. "Few Local People Suffer From Grip,"*Madison Eagle*. October 4, 1918, p. 1.

30. "Epidemic in Madison Causes Seven Deaths Within Week," *Madison Eagle*. October 11, 1918, p. 1.

31. "Fewer Deaths This Week From Influenza Epidemic," *Madison Eagle*. October 18, 1918, p. 1.

32. "Hospital Created By Magic To Handle Local Epidemic," *Madison Eagle*. October 25, 1918, p. 1.

33. "Ban Lifted And Madison Resumes Normal Life," *Madison Eagle*. November 1, 1918, p. 3.

34. "Epidemic Took Very Heavy Toll," *Madison Eagle*. November 15, 1918, p. 1.

35. "Epidemic in Madison Causes Seven Deaths Within Week," op.cit., p. 1.

36. "Fewer Deaths This Week From Influenza Epidemic," op.cit., p.1.

37. "Ten Deaths In Single Week." *Madison Eagle*. October 25, 1918. p. 1.

38. Telephone interview with Cathie Coultas by David Luber in June 2020.

39. "First Victim of Fresh Epidemic of Influenza." *Madison Eagle*. February 21, 1919, p. 1.

40. "New Settlement House A Beauty," *Madison Eagle*, November 21, 1924, p. 1.

41. See "Effect of Prohibition in Borough Arouses Interest," *Madison Eagle*, March 7,1919, p. 3, and Kenneth Haynes and Dorothy Fredrickson, "Prohibition," in "Madison Heritage Trails, *Madison Eagle*, March 15, 1979, p. 17.

42. Scott Christianson; Interactive by Chris Heller, "When the Empire State Building Was Just an Architect's Sketch, How One of the World's Most Famous Skyscrapers Was Built," SMITHSONIAN.COM, November 10, 2015.

43. See *Madison Eagle*, November 4, 1982, p. 29.

44. "The Lawrence Murder Case Ends," *Madison Eagle*, July 21, 1922, p. 4.

45. "Golden Hind Press a Family Affair for the Rushmores," *Madison Eagle*, May 12, 1966, p. 3.

46. "A Visit to the Golden Hind Press." *American Artist,* May, 1941.

47. "Sandburg Urges American Independence in the Arts," *Madison Eagle*, March 18, 1927, p. 2.

48. "City Dwellers Coming Here," *Madison Eagle*, January 11, 1929, p. 1.

49. "Madison and Drew," *Madison Eagle*, September 18, 1925, p. 4.

50. "The University and its Community," *Madison Eagle*, February 3, 1929, p. 1.

51. "Dr. Hough Reviews America's Position," *Madison Eagle*, April 13, 1934, p. 1.

52. "Lenox Sheaf Rose, Millionaire, Dies At Florida Estate," *Madison Eagle*, April 4, 1934, pp. 1,4.

53. Mayor Alan Brown's inaugural address is discussed at length in "Mayor Brown Makes Few Changes in Boro," and "Mayor Brown's First Message," *Madison Eagle*, January 5, 1934, both articles on p.,1.

54. "Rubber Balls, Dog House, Tires All Dug Up In Clearing Whippany River," *Madison Eagle*, April 19, 1935, p. 1.

55. "Commuting Ended," *Madison Eagle*, January 4,1935, p. 4.

56. Personal interview of Frank Valgenti, Jr, op.cit. (Chapter 8).

57. "They Are Not Dead," *Madison Eagle*, August 23, 1945, p. 12.

58 "First Lady's Gracious Manner Wins Approval of Madisonians On Visit Here Friday," *Madison Eagle*, March 22, 1945, p. 1.

59. "Mrs. Roosevelt In Talk at Drew Stresses Strength in Our Beliefs," *Madison Eagle*, January 11, 1951, p. 1.

60. Carl Shillet and Mike Tolhurst, *A Traveller's Guide to D-Day and the Battle for Normandy.* (New York: Interlink Books), p. 69

61. https://www.history.com/topics/world-war-ii/d-day

62. *Madison Eagle*, August 10, 1944.

63. Chris Spelker, "Eulogy for Frederick W. Hopper." College course paper, April 2019.

64. In-person interview by Herman Huber with Michael Piano, April 4, 2019

65. Telephone interview by Herman Huber with Mary Torbali, April 1, 2019.

66. In-person Interview by Herman Huber with Michael Sena, April 10, 2019.

CHAPTER 12: Rose City Blooms as Affluent Suburb

1. For an excellent analysis of the evolution of the suburb, see John Kramer, editor, *North American Suburbs: Politics, Diversity, and Change* (Berkeley: Glendessary Press, 1972). See also William H. Whyte, *The Organization Man* (New York: Simon and Schuster, 1956).

2. "Hizzon N. J. Griffiths," *Madison Eagle*, January 9, 1947 p. 10.

3. "Will Name Commission To Investigate Schools," *Madison Eagle*, October 16, 1947, p. 1.

4. "Mayor Raps Driscoll Delay in School Communism Probe," *Madison Eagle*, March 11, 1948, p. 1.

5. "Hear Stassen's Proposal For Stronger U.N.", *Madison Eagle*, Feb 5, 1948, p. 1.

6. *Madison Eagle*, October 12, 1950, pp.1, 4.

7. Richard E. Ecker, *Korean Battle Chronology: Unit by Unit United States Casualty Figures and Medal of Honor*) Jefferson, NC: McFarland and Co, 2005, p. 42.

8. https://www.abmc.gov/node/457260#.XBKxyxNKgWp.

9. "Officer Wins Top Medal." *New York Times*, June 16, 1951.

10. Telephone conversation, Sam Coursen, Jr. and Herman Huber, November 28, 2018.

11. Madison War Memorial Book Committee, *Always With Us*, Madison, NJ: 1998, pp. 243-253.

12. Telephone conversation, Evangeline Coursen Pouncey and Herman Huber, December 3, 2018.

13. Ibid.

14. "Residents Favor Bond Issue," *Madison Eagle*, February 5, 1948, p. 1.

15. "Sentiment -", Madison *Eagle*, June 28,1951, s.2; p. 2.

16. "The Suburban Slum --" *Madison Eagle*, March 15,1951, s. 3, p. 2.

17. "Eliminate Sub-Standard Housing," *Madison Eagle*, March 9, 1950, s. 2; p. 4.

18. "New Schools By Spring of 1949 If Voters Approve," *Madison Eagle*, January 29,1949, p. 1.

19. "About School Costs," *Madison Eagle*, March 9, 1950, s. 2; p. 2.

20. See *Madison Eagle* of October 25, 1956, pp. 1,6 for an account of Merritt's role.

21. "The Unforgettable Mr. Shoemaker," *Madison Eagle*, June 18, 1964, p. 10.

22. "Realtor Flays Master Plan Proposal," *Madison Eagle,* January 5, 1955, pp. 1, 4. This article lists Mr. Evans's objections to the plan and John Hutchinson's response, including the Eagle's comment about his political following.

23. *Madison Eagle*, December 31, 1959, p. 1.

24. "Smith Bequest Sets Up Trust For Many Denominations In Area," *Madison Eagle*, July 28, 1959, p. 2. The article also mentions that George Washington's papers will go to the national historic park in Morristown.

25. "Lloyd Smith, Master of Boxwood Hall, Died Saturday," *Madison Eagle*, July 7, 1955, p. 1.

26. "Planning Rad-Chem Activation," *Madison Eagle*, May 9, 1957, s.3; p. 1.

27. Clayton Hoagland, "Fairleigh Dickinson University," in Peter Sammartino, *A History of Higher Education in New Jersey* (Cranbury: A.S. Barnes, 1978), p. 155.

28. The Robinson visit was discussed in two editions of the *Madison Eagle*: "500 Greet Robinson" was a front page article in the December 23, 1948 edition and "Athletes and Others" appeared on page 7 of the December 30, 1948 edition. The latter edition also featured pictures of the Dodger great with Rev. Benjamin Richardson, the pastor of Madison's First Baptist Church, on page 1 and with Eagle publisher Charles McDermott on page 7.

29. "Four Colonial Errors Give Newark Eagles 6-4 Win Tuesday," *Madison Eagle*, September 13,1945, p. 1.

30. "Don Newcombe In Madison," *Madison Eagle*, December 8, 1949, p. 4.

31. "Phillies Catcher Signed by Kurns For 1948 Season," *Madison Eagle*, March 25, 1948, p. 13.

32. "Recreation Becoming More Important," *Madison Eagle*, April 1, 1948, p. 13.

33. "Mayor Again Raises Question of Paid Manager for Madison," *Madison Eagle*, January 6, 1955, p. 2.

34. "A Journalistic Question," *Madison Eagle*, December 15, 1955, p. 2.

35. "Chicago Too –," *Madison Eagle*, July 28, 1955, p. 2.

36. "Five Councilmen Censure Macmillan," *Madison Eagle*, December 15, 1955, p. 1.

37. *Encyclopedia Britannica*, Inc., https://www.britannica.com/biography/William-Shockley, accessed October 23, 2019.

38. According to a recent article by Glenn Zorpette in the December 2022 issue of the *IEEE Spectrum*, Brattain and Bardeen, working under Shockley's direction, invented a working point-contact transistor on December 16, 1947. By the end of that month, Shockley had developed (on his own) the basic design for the bipolar junction transistor, which would become the dominant transistor design into the late 1970s.

39. Joel Shurkin, *Broken Genius: The Rise and Fall of William Shockley, Creator of the Electronic Age.* (New York: Macmillan, 2006).

40. Ibid., p. 309.

41. "Smith and Macmillian Back Independent Candidates;" *Madison Eagle.* March 2, 1945, p. 1.

42. "Santa To Preside At His Usual Spot,", *Madison Eagle*, December 5, 1957, p. 1.

43. "British 'Cathedral' Publication Honors Dean Lynn Harold Hough," *Madison Eagle,* February 9, 1956, s 2; p. 2.

44. "Ralph E. Hersey Retired Thursday," *Madison Eagle*, April 7, 1960, p. 10.

45. "Colonial Little Symphony To Play At Madison High School Next Month," *Madison Eagle*, December 6, 1951, p. 18

46. Final Curtain Falls for Colonial Symphony," *Madison Eagle*, November 25, 2010, p. 12.

47. "Thrift Shop Climaxes 20 Years of Service," *Madison Eagle*, May 23, 1963, p. 1.

48. Cam Cavanaugh, *Saving the Great Swamp* (Frenchtown: Columbia Publishing Co., 1978), is an excellent account of the struggle to save the Great Swamp from development.

CHAPTER 13: Generations Clash in Turbulent Sixties

1. For a full account of local events surrounding the assassination of President Kennedy and the *Eagle* editor's editorial response, see the front page of the November 28, 1963, *Madison Eagle*.

2. "What Will the World Think," *Madison Eagle*, November 28, 1963, p. 1.

3. "'Marcy' Dodge, Man of Special Distinction," *Madison Eagle*, January 1, 1964, p. 3. Mr. Dodge's role in the creation of the Great Swamp National Wildlife Refuge is described in a companion piece on the same page entitled "1000 Acres of Great Swamp Named For Conservationist."

4. David H. McAlpin letter to Edna Lerley and Nancy Singleton, June 26, 1976, Dodge Collection, Madison Public Library, Madison, NJ.

5. For details of the visit of Martin Luther King to Madison, see the following issues of the *Madison Eagle*, January 30, 1964; February 13, 1964.

6. In a personal email to David Luber on December 4, 2023, Gary Ruckelshaus wrote that he had made the comment on several occasions as Madison's mayor speaking at Martin Luther King ceremonies "…because it was an extremely important event in my young life." Ruckelshaus wrote that there were several such occasions including one held at St Vincent Martyr Church.

7. Morris County Fair Housing Council, *Newsletter*, August 1964, Madison Public Library, Madison, NJ

8. George Kelsey, *Racism and the Christian Understanding of Man*, (New York, Charles Scribner's Sons, 1965), p. 175.

9. https://aaregistry.org/story/dr-george-kelsey-was-a-great-theologian/.

10. "Peculiar Status of Blacks in America," *Madison Eagle*, April 30, 1987, p. 19.

11. https://uknow.drew.edu/confluence/display/DrewHistory/George+Kelsey

12. Harold Dean Trulear, Ed., Donald Jones in *The Pastor Scholar Unsung Hero: The Legacy of George D. Kelsey*. Andover Newton Theological School, undated.

13. "Peculiar Status of Blacks in America," op.cit., p.19

14. "Rev. George Kelsey, 25-year Drew Professor," *Madison Eagle*, April 11, 1996, p. 19.

15. Note that added primary source materials on the Barbershop controversy can be found in the Madison Public Library archival files.

16. "Mayor Speaks on Criticism," *Madison Eagle*, May 14, 1964, p. 4

17. "Father Callagan Replies," *Madison Eagle*, May 14, 1964, p. 4.

18 John Dalena, Telephone Interview with Herman Huber, September 23, 2023.

19. "Chamber Supports Stand of Barbers," *Madison Eagle*, May 14, 1964, p. 4

20. "Says Chamber Opposes Bias," *Madison Eagle*, May 21, 1964, p. 1.

21. "Oxnam Underlines University's Role," *Madison Eagle*, May 14, 1964, p. 4.

22. "No Citizen Wants 'Seething' Town, *Madison Eagle*, May 14, 1964 p. 4.

23. "NAACP Charges," *Madison Eagle*, May 21, 1965, p. 1.

24. "Divided Town Quiets Down After Week of Turbulence," *Madison Eagle*, May 21, 1964, p.1.

25. This document is included in the Library archival files.

26. "Two Students Late, Refused Haircuts," *Morris County Daily Record*, October 3, 1964, p. 6.

27. "Barbers Demands Growing With Size of Membership," *Madison Eagle*, September 3, 1964, p. 1.

28. "Barbers Must Cut Hair of Negroes, State Declares," *Newark Star Ledger*, December 17, 1964, p. 6; see also George Cable Wright, "Madison, N.J. Barber Ordered to Cut the Hair of two Negroes," *New York Times*, December 17, 1964, p. 46.

29. "Are No Madisonians Vexed Over Local Racial Image?" *Madison Eagle*, December 31, 1964, p. 2.

30. "Townfolk Give Emerging Therapy for Massive Infection," *Madison Eagle*, March 18, 1965, p. 1.

31. "Who's Apathetic? Who's Indifferent? Who Needs Protection?" *Madison Eagle*, March 8, 1965, p. 8.

32. "The case of an Over-Ripe Conscience," *Madison Eagle*, October 7, 1965, p. 1.

33. Ibid., p. 1.

34. "Defends Mellen Attack as Pickets Debate," *Madison Eagle*, October 14, 1965, p. 1.

35. "Madison GI Escapes Viet Cong Offensive," *Madison Eagle*, February 22, 1968, p. 1.

36. The quoted reactions to President Johnson's April 1968 announcement by Jeannette Balber and Ronald Eisele appeared in "Johnson's Decision Stuns Local Leaders," *Madison Eagle*, April 4, 1968, p. 1.

37. "Question: Why Do They Hate Us So Much?" *Madison Eagle*, October 3, 1968, p. 1.

38. James Carter, "Campus Rock." *Journal of Popular Music Studies*, Vol. 32, No. 3, 2020, p. 51.

39. David Hinckley, https://Drew.edu/news/2016/04/14/when-rock-ruled. Retrieved May 5, 2021.

40. James Carter, op.cit., p. 53.

41. https://Drew.edu/news/2016/04/14/when-rock-ruled. Retrieved May 5, 2021.

42. https://www.rockhall.com/inductees. Retrieved May 19, 2021.

43. "Jefferson 'Airplane' finds home in Madison." *Madison Eagle*, July 25, 1968, p. 13 and Mark Ransom, "Airplane, Opera excel; crowd 'painfully quiet." *Drew Acorn*, October 11, 1968.

44. Masso, Richard. "Dylan concert provides for memorable experiences." *The Acorn*, April 19, 1996.

45. James Carter, op.cit., p. 71.

46. Bonnie Barrow, "Unclean and Undesirable," *Madison Eagle*, February 10, 1966, p. 8.

47. Walter H. Waggoner, "Barbers Curbed on Bias in Jersey," *New York Times*, February 22, 1966, p. 1.

48. "Madison Rallies to American Way of Life, *Madison Eagle*, March 3, 1966, p.1.

49. "Oxnam Underlines University's Role," op.cit., p. 4.

50. The positions of the Republican and Democratic municipal candidates in the 1967 Candidates Night forum were reported in "Local Candidates Offer Solutions to Problems,"

Madison Eagle, October 26, 1967, p. 2.

51. "Proper Use of a Jaw Bone," *Madison Eagle*, October 19, 1967, p. 6.

52. "New Developments May Fill Up Local Classrooms," *Madison Eagle*, Aug 4, 1966, p. 1.

53. "Landmark Becomes Prized Museum," *Madison Eagle*, September 17, 1970, p. 1.

54. "Fifty Years of Youth Experience Embodied In New Y.M.C.A. Building," *Madison Eagle*," Oct 8, 1959, p. 8.

55. "The Long Lasting Gift," *Madison Eagle*, January 3, 1963, p. 6.

56. "The Citizens' Committee: A Pool of Wisdom," *Madison Eagle*, May 2, 1968, p. 12.

57. "Former Mayor Opposes Charter Study Request," *Madison Eagle*, July 18, 1968, p. 3.

58. The July 31, 1969 issue of the *Madison Eagle* provided comprehensive front page coverage – pro and con – of the Charter Study report. In addition, the full text of the report, including the Minority Report, appeared on pages 9 through 11 of the July 31 issue of the newspaper.

59. "Commission Decries Campaign Of 'Fear And Distortion,'" *Madison Eagle*, October 23, 1969, p. 2.

60. Quoted praises to the slain civil rights leader and a description of the service appear on page 1 of the April 11, 1968 edition of the *Madison Eagle*. The headline article was entitled: "Residents Assess Dr. King Tragedy In Area"

61. Ibid., p. 1.

62. "Dr Kelsey: New Leader Could Be White," *Madison Eagle*, April 11, 1968, p.1.

CHAPTER 14: The End of an Era as Madison Faces New Challenges

1. *Geraldine R. Dodge. Last Will and Testament.* October 29, 1962. Eleventh Provision, 3(b), p.7. Photocopy, Madison Historical Society, Madison, NJ.

2. Sotheby Parke Bernet's characterization of the sale as cited in Barbara J. Mitnick, *Geraldine Rockefeller Dodge.* (Morristown, NJ, Geraldine R. Dodge Foundation, 2000), p. 117.

3. See "Thousands See Hints of Past They Never Knew" *New York Times*, October 7, 1975, p. 40.

4. Ibid., p. 40.

5. *Wall Street Journal.* October 10, 1975.

6. Mitnick, op.cit. p. 119.

7. Kathleen O'Brien, *Daily Record* (Morris) June 1978.

8. "Millionaires Footprints Fall in the Dust of Debris" *Madison Eagle*, June 22, 1978, p. 8.

9. Scott McVay, "Report of the Executive Director," Geraldine R. Dodge Foundation. *Report*, 1978, p. 7.

10. "Dodge Foundation trustees to act on local fund requests Sept. 4," *Madison Eagle*, August 11, 1977, p. 6.

11. *Geraldine R. Dodge, Last Will and Testament.* October 29th, 1962. Provision Thirteenth (e) 1-7 pp. 13f.

12. John J. Degnan, Letter to Robert Muir, Jr. Re: Estate of Geraldine R. Dodge. October 29, 1979. 4 pp. Photocopy, Madison Historical Society, Madison, New Jersey. The photocopy does not include copies of the exhibits attached to the original. See also: "'Dodge Estate May Face Report Delay." *Daily Record* (Morris), July 8, 1979.

13. "Editorially Speaking: Putting Off the Inevitable," *Madison Eagle*, October 4, 1973, p. 18.

14. "Mayor Questions Dodge Spending." *Daily Record* (Morris). June 3, 1979. See also "Attorney May Challenge Dodge Grants" *Daily Record* (Morris), July 19, 1979.

15. Mitnick, op.cit., p 116.

16. Much of this section was written by Louise Easton; she is quoting herself. The Glenn O. Head quotation in the following paragraph represents her memory of their interactions.

17. "Council Approves Underground Wiring," *Madison Eagle*, April 14, 1977, p. 1.

18. "Fruehling Explains Vote." *Madison Eagle*, April 14, 1977, p. 1. Also see "Other Ways to Renovate Downtown", *Madison Eagle*, Mar. 24, 1977.

19. Pat Luciano, private interview with Louise Easton on July 12, 2021.

20. "Falco building named most important in Madison," *Madison Eagle*, Dec.17,1981, p. 15.

21. Group interview with Jerry Stevenson, John Hatley, and Gary Ruckelshaus by Louise Easton at the Madison Commons clubhouse, February 2020.

22. Ibid.

23. Ibid.

24. "Life Among the Legislators," *Madison Eagle*. May 20, 1971, p. 10.

25. "Hubbard Concerned With Water," *Madison Eagle*. October 2, 1997, p. 6.

26. "70% Turnout Splits Vote In 3-Way Race," *Madison Eagle*. November 4, 1997, p. 1.

27. "Land-Hungry Developers Eye 'Green Acres' Sites." *Madison Eagle*. November 16, 1972, p. 1.

28. "Mayor Highlights Parks, Recreation," *Madison Eagle*. January 4, 1973, p.1. See also: "Council Pushes For Green Acres Approval," *Madison Eagle*. January 11, 1973, p. 1.

29. From a telephone interview with Connie Stober by David Luber in April 2020.

30 "To accept state funds," *Madison Eagle*. September 5, 1974, p. 1.

31. "Summerhill Park is the choice!" *Madison Eagle*. February 5, 1987, p. 1.

32. "Former resident recalls Green Acres homestead," *Madison Eagle*. November 6, 1986, p. 1.

33. "Democrats control Council in landside," *Madison Eagle*, November 8, 1973, p. 1.

34. From a telephone interview with Connie Stober by David Luber on October 1, 2019.

35. "Council winners are Baumgartner, Maione and Mantone," *Madison Eagle*, November 4, 1976. p. 1.

36. Much of this sidebar article is based on a series of personal interviews with Ms. Mantone by Louise Easton in June 2022.

37. "Making History," https://newsweneed.org, (Website for New Jersey Local Media).

38. "NJ Hills Group Converts to Nonprofit," *Madison Eagle*, April 7, 2022.

39. "Housing Bias Discussed," *Madison Eagle*, May 23, 1963, p. 3.

40. "Can checkerboard plan upgrade housing?" *Madison Eagle*, January 29, 1970, p. 1.

41. "Authority Condemnation Angers Citizens," *Madison Eagle*, August 2, 1979, p. 1.

42. Louis Riccio, Interviewed by Louise Easton at the Madison Housing Authority Office on Central Ave., May 2019.

43. "Senior Housing Should Be Explored," *Madison Eagle*, Feb. 14, 1980, p. 2.

44. "Borough gets $6.1 million for senior citizen housing," *Madison Eagle*, Sept. 3, 1981, p. 1.

45. "HUD gives ultimatum," *Madison Eagle*, October 27, 1983, p. 1

46. Ibid., p.1.

47. "Drew Housing Brings Concerns," *Madison Eagle*, Sept. 12, 1985, p. 1.

48. "Health services expanded," *Madison Eagle*, May 23, 1974, p. 1.

49. "It'll be Bottle Hill Day," *Madison Eagle*, August 1, 1974. p. 1.

50. "Bottle Hill Day is Saturday," *Madison Eagle*, September 14, 1989, p. 1.

51. "Bottle Hill Day," Supplement to the *Madison Eagle*, October 3, 2019.

52. Minutes of the Madison Public Library Board of Trustees, May 24, 1973.

53. "Bicentennial Jubilee," *Madison Eagle*, November 29, 1973, p. 1.

54. "Bicentennial committee seeks community input," *Madison Eagle*, May 16, 1974, p. 1.

55. "Committee issues appeal for help," *Madison Eagle*, September 12, 1974, p. 1.

56. "Markers to key historic homes in thre Borough," *Madison Eagle*, December 30, 1976, p. 1.

57. "Town-wide picnic Saturday," *Madison Eagle*, May 15, 1975, p. 1.

58. "The Bicentennial Ball," *Madison Eagle*, February 12, 1976, p. 4.

59. "Parade Highlights," *Madison Eagle*, September 2, 1976, p. 4.

60. "Santa Will Light Community Tree In Borough Center, *Madison Eagle*, October 24, 1946, p. 1.

61. "The Dying Year, 1877," *Madison Journal*. December 29, 1877, p. 2.

62. Personal interview of Carmen Toto, Jr. by Louise Easton on January 12, 2020

63. "A symbol of 'good over evil;' Madison lights its first public menorah," *Madison Eagle*, December 16, 1999, p.1.

64. Much of this section was written by Ms. Easton and it reflects her remembrances as a partner with Ms. Valk in the establishment and management of the *Madison Eagle* Christmas Fund.

65. "*Madison Eagle Christmas Fund*; Over 50 Years of Madison Neighbor Helping Neighbor," MECF, 2023. Mailer sent to Madison households.

66. Ibid.

67. "Dodgers prove they're champions," *Madison Eagle*, December 6, 1979, p.48.

68. Neal O'Donnell comments made on phone interview with Gary Ruckelshaus, January 14, 2024.

69. Peter Jilleba comments made on phone interview with Gary Ruckelshaus, April 19, 2020. Jileba died on May 3, 2020.

70. Ibid.

71. Tony Gero comments made on phone interview with Gary Ruckelshaus, April 17, 2020.

72. Steve Natale comments màde on phone interview with Gary Ruckelshaus, January 8, 2024.

CHAPTER 15: Community Action in the 1980s and 1990s In Order to Preserve a Unique Madison

1. "Bulging Museum Wall is Victim of Ice," *Madison Eagle*, March 8, 1973, p. 1.

2. "Success may not be so sweet," *Madison Eagle*, September 11, 1975, p. 6.

3. "Agrees With McKenna on Library Use," *Madison Eagle*, February 15, 1968, p. 11.

4. "Bulging Museum Wall is Victim of Ice," op.cit., p. 1.

5. "Load Forces Special Meeting," *Madison Eagle*, July 12, 1973, p. 1.

6. "Museum Repairs Debated," *Madison Eagle*, February 3, 1983.

7. "Ordinance 11-83," *Madison Eagle*, May 12, 1983, p. 20.

8. "A step forward for museum", *Madison Eagle*, October 27, 1983, p. 1.

9. This and much of the following paragraphs describing the decision to save the building were prepared by the former mayor and councilman, Gary Ruckelshaus, serving as a member of the Madison History Committee.

10. "Mayor leaving office on proud note," *Madison Eagle*, December 23, 1999. p. 1.

11. "Museum lease passed, with one 'no' vote," *Madison Eagle*, April 16, 1992, p. 3.

12. "Governor comes to town," *Madison Eagle*, October 9, 1997, p. 19.

13. "Mayor leaving office on proud note," op.cit., p. 1.

14. "Museum's renovation garners state preservation award," *Madison Eagle*, May 7, 1998, p. 3.

15. "Mayor appoints members to Historic Preservation Commission," *Madison Eagle*, October 28, 1993, p. 3.

16. "Conference hears preservation depends on details," *Madison Eagle*, March 28, 1996, p. 9.

17. 'Historic preservation law boosted, *Madison Eagle*, March 28, 1996, p. 1.

18. "Mayor leaving office on proud note," op.cit., p. 1.

19. The September 2, 1971 edition of the *Madison Eagle* provided comprehensive coverage of the immediate impact of Hurricane Doria on Madison (and Florham Park). See "Doria's Destruction Heaviest In Memory; We Just Kept On Pumping & Pumping," *Madison Eagle*. September 2, 1971, p. 1, and "Watery woes plague hundreds of Madison homeowners," *Madison Eagle*, September 2, 1971, p. 6.

20. "Name 3 Areas For Flood Relief Plan," *Madison Eagle*, December 14, 1972, p. 1.

21. "Drainage Approved," *Madison Eagle*, July 29, 1982, p. 1.

22. Residents Happy Over Flood Project. *Madison Eagle*. November 14, 1985, p. 1.

23. See "BOROUGH OF MADISON MORRIS COUNTY, NEW JERSEY CONTRACT   MA 83-11 SPRING GARDEN BROOK SECTION 3 IMPROVEMENTS NOTICE TO BIDDERS," *Madison Eagle*, July 26, 1990, p. 23.

24. "Historic Hostelry To Be Restored By Experienced Restaurateur." *Madison Eagle*. December 17, 1957, s 2; p. 2.

25. "New Name." *Madison Eagle*. June 19, 1986, p. 16.

26. "Historic Bottle Hill Inn closes doors; owner to pursue retail development." *Madison Eagle*. January 7, 1988, p.1.; Inn demolished to make way for bank. *Madison Eagle*, August 8, 1991, p. 1.

27. Coverage of the immediate impact of the fire was reported in "The Mead Hall Fire", *Madison Eagle* August 31, 1989. John Cunningham's fine book, *University in the Forest, The Story of Drew University*, 2nd ed, (Phoenix Color Corporation, 2002), pp. 342-346 also describes the fire and its impact. Other sources included the Drew University website; *Madison Fire Department History* by Robert Dunne, and conversations during and after the fire between W. Scott McDonald and former Madison mayor, Gary Ruckelshaus.

28. "Ceremony Officially Reopens Mead Hall", *Madison Eagle*, December 17, 1992, p. 3.

29. "Green Acres Approves Loantaka Project," *Madison Eagle*, Nov. 4, 1993, p. 1.

30. Email communication to David Luber from Gary Ruckelshaus on January 11, 2024.

31. "Land Deal Talks Step to Fruition," *Madison Eagle*, May 15, 1997, p. 1. and "Tree Hugging Works, Madison gets Gibbons Place Property," *Madison Eagle*, June 19, 1997, p. 1, 17.

32. "Council to vote for ordinance dedicating parkland on Belleau Ave.," *Madison Eagle*, Oct. 8, 1992, p. 4.

33. "Tree planting to become a private affair," *Madison Eagle*, May 22, 1990, p. 1.

34. "People worked above and beyond for park," Letter to the editor from Judy Mullins, *Madison Eagle*, June 16, 1994, p. 4.

35. "Rail station embankment 'scrubbed' for facelift," *Madison Eagle*, April 1, 1999, p. 1.

36. "Madison buds as 'Tree City' for 20th year," *Madison Eagle*, April 28, 2005, p. 2.

37. Ibid, p. 2.

38. "For seniors: Garden beds, walking trail," *Madison Eagle*, February 28, 2008, p. 14.

39. "Madison Rotary completes first phase project to plant 100 trees across town," *Madison Eagle*, November 15, 2023.

40. William Parkhust Tuttle, *Bottle Hill and Madison* (Madison Eagle Press 1917), p. 247.

41. "After oak's demise, replanting is mulled," *Madison Eagle*, December 12, 1996, p. 1.

42. "Boro named Tree City," *Madison Eagle*, April 17, 1986, p. 2.

43. "Let there be light – Part II: Madison Electric Co. then and now," *Madison Eagle*, May 24, 1984, p. 15.

44. "A Million Dollar Asset Given Away," *Madison Eagle*, Sept. 7, 1923, p. 1. See also "Your Electric Light and Power Plant Which Has About Been Given Away," *Madison Eagle*, September 21, 1923, p.1.

45. "Let there be light – Part II," op.cit., p.15.

46. "Higgs Company sues borough on new electric rates," Madison Eagle, December 24, 1980, p.1.

47. "Let there be light – Part II," op.cit., p. 15.

48. "Revised rates aim to keep big electric users," *Madison Eagle*, December 23, 1993, p. 1.

49. "Conley works diligently, and Madison reaps benefits," *Madison Eagle*, October 16, 2008, p. 2.

50. *Madison Eagle-Florham Park Eagle-Chatham Courier*, April 18, 1996, p. 6, for an extended discussion and explanation.

51. "Official looks to set record straight on surplus," *Madison Eagle*, May 27, 1999, p. 2.

52. "Mayor leaving on a proud note," *Madison Eagle*, December 23, 1999, p. 17.

53. Bond Ordinance 56-2019, approved December 19, 2020. Retrieved December 4, 2023. https://www.rosenet.org/725/Annual-Budget-Process.

54. "S&P Raises Madison, NJ's GO Bond Rating To 'AAA,'" The Bond Buyer, December 28, 2004. https://www.bondbuyer.com/news/s-p-raises-madison-njs-go-bond-rating-to-aaa. Retrieved December 4, 2023.

55. John T. Cunningham, "The Route 24 Missing Link", *The Madison Heritage Trail*, (Madison, NJ: The Madison Bicentennial Heritage Committee, 1985), pp. 316-318.

56. Ibid.

57. "Two route 24 connectors called needed by state, *Madison Eagle*, September 17, 1992, p. 14.

58."DOT adds Route 24 alternatives," *Madison Eagle*, October 23, 1980, p. 1.

59. "Traffic conditions bring resident demands for street cul-de-sacs," *Madison Eagle*, May 12, 1983, p. 1.

60. "Town Talk," *Madison Eagle*, April 24, 1980, p. 14.

61. "300 urge Route 24 'connections' be delayed or dropped." *Madison Eagle*, December 19, 1991, p. 31.

62. "DOT adds Route 24 alternatives, op.cit., p. 1.

63. Carla Cantor, "After 30 Years, a Jammed 2-Lane country Road Awaits Relief," *New York Times*, August 21, 1988.

64. "Governor snips ribbon, opens Route 24 freeway," *Madison Eagle*, November 19, 1992, p.14.

65. "The Lackawanna Electrics chug into the past," *Madison Eagle*. September 6, 1984, p. 13.

66. "About Us." NJ TRANSIT. [Online] https://www.njtransit.com/about/about-us.

67. "Morris & Essex to phase in new Arrow III trains." *Madison Eagle*. September 6, 1984, p. 13.

68. "Transit, NJ. New Jersey State Rail Plan; The New Jersey Railroad System; Final Report," 2015, pp. 3-11.

69. Ibid., pp. 3-11.

70. "Train station, once tired, now exemplar." Madison Eagle, May 10, 2007, p. 30.

71. "Three: Trio to be interviewed." Madison Eagle, January 10, 2008, p. 19.

72. "Train station, once tired, now exemplar," op.cit., p. 30.

73. "Madison raising rates for train station parking." Accessed January 2, 2024. https://www.nj.com/news/local/2009/08/to_all_the_freeloaders_who.html

74. "Train station, once tired, now exemplar." op.cit., p. 30

75. John Yang, Washington Post, November 3, 1992. Accessed January 3, 2024. https://www.washingtonpost.com/archive/politics/1992/11/03/candidates-finish-in-a-sprint/301d84f6-54f5-41e8-8597-17e35faa7fbe/

76. Christine Lee, "Madison's Rodin sculpture sold," *Madison Eagle*, https://www.newjerseyhills.com/madison_eagle/news/madisons-rodin-sculpture-sold/article_59bd-7de7-6eed-582e-855b-a0276fddc79c.html, accessed January 7, 2024.

77. Council President Gary Ruckelshaus was present with President Bush when these events

occurred and these are his written personal recollections, dated March 1, 2020.

78. Christopher Moore, "Bush rallies Madison crowd on final day of campaign," *Madison Eagle*, November 5, 1992, p.1.

79. Battey, Mrs. Sallie, New York Letter. *Madison Journal*, April 29, 1879, p.1.

80. Our History. The Shakespeare Theatre of New Jersey. https://www.shakespearenj.org/about-us/history. Accessed January 8, 2024.

81-85. Ibid.

86. "Theater; A Brand-New Stage for Shakespeare's World." *New York Times*, July 7, 1998. https://www.nytimes.com/1998/06/07/nyregion/theater-a-brand-new-stage-for-shakespeare-s-world.html. Accessed January 8, 2024.

87. "Our History. The Shakespeare Theatre of New Jersey". https://www.shakespearenj.org/about-us/history. Accessed January 8, 2024.

88. Ibid.

89. William Westhoven, "'Sweet sorrow' parting: Artistic director Bonnie Monte to exit Shakespeare Theatre of NJ." *Morristown Daily Record,* February 11, 2023. https://www.dailyrecord.com/story/entertainment/2023/02/09/bonnie-monte-leaving-shakespeare-theatre-nj-artistic-director/69888019007/. Accessed January 8, 2024.

90. This section was taken from a research paper prepared by James Burnet, IV for this book. A copy is available from the Madison Historical Society. A version of the paper, co-authored with Rachel Barry, appeared as an article in the May 2021 edition of *Madison Living*, pp. 7-8.

91. "Millennium event planners ready logo for year 2000," *Madison Eagle*, December 3, 1998, p. 1.

92. "Millenium logo," *Madison Eagle*, January 1, 1999, p. 1.

93. "Picnic to launch millennium fete," *Madison Eagle*, Feb. 25, 1999, p. 1.

94. "Picnic kicks off Madison Millenium fest," *Madison Eagle*, June 10, 1999, p. 8.

95. "A Great Reunion Indeed," *Madison Eagle*, November 4, 1999, p. 2.

96. "Time Capsule sealed with fanfare," *Madison Eagle*, December 2, 1999, p. 1.

97. "Madison revelers ring in new year," *Madison Eagle*, Jan. 6, 2000, p. 8.

98. "Quilters warmed by camaraderie in project," *Madison Eagle*, February 4, 2000 and "Tapestry Makers," *Madison Eagle*, June 1, 2000, p. 8.

99. "Martell benefit will be jazz blast," *Madison Eagle*, September 10, 2015, p. 14.

100. In a January 8, 2024 email to David Luber, Gary Ruckelshaus noted that following the first walk in 1995, Tony Martell established an annual target for the Walkathon Committee to raise $100,000, which it met or exceeded every year. This was confirmed by Sylvia Luber, who like Ruckelshaus served on the Committee from its inception.

101. Elwood Kerkeslager, *RoseNet Madison's Community Network Mission.1996*. Report to the Madison Borough Council. See also Kerkeslager, *Brief History of RoseNet*, 1999.

102. Gene Robbins, "Computerized 'RoseNet' planned to embrace the town," *Madison Eagle*. October 31, 1996, p. 1.

103. Nancy Adamczyk, RoseNet Technology Committee - Meeting Minutes. 2000.

104. "RoseNet cost for this year to hit $250,000." *Madison Eagle.* March 12, 1998, pp. 1, 19.

105. Gary Ruckelshaus, Video Recording: 1997 Mayor's Conference Opening Remarks. Madison: 1997).

106. Madison RoseNet - See Presentation Charts. Elwood Kerkeslager (Madison: 1997).

107. "RoseNet Draws Attention at International Conference." *Madison Eagle.* December 3, 1998, p. 2.

CHAPTER 16: The New Millenium

1. "Schools Go to Crisis Mode in Response to NYC Tragedy." *Madison Eagle.* September 13, 2001, p. 1.

2. "Superintendent Praises Response to Catastrophe." *Madison Eagle,* October 4, 2001, p. 7.

3. "Madison Feels Tremor of Terrorist Attacks," *Madison Eagle*, September 13, 2001, p. 1.

4. "22 from Our Area Among the Missing," Madis*on Eagle,* September 20, 2001, p. 3.

5. "Madison to Meet Tragedy with Unity," *Madison Eagle*, September 20, 2001, p. 1.

6. "Madison Unites in Mourning and Hope," *Madison Eagle*, September 27, 2001, p. 1.

7. "Why We Can Face Whatever is Ahead," *Madison Eagle,* September 20, 2001, p. 4.

8. "Fund to Aid Families," *Madison Eagle*, November 29, 2001, p. 1.

9. Personal interview with Fire Chief Louie DeRosa, III at the Madison Public Safety complex by David Luber, February 3, 2021.

10. Ibid.

11. "Rumor of 'Cheering' Called False." *Madison Eagle*, October 18, 2001, p. 1.

12. "Why We Can Face Whatever is Ahead," *Madison Eagle*, September 20, 2001, p. 4.

13. "9/11 probe hears of planning failures," *Madison Eagle*, November 27, 2003, pp.,1, 19

14. Linda l. Malone. "Morris County Census Trends, 1970 to 1980." 1986. See also "Blacks See Little Overt Bias Today," *Madison Eagle*, April 21, 1994.

15. www2.census.gov. [Online] 1990. https://www2.census.gov/library/publications/decennial/1990/cp-1/cp-1-32-1.pdf? p. 351.

16. www.census.gov/quickfacts. [Online] 2021. https://www.census.gov/quickfacts/fact/table/morriscountynewjersey,madisonboroughnewjersey/PST045219.

17. "Recognition of Dr. Charles Robinson," *Madison Eagle*, November 13, 1986.

18. "Civil Rights icon William Primus Mourned," *Madison Eagle*, October 15, 2015, pp. 1, 19.

19. Website of the Urban League of Morris County, www.ulmcnj.org.

20. In-person interview with A. Caig Dunn by Herman Huber, October 2021.

21. "Kenisha Tucker: Helping Bring Madison's Hidden Figures to Light." *Madison Living Magazine*, August 2021, pp. 6-7.

22. See "Hidden Figures of Madison," https://storymaps.arcgis.com/stories/b2efb33d974945bcb17c9702099bbcfe.

23. "Darwin Ray Chang" Obituary, *Madison Eagle*, October 15, 2015, p. 12.

24. *Downbeat Magazine*: List of "Great Jazz Rooms" featured the Shanghai Jazz Rooms. 2021.

25. Personal interview with Waseem Chaudhary, Daniel Chaudhary, and Shaan Chaudhary

at the Waseem Petroleum Group office in Madison by David Luber, March 10, 2022. See also "Mosque Vote Nears," *Madison Eagle*, September 30, 2021, p. 19. and "Board Hearing Mosque Plan," *Madison Eagle*, August 12, 2021, pp. 1, 5.

26. "Madison Mosque Plan Approved," *Madison Eagle*, October 6, 2021, p. 1.

27.Personal interview with Dora Ramirez by Maria Slabaugh, January 17, 2022.

28 Ibid.

29. Personal telephone interview with Jan Figenshu by David Luber and Maria Slabaugh, January 19, 2022.

30. Dora Ramirez interview, op.cit.

31. Affordable-housing units planned at Civic Center," *Madison Eagle*, November 26, 2020, page 1.

32. "Library Roof Project Precedes Interior Renovation, Redesign," *Madison Eagle*, August 22, 2022.

33. "Town hall renovation plan questioned," *Madison Eagle*, April 26, 2001, p. 1.

34. "Madison told to upgrade its courtroom," *Madison Eagle*, July 25, 2002, p. 1.

35. "Council plans to move court upstairs," *Madison Eagle*, January 30, 2003, p. 1

36. "Madison eyes first bonding after 13 years," *Madison Eagle*, February 26, 2004, p. 1.

37. "American Dream in Reach," *Madison Eagle*, October 9, 2014.

38. See John T. Cunningham, *On the Right Track. A History of the Madison Y.M.C.A.* (Madison, Y.M.C.A. 1990).

39. "Quarterback O'Donnell scores game winner for YMCA," *Madison Eagle*, April 12, 2001, p. 1.

40. Personal interview with Diane Mann by Herman Huber, July 21, 2020.

41. "Madison YMCA breaks ground on $16 million expansion project.," *Morristown Daily Record*, August 30, 2019.

42. Cunningham, op.cit., p. 13.

43. "Club, Contractors, Donors Celebrate Landmark's Rebirth," *Madison Eagle*, February 5, 2009, p. 1.

44. Michal Sherer Holzman, "History of the Thursday Morning Club," 2017.

45. The public report by Astrid Baillie was issued in 2018.

46. "Step back in time at 'Bottle Hill' home," *Madison Eagle*, December. 6, 2007, p. 10.

47. "Drew Forest Preserve," https://drew.edu/about/campus-facilities/conferences-events/event-rentals-facilities/drew-forest-preserve/. Viewed December 10, 2024.

48. "Biodiversity and Ecological Restoration at Drew," https://drew.edu/academics/environ-mental-studies-sustainability/environmental-studies-sustainability-department/biodiversi-ty-and-ecological-restoration-at-drew/ Viewed December 10, 2024.

49. "Buried Valley Aquifer System," https://en.wikipedia.org/wiki/Buried_Valley_Aquifer_System

50. William Westhoven, "Drew University, Madison sign 'landmark' deal to pur-chase, preserve forest." Originally in *Daily Record*, November 8, 2024. Accessed December 10, 2024. https://www.dailyrecord.com/story/news/2024/11/08/

drew-university-madison-nj-deal-save-forest-housing/76108599007/

51. "Rare owl spotted in Drew Forest." Accessed Dec 11, 2024. https://www.friend-softhedrewforest.com/blog/rare-owl-spotted-in-drew-forest#:~:text=Drew%20 University%20student%20Daniel%20Magda,species%2C%20in%20the%20Drew%20 Forest.&text=MADISON%20%E2%80%93%20The%20barred%20owl%2C%20a,Magda%20 in%20the%20university%20woods.

52. "'Geraldine' will remain in Madison," *Madison Eagle*, July 11, 2013, p.1.

53. *A History of the Lyons Madison Theater*. Barton Ross & Partners, LLC. August 2020.

54. In-person interview with Sandy Kolakowski, June 2, 2022, by Herman Huber.

55. "Madison caters to hunger for arts," *Madison Eagle*, Sept 9, 2004, p. 4.

56. "Making local scene as vibrant an arts…and CMS collaboration": see letter to the editor of the *Madison Eagle* entitled "The arts are music to Madison's ears", November 16, 2006, p. 4.

57. "Weekly meetings grew to over a dozen": see Woody Kerkeslager article entitled "Heralding a center for arts and culture," *Madison Eagle*, September 9, 2004, p.T2.

58. Dr. Robert Butts: "History of The Baroque Orchestra of New Jersey," Private Report, January 2021. A copy of the report is available from the Madison Historical Society.

59. Dr. Anne Matlack: "A History of Music at Grace Church," Private Report, February 2021. A copy of the report is available from the Madison Historical Society.

60. Joanne Spignor, Private Report compiled from MHSEF and MEF files, July 8, 2020. See also "New foundation aims to make 'a top high school even better'," *Madison Eagle*, May 29, 2003, p. 3. and "High school foundation takes first steps to go district wide," *Madison Eagle*, February 11, 2010, p. 2.

61. MEF website: https://www.mefnj.org/.

62. "Snow snarls traffic," *Madison Eagle*, January 29, 1987, pp. 1, 2.

63. "Opinion: Blizzard hit hard but Storm of the Century?" *Madison Eagle*, March 18, 1993, p. 4.

64. "Town blasted by 25 inches of wintry snow," *Madison Eagle*, January 11, 1996, pp. 1, 19.

65. "Madison weathers challenge of Irene," *Madison Eagle,* September 1, 2011, pp. 1, 15.

66. AON Benfield Impact Forecasting, May 14, 27, "Hurricane Sandy Event Recap Report."

67. "Madison powerless against Sandy," *Madison Eagle*, November 1, 2012, p.1.

68. "Madison storming back after Sandy," *Madison Eagle*, p1 & p.19 and "Madison Remembers Hurricane Sandy, Two years After the Storm," *Madison Eagle*, October 29, 2014, p.1.

69. "Editorial: The misery and charity of 'Sandy," *Madison Eagle*, November 5, 2015, p. 4.

70. "Just in case, Madison Y2K crew will stand by," *Madison Eagle*, December 16, 1999. p. 8.

71. "Madison mayor promotes 'Covid-19 Crises Response Toolkit,'" *Madison Eagle*, April 7, 2020, p. 1.

72. Rachel Barry, "Madison Comes Together", *Madison Living*, May 2020, pp. 6-8.

73. "3-D project makes Madison Junior School teacher a 'Mazda Hero'", *Madison Eagle*, December 6, 2020.

74. Rachel Barry, opt.cit., pp. 6-8.

75. "Madison Area YMCA Distributes More Than 1,300 Food Boxes", *Madison Eagle*, October 15, 2020.

76. "Madison Eagle Christmas Fund (MECF) Responds to Growing Needs Amidst Pandemic," *Tap Into Madison: Your Neighborhood News Online*, November 16, 2020. See also Stacey Smollen, "Madison Eagle Christmas Fund", *Madison Living*, December 2020, pg. 9. Additional input provided by Ms. Smollen via personal email to Susan Simon in August 2023.

77. "Food Distribution Through Boxcar," *Tap Into Madison: Your Neighborhood News Online*, April 27, 2020.

78. "Virtual Holiday Arts Festival", *Tap Into Madison: Your Neighborhood News Online*, November 4, 2020; See also "Madison Offering Virtual Holiday Entertainment This Saturday", *Tap Into Madison: Your Neighborhood News Online*, December 4, 2020.

79. The potential loss of the Drew Forest and the need to combat climate change are closely related issues as forest areas effectively remove carbon dioxide from the atmosphere.

80. "Climate Change is Speeding Towards Catastrophe. The Next Decade is Crucial, U.N. Panel Says," New York Times, March 21, 2023.

81. *"There's No Escaping Climate Chaos,"* Opinion by Jonathan Mingle, *New York Times*, July 15, 2023, p. A18.

82. By the end of 2023, Madison had been named 'Sustainability Champion' among all mid-sized New Jersey towns (towns with populations between 5,000 and 40,000) for four straight years. See "Madison is again named 'Sustainability Champion' among mid-sized towns," *Madison Eagle*, November 23, 2023, p. 7.

83. *2020 New Jersey 80x50 Report*, Executive Summary, New Jersey Department of Environmental Protection: https://dep.nj.gov/wp-content/uploads/climatechange/nj-gwra-80x50-report-2020.pdf.

84. In 2022 the Climate Action Ad Hoc Committee included: Council member and committee chair Rachel Ehrlich, Kathleen Caccavale, Peter Fried, Mary Ellen Hennessy-Jones, Lisa Jordan, and Kirsten Wallenstein.

85. Climate Action Ad Hoc Committee, "2022 Climate Action Report," January 23, 2023, Madison, NJ.

86. Ibid.

87. Climate Action Ad Hoc Committee, "2023 Climate Action Annual Report," presented by Council member and committee chair Rachel Ehrlich, June 26, 2023, to Madison Borough Council Meeting.

88. "Madison tacks on $1 million to share of cost for affordable housing project," *Madison Eagle*, May 23, 2023.

INDEX

www.ingramcontent.com/pod-product-compliance
Lightning Source LLC
Chambersburg PA
CBHW081528120626
46550CB00009B/2650